FRONTIERS OF VIOLENCE IN NORTH-EAST AFRICA

Zones of Violence

General Editors: Mark Levene and Donald Bloxham

Also available in the Zones of Violence Series

Alexander V. Prusin, The Lands Between: Conflict in the East European Borderlands, 1870–1992

Mark Biondich, The Balkans: Revolution, War, and Political Violence since 1878

FRONTIERS OF VIOLENCE IN NORTH-EAST AFRICA

GENEALOGIES OF CONFLICT SINCE C.1800

RICHARD J. REID

OXFORD
UNIVERSITY PRESS

*This book has been printed digitally and produced in a standard specification
in order to ensure its continuing availability*

OXFORD
UNIVERSITY PRESS

Great Clarendon Street, Oxford OX2 6DP
United Kingdom

Oxford University Press is a department of the University of Oxford.
It furthers the University's objective of excellence in research, scholarship,
and education by publishing worldwide. Oxford is a registered trade mark of
Oxford University Press in the UK and in certain other countries

© Richard J. Reid 2011

British Library Cataloguing in Publication Data
Data available

Library of Congress Cataloging in Publication Data
Library of Congress Control Number: 2010943357

ISBN 978-0-19-921188-3

Contents

PART III: COLONIALISMS, OLD AND NEW

PART IV: REVOLUTIONS, LIBERATIONS, AND
THE GHOSTS OF THE *MESAFINT*

Acknowledgements

In terms of the management of this project, I would like to mention at the outset Christopher Wheeler and Matthew Cotton at Oxford University Press, and the general editors of the series, Donald Bloxham and Mark Levene, for their encouragement and helpful comments at the draft stage. Friends and fellow practitioners who have likewise provided guidance and inspiration—if sometimes unknowingly—include Christopher Clapham, Dan Connell, the late Richard Greenfield, Wendy James, Douglas Johnson, Gaim Kibreab, Alex Last, Tom Ofcansky, Izabela Orlowska, Martin Plaut, Gunther Schroeder, and Alessandro Triulzi. I must record my profound thanks to informants, colleagues, and friends from both Eritrea and Ethiopia, many of whom I cannot name individually but who have contributed ineffably to whatever understanding of the region I can claim to have. Some deserve special mention, however, and in Ethiopia I am grateful to Alemseged Girmay, Amira Omer, Eyob Halefom, and Gebretensae Gebretsadkan, while Yemane 'Jamaica' Kidane has been generous with time, information, and opinion. My visits to Addis Ababa were greatly enhanced by Patrick Gilkes' wonderfully open-handed help and advice. In Eritrea, I am more grateful than I can say to Alemseged Tesfai, while trips to Asmara would have been so much less productive without the help of Azeb Tewolde and her staff at the Research and Documentation Centre, and also of Brook Tesfai, Mekonen Kidane, Seife Berhe and Zemhret Yohannes. I want to reserve special mention for my two old buddies in Asmara, Abraham Keleta and Eyob Abraha, who have always made it worthwhile, no matter what. Closer to home, the team at Chatham House in London—Sally Healy, Roger Middleton, and Tom Cargill—have provided much in the way of inspiration and expertise. Then there is my wife Anna, who has lived with north-east African violence on a daily basis for some time now, more than anyone sane has a right to expect. I thank her with love and amazement. It is never more important than in a book on north-east Africa to point out that none of the above bear any responsibility for the interpretation which follows; some, indeed, will heartily disagree with it.

Finally, I would like to dedicate this book to the memory of an old friend who died before its completion, Amanuel Yohannes. Amanuel taught me more about the region than anyone else, and especially how to think differently about its past and its present; I owe him a great deal, though I never got to tell him just how much.

RJR, LONDON

List of Maps

Glossary and Abbreviations

AAPO	All Amhara People's Organisation
Andinet	'Unity', youth wing of the UP in the 1940s
ANDM	Amhara National Democratic Movement
Anyanya	Southern Sudanese guerrillas from the late 1950s onward
ascari	African troops in the Italian colonial army
banda	irregular militia
baria	derogatory Tigrinya term for the Nara, implying 'black slaves'
blatta	title given to learned men, counsellors
BMA	British Military Administration
BPLM	Benishangul People's Liberation Movement
dejazmach	noble title, lit. 'commander of the gate'
Derg	informal name for Ethiopian government 1974–91, lit. 'Committee'
EDU	Ethiopian Democratic Union
ELF	Eritrean Liberation Front
ELM	Eritrean Liberation Movement
ELPP	Eritrean Liberal Progressive Party
EPDM	Ethiopian People's Democratic Movement
EPLF	Eritrean People's Liberation Front
EPRDF	Ethiopian People's Revolutionary Democratic Front
EPRP	Ethiopian People's Revolutionary Party
fitaurari	noble title, lit. 'commander of the vanguard'
gada	Oromo age grade system
GPLM	Gambella People's Liberation Movement
gult	fief
habesha	common, informal term for highland Ethiopians and Eritreans
IGAD	Intergovernmental Authority on Development
Jiberti	Amhara and Tigrinya populations who are Muslim

kebessa	Eritrean highland plateau
Kebre Negast	Glory of the Kings
lij	title for children of nobility, lit. 'child'
metahit	Eritrean lowlands
ML	Muslim League
na'ib	title of Ottoman governor of Massawa, lit. 'deputy'
negus	king
negus negast	king of kings (emperor)
NFD	Northern Frontier District (Kenya)
NIF	National Islamic Front
OAU	Organisation of African Unity
OLF	Oromo Liberation Front
ONLF	Ogaden National Liberation Front
OPDO	Oromo People's Democratic Organisation
PFDJ	People's Front for Democracy and Justice
ras	noble title, lit. 'head'
sha'abiya	'popular', nickname for EPLF
shangalla	derogatory Amharic term for peoples to the west of Ethiopian highlands, in Sudan
shifta	bandit, rebel
shiftanet	banditry, rebellion
SPDO	Sidama People's Democratic Organisation
SPLM/A	Sudan People's Liberation Movement/Army
SYL	Somali Youth League
TFG	Transitional Federal Government
TNG	Transitional National Government
TPLF	Tigray People's Liberation Front
UIC	Union of Islamic Courts
UP	Unionist Party
Woyane	lit. 'revolt', referring to 1943 uprising as well as a nickname for TPLF
zemene mesafint	'era of the princes'

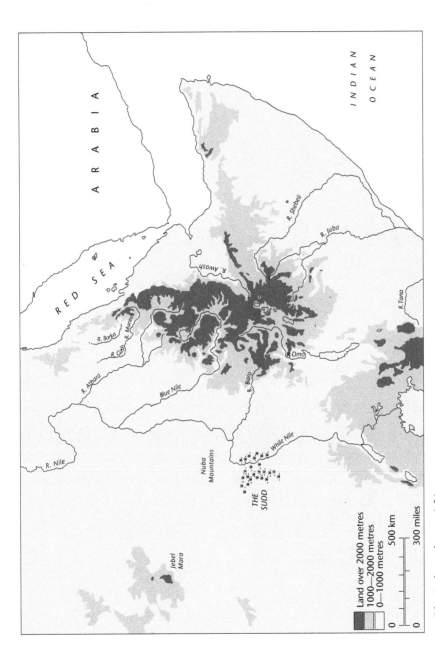

1. Physical north-east Africa

Source: J. Markakis, *National and Class Conflict in the Horn of Africa*, Cambridge University Press, Cambridge, 1987

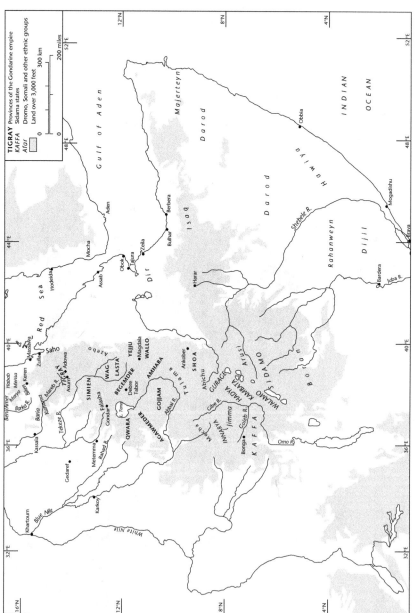

2. The region during the *zemene mesafint*

Source: J. E. Flint (ed.), *Cambridge History of Africa Vol. 5. c.1790–c.1870*, Cambridge University Press, Cambridge, 1976; this version adapted to R. J. Reid, *A History of Modern Africa*, Wiley-Blackwell, Oxford, 2009

The following labels appear on the map:

TIGRAY Provinces of the Gondarine empire
KAFFA Sidama states
Afar Oromo, Somali and other ethnic groups
Land over 3,000 feet

0   200 miles
0   300 km

Gulf of Aden
Red Sea
INDIAN OCEAN
White Nile
Blue Nile

Khartoum, Karkoj, Gedaref, Kassala, Metemma, Gondar, Rabad R., Takeze R., Baria, Barko R., Bilen, Keren, Marya, Habab, Beni Amer, Zulla, Massawa, Saho, Hodeida, Mocha, Aden, Assab, Obok, Tajura, Zeila, Buhar, Berbera, Obbia, Mogadishu, Bardera, Juba R., Brava

Kumaila, Mareb R., Axum, Adowa, TIGRA, Falasha, L. Tana, QWARA, SIMIEN, Azebo, WAG, LASTA, Debre Tabor, BEGEMDER, AGAWMEDER, GOJJAM, Abbai R., AMHARA, WALLO, Magdala, YEJIU, Ankober, SHOA, Abichu, Tulama, GURAGE, Arusi, Boran, ARUSI, SIDAMO, WALAMO, KAMBATA, HADIA, INNARYA, Jimma, Gibe R., Gojeb R., Bonga, KAFFA, Omo R., Macha R., Harar

Majerteyn, Darod, Isaq, Dir, Shabele R., Rahanweyn, Dijil, Hawiye

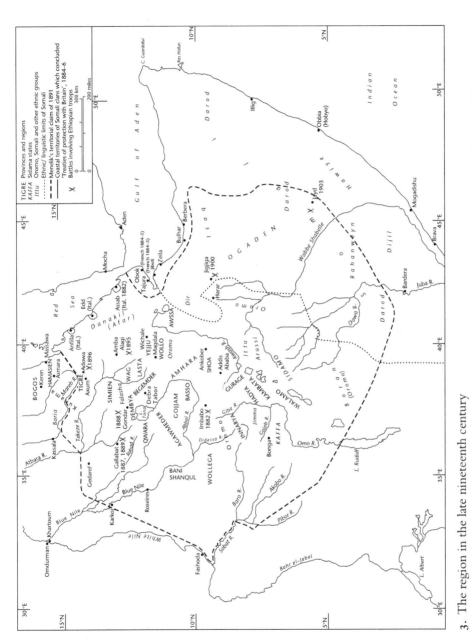

TIGRE Provinces and regions
KAFFA Sidama states
Ittu Oromo, Somali and other ethnic groups
.... Ethnic/ linguistic limits of Somali
━ ━ ━ Menelik's territorial claim of 1891
Coastal territories of Somali clans which concluded
'Treaties of protection with Britain', 1884–6
X Battles involving Ethiopian troops

0 ___ 200 miles
0 ___ 300 km

3. The region in the late nineteenth century

Source: R. Oliver and G. N. Sanderson (eds), *Cambridge History of Africa Vol. 6, c.1870–c.1905*, Cambridge University Press, Cambridge, 1985

4. Imperial Ethiopia, mid-twentieth century

Source: P. Henze, *Layers of Time: A History of Ethiopia*, Hurst, London, 2000

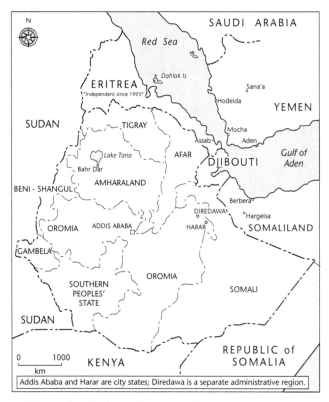

Addis Ababa and Harar are city states; Diredawa is a separate administrative region.

5. The region in the early twenty-first century

Source: P. Henze, *Layers of Time: A History of Ethiopia*, Hurst, London, 2000

Prologue

The Past in the Present

In the first few years of the third millennium, the region of north-east Africa is as enmeshed in conflict as it has been for several decades. Somalia is engulfed once more by violence, the result of both factional fighting and the Ethiopian invasion; Ethiopia itself is politically tense, its government confronted with armed insurgency among the Oromo in the south and the Ethiopian Somali of the east; the Sudanese peace agreement looks impossibly fragile, and violence has flared in contested areas between north and south; Eritrean and Djiboutian forces are engaged in a standoff across their common frontier; and—the epicentre of so much regional conflict—the Eritrean–Ethiopian border remains highly militarized, with armies representing two competing national missions glaring at one another with malicious intent. It is this last conflict which best illustrates the analytical parameters of this book. Eritrea and Ethiopia, the two key state-level actors in the account which follows, appeared to be on the brink of renewed war in the early twenty-first century: scores of thousands of troops were dug in on either side of a border which was as torturous as it was disputed, and the governments in Asmara and Addis Ababa seemed as far away from any kind of *rapprochement* as they had been at any time since the Algiers Agreement in December 2000 supposedly ended the original conflict. In fact, while the Algiers Agreement had ended a battle, or series of battles, it had not addressed the causes of the war itself. That war had begun, ostensibly at least, in May 1998—but as this book will argue, it had been going on for some considerable time before that, interrupted by brief periods of armistice, quiescence, and even, apparently, sporadic goodwill. Its genealogy, in fact, can be traced back through the twentieth century and into the nineteenth. It is clear that what happened in May 1998 was only the latest manifestation of a war which had been going on for a very long time. The conflict represented the crystallization of a number of intertwined historical grievances, the opening up of so many fault lines, and constituted another episode of extreme violence in a regional cycle of conflict stretching back more than two centuries.

In the early years of the twenty-first century, beyond the northern highlands themselves, the Eritrean–Ethiopian war had had a profound effect on the wider region, either sparking new, proxy, conflicts or joining up with extant ones. It was in Somalia in particular that the implications of the war between the two countries were clearest, and where the violence inherent within their respective political cultures was most dramatically manifest. Somalia had imploded in the early 1990s, but in the first years of the twenty-first century violent instability there had taken on new forms. In a world increasingly defined by post-9/11 allegiance, Eritrea sought to shore up the Union of Islamic Courts in Mogadishu, a government which appeared to have at least some semblance of local support but which the United States believed sponsored, and provided a base for, Islamic terrorism. When at the end of 2006 Ethiopia invaded what remained of 'Somalia', the US—after initially, so it is claimed, advising against such an act—came to support it,[1] and the stated objective was to overthrow the pernicious al-Qaeda-succouring Islamic government. Within a few months, entirely predictably, an insurgency had erupted against the Ethiopians, while the Eritreans were widely believed to have been arming the insurgents themselves. A proxy war had begun, compounding the stand-off on the Ethiopian–Eritrea border itself and—temporarily at least—replacing actual fighting along that frontier. At the same time, Eritrea found itself threatened with the 'terrorist-sponsor' label by the US. This was a ludicrous accusation by a misguided administration. Yet what was certainly true was that there appeared to be no regional crisis which the Eritrean government would not exploit for foreign policy gains against Ethiopia: it reached out to the Southern Sudanese government, raising the issue of Eritrean support for South Sudan's secession from Khartoum, even as the Comprehensive Peace Agreement itself appeared increasingly fragile; it at first provided military support to, and then sought to build alliances among, a range of Darfur rebel factions which for a time at least—like their Somali counterparts—saw Asmara as a safe haven. Eritrean President Isaias Afeworki saw himself as a peace-broker; his critics detected the whiff of megalomania, and at best saw him as a troublesome meddler. Meanwhile Ethiopia provided succour to armed groups opposed to the Eritrean state; Eritrea, in addition to their Somali connections, trained and armed insurgents among the Oromo and anyone else in a position to direct their fire at the government in Addis Ababa.

The governments of Eritrea and Ethiopia themselves were in increasingly precarious positions at home, their power based upon greater or lesser degrees of violence or the threat of it against sizeable sections of their own populations. Governments—indeed entire state apparatuses—which had grown out of guerrilla movements were ever less secure and drawn to various forms of violence in the attempt to stabilize themselves: in both Ethiopia and Eritrea, the 'new' political elites were imbued with a militarism and a faith in armed force which had been forged in mountains and barren places during their armed struggles. Yet these 'new' elites had much in common with their political forebears in that their visions of statehood had been conjured up on the periphery and carried through blood sacrifice to the embattled centre to be made flesh. Given to armed adventure and intrigue, these 'new' governments now sat, trembling and suspended, at the centre of a web of interlinked conflict, linked by almost imperceptible, but remarkably resilient, threads to the past as well as to the wars of the present, and indeed those to come.

In Ethiopia, the coalition government of the Ethiopian People's Revolutionary Democratic Front (EPRDF) was faced with a growing armed insurgency in the Ogaden, the Somali-dominated 'Region 5', where the Ogaden National Liberation Front (ONLF) demanded the right of self-determination from Ethiopia. There was also an ongoing insurgency among the Oromo, led by the Oromo Liberation Front (OLF), and among an array of smaller ethnic groups along the western border with Sudan. These peoples remained violently irreconcilable to the Tigrayan–Amhara order at the centre of Ethiopian political life; elections of a kind might be staged to present the image of pluralism and accountability, but the violence at the heart of the Ethiopian political system remained overt, whether in Addis Ababa itself or in the outlying provinces. Prime Minister Meles Zenawi was no more willing than his predecessors to brook dissent, whether ideological or ethnic. The system of ethnic federalism now in place was only the latest, albeit markedly sophisticated, in a line of political strategies to secure some degree of unity and cohesion across the Ethiopian region stretching back to the *zemene mesafint*, and indeed earlier. In Eritrea, meanwhile, armed irreconcilables were likewise gathering, within and on the borders, albeit on nothing like the scale of the insurrections confronting the Ethiopian Government. More importantly for Eritrea, in the immediate term, was the marked degree of militarization in political and cultural life, as the spectres of wars past, present, and future haunted public discourse, and ensured the maintenance of a captive army of young men and women whose lives were being sacrificed to the

service of an ungenerous state. Levels of oppression were heightening year
on year, as the Government became ever more wary of enemies both within
and without; Eritreans were told daily that the Ethiopians could attack at any
time, but increasingly there were neither *panem* nor *circenses* as a reward for
the resultant loss of freedom which—contrary to Jefferson's dictum—flowed
directly from apparently eternal vigilance.

The region was characterized by a series of interconnected conflicts, a
spatial network of violence which—it was increasingly clear—would need
to be understood by those who would promote 'peace' across north-east
Africa and the Horn.[2] Yet what was perhaps less commonly recognized was
the antiquity of many of these wars, and their profoundly historical nature:
in other words, there were *temporal* as well as *spatial* networks of violence,
indicating a depth which was rather more difficult to grasp than mere surface spread. It will be argued in this book that while novelty can indeed be
identified in the contemporary situation—most obviously in terms of the
political contexts with which much violence as well as interethnic and
interstate relations have occurred—there are much clearer lines of continuity than discontinuity in the modern history of the region. The key crises
and the major fault lines—the *frontiers* concept developed in the first chapter—have deep roots, and much of what has happened in the early years of
the new millennium represents a continuation of, or a reversion to, well-
established precedent in terms of intra-regional relations, at the level of state,
ethnicity, and locale, however shifting those definitions may be. Cyclical
patterns of hegemony and subjugation, and the creation of militarized communities and identities based on alternating ideas about defence and aggression, are discernible over a period of two centuries or more, and make it
possible—indeed essential—to talk of genealogies of conflict and identity
over this timeframe. Claims for novelty—for which 'revolutionary' liberation movements have an especial propensity—should not be overlooked;
but nor should they blind us to the deeper roots of groups and movements
and ideas, even in the face of prevailing vernacular wisdom.

It has become clear in the course of the late twentieth and early twenty-
first centuries that an appreciation of *la longue durée* in terms of the history
of violent conflict in this region is long overdue; certainly, several contemporaneous and cumulative dynamics have produced an era of continuous
conflict since the late eighteenth century. This era has been characterized by
markedly intense, cyclical, and increasingly institutionalized violence
between, and systematic persecution and/or marginalization of, particular

population groups. This is not, then, a particularly happy book, but there is no reason why it should be: the region's troubled present is rooted in a troubled past, and an appreciation of the *longue durée* is at the heart of this project. The region of north-east Africa is conceived here as stretching, on a south–north axis, between the southern Somali coast and the Eritrean shoreline, between Mogadishu and Massawa, and encompassing the vast range of mountains and plateaux known as the Ethiopian Highlands and its adjacent lowlands; and this region is distinctive vis-à-vis many other parts of Africa both temporally and spatially. In terms of timescale, it is possible to trace patterns of conflict over a remarkably long and continuous period, owing chiefly to the relative wealth of source material, both indigenous and external, relating to the area. While the actions, ideologies, and visions of literate Semitic-speaking elites were recorded in chronicles and ecclesiastical records from the middle of the first millennium AD onwards, foreign visitors penetrated the states and societies of the region much earlier, and in greater numbers, than most other parts of Africa, especially Europeans from the sixteenth century. In spatial terms, too, the region is noteworthy for it has an historically rooted, geopolitical coherence—notwithstanding its cultural, linguistic, and environmental diversity—which means that the competition for space, resources, and political power within it was remarkably intense. This was a region in which a series of interlocking competitions linked the Tigre and Tigrinya, in the north, to the Amhara further south, to the Oromo and Somali still further south, and in turn linked these to the Afar in the east, and the Sidama and others in the west and south-west. Ultimately, indeed, it was this very competition which would give birth to the modern nation-state—or empire-state, perhaps more accurately—of Ethiopia at the end of the nineteenth century, and in that sense it might be argued that 'Ethiopia', insofar that it is at base the culmination of so much spatially defined conflict, is indeed much older than we might assume.

PART
I

Setting and Approach

I

Interpreting the Region

Peoples and places

It is important at the outset to provide the framework—in terms of physical geography and human settlement—within which our discussion is situated. It will be clear that the integrated history of this complex region cannot be understood without first appreciating its environmental and ecological diversity, and the socio-economic systems which have resulted. These systems are evidently subject to continual change and adaptation, and it is not our intention here to provide a 'static' picture, for just as peoples and communities migrate, so too do identities and senses of belonging, according to time, space, and circumstance—this, indeed, is a theme which will surface at various stages in our story. Nonetheless, it is important to attempt a 'snapshot' of the human protagonists in our narrative and their physical environment, before turning to the interpretation of these—interpretation, that is, both by outsiders and by the peoples themselves. The book is concerned with a broad corridor of conflict which has the Ethiopian Highlands (and their Eritrean extension) as its centrepiece; it incorporates these highlands and their escarpment and lowland peripheries, stretching between the modern Eritrean Red Sea coast and the southern, western, and eastern foothills and lowlands of present-day Ethiopia. In particular contexts, the Sudanese and Somali frontier zones must be considered, but only insofar as these relate to the core themes of ethnic and religious conflict, the irruption of external influences, and the violent state- and empire-building which takes place in the central and northern Ethiopian Highlands in the course of the nineteenth and twentieth centuries.

The region thus defined comprises remarkable diversity in terms of physical terrain, vegetation, and climate; geographical difference explains much of the conflict and competition under examination, and indeed these physical borders—the demarcations imposed by nature, as it were—are doubtless the most important in the first instance. Particular geographies have facilitated particular economic systems, and thus have reinforced notions of ethnic uniqueness and difference. In the broadest terms, the volcanic fertility of the highlands—where rain falls relatively abundantly—is in contrast with the dry, hot coastal lowlands of Eritrea, Djibouti, and Somalia, the Nile floodplains of eastern Sudan, and the savannah scrub of northern Kenya. In Ethiopia, these surrounding hot lowlands of desert and steppe, known as *Quolla*, reach to 1500 metres around the foothills of the great massif. Beyond this is a sub-tropical zone, or *Woyna Dega*, which reaches to around 2500 metres and which is cooler, wetter, and contains pastureland. Beyond this still is the high mountainous zone, which is temperate and wet, known as *Dega*. The Ethiopian tableland itself is a natural centre of centralized civilization, protruding skyward to dominate north-east Africa, and has the greatest concentrations of population, although it is characterized by natural divisions in the form of river beds, valleys, and deep gorges which have separated communities at key moments in the region's history. An important feature of this landscape is the distinctive mountainous *amba*, with sheer sides and flat tops. Most dramatically, the Rift Valley splits the highlands into two, western and eastern, zones—a landscape which has had a profound influence on Ethiopian history.

Eritrea's highland plateau—the *kebessa*—is an extension of the Ethiopian Highlands, and is flanked in the west by lowland plains, which stretch toward Sudan and are extremely fertile; and to the north and east, by a hot, arid coastal plain which links up with Djibouti. The two broad Eritrean zones, therefore, are the *kebessa* and the lowlands, or *metahit*, although there are important sub-regional differences in habitat and culture within these. The Somali landscape is characterized by mountains in the north and north-east, which abut the eastern Ethiopian highlands, but more generally by hot savannah with irregular rainfall. This is a region which has been especially prone to drought, and water scarcity has had a huge impact on human relations across the Ethiopian–Somali and the Ethiopian–Kenyan borderlands. But even the well-watered highlands have experienced periodic drought, and states and societies have been vulnerable as a result, which has coincided with, and indeed spurred, massive political and social change. There are a number of examples of this through the period under examination. Food shortages in the north in the 1860s were both the symptom of prolonged violence and economic collapse, and the cause of further socio-political insecurity; the major famine of 1888–92 drove much political violence in that critical moment in the region's history; the prolonged drought across the Sahel belt in the 1970s and 1980s is crucial to understanding the instability of the Ethiopian state and the political cultures which emerged around liberation struggle. The pressures facing pastoralists and farmers alike, and the broader competition over resources, have fuelled a great deal of conflict across the region.

These various landscapes are inhabited by—indeed have been instrumental in the creation of—a vast array of ethnic and linguistic groups. In terms of human populations, clearly, the 'zone of violence' envisaged here involves primarily the Tigrinya of highland Eritrea and northern Ethiopia, the Amhara of central Ethiopia, and the Oromo and Somali of southern and eastern Ethiopia. However, a range of other, invariably smaller, groups, notably in south-west Ethiopia and along the western flank of the corridor—no less important, and in certain contexts even more important than their better known neighbours—need also to be considered, including Gurage, Welayta, Sidama, Hadiya, Kambata, Kaffa, Beni Amer, and Beni Shangul. Most commentators have categorized the peoples of the region as belonging to one of three major blocs—Semitic or Semitized, Cushitic, and Nilotic or Sudanic—according to a range of variables, including language group and genetic origins. In a handful of cases, these divisions are a little misleading, as some population groups in fact straddle more than one such category. The Nilotic groups are strung out around the edges of our zone, from the Kunama and Nara in the western lowlands of Eritrea and adjacent Sudanese and Tigrayan borderlands, to the various groups along the Ethiopian–Sudanese frontier zone, including the Berta, Anuak, Koman, and Beni Shangul. These groups have been historically referred to in pejorative terms by highlanders—the Nara, for example, have been called in derogatory Tigrinya *baria*, implying 'black slaves', while the Beni Shangul have commonly been referred to as *shangalla* in Amharic, although the term is applied to all 'black' peoples to the west. Some practice mixed farming, though many remain primarily pastoralist, and many are Muslim.

The Cushitic category contains a vast array of peoples, spread across the region. Some pre-date Semitic populations by some distance. Thus the Agaw are clustered north of Lake Tana and west of the Takkaze river, and are also represented in Eritrea by the Bilen around Keren. Then there are the Beja: although in various contexts, both past and present, the 'Beja' are referred to as a distinct ethnic group—such as in Eritrea, where they are also known as Hedareb—in other contexts it is more properly a linguistic term. Beja-speakers inhabit the north-east African coast from Egypt to Eritrea, and inland occupy swathes of eastern Sudan and northern and western Eritrea. Today they include, among others, some Tigre (the second largest cultural and linguistic group in Eritrea after the Tigrinya), sections of the Beni Amer, and Hadendowa ethnic groups of Eritrea and eastern Sudan. Most are Muslim agro-pastoralists. The Saho and the Afar, or Danakil, are Cushitic, largely Muslim, groups straddling central-eastern Eritrea and north-east Ethiopia, while the largest single Cushitic grouping in Ethiopia is, of course, the Oromo, who have a common language but who have diversified in culture and economy. While largely pastoralist in origin, migrating into the highlands from the sixteenth century onward, they have become urban dwellers and settled farmers in some areas, just as others retain their pastoral roots; some Oromo are Christian, others have absorbed Islam. In the broadest terms, the more southerly Oromo tend to be Muslim—in Hararge, Arsi, and the Gibe region—while those in Welega, Wollo, and Shoa are Christian; some have become so assimilated into high-land *habesha*[1] culture that they speak Amharic as their mother tongue—one of the challenges for the emergence of a coherent Oromo consciousness.[2] Yet in some areas migrating Oromo have themselves absorbed and assimilated conquered groups, notably in the Gibe region of the south-west. In sum, there is no singular 'Oromo experience' but rather many such experiences, although as we shall see certain key narratives have been extracted from Oromo history, and a discernible Oromo 'culture' identified and clarified. The Somali are also Cushitic, associated primarily with pastoralism in the great plains of the east, although again others have become farmers. Most Somali are Muslim, one of the key dynamics in the region's history. In the fertile south-west of Ethiopia are other Cushitic language groups, such as the Konso, and others are clustered together under the term Sidama; these include Kambata, Gimira-Maji, and Janjero. They inhabit a complex cultural and ethnic zone which has been much prized by central state-builders owing to its natural wealth; hoe agriculture is common, while there is a mixture of Christianity, Islam, and indigenous belief systems. In this area, mention should also be made of the Omotic cluster of communities—peoples living along the Omo River—which comprises remarkable linguistic and cultural diversity, including the Kafa grouping. There is no common religion here and peoples are both pastoralists and grain cultivators.

The Tigrinya of highland Eritrea and Tigray, and the Amhara of the great Ethiopian massif comprising Wollo, Gondar, Shoa, and Gojjam in Ethiopia, continue to be the main shapers of political destiny to the present day. They have much in common in the way of culture and custom, but there are regional differences amongst the Amhara, and between the Tigrinya north and south of the Mereb River; nonetheless Tigrayans and Amhara have competed for political dominance of the region for a millennium or more. They are primarily plough farmers, while also keeping some livestock, and represent the central Semitic bloc. The Semitic or 'Semitized' bloc also includes a range of other groups, including some Tigre-speakers, of which the Beni Amer are the largest grouping, the Rashaida along the Red Sea coast, and 'pockets' amidst Cushitic populations, notably the Adari of Harar, and the Gurage south of Shoa. Some of these have become 'Semitized' through extensive intermarriage as well as through political and military absorption, much as swathes of the Oromo population have become assimilated. Although highland Semitic culture is associated with Christianity, sizeable numbers of Amhara and some Tigrinya are also Muslim (known as *Jiberti*), as are the inhabitants of Harar and most Gurage.

While a broad historical overview would suggest ongoing rivalry between the Tigray-Tigrinya and Amharic segments of the Semitic bloc, and the struggle of the Cushitic and Islamic 'south' against the domination of the Semitic and Christian 'north', it is also the case that the various cultural, ethnic, and linguistic fault lines of the region—the zones of identity, as it were—are intertwined and overlapping. It is true, moreover, that ethnic identity has been flexible and fluid, historically—doubtless it is ever thus, and this should not be especially startling—and that an instrumentalist interpretation of ethnicity would suggest that particular identities have become solidified in the last century or so owing to the formation of the modern state of Ethiopia. In other words, the Amhara as a hegemonic group have become rather clearly defined as a result of the state-formation process, and indeed a number of communities—across the south and south-west, notably—have in turn sharpened their own ethnic edges in response to Amhara dominance. Yet I would argue that regardless of whether particular groups expanded or contracted according to political circumstances, such identities did indeed have deep roots and defined characteristics which were less concerned with biological descent than with cultural traits—in the case of the Amhara, for example, the Amharic language and Orthodox Christianity, with its attendant cultural apparatus. There are institutions and accoutrements associated with *being Amhara* which are as important to understanding the longevity and depth of the *ethnie* as any sense of *who exactly* is Amhara at any given point in time. In sum, it is not that ethnic categories are formed purely according to the instrumentalist model, it is rather that such group-ings contract or expand according to circumstances, and that such an epi-sodic process represents a shifting frontier of identity and cohesion.

There can be little doubt, too, that marginalization produces indignant cohesion, often compelling groups with loose structural and cultural affili-ations into larger communities. This can be seen, for example, along the Ethiopian–Sudanese border, a zone of sporadic, low-level conflict through-out the twentieth century. The 1980s witnessed the emergence of Berta militia in Beni Shangul, and Anuak militia in Gambella: in the latter prov-ince, Nuer and Anuak competed for political dominance, a struggle which was heightened in the 1990s with the arrival of Amhara, Tigrayan, and Oromo settlers. This was the latest stage in a cyclical push-and-pull experi-enced by the peoples of the region between Sudan and Ethiopia, an experi-ence which has clearly led to sharpened self-definitions on the part of the communities themselves—manifest, for example, in the creation of the Gambella People's Liberation Front and the Benishangul People's Liberation Movement (dominated by the Anuak and Berti respectively).[3] These devel-opments have served to increase the 'visibility' of the ethnic periphery across north-east Africa—scholarly analysis since the 1980s has certainly tended to focus on the overtly *ethnic* aspect of much regional conflict.

Toward a new regional historiography

Several broad groupings and thematic approaches in the literature are par-ticularly important. In terms of the older literature on Ethiopia—up to the 1970s, broadly—there is what we might generally term the 'Greater Ethiopia' or Ethio-centric school, which ultimately saw both Ethiopia and the wider region from the perspective of Addis Ababa. Within the essentially benevo-lent imperial state conceptualized by such writers came not only the recently conquered but generally pacific Cushitic (including Oromo), Nilo-Saharan, and Omotic peoples of the south and south-west, but also the incorporated Somali of the Ogaden and Eritreans in the north. Much of this older work was concerned with the state-building travails and successes of the eighteenth and nineteenth centuries. This is in overall contrast to the more recent literature, which has tended to focus on the twentieth century, and the period after the 1950s and 1960s in particular. There are exceptions to this general trend—the work of Donald Crummey, notably, and the necessarily elongated projects of archaeologists—but little new work has been done on the pre-1900 era for some years now. 'Greater Ethiopianists' were concerned, above all, with the essential continuity of 'Ethiopian' (or at least Semitic) civilization from the early centuries AD onward, the resilience and adaptability of that civilization, and—notwithstanding the trauma wrought upon sections of the population by Solomonic mythology—its assimilationism. This older generation of scholars was also characterized by its tendency to *particularize* Ethiopia and Ethiopian-ness, to the extent that academics who 'did Ethiopia' regarded themselves rather self-consciously as a breed apart from other Africanists, and were regarded as such by the latter. The two rarely intersected.[4] Scholars of the region were in thrall to the mountainous mysticism of Ethiopian antiquity and to the supposedly rarefied environment facilitated by literate Semitic culture.

Increasingly, set against this was the more ethnically or regionally based nationalist literature which began to reflect the aspirations of those very groups (or elements within them)—chiefly Eritreans, Oromo, and Somali—who kicked against the centrism of 'old Abyssinia' and in so doing were in fact demanding a new perspective on the region's history. The most noteworthy branch of this was the emergence of Oromo nationalist literature,[5] but there were others and, increasingly, anthropologists (and to a lesser extent historians and political scientists) worked among the smaller minorities of the southern and south-west fringes: those on the borders of Kenya and Sudan and squeezed between self-possessed hegemonic blocs. In many respects this amounted to an examination of the peoples living on Menelik's southern battlegrounds of the late nineteenth century. This coincided with studies of the ethnic federalism of the post-*Derg* state, some of which sought to historicize Ethiopia's multi-ethnic challenge; at the same time, however, those writing on Eritrea and Somalia soon had new tests of their own. Somalia collapsed in the early 1990s, descending into an apparent chaos which was hotly contested by a series of 'warlords' and which was only partially alleviated with, first, the emergence of Somaliland as a *comparatively* stable would-be state in the north, though lacking international recognition at the time of writing; and, second, the emergence of the Islamic Courts Union, who were considered threatening enough to warrant military action by Ethiopia at the end of 2006. But, basically, Somalia—the supposedly heterogeneous ethnic nation in Africa *par excellence*—had ceased to be. Further north, while the first few years of Eritrean independence created many new admirers and caused many an enthusiastic thesis to be written on the virtues of EPLF-led nationalism, the war with Ethiopia, and the political oppression which swiftly followed, led scholars to either wonder where it had all gone wrong or to write 'told-you-so' pieces, depending on where they had positioned themselves in the 1980s.

In developing its particular interpretation of the region's history, then, this book is building upon, or has been inspired by, a range of scholarship both old and new. Several key works need to be noted at the outset, most of them clustered, not coincidentally, between the mid-1980s and the early 1990s—a period of radical rethinking about the contours of, and approaches to, north-east African history.[6] One scholarly collection of major significance in the reinterpretation of Ethiopian history was *The Southern Marches of Imperial Ethiopia*, published in 1986 and edited by Wendy James and Donald Donham, which signposted a number of important shifts.[7] The following year, John Markakis published his immensely valuable regional study, *National and Class Conflict in the Horn of Africa*, which, while it is now a little dated in certain aspects, was extremely prescient in drawing out the interconnectedness between, and striking array of, conflicts emerging across the north-east African region, in Ethiopia, Sudan, Somalia, and Eritrea.[8] The scholarly deconstruction of the Ethiopian region continued apace, and two further studies were significant. The first, though perhaps less well-known, was Bonnie Holcomb and Sisai Ibssa's provocative *The Invention of Ethiopia*, which gained in intellectual courage what it may at times have lacked in scholarly rigour.[9] It was among the first academic shots fired on behalf of the Oromo, studies of which were beginning to demand a revised history of the Ethiopian imperium. John Sorenson's equally provocative and stimulating *Imagining Ethiopia* argued essentially for the demystification of 'Ethiopia', and a more honest analysis of what it represented to various parties both within and outside the country itself.[10] Finally, what was in effect the sequel to James and Donham's *Southern Marches*—*Remapping Ethiopia*—was published in 2002, in which James and Donham were joined as editors by Eisei Kurimoto and Alessandro Triulzi.[11] The title encapsulated the spirit of the body of work which had emerged over the previous 15 years.

Meanwhile, again, feeding into this revisionism was the burgeoning literature on, most notably, Eritrean and Oromo nationalisms—very different beasts, no doubt, but each responsible in their own way for the remapping exercise taking place through the 1980s and 1990s. It is inadvisable at this stage to attempt even a brief survey of this canon of work—we will have occasion to examine and utilize it in due course—but suffice to say it was of immense importance in pioneering the unravelling of the many mythologies at heart of *Ethiopianism*. Inevitably, of course, such revisionism has created mythologies of its own, not least the result of the aggressive optimism which lay at its core, and in different ways Eritrean and Oromo nationalist revisionism has each encountered serious problems—the former because of the failures of the Eritrean state,[12] the latter because of the deep fissures within Oromo studies and the Oromo struggle[13]—but this scarcely detracts from its historiographical significance.

Taken as a whole, this body of literature, disparate though it was in many respects, signified a radical shift in regional historiography, typically characterized as moving away from centre-biased analysis and toward the 'peripheries', borderlands, and the constituent yet marginalized parts of the old Ethiopian empire. The current work builds on the critique initiated by these volumes of the 'centrist' or 'Greater Ethiopia' school, exemplified by Donald Levine's glibly optimistic thesis—recently revised but essentially unchanged a quarter of a century after it first appeared—that Ethiopia has been and can continue to be a contented amalgam of ethnicities, cultures, and languages.[14] My own view is rather more sympathetic to that expressed by Ernest Gellner, who, echoing Lenin's remarks about Tsarist Russia, asserted that '[t]he Amhara empire was a prison-house of nations if ever there was one'.[15] But this was an overly simplistic, if pithy, summation, and our understanding of Ethiopian history, politics, and culture—and that of the surrounding region—has become rather more sophisticated since the 1980s—at least, it has changed quite dramatically. In part, this has been a case of scholars catching up with events on the ground, certainly in the early 1990s with the overthrow of Mengistu in Ethiopia and Siad Barre in Somalia, and the appearance of an independent Eritrea. In many respects the ELF and then the EPLF in Eritrea had led the way in this exercise in regional 'remapping', violent pioneers whose military success had forced the most dramatic reconfiguration of political reality and scholarly received wisdom alike; in many respects, perhaps, they have never really been forgiven, in certain quarters at least. At any rate, while just a few years earlier most had been fixing their gaze, essentially, on Addis Ababa and Shoa, and seeing the region from the viewpoint of this particular centre, now scholars and commentators witnessed the encroachment of the so-called 'periphery' on the centre, and understood that the history of the region was rather more nuanced than had often been supposed. The Ethiopian empire-state would be dissected by scholars and soldiers alike.

It is wholly understandable, and very welcome in many respects, that so much work has tended to focus on the modern era; it has, however, come at a price, namely a neglect of the deep past and *la longue durée*. Pre-colonial African history more generally has, of course, experienced something of a dramatic decline since the 1970s, and no doubt scholarship on north-east Africa reflects that trend. In north-east Africa, of course, the concept of 'pre-colonial' is problematic. It has no applicability in Ethiopia itself, unless we wish to talk of the various subject peoples of the south and west in these terms, a people who have only recently begun their struggle against Amhara-Tigrayan domination—and many do, of course. More conventionally, work on 'pre-colonial' Eritrea is virtually non-existent, for various reasons, although a recent special edition of the *Eritrean Studies Review* on 'Eritrea on the eve of colonial rule' suggested what might be done.[16] Archaeological work in Eritrea is in its troubled infancy.[17] Meanwhile, those interested in the pre-colonial history of the Somali must continue to rely on the most recent edition of Ioan Lewis' classic monograph.[18] As for Ethiopia itself, work on the pre-1900 period has been reduced to a trickle. Donald Crummey's recent weighty study of land and society was the product of many years' research,[19] while the 1986 Donham and James volume contained some important insights into the late nineteenth-century peripheries of imperial Ethiopia.[20] The Oromo in particular have begun to be studied in these terms, not coincidentally in the era of ethnic federalism in Ethiopia and of continued Oromo insurgency.[21] Many have attempted to historicize this conflict, sometimes very self-consciously—although it is interesting that this was never really attempted in the Eritrean context,[22] doubtless reflecting the liberation movement's own somewhat inhibited view of the past. Certainly, it is as though the big states had been 'done', and there was a brief flurry of attention directed toward smaller, less 'visible', but increasingly armed ethnicities in the Rift Valley, in northern Kenya and southern Ethiopia in the early and mid-1990s. Contributors to Fukui and Markakis' examination of ethnic violence in the Horn, or Kurimoto and Simonse's volume on age systems across the region, often rooted their analyses in the nineteenth century.[23] As for the dramas of the nineteenth-century Ethiopian highlands, the last word, it seemed, had gone to the generation working on these in the 1960s and 1970s, with only fast-moving, cinematic retellings appearing on bookshelves, such as, most recently, Philip Marsden's version of the Tewodros story.[24] However, exceptionally, and rather more importantly, James McCann's work on Ethiopian environmental history incorporated the nineteenth century, and—as was only appropriate to the subject-matter—carried the analysis into the late twentieth century,[25] and Izabela Orlowska's doctoral research on Yohannes IV should be mentioned here, too.[26] Clearly, it is not that *nothing* has been done, but that there has been so little of it. The problem is that, as a result, there has been a failure to more deeply historicize some key phenomena so apparent across modern north-east Africa, not least warfare.

I have argued elsewhere that the role of war in Africa's deeper history has been a comparatively neglected subject to date, but that the Ethiopian region is rather better served than most.[27] In our region, warfare has been given its historical place in a number of studies concerned with the expansion of the Solomonic state, particularly bellicose (and successful) monarchs, and the necessity of defence against a range of external enemies, culminating in those from Europe. In much of the Ethio-centrist literature, indeed, all roads lead to Adwa, and in almost no other corner of pre-colonial Africa has a battle been awarded such nation-building significance as to be virtually European.[28] More generally, Ethiopia since the 'Solomonic restoration' has been defined as a militaristic polity, smiting enemies and imposing itself—and its grand (written) narrative—on the highland environment. Some excellent work has indeed been produced on soldiers, weapons, and battles, and the current study owes much to them. But these older celebrations of both sword and pen in the great sweep of Ethiopian history were rarely concerned with analyses of social and political violence, or with the economic, cultural, and ethnic dimensions to war which was itself hardly problematized. It is also true that, as noted above, the role of war and violence in the pre-1900 past has largely been set aside in favour of more contemporary analyses of violence, more often undertaken by anthropologists than historians. Once more, this has reflected concern for actual events. The collapse of the Ethiopian and Somali states—temporary in the case of the former, rather more enduring for the latter—in the early 1990s was at least in part brought about by localised, anti-state, ethnically cohesive (or ethnically inspired) violence; as the 1990s progressed, a host of

small but often deadly armed organizations grew up alongside older
movements such as the Oromo Liberation Front to challenge the existing
order. Meanwhile the supposed *pax* between Eritrea and Ethiopia proved
to be a mere suspension of hostilities.

A great many of these conflicts have been examined in considerable
depth by specialists, and again this book owes much to their analyses.
However, while these studies often lay stress on the essential *novelty* of such
violence—environmental catastrophe, the failure of the state and of state-
building projects, and the conjunction of arms and newly radicalized ethnic
and/or 'national' identity, all since the 1970s—it is my contention that these
conflicts are in fact much more deeply rooted in the past than might be
assumed, and are indeed intrinsic to understanding the political and social
evolution of the region. In essence, like some previous scholars of north-east
Africa, I too believe in continuity; unlike them, however, I do not perceive
a continuous state, but rather a continuous state of violence upon which is
founded the modern polity—whether Ethiopia, or Eritrea, or indeed Sudan
and Somalia—which is in turn defined by violence. The nation-states which
have emerged in the early years of our millennium are built less on negotiated settlement—although inevitably this is a core component of state-
building—and rather more on cyclical conflict whose periodic cessation is
only part of the political and social equipment seen as necessary to the consolidation of those states. Such equipment has been refined over the last two
centuries or more; and, within the states themselves, actors who see themselves as marginalized continue to draw on past experience and to consider
violence as the natural means to 'resolution'.

The fertile frontier: borderlands and frontier societies in north-east Africa

The title, 'frontiers of violence', alludes to the conceptualization of the
region's history over the two centuries which is at the core of this book. It
is contended here that the region can be characterized in terms of tectonics—a mosaic of fault lines and frontier zones, shifting borderlands which
are not 'peripheries' but which have defined the very nature of the states
and societies themselves. As communities compete over ideologies and
resources, frontiers of violence have opened up across the region: sometimes

the communities pre-date the frontiers, which are thus formed by expanding
polities, at other times the frontiers have emerged first, and serve to forge
the communities. In that sense we are interested in the ways in which particular societies have grown up *within* and *because of* the violent frontier—
Oromo expansion, for example, or the liberation struggles in the north in
the twentieth century—and also how other (often larger) states have been
fundamentally shaped by the experience of these frontiers: i.e. states are
ultimately defined by their turbulent borderlands, which are thus not
'peripheral' but are seedbeds, zones of interaction which are as constructive,
creative, and fertile as they are destructive and violent. Thus the concept of
the *fertile frontier* is true often in a literal sense—borderlands are the result of
societies and cultures pushing into resource-rich lands—but it is *especially*
true in the sense that out of these frontiers come new ways of being, of
organizing, and self-perceiving and perceiving others. The fertility of the
frontier—the vitality of violence, if we prefer—is crucial to understanding
the region's modern history; tectonics helps us rethink the political con-
figuration of the 'Greater Horn' over *la longue durée* in terms of fault lines, at
times dormant, at other times explosive, as states and societies and cultures
invent and reinvent themselves according to current political and economic
exigencies.

Although it is hoped that this model may be more widely applicable to
other parts of the world which are clearly historically turbulent, our region
does have some unique features—or at least a combination of dynamics
which renders the region both particularly violent and markedly creative:
its peculiar historical experience of contemporaneous European imperialism and African imperialism; the very experience of 'African-on-African'
imperialism in the form of modern Ethiopia; particularly deeply rooted
(and literate) ideologies of governance, ethnic election, and social organization (among the Tigrinya, Amhara, and Somali); as a result, especially
clearly defined and historically rooted (even if at times shifting) notions of
ethnic community; the presence of competing global faiths; remarkable
geographical and thus cultural diversity within a historically discrete and
coherent zone of interaction; proximity to the strategically and commercial vital southern Red Sea zone; climatic variability, thus giving rise to
fierce competition over resources; large-scale and long-term population
movement across the region. While many other regions have had a number
of these features in place, few have all of them, and this is what renders
north-east Africa so dynamic and its frontiers of violence so fertile.

The analysis presented here owes much to Frederick Jackson Turner's seminal thesis—that the moving frontier had fundamentally defined the history of the United States, shaped its political and social structures, and the ways in which Americans thought about themselves—and the criticisms that have been made of it over several decades. My own interpretation has likewise drawn inspiration from Dietrich Gerhard's revisiting of the Turner thesis in 1959,[29] and, above all, from Kopytoff's work on the African frontier and political culture.[30] The study of borders and frontier zones has long been, in different ways, of interest to scholars of north-east Africa, but there is no doubt that in recent years it has attracted more attention.[31] I have attempted to build on some of Kopytoff's core ideas in relation to north-east Africa, which provides an excellent laboratory for the purpose. It is important to be clear about our typologies, which are basically three. The first is the squeezed zone between states, contested areas between the expanding imperial frontiers of competing polities. This zone produces militant identities and political cultures and frontier mentalities of its own, built on regional fault lines. Second, we have deep-rooted ethnic or 'national' boundaries, which can be both internal and external, and which can shift continually—in terms of categories of population and the location of the frontier. Thirdly, there are the physical frontiers and borderlands between environmental and economic zones (and even within these); and these clearly make a contribution to the formation of the first two typologies. Periods of economic and environmental stress rendered these frontiers highly volatile and competitive zones, where human suffering but also economic opportunity and political creativity coexisted. It is also the case, of course, that insofar as borders are 'shifting'—although it is argued in this book that the broad frontier zones remain remarkably consistent over two centuries or more—some borders or fault lines are 'dormant' at particular moments while others become 'live'. This is resonant, clearly, with the idea of identities also shifting. The margins make the metropole: they fundamentally influence and shape it, place overt and covert political and economic and cultural pressures on it, while, of course, often the metropole itself is *from* the margins originally, or otherwise a direct product of it. *The very nature of society in north-east Africa, thus, is defined by its rough, contested edges.* The border reflects the essence of the state itself, in Ethiopia and Eritrea, and indeed Sudan.

Frontiers, then, frequently produce highly militarized societies—especially when we recognize the frontier not simply as a no-man's-land between mature polities, but as a *fault line* and, often, a contested zone. Such a zone of conflict and competition—and this does not preclude the zone being a conduit, or indeed a 'land of opportunity'—produces particular kinds of societies and degrees of conflict; the fault line is representative of deeper political tectonics, and this is clearly demonstrated across north-east Africa. Again, as will become clear, I will argue for the interpretation of the Eritrean–Ethiopian frontier zone as the epicentre of much of the region's violence. It is not, I would suggest, overly deterministic to argue that the fault line does indeed have a profound impact on the societies and communities which grow up there: the Eritrean frontier zone, for example, demonstrates this very well. Here, we can see the national liberation movement of the late twentieth century as the product of a much deeper competitive and contested environment. More broadly, Ethiopia and its immediate neighbours constitute a region which may be described—echoing, but in many respects distinct from, Gellner's idea about the prison-house of peoples—as a *mosaic of fault lines and frontier zones*. This violent competitiveness, and importantly its antiquity, in turn explains the strength of ethnic identity and group consciousness across the region. Moreover, as a region relatively free of the processes of colonial invention, it offers us insights into African political and ethnic evolution which might be possible elsewhere, were it not for the fact that scholars are unable to study local constellations for the bright lights of colonialism. It is also the case that the frontier zone itself *exercises a profound influence on the wider region*—it does not merely exist of and for itself. Metropoles are frequently *defined by what happens in their adjacent frontier zones*—it is not merely a matter, as Koptyoff implies, of pioneers from the metropole going forth and building new societies there. These fault lines are merely the surface manifestation of deeper political tectonics, and thus shape profoundly the kind of *ethnies* and communities and nations which press in on them from every direction. In this context do we thus recall the work of Fredrik Barth on how ethnic communities define themselves according to their boundaries, and what lies beyond them[32]—and, I would suggest further, what happens *within* those frontier zones and corridors of competition. In these places, political and cultural creativity flourish and violence has a vitality that is sometimes unpalatable to the squeamish observer; to be sure, such creativity has often had brutal results, but it has been a crucial part of the process of invention and formation and, ultimately, construction as well as destruction.

2

The Shadows of Antiquity

Axum and its aftermath

The Axumite empire has cast long shadows over the region's history, and these can be understood from two perspectives. First, there are the very tangible ways in which the ideological, political, and ethnic nature of Axum had repercussions long after the state's demise, and of course the manner in which it actually collapsed likewise had a profound impact on the shape of political and social relations across the region. Second, the undoubted intellectual and material legacy of Axum has been claimed and contested by a number of successive regimes seeking—in different ways—both continuity and legitimacy. The partial mythology—and it is only partial—persists that 'Ethiopia', in its medieval, early modern, and more recent manifestations, is the successor to Axum, and the rightful inheritor of its physical and intellectual legacy. Yet even within this collective inheritance, tensions have existed over whether the southern Semites, the Amhara, can really lay any claim to what was in essence a northern Semitic, Tigrinya civilization; certainly, few groups south of the tenth parallel would consider themselves to have been part of the supposedly seminal cultural experience that was Axum. Lately, however, a new challenge has come—as in so many other respects—from north of the Mereb River. Eritrean independence and consequent nationalist revisionism has meant the split of the Axumite inheritance across an international frontier, and a violently contested one at that, and the assertion that Axum was at least as much an 'Eritrean' as an 'Ethiopian' civilization, notwithstanding the fact that these appellations are meaningless for the period under discussion. Recent discoveries of pre-Axumite sites in Eritrea caused much excitement among archaeologists,[1] and apparently some bitter resentment on the Ethiopian side of the border: Eritrea's extant archaeological inheritance came under attack by Ethiopian soldiers in 2000, who attempted to destroy an important pre-Axumite stele at Metara.[2] It seemed that the battle over boundaries, identities, and regional hegemony had also become one of who had a stronger claim to antiquity—a curious juxtaposition alongside the revolutionary militancy of the former guerrillas in power in Asmara and Addis Ababa.

Axum had been one of the great civilizations of the ancient Eurasian world, with its roots in an indigenous agrarian culture with links across the Red Sea to southern Arabia between the fifth and third centuries BCE. Axum's mercantilism had a violent aspect, and royal inscriptions from the fourth century onward attest to military campaigns across the Red Sea, leading to the establishment of military garrisons in southern Arabia, to wars against the Nubian kingdom of Meroe in central Sudan, and to the conquest of various peoples in the immediate vicinity of Axum itself. Ezana was the self-styled 'king of kings'—an epithet which would be inherited by the emperors of Ethiopia many centuries later—while Axum itself, dominant between the second and eighth centuries CE, was in truth one of a number of states vying for power in the southern Red Sea region. It was a distinctively Semitic, highland civilization which made much of military glory—few do not, of course—but which also, in time, made much of its proselytizing Christian mission across the wider region. In religious centres, such as Debre Damo, a new monastic zeal emerged around the principles of communal living, obedience, and self-discipline and was introduced into the provinces of Wag and Lasta, south of Tigray;[3] Christianity was also growing among the non-Semitic Agaw speakers of northern Wollo. Already by the middle of the first millennium CE, the interaction between Christians and non-Christians in the northern highlands had an ethnic element to it, and the notion of what it was to be *Axumite* was being formed very sharply along the lines of religion, ethnicity, and language.

These definitions would become all the more marked in the centuries which followed, the period of Axum's slow, apparently inexorable decline. Out of the violence and chaos of Axum's collapse emerged the Zagwe dynasty, itself Agaw—a problem in terms of posterity, as we see below. In fact the Zagwe era, beginning in the mid-twelfth century, was one of the most remarkable in the region's early history.[4] The Zagwe presided over an energetic Christian expansion through the northern and central Ethiopian highlands, as well as a notable commercial and cultural interaction with Egypt and the wider Middle East; the dynasty was also responsible for the creation of some of Ethiopia's most remarkable architecture. Despite their considerable

achievements, however, weaknesses in the Zagwe state had begun to appear
by the early thirteenth century. Unable to forge broader unity, the Zagwe
were also undermined by their own repeated succession disputes, which in
turn encouraged the emergence of anti-Zagwe movements among the
Semitic-speaking Tigrayans and Amhara; they were, in many ways, the 'natural' ethnic and cultural enemies of the Cushitic, Agaw-speaking Zagwe, and
certainly in terms of their own self-image the rightful claimants to the
Christian Axumite inheritance. The most potent challenge ultimately came
from the Christian community in Shoa, which had grown prosperous from
the eastbound trade routes and which—critically—had the support of the
local church. The Shoan rebellion started in 1268 and was led by Yekuno
Amlak, who won a series of battles across Lasta and Begemedir culminating
in the death of the last Zagwe king in 1270. Yekuno Amlak declared himself
ruler and set about creating a new moral and ideological order.

Violence and mythology: the new Zion

The non-Semitic origins of the Zagwe would allow the insurgents of the
1260s and subsequent chroniclers to talk of their illegitimacy. While the
Zagwe had sought legitimacy by creating the myth that they were descended
from Moses, and assiduously sought moral authority through impressive
churches of rock, none of this impressed later chroniclers, who probably
destroyed much of the dynasty's own literary endeavour and depicted the
Zagwe as lacking any 'Israelite' connection. In order to assert its own legitimacy, the new dynasty claimed to be a restoration of the 'Solomonic' line.
It sponsored the narrative at the centre of the *Kebre Negast* ('The Glory of
the Kings'[5]) that the rightful rulers of the Christian kingdom must be
descended from the union of King Solomon and Makeda, the Queen of
Saba, or Sheba; the Zagwe had represented an illegal hiatus, while the newly
restored Solomonic kings were associated with the ancient and glorious
kings of Axum. In real terms, it seems fair to say that only insofar as the monarch was once again a Semitic-speaker can Yekuno Amlak's advent to power
be considered a 'restoration'; but the *Kebre Negast* was a powerful vindication.
Its central point was that the 'greatness of kings' was related to possession of
a sacred emblem (namely the Ark of the Covenant), and a blood connection
with a God-anointed elect. While some scholars have dated at least some of

the text to the sixth century, it is more likely to have originated in the thirteenth century as a piece of anti-Zagwe propaganda, and was redacted in the early years of the fourteenth century. In many respects, it is a composite work, incorporating oral and written traditions from both the Ethiopian region and the Middle East, but above all it was used to bathe the new state in military glory and legitimacy, and hail the 'restored' lineage. In fact, the early decades of the new dynasty's existence were precarious, with Yekuno Amlak facing much opposition, and it was only under his grandson, Amda Tsion (1312–42) that the state was able to establish itself firmly in the Christian heartlands and indeed embark on expansion.[6] The *Kebre Negast* was therefore crucial in terms of legitimization, for who could argue with a kingship descended from Solomon, and his son Menelik, who had taken the Ark of the Covenant to Ethiopia? Thus was made explicit the covenant between God and Ethiopia, which was now Israel's successor, the new Zion; *habesha* Christian highlanders were developing a distinctively chauvinistic view of themselves and their geopolitical environment. Yet there was perhaps more to it than meets the eye. The 'final' redaction of the text was undertaken by a team of Tigrayan monks in the early fourteenth century, at a time when the north was in revolt against Amda Tsion; one argument, therefore, is that the *Kebre Negast* was actually a Tigrayan script, a northern riposte to southern 'usurpation', namely that of the increasingly ambitious and hegemonic Amhara.[7] Tigray, after all, had a much stronger claim to the Axumite inheritance than any other parvenu Christian province.

Whatever the case, the *Kebre Negast* provided the foundations for a uniquely *habesha* polity; the 'nation' thus born in its narrative was superior to all others in faith, in culture, in blood, and, blessed by God, Ethiopians now had a mandate to carry fire and sword among pagans and Muslims alike across the surrounding area. Their violent expansion was just and righteous, a form of holy war which defined the Solomonic state in the centuries to come. Much of this war was documented in glorious detail in royal chronicles, composed in the style of the Old Testament and redolent of the trials and triumphs of the early kings of Israel.[8] These were doubtless inspired, of course, by the *Kebre Negast* itself, which is a violent book: soon after becoming king, Menelik I—also David II—

> waged war wherever he pleaseth, and no man conquered him, but whosoever attacked him was conquered, for Zion himself made the strength of the enemy to be exhausted. But King David II with his armies and all those who obeyed

his word, ran by the chariots without pain, hunger or thirst, without sweat and
exhaustion...

In this way, successful wars are waged against enemies as far flung as Egypt
and India.[9] Righteous violence became legitimized through Solomonic
mythology and came to occupy a central role in *habesha* political discourse
and action, as real and as vital to nineteenth- and twentieth-century rulers
as it was to early Solomonic monarchs. From the outset, moreover, the
Solomonic state was wedded to a militant monasticism, which pushed forward the frontiers of Christianity as the state itself expanded. Monks and
monasteries were as much at the forefront of *habesha* imperialism as soldiers
and governors.

The Christian state increasingly defined itself against a range of external
enemies, and indeed its rivalry with the Islamic states and societies to the
east and south-east was prolonged, and episodically violent. In the first
instance it was concerned with the control of trade routes which fanned out
from the port of Zeila on the Gulf of Aden, and around which a series of
Muslim settlements were founded, reaching as far as south-east Shoa. Islam
had been gradually introduced to north-east Africa via the Somali coast,
linking the region with Muslim trading networks which were stretching
out across the western Indian Ocean from the Persian Gulf.[10] The early
Solomonic state had undoubtedly accrued considerable benefits from working with Muslim merchants—notably in terms of the slave trade—but the
trade routes themselves were soon the focus of fierce competition between
Christians and Muslims, and Amda Tsion's victories toward the east meant
that Muslim settlements were required to recognize his suzerainty. Islam was
disunited in the region—many Muslims were content to accept Solomonic
hegemony, as it meant commercial gain in some respects, while there was
also bitter rivalry between settlements as well as ethnic diversity—and the
key sultanate of Ifat, under the Walasma dynasty, was ultimately overcome in
the 1330s. But a radical anti-Christian element survived in Ifat, and sparked
into life in the late fourteenth century when an abortive coup attempted to
overthrow the sultan, Ali, who was seen as overly friendly with the
Ethiopians. Ifat, indeed, collapsed temporarily under the weight of these
disturbances; the Walasma family took refuge for a time in Yemen, but they
later returned to found a new settlement further east, close to present-day
Harar. Meanwhile, by the early fifteenth century, another Islamic state, Adal,
had become established nearby—in the area of modern north-west Somalia,

southern Djibouti, and north-east Ethiopia—but out of range of direct Christian control, if not of their marauding armies which visited regularly in the course of the fifteenth century.

Adal would become the focus of concerted Islamic resistance against *habesha* domination of the region.[11] The Ethiopian defeat of Adal's ruler Muhammad in 1516 led to a crisis for the sultanate: as the capital was transferred to Harar, Ahmad ibn Ibrahim al-Ghazi, a prominent soldier, emerged as kingmaker, having Sultan Abu Bakr killed, putting his brother in his place, and having himself titled Imam. The broader context was the rise of Ottoman power in the Red Sea region, and with it a more confident, aggressive Islam, and contemporaneously a weakening of Ethiopian power stemming from problems at the centre through the late fifteenth century. Imam Ahmad was a messianic leader, successfully preaching the need for *jihad* against the Christian state among the Somali and Afar—although quite how much these Cushitic soldiers were moved by religious fervour is a matter of debate, and environmental factors may have been at least as important. He urged self-discipline and abstinence, and his militant message—the purification of Islam in the region, and the wresting of the Ethiopian state from the unbelievers—received support (and doubtless inspiration) from imported missionaries, adventurers, and activists from the Arabian peninsula. The links between nascent Somali Islam and Arabia were clearly already significant. In the course of the 1520s, Ahmad—also known as 'Gran', the left-handed—reorganized Adal, revitalized the ruling dynasty, and set about the systematic recruitment of the Somali, who had become increasingly Islamized over several decades; and in 1529, he led his *jihad* into the Ethiopian highlands armed with Ottoman guns and temporary Muslim unity. As his army advanced, it was joined by Cushitic communities hopeful of regaining their independence from Solomonic control, and success came quickly: by the mid-1530s, the Islamic forces had swept into the Ethiopian heartlands. The Ethiopian emperor, Lebna Dengel, however, remained at large, and fought a rearguard action until his death in 1540; and before he died, he succeeded in sending a desperate message to the Portuguese, his new allies with whom he had been in contact since around 1520 and who had themselves recently arrived in the southern Red Sea area. The Portuguese contributed a small force equipped with firearms and Ahmad's increasingly over-stretched army was decisively defeated in 1543. The Christian church was thus preserved, and the image of 'fortress Ethiopia' underlined. But much damage had been done. In the 1550s, as Galawdewos tried to refashion the Solomonic state with the remnants left to him, Ethiopia was characterized by a loss of con-fidence as well as much material damage and immeasurable human losses. Certainly, the events of the sixteenth century were burnt into the 'popular' and 'institutional' memories of Ethiopians, as we see in Part II; they also cast a shadow over future Christian-Muslim relations, however economically interdependent adherents to the two faiths were. But Christian Ethiopia remained conscious of its precarious position surrounded by Muslim ene-mies—something which would echo down to the present day in terms of Ethiopia's internal politics, and its relations with neighbouring states, nota-bly Somalia and Sudan.

Between the sixteenth and the eighteenth centuries, the shrunken Ethiopian state attempted to stabilize and consolidate, and for a time—during the Gondarine period—it did so. But centrifugal tendencies, an over-powerful regional nobility, and lack of clear succession rules weakened the Solomonic state, which was also fundamentally transformed by the arrival of the Oromo. The Oromo 'appeared' in the *habesha* line of vision in the aftermath of Ahmad's *jihad*, were of increasing significance in the remak-ing of the Solomonic state at Gondar, and were instrumental in the demise of the monarchy and the forging of a new era—and ultimately, of a new political reality. Although the Oromo migrations were only one factor in a crisis-laden and bloody sixteenth century, their impact would endure.[12] Oromo played many roles, and came in many guises; their past, indeed their present, is contested, and it is to their story that we must now turn.

The Oromo frontier

There can be few peoples in African history who have been as misunder-stood, and indeed as misrepresented, as the Oromo—or pejoratively 'Galla' in the older literature. They have been, arguably, even more demonized by Ethiopian chroniclers of various hues and over a longer timeframe than the Somali, historically the other great rival 'bloc' confronting the Amhara in north-east Africa. The tone was set early on by the monk Bahrey, whose 'History of the Galla' was produced in 1593.[13] In many respects Bahrey's 'History' tells us rather more about the problems of the Solomonic state than it does about the Oromo, as the latter are juxtaposed throughout against the society within which Bahrey was writing. He explained Oromo success as being due to the failure of the Ethiopian state to properly mobilize its resources, for example; he bemoaned the fact that Solomonic society comprised a number of privileged classes which no longer did any fighting, or indeed much of any use at all, while the Oromo were dedicated to warfare and moved 'as one' into the highlands, an unstoppable force both numerous and ferocious. Bahrey exaggerated both their numbers and their ferocity, but he created images that endured. By the nineteenth century it was *de rigueur* for European travel accounts to contain historical prologues outlining the savage invasions of the 'Galla', which gripped the European imagination and became a central part of the narrative which described the Christian kingdom as a highland fortress resolutely defending itself against savage neighbours. There was something in the story that reminded some writers, at least, of the decline of Rome, and Henry Salt could not resist the temptation to consider the Oromo as the region's Goths and Vandals. Yet they were also Philistines to Ethiopia's Israelites, and indeed 'the feelings of the Abyssinians towards the Galla partake of the same inveterate spirit of animosity which appears to have influenced the Israelites with regard to their hostile neighbours'.[14] In another source, the Oromo were the 'savage hordes' which had 'rent asunder the once powerful empire of Abyssinia, and arrested...the progress of Christianity, civilization, and refinement'.[15] They had their admirers—Victorian Britons were ever keen to applaud noble savagery—and in the 1860s Blanc considered the Wollo Oromo 'a fine race, far superior to the Abyssinian in elegance, manliness, and courage';[16] but rather more common was the view expressed by Markham in 1869, who declared that the Oromo were 'untameable people, resolved either to conquer or die...They are a cruel set of bloodthirsty robbers'. They had thrown 'a once civilized people more and more into barbarism and anarchy', and the resultant violence had 'plunged the wretched country deeper and deeper into anarchy'.[17] Thus were the Oromo made scapegoats for much that was held to be 'wrong' with highland state and society in the nineteenth century.

The generally accepted account[18] is that the prolonged period of destructive warfare in the first half of the sixteenth century had weakened the Christian kingdom's defences, leading to its shrinkage and consolidation around a northern core, particularly under Sarsa Dengel between the 1560s and the 1590s, and facilitating the gradual advance of groups of pastoral Oromo into the southern highlands. Sarsa Dengel withdrew many of his southern garrisons—which were increasingly becoming mere islands of Solomonic 'authority' in the midst of Oromo populations—and redeployed them in the north, thus reducing the level of resistance the migrants might otherwise have encountered. The Cushitic Oromo originated in the broad zone between the grasslands north-east of Lake Turkana and the south-east Ethiopian foothills, and in the course of the late sixteenth century they began to move into the southern third of present-day Ethiopia. They also moved in the vicinity of Harar. They were in search of better pastureland, although their point of origin suggests that they also practised some agriculture; almost certainly, their spread—like that of the Somali—was related to overpopulation and overgrazing. There was a significant number of Cushitic speakers—mainly Somali—in the Adal forces of Ahmad ibn Ibrahim. It seems reasonable to suppose that these *jihad*-ist fighters were in fact part of a larger Cushitic movement. Many converted to either Christianity or Islam, depending on the states and societies they encountered; however, it is the Muslim Oromo who are frequently portrayed in contemporary and later sources as 'barbarous hordes', closing in on Christian 'fortress Ethiopia'. Certainly, the advance of the Oromo into the central highlands was to some extent related to the shift in Amhara settlement to the north and west, but this was pull as well as push: the Amhara state was repositioning itself toward the Red Sea coast, seeking trading contacts with the Ottoman Turks at Massawa. Overall, it was a process of relocation that was reflected in the creation of the royal capital at Gondar in the 1630s.

As they moved, they both assimilated others, and were themselves assimilated.[19] There was nothing uniform or monolithic about the movement itself, of course: Oromo identified themselves as belonging to one or other of the two main branches, namely Borana (west, south, and centre of the Oromo population) or Bayratu (in the east), and then as members of one of the numerous clans within those branches, and as members of particular age-sets and lineages. But what they shared was a highly complex, sophisticated, and distinctive system of social and cultural organization; it was a system which would have an enormous impact on the peoples of the region, including the highland cultures of the Amhara and Tigray. Initially, their culture had its greatest impact in the military sphere, particularly through their complex age-grade system, known as *gada*.[20] *Gada* was remarkable for its pervasiveness, affecting all aspects of society; and although it is as much as anything else a philosophical tradition and the embodiment of a set of cultural values, it is most commonly associated with a militaristic pastoralism within which a man could gain honour and influence in society by attacking neighbouring societies and killing. The *gada* system defined male activities in eight-year segments. The pastoral nature of Oromo life meant the necessity of a loose, decentralized, egalitarian society which was ultimately led by officials who were elected by the particular *gada* rank responsible for government. The *qallu*, leaders who represented the forces of nature, exercised a loose authority over religious and political matters; they validated the leadership of the *gada* council drawn from a list of approved individuals. Oromo men, in order to reach the *qallu* grade, needed to have gone through the key aspects of life, notably marriage and military service. Success in the latter led to the former, very often, and so violence was periodically exercised on neighbouring peoples in order to permit young men to prove themselves. Certainly, one of the enduring historical images of the Oromo is of militaristic, proud, pastoralists, given to bursts of controlled violence; the influence of *gada*, arguably, was such that it led over the longer term to a wholesale change in the organization of highland Christian society after the sixteenth century.[21]

The mammoth clash between the Solomonic state and Adal had left the way clear for Oromo expansion, especially into central Shoa which had been situated on the fault line between Ethiopia and Adal, and which following the fighting constituted a depopulated borderland. Indeed Shoa now became one of the key battlegrounds between the Amhara and Oromo, and the Amhara-dominated parts of Shoa constituted a centre of anti-Oromo sentiment and propaganda. Sarsa Dengel was more or less constantly engaged in campaigns against the Oromo throughout his reign, and although he won victories against them in pitched battles in 1569, 1573, and 1578, in the longer term these were largely irrelevant: 'they kept on coming', in Levine's words.[22] In the 1550s, Oromo were beginning to move into both the former Christian provinces of the south, and the former Islamic sultanates of the Rift Valley; by the end of the sixteenth century, they were present in the heartlands of both Ethiopia and Adal. In time, they moved into the west and south-west, where Oromo pioneers encountered extant state systems which had been tributary to or influenced by the Solomonic state; here, the Oromo were influenced by what they found, and their pastoral egalitarianism was inverted in favour of agricultural and commercial monarchies.[23] These Oromo kingdoms asserted themselves over the Sidama and Omotic peoples of the region, and would remain essentially independent until Menelik's campaigns of territorial expansion in the 1880s and 1890s. Other groups of pioneers headed for the uplands, their movement and settlement facilitated by local depopulation and war-weariness; as they encountered different physical environments, socio-political differentiation developed. Again, there was no uniformity of response to or interaction with the communities they met. Some Oromo continued as pastoralists, others took to sedentary agriculture; many prac-tised both. While large numbers of Oromo came to identify closely with the host society, others held themselves apart, or only selectively adopted certain aspects of the host society and culture. Importantly, where Oromo pioneers settled and became Christian, it was increasingly rare for them to act in political unison as Oromo, a description which only had meaning below the public horizon—often only at the level of family; in time, they intermarried with the Amhara and other Semitic groups, and such cultural integration often led to the dissipation of the cultural frontier in the public space of the Ethiopian polity.

It was certainly clear, in time, that the Oromo were permanent settlers, especially across Shoa, Gojjam, and Wollo, where they continued to settle through the seventeenth century. Strategies of cohabitation were required. In the early seventeenth century, Emperor Susenyos implemented one such strategy which aimed at the integration of the Oromo into the political life of the Solomonic state; it was a project fraught with danger, although Susenyos' confidence doubtless stemmed from the fact that he had in fact lived among the Oromo and had married the daughter of a *gada* official. He sought to integrate Oromo military units into his army, and indeed used these to subdue rival branches of the Oromo, such was their disunity.[24] In the late seventeenth century, Iyasu sought to bring more Oromo into impe-rial service, and in this way did Oromo come to fill ever more prominent roles in the *habesha* political and military establishment. On one level, it was a highly successful policy of co-option on the part of the Amhara; but from a different perspective, it was the Oromo who had co-opted the Solomonic state, becoming a force to be reckoned with at the centre of imperial power in the eighteenth century, and uneasily sharing power with the Amhara and the Tigrinya—a situation which has persisted, in different guises, down to the present day.

In Gondar and its environs there was a swelling Oromo population—farmers, soldiers, courtiers, senior figures at the Gondarine court. New Oromo populations flowed in on the eastern flanks of the kingdom, while the state expanded into new borderlands north and west of Lake Tana. While they may have been associated with recent disasters, they also repre-sented a new and dynamic element in Ethiopian society. Oromo leaders were increasingly powerful, as the monarchy came to depend on them to shore up its position against the Amhara nobility. In the second half of the seventeenth century, for example, Fasilidas had forged alliances with the Oromo elite at Gondar during a theological controversy within the Orthodox Church which had isolated the monarchy from many Amhara noblemen. In the 1720s, Bakaffa had attempted to purge the court nobility, and used newly armed Oromo as a counterweight to the increasingly unreliable imperial guard, as well as deploying them in the suppression of regional revolt.[25] But it was the long-lived, powerful matriarch Mentewwab— Bakaffa's consort and, after his death, the head of an extensive political family known as the Qwarrana—who simultaneously buoyed the ailing monarchy and sowed the seeds of its destruction by allying it with the powerful Wollo Oromo through a series of political marriages.[26] This intricate network of alliances was supposed to protect the monarchy from a range of enemies, within the court and beyond Gondar—many of whom questioned the legitimacy of the Qwarrana, who had Agaw roots—but even Mentewwab came to realize the dangers of making the Oromo such an integral part of the political centre. She realized the power of Oromo king-makers too late, attempting to develop a Tigrayan counter-balance to Oromo power through *Ras* Mikael Sehul in the north. But in fact Mikael was himself able and willing to take advantage of widespread (and perennial) *habesha* fears of imminent decline, and playing upon the image of Gondar as the ailing heart of empire, riddled with vice and infidelity, and, most important of all, full of Oromo soldiers, courtiers and administrators who had no right to be there. It was, at least in part, the ethnicization—indeed, racialization—of political catastrophe which finally crushed the medieval Ethiopian state, and ushered in the period of overtly violent political culture known as the *zemene mesafint*; it also set the tone for much of what was to follow in terms of the region's political development.

PART
II

Violence and Imperialism

The 'Long' Nineteenth Century

3

States of Violence, to *c.*1870

Haunted house: the wars of the *mesafint*

The conflicts which erupted in the 1760s and 1770s were a long time coming. They finally shattered the façade of unity—of political and ethnic homogeneity—much trumpeted at the apex of the medieval Ethiopian state. Yet although the 'basic' narrative is reasonably well-known,[1] this remains an era on which much work needs to be done in order to fully understand its rich social, political, and ethnic dimensions and implications. The *zemene mesafint* was the crystallization of many of the evolving crises experienced by the *habesha* polity dating to the mid-sixteenth century, including the ever sharpening religious frontier between Christianity and Islam, the regionalism and centrifugal forces which would ultimately destroy the Ethiopian state, and the migration of the Oromo. The processes and dynamics which were unleashed from the late eighteenth century, moreover, would come to define the region's history long after the supposed 'reunification' of Ethiopia in the middle of the nineteenth century. The patterns of violence, and the reasons behind such violence, exist to the present day.

There is much we know about the *zemene mesafint*, but there is much we do not; and it remains the case that scholars rarely connect the events of this era to those of a later epoch. Viewed in bold colours, the century and a half between the 1770s and the 1920s is supposed to represent some kind of linear progression toward Ethiopian 'modernity', the latter manifest in the functioning state fashioned by Menelik and Haile Selassie. The *zemene mesafint*, from this perspective, is treated as a form of temporally determined 'pre-modern savagery', in much the same way as escalations of violent conflict in the nineteenth century have been regarded in other parts of the continent. It is history as prologue—albeit a necessary one, as otherwise the

essential modernity of the Ethiopian state-building exercise at the end of
the nineteenth century cannot be emphasized to the same extent—and
what happens next is, again, linear progression. The *zemene mesafint* is bloody
and terrible, and, at least implicitly, against the natural order of things; and
then comes 'restoration' and 'reunification', and Ethiopia not only 'survives'
but expands. In some respects, the Ethiopian 'model of modernity' follows
that set up for European colonial rule elsewhere on the continent.

This was an era of the nobility's dominance over the monarchy, and one
during which 'Ethiopia', in its medieval and early modern form, did not
exist in any practical, tangible shape—save for the fact that an emperor still
existed, lingering in Gondar in an impoverished state while politics rushed
on around him. Importantly, however, 'Ethiopia' did indeed survive as an
idea, powerful in the imagination—and it was this which caused contemporary chroniclers to despair about the awful illegitimacy of the violence
which defined the era, and lament that 'the Kingdom has become contemptible to children and slaves . . . a laughing stock to the uncircumcised . . . a
worthless flower that children pluck in the autumn rains'.[2] Imperial authority was paralysed by intrigue and by an impossibly entangled web of tactical
alliances and counter-alliances. Whatever power was still wielded by the
emperor Iyoas, and indeed of the ageing matriarch Mentewwab, was
contingent upon the advantages which others could derive from royal commands. Politics was increasingly a matter of ethnicity and of region. The
royal family, with Agaw roots, had sought to shore up its position through
intermarriage with other powerful groups, not least the increasingly important Oromo of Wollo province. When it was feared that an ethnic imbalance
might destabilize the delicate arrangements at Gondar, redress was sought
elsewhere, notably in the form of the Tigrayan leader Mikael Sehul, who
had been appointed governor of the north. But Mikael was no more interested in the restoration of Solomonic glory than the Oromo nobility now
so central to the functioning of imperial power. He too sought political pre-
eminence, and indeed had the advantage—as governor of Tigray—of access
to coastal commerce and thus the ability to acquire firearms.[3] Further south,
the Amhara may have been resentful of his being Tigrayan, but Mikael was
able to play on the fears harboured by traditionalists and conservatives that
Ethiopia was facing disaster, and at any rate he was, for many, a better option
than any of the Oromo now flooding the streets of Gondar as soldiers,
courtiers, and administrators. In Bruce's indubitably embellished account,
Mikael at one point proclaims the 'Galla' 'the enemies of [this] country . . .

I am much deceived if the day is not at hand when [the emperor] shall curse
the moment that ever Galla crossed the Nile'.[4]

Among the Oromo themselves there were tensions between those who
were 'assimilated' into the Solomonic state and those who were not, and
such strains exploded into open war in 1766. Out of desperation, and fear-
ing that Gondarine society would be destroyed by intra-Oromo strife, Iyoas
called on *Ras* Mikael to save the state. It was a plea which highlighted the
insoluble dilemma faced by the monarchy: unable to withstand the power
of regionalism, they had turned to the clearest manifestation of potent
regionalism to protect the Solomonic inheritance. He responded by mar-
shalling his army and defeating, first, the unstable royal faction, followed by
the Wollo Oromo themselves. Bruce recorded: '[T]here was no safety but in
Ras Michael', who was now possessed of 'supreme power, both civil and
military'.[5] In 1769, Iyoas, quickly becoming fearful of the *Ras*'s strength,
ordered Mikael back to Tigray and attempted to form a coalition of anti-
Tigrayan forces, loyal Oromo included; Mikael refused, marched on Gondar,
and had Iyoas murdered. It was arguably the most significant *coup d'etat* in
the region's history until the removal of Haile Selassie in 1974. In effect, the
Gondarine era was brought to a close, and in many respects the Solomonic
state was finished. In Gondar itself, emperors would come and go, some dal-
lying longer than others, but each one merely the titular head of an empire
which to all intents and purposes no longer existed. The *zemene mesafint*
may have begun as a 'civil war', but it became rather more than that, morphing into bloody competition between territorially and, increasingly, ethnically defined polities, from the region of the Eritrean highland plateau
(the *kebessa*) and adjacent lowlands, down through Tigray and the central
Ethiopian Highlands. It was an era in which the power of Tigray grew,
portentously connected in no small measure to the slave and arms trades of
the Red Sea, and during which the importance of the Oromo in altering
the ethnic and cultural shape of the central highlands was profound. In the
meantime the Amhara provinces sought to hold their own against both; and
in the longer term, it was the ability of Shoa to supplant Tigray, marginal-
izing the latter province in political and economic terms, which defined the
later decades of the nineteenth century.

While the 1770s were characterized by a series of schisms within the
increasingly decrepit Solomonic order, in the course of the 1780s a faction
of families known as the Warrashek became prominent.[6] They came from
the Yajju region of Wollo, and were ultimately descended from a group of

Oromo families which had married into the imperial court in the course of the sixteenth century. Although originally from a region in Wollo that had been exposed to Islamic influence, the leading members of the Warrashek faction were Christian by the late eighteenth century—although names such as Ali clearly show an Islamic influence. Ali Gwangul was in many ways the founder of the dynasty, establishing hegemony over the rump Solomonic polity in the 1780s and 1790s. By the early years of the nineteenth century, *Ras* Ali II of the Warrashek was the dominant figure, based at Debre Tabor to the east of Lake Tana. Ali's mother, Menen, was a powerful and charismatic figure, and belonged to an Ethiopian tradition of influential matriarchs stretching back several centuries. In essence, the Warrashek represented the dominance of the central Amhara provinces, the old heart of the Gondarine empire, but new frontiers and conflicts were opening up. Warrashek hegemony was increasingly challenged from the north, notably, Tigray under Wube from the 1830s. For a time, Wube was a serious contender for the Solomonic inheritance—had he won a major encounter against the Warrashek at Debre Tabor in 1842, he might have been able to claim it—but he failed, and retreated back north. Ali's Amhara domain was, for the time being, more powerful than Tigray, a fact at least tacitly acknowledged by Wube; yet Tigray remained a major, and increasingly important, player in *habesha* politics.

In addition to this essentially 'northern' struggle, challenges came from the southern mountains in the form of Gojjam, lying south of Lake Tana, and Shoa, further south-east.[7] These historically Amharic provinces were also deeply infused with Oromo immigration. Gojjam and Shoa were well-positioned to gain access to the rich lands of the south—later the great prize of imperial expansion—while Shoa in particular was also able to reach toward the Red Sea trade at its southerly end from the early nineteenth century. Gojjam and Shoa—the former under Berru and his son Goshu, the latter under Sahle Selassie, grandfather of Menelik—began to accumulate both political and economic muscle in the early decades of the nineteenth century, and were the key rivals in the southern-central bloc of the *zemene mesafint*. The Shoans in particular showed themselves interested in the Solomonic restoration, an increasingly potent notion as the first half of the nineteenth century wore on, and indeed Sahle Selassie was using the title *Negus* by the early 1830s. Yet the more potent attempt to consolidate imperial power and claim the Solomonic inheritance would in time come from an ostensibly unlikely direction—the province of Kwara, closer than Shoa

to the old imperial heartland at Gondar, but a peripheral, borderland territory nonetheless, located in the foothills between the Ethiopian Highlands
and the central Sudanese riverine plains. There, Kassa Haylu—later
Tewodros—would gradually gather strength.

It is axiomatic to suggest that contemporary European sources must be
treated with caution in this context; 'Western' observers had a tendency to
exaggerate and misunderstand the level of violence they were witnessing,
and to emphasize above all else the prevalence of war, or what passed for it,
among savage tribes endlessly at one another's throats.[8] What they were
witnessing, in fact, was vicious total war, ruthlessly rational in economic and
political terms. It was cyclical economic war aimed at the capture of agricultural resources and livestock, or the destruction of these so that enemies
could not benefit from them. This form of economic war was especially
virulent during periods of climatic instability, drought and hunger—as in
the 1860s, notably, as well as later in the nineteenth century. While pitched
battle between 'professional' armies appears to have been common enough,
there was scarcely any differentiation made between combatant and non-
combatant when it came to the targeting of particular communities by
those armies. Peasant farmers were deliberately attacked, periodically dis-
persing communities into hills and forests away from vulnerable positions
on open ground, or else pushing them together into fortified settlements.[9]
Regional chiefs pursued terroristic tactics against populations in enemy territory in order to achieve hegemony and secure resources. Violence was not
something that happened on distant appointed fields, but was lived by ordinary Tigrinya, Amhara, Oromo, and a host of others across the region.

Europeans were drawn to the depiction of the Oromo as savage hordes,
destroying a once-great civilization, as we saw in Chapter 2. Nonetheless, it
is clear enough that particular divisions of Oromo across the north and
north-east highlands were frequently the decisive military and political factor throughout the decades of the *zemene mesafint*. In Gojjam, Lasta, and
Wollo, the ethos and organization of Oromo forces, and their deployment
of substantial corps of horsemen, made them formidable enemies as far as
various Tigrayan and Amhara overlords were concerned.[10] The latter, indeed,
frequently required Oromo support in order to make good, through armed
force, political claims over the longer term. Thus were the Oromo involved
in key struggles across the region, including Tigray itself. Plowden, well-
acquainted with mid-nineteenth century realities, noted that the Oromo of
Wollo and Shoa 'are always in a state of more or less active warfare', and

recorded one Oromo as sneering,' "What do you Amharas know of fighting? It is the same to us, and as regular, as breakfast and supper are to you.
What was a horse made for but to fight on, and a man made for but to die
like a man when his time comes?" '[11] As Blanc suggested some years later,
'[e]very Galla is a horseman, and every horseman a soldier; and thus is
formed a perfect militia, an always ready army, where no discipline is
required, no drill but to follow the chief'. Yet Blanc was careful to point out
that there was no such thing as a single 'Oromo nation', and that they were
deeply divided according to lineage and region;[12] this was to the advantage
of the *habesha* rulers who were frequently able to co-opt Oromo groups
into their own wars.

Between the 1800s and the 1840s, as competition heightened between
Tigray, the broad Amhara zone comprising Gojjam, Gondar, and
Begemeder, and Shoa with its particularly large Oromo population, successful armies required ever larger numbers of both foot soldiers and
horsemen, as well as of firearms, and thus ever greater access to the
resources to fund these forces.[13] The cumulative effect was a dramatic
militarization of political culture and discourse which has defined the
region subsequently. As Gobat wrote in 1832:

> The supreme judicial and executive power, including both the administration
> of the civil law, and military offices, are intimately connected in Abyssinia,
> being deposited in the hands of a single individual; for all the governors are
> both civil judges and military chieftains.[14]

For the broader population, the outcome was episodic suffering on a large
scale, with chronic insecurity of life and property across the central and
northern highlands, and as huge refugee movements away from zones of
conflict brought about severe economic hardship. Evidence from throughout the period indicates that non-combatants, including (indeed especially)
women and children, caught up in the violence were likely to be either
killed or enslaved. These were not merely the clashes of noblemen and their
professional armies on appointed fields, rather this was terroristic social violence on a dramatic scale. Soldiery itself was indeed becoming ever more
'professional' in the course of the nineteenth century, certainly insofar as
there were ever larger numbers of men whose time was largely dedicated to
armed service; Plowden wrote extensively of a distinctive and powerful
military class.[15] Armies themselves were supplemented by large numbers
of scavengers, fortune-hunters, and sundry hangers-on, all armed, if less

impressively than the warrior class, and predisposed to inflict damage on communities where profit was to be had as a result. Clearly, too, cultures of violence developed whereby the chase, the action, was an end in itself; brutal and brutalized, the perpetrators of the violence, which spread out beneath the grand political ambitions of the central figures of the period, were evidently in thrall to the notion of *gedday*, killing, for its own sake. The militarization of broader society was both cause and effect: all men carried arms, wrote Plowden, which was necessary even among a numerous 'middle class' of landholders who needed to protect themselves from marauding soldiers and nobility alike.[16]

In the mid-1840s, one traveller recorded grimly that

> the whole country was always more or less in a chronic state of war. If the two ruling princes [*Ras* Ali, west of the Takkaze, and Wube in Tigray] were not at war with each other, they were either fighting their neighbours or quelling rebellion among their own subjects.[17]

It seems possible to argue that it was through such violence that ideas about both sovereign statehood and the political utility of armed force were developed in their modern Ethiopian context—much as, for example, the wars of the princes in sixteenth-century Europe gave rise to military professionalism and laid the foundations of the nation-state. If it is the case that '[t]he origins of Europe were hammered out on the anvil of war',[18] then it holds true of much of Africa, too, and certainly north-east Africa. Plowden's description from 1844 of *Ras* Ali, Oromo by birth, and controlling a vast realm of Amhara territory from Gondar to Harar, illustrates the essential point that 'the spear and buckler have outweighed the law',[19] echoing Machiavelli's assertion that 'war is just when it is necessary' and subsequent debates in Europe about the legal framework required to facilitate war.[20] As Plowden explained, '[t]he chief power being entirely military, the soldier occupies the principal place; the Ras, and all the great men of the country, are of that class, and have absolute sway'.[21] It was a precarious and unstable existence, as recognized by *Ras* Welde Selassie in a revealing (if somewhat embroidered) conversation with Henry Salt around 1811:

> Even should I be successful [against Gondar] as I have every reason to expect, still I have not the means of ensuring any permanent settlement of affairs. It is my most heartfelt desire to see the King reinstated in all the dignity of his office but how can I give him ability? And all rule in this country depends on the energies of a chief himself—or how can I prevail [?] when I am obliged

to return to my own Government (from which a long absence is absolutely incompatible with my interests) affairs reverting as they have so often done to the old system. When I march into the country they will, as before endeavour to appease me by every humiliation they can employ and for a time agree to all my measures, but no sooner is my back turned than they plunder the King, refuse their proper tribute...

'Besides', he tells his European interlocutor, with (one imagines) a weary sigh, 'I am old now, and when I am dead all will come again to confusion'.[22]

While the central and northern highlands were embroiled in these con-flicts, rapid change was also taking place in the south, with the emergence of, and fierce competition between, several key Oromo states situated both at the end of vital trade routes and in richly productive areas.[23] State-formation here came about through a series of dynamics. Alongside the Omotic kingdoms of Yam (or Janjero), Kaffa, and Walayta, further north there were the Oromo monarchies forming in the first half of the nine-teenth century, including the so-called 'Gibe' monarchical states (founded in the area of the Gibe river) of Limmu-Enarea, Jimma Abba Jifar, Gera, Gomma, and Guma, there were also the Oromo principalities of Leqa, Qellam, and Naqamte. The Gibe monarchies were the product of complex processes of socio-political transformation: Oromo groups migrating into the area absorbed both people and ideas, and gradually made the shift from pastoralism to sedentary agriculture. This meant a long-term dilution of egalitarian social organization based around *gada*, the age regiment system, and the creation of social differentiation and political hierarchies similar to the extant political systems of the Ethiopian Highlands. Wars of expansion led to the enhancement of the position of war leader (*abba dula* in the *gada* system) which in several cases evolved into a monarchical institution. Additionally these were polities which fed off the increasingly lucrative trade routes running between the lower Nile basin and the southern Red Sea. Certainly, by the early nineteenth century, key states which had emerged as a result of these dynamics included Jimma Abba Jifar—named after its founder king, Abba Jifar I, who reigned 1830–55[24]—and Enarea, which reached its height under Abba Bagibo (reigned 1825–61) before being eclipsed by Jimma.[25] Another dramatic example is the state created by Jote Tullu in Wallaga in the later nineteenth century, which used military power to exploit the Ethiopian–Sudanese frontier commercial network. On the eastern side of the Great Rift Valley, Harar, the successor to Adal and a city-state which was becoming a major centre of Islamic influence, successfully resisted repeated attempts by local Oromo to overrun it, and indeed managed to convert some Oromo in the vicinity to Islam.

Thus did great territorial borderlands open up across a huge area of modern northern and central Ethiopia, characterized by a series of ethnic as well as multi-ethnic polities in competition with one another over space, economy, ideology, and belief systems. In a process of violent symbiosis, these various borderlands and frontier zones both cardinally defined the communities in and around them, and in turn were shaped by adjacent polities. It was a vortex of competition characterized by frequent minor armed clashes, and a handful of major battles. Campaigns which often stretched over months and years had a devastating impact on local populations, which were not only the target of the violence but which had to endure the garrisoning of troops on their lands for long periods at a stretch. Although it may be a characteristic of the region's deeper past, too, there can be little doubt that the nineteenth century witnessed a growing gulf between military and peasantry, and a growing belief among the latter that the former were rarely to be trusted, and only to be welcomed cautiously and often under duress. Above all, this was an era in which violence had primacy in political culture and in which militarism was both the means to an end and an end in itself in public affairs, thus creating models for political interaction according to which the region continues to function. Violence and militarism in nineteenth-century northeast Africa became self-perpetuating and cumulative.

Before the *zemene mesafint* fell into historiographical obscurity some twenty years or so ago, there was debate over the nature of the conflicts themselves—notably, whether centred on class, region, or ethnicity. While 'classic' accounts such as that by Abir couched their analyses in terms of 'Galla' (Oromo) domination and Tigrayan and Amhara struggles against it,[26] Crummey warned against the 'inadequacies of ethnicity as an explanation of politics in Christian Ethiopia during the Zamana Masfent', and instead placed emphasis on 'the social framework of political power'.[27] Class, he asserted, was crucial—particularly in terms of struggles between the nobility and the monarchy, and *within* the nobility itself. Much of this discussion needs to be understood in its intellectual context, namely the then-current conversation concerning Ethiopian 'feudalism' and its similarities to medieval European socio-political structures.[28] There can be little doubt that social status (and the mobility which characterized it) was a key factor in the pursuit of conflict; violence was often driven by 'class', loosely defined, in terms of access of economic and political resources. Regionalism drove conflict, too, for the same reasons—nor were regions always defined in 'ethnic' terms: witness the ongoing intra-Amhara violence, notably the often bitter competition between Shoa, Gojjam, and Gondar, and that between Tigrinya communities on either side of the Mereb River. But ethnic, cultural, and linguistic consciousness was also critical, and increasingly so; the analysis presented here rests on the argument that the militarization of politics involved the utilization by a range of groups and communities of various forms of identity (class, *ethnie*, territory), and that violence both was driven by and helped enhance, these cohesions. It is certainly the case that ideas about *ethnie*, nation, and cultural community were at the forefront of violent conflict, and both grew up within and were defined against the frontiers which define our story.

This period witnessed an expansion of Red Sea commerce, and in particular the expansion of the north-east African slave trade with the heightened demand for slaves in the Arabian peninsula and the Middle East.[29] The marked increase in slaving violence across the north-east African highlands and into their lowland environs in the course of the nineteenth century had a profound influence on state-formation in the region. In the middle of the eighteenth century, Jeddah was already a major destination for slaves from the region, both *habesha* and Sudanese, although the former, especially females, reportedly fetched higher prices on account of their supposed physical beauty. *Habesha* slavers themselves preyed on the Sennar borderlands, and on Oromo and *shangalla* communities further south;[30] the Gash-Barka lowlands constituted another important hunting ground in the mid-nineteenth century.[31] But this was no one-way traffic: the north-west borderlands of Ethiopia were vulnerable to 'Arab' slave-raiding incursions, while along the western frontier Oromo and other slave raiders were regular visitors.[32] The so-called 'Baria', observed Parkyns in the mid-1840s, regularly raided for slaves into the northern highlands.[33] Slaving warfare was one of the key forms of the economic war of the nineteenth century; it was also violence which was racially motivated and justified. The armies that preyed on dispersed mixed-farming communities along contested borderlands represented an ever more complex and large-scale military organization, which in itself represented expanding and ever more sophisticated state-formation. Such statehood increasingly defined the parameters of both warfare and economy across the region.

Slaves, cotton cloth, and horses were traded at markets along the Sennar–Ethiopian borderlands; Metemma was an important commercial centre.[34]

Slave merchants made their way via burgeoning trade routes to the Red Sea hinterland, often across considerable distances, for example the 'Sidama' groups, reported Gobat, were heavily involved.[35] In the 1770s, Bruce noted that the settlement of Digsa, in Akele Guzay, was a key market town for slaves, especially children, from whence many were presumably dispatched coastward.[36] Adwa in Tigray was likewise a key transit point for slaves: Salt reckoned about a thousand passed through annually, some of whom were sent onward to Massawa, and others to smaller ports further north, as traders sought to avoid the customs duties levied by the *na'ib*.[37] Shortly after acceding to power, Tewodros had famously abolished the slave trade as part of his putative 'modernization' programme, but by the end of the 1850s the commerce was thriving[38]—indeed it is unlikely that Tewodros' proclamation had made any real difference. Slaving continued to be a central component within the larger umbrella activity of warfare, and remained so in the 1890s, when Menelik's soldiers took slaves in the north-west during skirmishes with the Mahdists;[39] in the 1870s and 1880s, meanwhile, swathes of the *kebessa*, especially Hamasien, had been devastated by the slaving which became a lucrative sideline during the Ethio-Egyptian conflict. Many of these, again, made their way to Arabia, Wylde recalling that 'when I first went to the Red Sea as British Vice-Consul with headquarters at Jeddah, the Hedjaz was full of Abyssinian females...that had been taken from the Hamasen'.[40] Against the violent background of the *zemene mesafint*, then, regional commerce was thriving—and while it is clear that recurrent conflict was frequently inimical to the successful flow of trade and economic development more generally, there can be little doubt, by the same token, that the promise of economic gain (whether the control of trade routes or the capture of resource-rich territory) drove a great deal of the violence of the nineteenth century.

The politics of *shiftanet*: Tewodros and the frontier state

The period between the 1850s and the 1890s was a formative one in the modern history of the region, although there was considerable continuity from the early nineteenth century. It was an era which witnessed the culmination of a process of militarization in terms of Ethiopian political culture originating in the mid- and late eighteenth century. The story of Tewodros[41] in many ways encapsulates the story of Ethiopia over the past two centuries or more: the advance of the 'periphery' on the 'centre', with the latter thus fundamentally defined by the former; the level of institutionalized and cyclical social and political violence; and, closely connected to the first point, the prevalent but much misunderstood role played by *shifta* in the evolution of the region's political culture. Born Kassa Haylu in around 1818, Tewodros was from an increasingly unstable and contested borderland between present-day Ethiopia and Sudan—namely, the lower-lying Kwara area to the west of Lake Tana and Gondar. A religious education made him deeply pious, but also critical of the established church, as he understood it. His early life was played out against the backcloth of the *zemene mesafint*: apparently in some way related, on his father's side, to several key regional overlords of the early and mid-nineteenth century, enabling him to claim a degree of status—the *habesha* nobility was an intricate web of inter-familial relationships—he served in the household of one of them, that of his half-brother in Kwara. Normally, such service should have led to his being rewarded with land—a portion of a *gult* estate—on which he could have sustained himself as an aspirant noble. On the death of his patron, however, Kassa received no such reward, and following a period in the service of Goshu of Gojjam, he 'rebelled' and became *shifta*, established practice for frustrated or disenchanted nobility.

The *shifta* phenomenon deserves some brief consideration at this point, crucial as it is to an understanding of the political culture of the region. We will see later in the book how important *shifta* are at particular times and in particular places—from the Ethiopian region of the nineteenth century, to the politically turbulent Eritrean borderlands in the 1940s and 1950s, to the supposedly irredentist Somali movement in northern Kenya in the 1960s (known as 'the Shifta war'). It will be clear that the term *shifta* itself has changed over time, according to context; as Crummey explains, the word is derived from the Amharic *shiftanet*, meaning 'banditry', which itself stems from *shaffata*, 'to rebel'.[42] It was an ambiguous term, referring both to common banditry as well as (often in romanticized hindsight) to heroic aristocratic rebellion; indeed it seems that over time the word became more associated with the former and less with the latter. Across north-east Africa in the course of the twentieth century, it found its way into English usage and came to mean 'any armed band at odds with the state' as well as low-level criminal behaviour, and was used derogatively to refer, for example, to the

guerrillas of the Eritrean liberation movement in the 1980s.[43] In the nineteenth century, *shifta* were both bandits and rebels, depending on the beholder;
they took to the bush or mountains and defied authority for a range of reasons, whether quick pecuniary gain through banditry or political disenchantment and ideological revolt.[44] Their presence in frontier zones and borderlands
enhanced the perception of those places as dark and dangerous, possessed of
a sinister fertility from which grew challenges to the order of things.

Shiftanet, rebellious activity, flourished throughout the nineteenth century,
and indeed was both a cause and a symptom of the *zemene mesafint*. *Ras
Mikael*—later the self-appointed guardian of the Solomonic order—began his
career as a *shifta* in the 1750s; in the following century, both Tewodros and
Yohannes came to power through *shiftanet*. Thus, being *shifta* in some senses
appears to have been something of a political and military apprenticeship, in
which aspirant leaders acquired skills at arms and developed strategies of command and organization; arguably, the same has proven to be the case of the liberation fronts in the later twentieth century. *Shifta* were fundamental to the
evolution of *habesha* political culture. They were both cause and symptom, again,
of political instability; they were often the direct manifestation of the 'frontierism' which characterized and shaped political discourse across the region,
and they represented, in different ways, the centrifugal forces with which
would-be centralizers continually had to grapple.

The young Tewodros was effectively a product of the north-west frontier.[45] Early skirmishes with the Egyptian forces as they consolidated their
control over northern and central Sudan in the 1840s had had a profound
impact on his understanding of regional dynamics, and indeed of the world
beyond. A major defeat at the hands of the better trained and better equipped
Egyptians in 1848 taught Tewodros some valuable lessons in the military
arts; his motley bands of variously motivated *shifta* were no match. This was
a defeat which doubtless convinced Tewodros of the absolute primacy of
armed force, a lesson which would be a crucial one, too, for future genera-
tions of those who, like Tewodros, sought the capture of the state from the
neglected borderlands and oppressed peripheries. Certainly, Tewodros was
convinced—and would remain convinced, until taking his own life in the
face of an inexorable British advance twenty years later—that armed might
was right, and that there was no political problem which could not be
approached through the use of mass, concentrated force. Following the
defeat by the Egyptians, there were a series of notable victories over key
regional overlords closer to home, in the course of the early 1850s.[46] His

growing success won him the respect of the Warrashek, who acknowledged him in his position as governor of Kwara province—a hollow gesture, as he was already effectively in control of it; he went on to consolidate his position, accumulating more governorships, and even marrying the daughter of Ali, the Yajju prince. His success was founded on a brilliant combination of tactical and strategic intelligence, passionate leadership, and the occasional stroke of good fortune, as well as errors by his enemies. By the early 1850s he was in a position to challenge the key leaders of the northern and central highlands, defeating first Goshu, and then, in mid-1853, his former patron Ali at the battle of Ayshal; in some respects, this ended Yajju pre-eminence, and thus the era of princes itself. However, Tewodros had yet one major fight to win—which he did in early 1855 when his army crushed that of Wube, governor of Tigray and Semien, and erstwhile competitor for the Solomonic inheritance.[47] His subjugation of Wollo and Shoa, in the eastern highlands, lent further apparent legitimacy to his coronation as Tewodros II, King of Kings. His belief in the need to establish a monopoly on the use of force, and to deploy that force in the direction of political challenges, seemed vindicated. What followed was an aggressive renaissance of the Solomonic ideal, around which would be built the notion of a perennial, unified Christian kingdom which would be regionally dominant.

Sheer armed force would also serve to resolve the issue of Tewodros' dubious ancestry, for the problem was that his lineage was weak. Many regarded him as a usurper, and for much of his career as 'king of kings' a great many contemporaries refused to accept that he was of Solomonic descent.[48] Yet his claim of descent from Fasilidas was accepted—again, his extraordinarily effective violence ensured it—and he was crowned by the (Egyptian) head of the Orthodox Church. His very choice of throne name suggested an amalgamation of hubris and insecurity, alluding to a long-standing Orthodox belief that a monarch named Tewodros would come to save the kingdom, and rule for a thousand years. It was a popular fiction, but the historicization of violent conflict was the defining feature of nineteenth-century *habesha* statehood, and was underpinned by ideas about destiny and inheritance.[49] These ideas—resting at the heart of the Ethiopian world-view—awarded Ethiopia a belief in a grand narrative arc, which in turn was translated into an aggressive potency as an empire-state. It would be among the most dangerous legacies to the modern era.

In truth, Tewodros' command of his realm was never more than slender, for all its righteous violence; rebellion was frequent, and his response to it ever more bloody. Again, this was conflict not simply between ever more professionalized soldiery, but escalating violence between militarized and armed peasant communities, so that the lines between combatant and non-combatant became ever more blurred. While Tewodros' soldiers were sent against the troops of defiant chiefs, they were also sent against 'civilian' settlements who quickly learned to defend themselves against soldiers from whatever direction. Within months of his coronation, there were revolts in Gojjam, in Tigray, in Begemeder. 'My people', he reportedly told the missionary Henry Stern, 'are bad; they love rebellion and hate peace; delight in idleness, and are averse to industry; but, if God continues to me my life...I will eradicate all that is bad, and introduce all that is salutary and good'.[50] His transferral of illegitimacy onto those he aspired to govern is noteworthy; at any rate, his professed policy of purification would be a gory one indeed. Stern's assessment is colourful:

> The King's relentless severity towards rebels and traitors does not, however, in the least damp the aspiration for power, or the passion for dominion. Men and women are continually scourged and mutilated; whole regions of wild hordes are sent to desolate and lay waste suspected and disaffected districts; whole clans are proscribed and outlawed; and yet all these extreme measures and sanguinary edicts fail to enforce obedience, or to win the nation's fealty.[51]

Stern, writing in the early 1860s, opined that, while Tewodros was unable to prevent continual rebellion, he had had some success against 'theft and murder', and ordinary criminality.[52] A near contemporary, Dufton, advised his readers: 'There are those who think they have described the man when they have stigmatised him as an inhuman despot, a bloodthirsty tyrant, a Nero, a worse than King of Dahomey'; but, no, exclaimed Dufton, Tewodros 'is not all devil!'[53] Later assessments were less sympathetic. The weight of a huge and more or less permanent army was enormous on land and people, and the military revolution proved self-consuming;[54] indeed, in a curious twist, 'peace' was actually anathema to the *shifta* state, for, once created, such an army could not be unmade, and violence became an end in itself. 'From 1860 to 1868', wrote Blanc, 'he seems little by little to have thrown off all restraint, until he became remarkable for reckless and wanton cruelty',[55] as he confronted such sworn enemies as Tigrayan rebels, the governor of Gojjam, the defiant Wollo Oromo, and the Shoans—and, of course, as we see below, Muslims.

The emperor, his violence sanctioned by God and facilitated by destiny, had no option (he told anyone who would listen) but to confront his wayward subjects with force; he 'complained bitterly of the conduct of the Abyssinians in general, whom he styled "a wicked people" '.[56] He could not control the ramifications of his own violent revolution. Uprisings were habitual from the early and mid-1860s.[57] Moreover, an army had been created which was in need of continual action, yet whose tactics rendered 'success' by any standard impossible, as well as causing the soldiers to be hardly better off than the peasantry itself. Ultimately, this was a 'war of extermination' between soldier and peasant, with atrocities committed on both sides; killing was commonly attended by physical mutilation, and the deliberate targeting of troublesome communities and indeed entire regions was the key feature of this warfare. The economic effects, as during the early decades of the nineteenth century, were dire, as harvests were destroyed through scorched earth tactics, propelling prices for basic foodstuffs skyward.[58] Starving and unruly soldiers increasingly preyed on destitute communities for whatever meagre sustenance they could find,[59] with supposedly 'disloyal' districts targeted in particular.[60] It was a scenario which would be ever more familiar in the twentieth century.

Military reorganization, above all, was Tewodros' key aim. In part this was the direct result of the experience of the increasingly violent political environment of the highlands: might was right, and armed force had become paramount. There is some evidence, too, that the militarization of politics in the late eighteenth and early nineteenth centuries had produced swollen militaries which needed to be controlled, and Tewodros sought to do this by creating a single, unified, 'national army'. He also attempted to regularize the payment of a salary to soldiers, and to prevent the looting and requisitioning that was standard military practice. He reformed organizational and command structures, and sought to equip his entire army with guns.[61] There was also the issue of an increasing hostile external environment, notably in the form of Egypt in the Sudan and in the Red Sea. Tewodros knew what guns could do, and sought the import of modern arms—commercial activity which brought him ever closer into the orbit of external powers, most obviously Egypt and Europe. Tewodros' perception of Muslims circling Ethiopia, slowly strangulating it, meant that overtures to Europe served a dual purpose, namely the acquisition of firearms and the creation of religious alliances against common enemies.

Yet his military reforms, and the necessarily political changes they entailed—the garrisoning and recruitment of troops, the placement of loyal

political establishments in the regions—were met with increasing levels of
resistance, which were in turn fuelled by his land confiscations. In many
provinces he was simply not recognized, and was rejected as an interloping
and over-mighty *shifta*. His response to violence resistance was even greater
violence, and by the early 1860s he had largely undermined his own best
efforts to both regulate armed force and establish his monopoly on the use
of force. Provincial rebellions were met with severe counter measures—
scorched earth tactics, notably, and the brutal treatment of populations
which he suspected of disloyalty—and much of Tewodros' reign was, in
truth, spent on campaign. In the final analysis he knew only violent answers
to political problems, and the cyclical conflict which spiralled beyond his or
anyone else's control in the course of the 1860s seemed to bear out the
lessons of the *zemene mesafint*—that violence begat violence, and that political failure resulted from an inability to control the armies which had become
an intrinsic part of Ethiopian political culture. When in his frustration at
perceived enemies everywhere he attacked and partly destroyed Gondar, in
1866, there was outrage and condemnation. Many called into question, once
again, his background and lineage.

If his early career had been defined by a strange fanaticism, his later life
was characterized by a violent paranoia, even if it has been in the interests
of subsequent story-tellers to exaggerate the tales of madness and bloody
extremism. But there is enough in the contemporary source material to suggest that he soon came to be seen as a violent transgressor, noted for a level
of overt and violent brutality that was generally deemed unacceptable—
destroying churches, burning people alive or starving them to death, mas-
sacring prisoners of war, destroying wholesale the herds of cattle which
were the livelihoods of communities.[62] In the words of a local chronicler,
'everyone held the King in dislike for he had resort to punishments hitherto
unknown in the land'.[63] In European texts, he is the embodiment of the
crazed oriental despot, the stuff of Victorian nightmares; but we must be
careful not to lift his violence out of context. His was the violence of a
political culture born of the *zemene mesafint*, the violence of that era writ
large. An exemplary product of the fertile frontier, he did not *imagine* there
were enemies everywhere; there *were* enemies everywhere, but his response—
entailing extreme armed force—merely served to exacerbate extant fissures
and conflicts, as would be the case a century later under the *Derg*. He may
well have been a paranoid individual, and there is little doubt that such

paranoia prompted the assault on Gondar—and other acts considered 'illegitimate' in the eyes of contemporary beholders—but it was also indicative of the fact that Tewodros' state was restless and uncertain of itself, uncomfortable with the political inheritance it claimed for itself. There was no clearer sign of that instability—at least in the European mind—than the imprisonment of a number of Europeans, including missionaries, following the apparent lack of interest in Tewodros' struggles on the part of the British Government. The chief resistance to him came from Gojjam, Wollo, and across the north, including Semien and parts of Tigray.[64] Repeated peasant uprisings overthrew his authority and that of his soldiers, and no amount of vengeful violence—of which there was a great deal—could restore his power. By 1867, he was largely confined to a rump state in the eastern highlands with perhaps 15,000 men, around the great rocky outcrop of Magdala, surrounded by enemies.[65] In one of the most expensive overseas military operations mounted by the Victorians, the British Government appointed General Napier to lead a force of 42,000 men, from the Gulf of Zula on the Eritrean coast up into the highlands, to confront Tewodros and free the captives. It was a remarkable expedition, although its progress was greatly eased by the fact that the north was in arms against Tewodros, and there were several local leaders there—including *Ras* Kassa of Tigray, the future Yohannes—who were willing to assist the British.[66] Napier's job would have been rather more difficult, perhaps impossible, had this not been the case—a lesson forgotten by the Italians a generation later. The British reached Magdala, where Tewodros, besieged and outgunned, committed suicide rather than fall into the enemy's hands.[67]

A standard view is that Tewodros was both reformer and upholder of tradition, harbinger of change as well as embodiment of continuity. There is evidence that he attempted to introduce certain changes in military organization, and improvements in technology capacity (again usually of a military nature) and political administration. But too many historians tend to mistake this for something called 'modernization', which denotes some kind of inexorable forward movement, largely inspired by expanding Europe and the models of organization it supposedly offered. Tewodros, rather, needs to be seen as the beginning of an era of high violence, his reign marking the beginning of an era—not yet at an end—defined by the hegemony of armed force in political affairs. Tewodros may indeed at times have dreamt of the equipment enjoyed by European armies; he was also a remarkable man, possessed of considerable talent, and vision and energy—

the past is, surely, marked by them. But he was a product of the peculiar political, cultural, and intellectual environment that was the northern Ethiopian Highlands in the late eighteenth and early nineteenth centuries; he was at least as concerned with looking backwards, into some half-imagined, dimly perceived past, as he was about the future. Yet in many respects the debate about the opportunities and capacities for 'modernization' dominated foreign discourse about Ethiopia for the next century— and indeed came to concern the thoughts of many Ethiopians, once some of the political and intellectual elite had glimpsed this other world for themselves. As for Tewodros himself, he was concerned first and foremost with acquiring the equipment with which to combat Ethiopia's sworn enemy—Islam, whose representatives had stolen piece by piece the ancient kingdom's rightful inheritance.

No doubt external models provided some impetus for so-called 'modernization'; modern Ethiopia has indeed been seen as an exemplar of the defensive modernization which characterized a number of states in northern Africa, along with the Ottoman Empire and Japan (in the course of the nineteenth century), dominated as this period was by European imperial expansion. No doubt, too, the combination of the attractions of neo-Solomonism along with the perceived threats on external frontiers prompted several provinces toward a greater degree of unity and cohesion—the overcoming of internal frontiers, in other words, in order to pay closer attention to the external. Yet there is something rather too neat in this model of political development. In the quest for the reassuringly solid notion of modernization, this paradigm has tended to downplay the violence of the era, and the role played by armed force—and its dramatically enlarged scale in the course of the nineteenth century—in bringing about a coerced unity. The rough edges are largely removed; and in any case, the Ethiopia that was born of these developments remained an intrinsically unstable political, territorial, and indeed ideological entity. The nineteenth-century Ethiopian region witnessed something of a violent revolution, and, again, a dramatic expansion in the scale of warfare, its organization and objectives. There can be little doubt that, at least in part, this was itself driven by external stimuli in the form of new territorial and religious threats. It was a process which began during the *zemene mesafint*; and one of the chief legacies of the *zemene mesafint* was not simply a widely held belief in the primacy of armed force and the utility of political violence, but in the means to put this into effect—namely, a greatly enlarged soldiery.

The conflicts of the *zemene mesafint* had produced cultures of violence and had swelled communities of armed men, better organized and more effectively channelled than previously, creating a more professional military ethos ably supported by the militias which could be conjured up according to need. It was these which ensured the success of the programme of political and territorial enlargement initiated by Tewodros. The enlargement of armed force enabled a succession of rulers—temporarily, at least—to overcome the 'internal' borderlands (political, ethnic, and physical) which had long fragmented the political environment of the Ethiopian Highlands. But a swollen militarism also led to a dangerously restless violence across the region which would periodically destabilize the very polity that it had brought into being.

Tewodros has iconic status in the region's history. He was, and has been, many things to many people: *shifta*, restorer of order and unity, nation-builder and modernizer, bloody tyrant, tragic hero. As with the era to which he supposedly put an end, the *zemene mesafint*, we know a great deal about Tewodros, and yet we also know very little—certainly in terms of what he represented. He embodied the essential violence at the heart of political discourse in the Ethiopian Highlands, even if he was the extreme manifestation of it; he also foreshadowed the supposedly 'modern' phenomenon of the margins seizing the centre—whether *shifta* or guerrilla—and becoming the 'established' order, although in fact this is a recurrent theme in the history of African political development more broadly, and certainly of African violence. Above all, he should not be seen as some essential 'stage' in a model of linear political development, a link between the bloodletting savagery of the *zemene mesafint* and the emergence of the modern nation-state: he was the past, and he was the future. Certainly, he contributed to the reinvention of Solomonism, or if we prefer the invention of neo-Solomonism, which encapsulated something of a 'new' vision of Ethiopia. But his actual history reflects the realities of violent statehood, insurgency, and counter-insurgency: he was unable (or unwilling) to move beyond these realities, and forge 'new' ones. Critically, for our purposes, his was *shifta* statehood, often brilliant in the context of the politics of armed force, but restless and unstable; it was a form of government which would re-emerge in the course of the later twentieth century across the region, manifest in the modern leadership of the TPLF in Ethiopia and the EPLF in Eritrea. In more than one sense, *shifta* statehood embodied the violent frontier which has defined political culture in the region.

Frontiers of faith

The frontier between Christianity and Islam across north-east Africa was, over the longer term, a shifting one; and while it would be misleading to depict the religious history of the region as characterized by conflict alone, it is clear that the positioning of that frontier, and the relative importance of the events and interactions along it, periodically had an enormous impact on the political and cultural evolution of states and societies along a broad arc linking Somalia, Ethiopia, and Eritrea. Violence erupted along and around the frontier episodically, and sometimes with long-term consequences. Islam and Christianity have co-existed uneasily in the southern Red Sea and lower Nile valley region for nearly a millennium and a half, and the sanguine perspective might be that it is remarkable the extent to which religious conflict has generally been managed and controlled. Although at least one scholar of Islam has seen the Eritrean conflicts of the later twentieth century in primarily religious terms,[68] and there is no doubt that the faith-driven component has often been played down here, the fact remains that Christians and Muslims have often fought on the same side, or against one another, for reasons other than matters of the spirit. Arguably, for example, recurrent violence between the Amhara and the Somali has often been economic and political rather than religious *per se*, notwithstanding the fact that, as Ernest Gellner put it, each group possessed a rival edition of The Book.[69] Faith, in other words, often lubricated the machines of war, but it was not necessarily the Faithful who built them.

African Islam, at least south of the Sahara, has been strongly influenced by Sufism. This has made it much more eclectic, flexible, and less vulnerable, if not wholly immune, to external stridency than might otherwise have been the case. Although there has been and continues to be disagreement about the precise nature of Sufi influence in Africa, the emphasis placed by Sufism historically on personal piety and exemplary behaviour, in the words of Knut Vikor, has been rather more important than 'its external functions as a focus for political combat and *jihad*'.[70] In other words, African Muslims have been historically less responsive to the call to arms than others of the Faith. Second, and more directly pertinent to north-east Africa, it has been suggested that Somali 'xenophobia' has likewise rendered Islam in that area comparatively immune to external influence. This goes some way to explaining what Iqbal Jhazbhay terms 'the relative inter-faith détente that has existed between Christian and Islamic spheres of influence in the Horn of

Africa'. Somali Islam 'appears to be solidly located within a tradition of regional, geo-cultural, peaceful co-existence between Christianity, Islam and indigenous animistic tendencies'.[71]

That said, there *was* a great degree of religious conflict. The collapse of the Gondarine state coincided with a rejuvenation of Islam in north-east Africa and the Red Sea zone more generally, and there was a significant religious element to the *zemene mesafint*. The nineteenth century witnessed a marked increase in intra-faith violence, both because of more aggressive Islamic presences across the region, in various guises, and because the 'restored' Ethiopian state of Tewodros and Yohannes was deeply rooted in a sense of Christian mission. In the early nineteenth century, Muslim influence in the Ethiopian region was rejuvenated because of the expansion in Red Sea trade, and the strengthening links this brought with the Arabian peninsula and the Middle East. North-east Africa became much more closely connected to the Islamic world in the course of the nineteenth century; there was also something of a revival of the *hajj* from Ethiopia to Mecca. Importantly, these new connections were developing at a time when the Muslim world itself was witnessing the emergence of a series of revivalist movements which sought the restoration of 'pure' or 'fundamental' Islam, and a more rigorous enforcement of the *shari'a* or Islamic legal code. Often, these revivalist movements were messianic, predicated on the imminent arrival of the 'Mahdi', or saviour, who would oversee the restoration of a purified Islam on earth; revivalist movements asserted that innovation within, and deviation from, pure *shari'a* was wrong, and they often advocated *jihad*, violent confrontation sanctified by God, in order to bring about purification and orthodoxy. The result was that often their enemies were not simply Christians or other 'infidels', but Muslims who were held to have lapsed and wandered from the righteous path. While some of the most important such movements emerged far beyond the African landmass—Shah Wali Allah's challenge to fading Mughal power in India in the eighteenth century, for example—it was the appearance of the alliance between zealous reformer Muhammad ibn 'Abd al-Wahhab and local chieftain Muhammad ibn Saud in the Arabian peninsula in the eighteenth century which had the most direct impact on the Red Sea world and north-east Africa.

The rapid development of commercial enterprise across north-east Africa—in the form of long-distance caravans which penetrated across the highlands and into the west and south—was largely under the direct control

of Muslim merchants.[72] The result was the further Islamicization of the
Oromo in those areas being brought into the Red Sea and Gulf of Aden
commercial orbit. Meanwhile, the continued spread of those Oromo who
were already Muslim in the late eighteenth and early nineteenth centuries
provided Muslim merchants with a base within which and from which to
establish ever greater influence. The founder of the Enarea kingdom, a
merchant-adventurer named Bofo Abba Gomol, for example, quickly
adopted Islam and employed Muslim scribes, traders, accountants, and
counsellors in the process of consolidating his power. The capital of Enarea,
Sakka, boasted a community of busy Muslim merchants, but also hundreds
of *ulama*, religious scholars.[73] Sufi brotherhoods, again, were instrumental
in the spread and establishment of Islam across the region. In the east and
south-east, Islamic political culture was increasingly centred on the strategically positioned city-state of Harar, and although the Somali to the south
were politically fragmented, the Afar had developed a sultanate in the central Danakil area. The Qadiriya, a prominent Sufi order, had been active in
the Harar area for some time prior to *c.*1800, but in the course of the nineteenth century the brotherhood spread further among the Somali and also
into parts of present-day Eritrea. Reformist orders such as the Salihiya
were active in the Ogaden from the 1850s, attracting the displaced and
those seeking refuge from conflict to their farming communities. In the
north, the Eritrean region saw the expansion of the Mirghaniya from the
1860s. Often, Muslim settlers married into chiefly families—much as they
had on the east African coast—and gradually brought those lineages and in
time entire communities over to Islam.

In Wollo in the eighteenth century, converts were brought to the faith
through the activities of Shaikh Muhammad Shafi, the major Sufi leader of
the region.[74] A student of theology, law, and the Arabic language early in life,
he was initiated into the Qadiriya brotherhood and became one of its key
figures, a successful recruiter with an increasing personal following; as he
grew in stature, he acquired a reputation for learning, saintliness, and the
performance of miracles. Notably, he had uneasy but peaceable relations
with local Wollo chiefs, many of whom were themselves Muslim; he avoided
their courts, and in fact in his later career preached increasingly of the need
for *jihad* in order to both purify existing Islamic practice and to extend
the faith itself. Indeed, he had even attempted to solicit support for *jihad*
in Wollo while on pilgrimage to Mecca, but the Meccan authorities
were largely unmoved. But he did succeed in establishing a permanent

settlement—*Jama Negus*, the community of the king—inhabited by a large, devout, and militant following. From among their number—in much the way that medieval Christianity had spread in the northern mountains—came clerics in a similar mould to Muhammad Shafi, consolidating and spreading Islam across the region.

And yet this was an eclectic, flexible Islam: new Muslim converts continued to venerate the shrines of local saints, and the pilgrimage to Mecca and the worship of Muslim saints were frequently combined with pre-Islamic practices and cults, notably among the Oromo, such as sacrifice and possession. Indeed it was because of such practices that reformers such as Muhammad Shafi in Wollo had urged the need for purification. Precise numbers are impossible to come by, but clearly conversion to Islam in the course of the nineteenth century was indeed considerable. And Islam went beyond communities of clerics and merchants: Ethiopian Islam could be found within the political establishment, and among farmers and herders. Mixed communities were common, and it is indeed the case that Christians and Muslims could and did live entirely harmoniously. Many ruling families themselves were mixed, with coexistent Christian and Muslim branches.

However, while such harmony might exist at the local level, larger tensions—more entrenched frontiers of faith—were developing as the nineteenth century went on. It was against this spread of Islam—among the southern Oromo, in the eastern Somali region, and to the north in Tigray and parts of modern Eritrea—that the Christian neo-Solomonic monarchs began to carve their own 'new' states in the central and northern highlands from the mid-nineteenth century. Tensions within the Ethiopian region, as well as conflict with external Muslim enemies, came about not least because at the ideological core of the highland state was the linking of Christianity and *habesha* identity. In other words, Muslims could not be 'true' Ethiopians. They were the enemy within, as well as the enemy beyond, for Solomonic rulers who were deeply concerned with the threat from both. Tewodros and Yohannes frequently spoke of Ethiopia's deeper history as well as their contemporary concerns using the language of religious struggle. Muslims were traders, and therefore involved in grubby work, unlike the Christian warrior nobility; one contemporary source in the mid-nineteenth century suggested that '[f]ew [Muslims] are soldiers, they being esteemed by the Christians as cowardly and effeminate'.[75]

Tewodros' spiritual mission was effectively his foreign policy, his view of Islam shaping his view of the region, and the world. He was deeply spiritual as a youth, receiving a religious education,[76] and apparently from a young age he saw it as his mission to 'restore' an imagined glorious past, doubtless in large part inspired by the *Kebre Negast* itself, and to wrest back from Muslim antagonists, who had gradually encroached on the former Ethiopian empire, all those territories once ruled by the King of Kings. His ambition was remarkable, and was indeed duly remarked upon by most Europeans who encountered him: Tewodros wanted the restoration of Jerusalem to Ethiopian control, and the destruction of Mecca; his territorial vision (which he considered his birthright through the union of Solomon and Makeda of Sheba) encompassed everything from Egypt to Zanzibar, from Arabia to the Holy Lands and Mesopotamia.[77] Dufton asserted that Tewodros' ambition, simply put, was that 'Mohammedanism must disappear from his country; and not only so, he would wipe it off the face of the earth ... Theodore is the first and only patriot Abyssinia ever saw'.[78] Tewodros was the enraged incarnation of the chauvinism and mythology contained within the *Kebre Negast*; he was the product both of the violent political culture brought about by the *zemene mesafint* and of a fertile religious imagination inspired by the myths surrounding Ethiopia's antiquity—a deadly combination. In some respects he was an oddity, too, in that his ire was also frequently directed at the Church itself, and in that he belonged rather more to the tradition of militant monasticism than to that of monarchical pomp.

In the end, of course, Tewodros had believed that a natural alliance lay with the Christian powers of Europe, and could not understand why the latter appeared less than interested. Considering the great struggle to which he supposedly dedicated his life—the destruction of Islam—it was a terrible irony indeed that he would end his own life as a British force advanced on Magdala, determined to destroy him. Yohannes may have been cleverer, in some respects, at balancing the various issues confronting him, but he certainly shared Tewodros' hatred of Islam, and in that regard the two men were very much exponents of the Christian nationalism that lay at the heart of the neo-Solomonic restoration. In the early 1880s, with the rise of the Mahdist state on his north-west border, Yohannes was anxious about the loyalty of his own Muslim subjects, and the possibility of a general uprising.[79] He, too, had a highly developed sense of the past and its political utility: his wars—both actual and verbal—with Islam were repeatedly historicized, as he reminded would-be European allies that Ethiopia had always had to fight the Muslim aggressor in the past. In particular, his reference point was the early sixteenth-century invasion by Ahmed Gran, around

which much memorial verbiage was constructed;[80] in the mid-1890s, the
Russian Bulatovich would note that Gran 'was an outstanding personality
and to this day still lives in the memory of the people, who ascribe to him
supernatural qualities'.[81] Yet apparently somewhat less fanatical than
Tewodros, at least in terms of political vision, Yohannes' main concern was
rather more specific than that of his predecessor—namely, the Egyptian
presence on the Red Sea coast. And even in this he was prepared to be
rather more placatory than Tewodros, clearly setting considerable store by
diplomacy rather than simply force of arms.

Yet a willingness to negotiate over the contested northern frontier was
only politic, and was in some respects indicative of feelings of insecurity—
after all, Yohannes had seen at first hand what might happen if the ire of a
foreign power was aroused. Nor should Yohannes' diplomatic overtures dis-
guise his own very real intolerance of Islam within his realm. Muslims in
Tigray, Wollo, or Amhara might be allied to the hated 'Turk', he thought,
and used as enemies behind the frontline; the fear of a Muslim uprising
against Christian rule within the provinces was genuine, and grounded in
some historical experience. In order to address this threat, Yohannes moved
aggressively against the Muslim community in Wollo, and forced the conversion to Christianity of many Muslim leaders and their followers. But
here, professions of faith and loyalty to Yohannes were both insincere and
perceived to be insincere, and indeed many Wollo Muslims fled south, thus
providing further impetus to Islamic missionary activity in the southern
marches in the later nineteenth century. Ultimately, Yohannes' more immediate religious antagonists were not within his borders but on them, in the
form of both Egypt and the Sudanese Mahdists.

Menelik was cautious enough to grant freedom of religious practice,
apparently in an attempt to assuage Islamic movements across his realm. But
the royal court and the 'new' Ethiopian state were to remain resolutely
Christian institutions. The events of the long nineteenth century had confirmed in the minds of the Ethiopian political establishment the absolute
need to be watchful of potential Muslim enemies. It was a 'lesson' deeply
ingrained in *habesha* political culture, and in any case was of some considerable antiquity. The story of Menelik's own heir, *Lij* Iyasu, makes the point
clearly enough: while probably not an actual Muslim convert, he nonetheless sought a greater degree of integration of Muslims into government,
including the members of some prominent Muslim dynasties. He showed
some sympathy to the Somali Islamic resistance against the British and the

Italians, and, with the 'Great War' in Europe already underway, made over-tures to the Ottoman Empire, apparently seeking an alliance. It was all too much: he was deposed and excommunicated in 1916, though he escaped and remained at large—a rallying point for future opposition—for a number of years.[82] Yet in the course of the twentieth century, his successor—*Ras* *Tafari*, later Haile Selassie—would assiduously position Ethiopia as a Christian ally of the West in a predominantly Muslim and increasingly hos-tile part of the world. This was no mere rhetoric, for the Christian state was itself a product of external as well as internal borderlands.

4

Borderlands, Militarism, and the Making of Empire

Resurgent Tigray

The rise of Tigray had been signposted several decades before the emergence of Yohannes. Modern Tigrayan nationalist writing—scholarly and other-wise—has described a gradual but inexorable erosion of Tigray's rightful place as both the birthplace and the guardian of 'Ethiopian' civilization following the decline of Axum, and Yohannes as its (temporary) saviour. Indeed, Yohannes himself is often credited with giving birth to modern Tigrayan nationalism itself, while he is also, in many respects, the single most important reference point in the modern Tigrayan struggle for self-fulfilment and 'repositioning' in the Ethiopian political order.[1] Tigray's resurgence was in large part con-nected to the expansion in trade to which it had better access than many poli-ties of the southern interior. As Valentia declared in 1808:

> Abyssinia is at present...torn by civil dissension, as it has been for many gen-erations, owing to the great power vested in the governors of the Provinces...The Province of Tigre, being the only one that has any commu-nications with the Arabians, is considered as the most important.[2]

Yet even within Tigray itself there were significant regional tensions and politi-cal cleavages, and despite the geopolitical importance of the province there was no real Tigrayan 'unity' until at least the 1830s.[3] *Ras* Welde Selassie's death in 1817 was followed by several years of conflict until Sebagadis, previously a close ally of the late *ras*, seized control in 1822; throughout this period, Tigrayan political leaders simultaneously aspired to the reassertion of Tigrayan-Amhara power over the old Ethiopian polity, and viewed with distaste the prevalence of Oromo leaders in the old Gondarine power structures, a situation, of course, which they also ascribed to Amhara weakness. A broad coalition led by the Yajju noble *Ras* Marye Gugsa, however, invaded Tigray in 1831 and defeated Sebagadis—ironically, perhaps, using Oromo cavalry whose predations across Tigray lingered long in the memory—whereupon *Ras* Wube was placed in charge.[4] Wube succeeded in achieving some degree of unity, not least by co-opting the family of the executed Sebagadis, and dominated northern politics for two decades. As well as arguably creating modern Tigray, Wube positioned the region at the forefront of both external contacts, with regular access to the Red Sea coast, and the struggles of the *zemene mesafint*; he might have laid claim to the Solomonic inheritance himself, but for his defeat at the hands of Tewodros in 1855. Tigray's increased geopolitical importance exacerbated its conflicts with rivals further south; at the same time, Tigrayan rulers had problems of their own with the frontier districts of the coast and the lowland plains, over which they had little direct control but in which Tigrayan forces frequently conducted military operations—not least to secure commerce. Ultimately, Tigray occupied the somewhat anomalous position of jostling for position at the heart of the Solomonic state, while simultaneously becoming something of a political, economic, and indeed ethnic frontier zone. It is a curious role which in many respects Tigray's political leadership has yet to address.

The future Yohannes IV, Kassa Mercha, was born in 1831 into impeccable aristocratic stock,[5] able to claim both Solomonic blood through the line of his paternal grandmother, and Tigrayan nobility with blood links to the prominent eighteenth-century family of *Ras* Mikael Sehul—the man whose actions had effectively ended the Gondarine monarchy and heralded the *zemene mesafint*. In the course of the 1860s, Kassa had consolidated his position as one of the major leaders of the north, a key *shifta* in opposition to Tewodros' gradually imploding state, and when the British passed through his territory in 1868 Kassa proved himself an eager ally. He succeeded in winning Napier's support in the form of a significant batch of modern firearms which placed him in a strong position in the forthcoming succession conflict. The short-lived reign of Takla Giyorgis II—formerly Gobeze of Lasta, and an erstwhile ally of Kassa, who defeated him near Adwa in 1871—was followed by Kassa's proclamation as Yohannes IV in early 1872. As with Tewodros, a former *shifta* had become *negus negast*, albeit one with a rather stronger claim to the Solomonic inheritance. Yohannes, faced with rivals both within and outside Tigray (among the latter, Menelik of Shoa), made strenuous efforts to demonstrate his bloodlines to the Solomonic dynasty,

and had himself crowned at Axum; his coronation ceremony drew on
'ancient' tradition and practice, and thus was emphasis also duly placed
on Tigray as the root of *habesha* culture and civilization.[6]

Yohannes steeped himself self-consciously in tradition, but his base in
Tigray also brought him into contact with an external world at a time when
European commerce and influence were becoming significant. The world
beyond was encroaching, but Yohannes' immediate task was to consolidate
his position within both Tigray and Ethiopia. To do so required a deft combination of tact and force. In contrast to his predecessor, he was willing to
allow local notables to accumulate a certain amount of authority, and was
not so swift to enforce submission as Tewodros had been. He proved himself
prepared to use armed force to bring recalcitrant districts to heel—Yohannes' polity remained a fundamentally military one, and he presided over a
marked degree of militarization and war-readiness—and he did so in both
Gojjam and Shoa, notably; but he nevertheless tended to confirm local
nobilities as rulers and, rather more cunningly than Tewodros, he built intricate webs of alliance by playing off regional overlords against one another.
Thus were Gojjam, under Takla Haymanot, and Shoa, under Menelik, set
against one another, unable to build the kind of broad front against Yohannes
that might have seen the latter rendered impotent.

It was a precarious business, and arguably Yohannes was never truly secure.
Many in the regions continued to undermine and defy him; despite offering submission in the mid-1870s, for example, Menelik was at the very least
ambivalent in his professed 'loyalty' to the Tigrayan *negus negast*, and spent
much of Yohannes' reign biding his time and pondering a move against his
supposed master. Nonetheless, Yohannes was able to enforce proclamations
of loyalty from Menelik in Shoa, and from Takle Haymanot in Gojjam, so
that by the late 1870s he was regarded as having 'pacified' the region.[7] In
1884, it was supposedly boasted that 'a child could pass through his dominions unharmed', following his successful bringing to heel of such 'turbulent
tribes' as the Azebo and Wollo Oromo, among others; he had increased trade
through his domains, while '[t]he peasant and cultivator were also better off
and less molested by the soldiery', as he was apparently more successful than
Tewodros at disciplining the armed forces at his disposal.[8] He also managed
to stabilize his position somewhat by adopting a more conciliatory stance
toward the Church, reversing Tewodros' policy by restoring some land to it.
He took the title *Negus Tsion*, King of Zion, and was ruthless in enforcing
religious unity, or at least suppressing open dissent; he was no less brutal in

his persecution of Muslims than his predecessor. Even so, it seems that Yohannes—and those close to him—were careful to use the language of magnanimity and mercy in dealing with his enemies (Christian and Muslim alike), in stark contrast to Tewodros' Old Testament smiting and righteous rage.[9] In this way did Yohannes manage to head a rough coalition which was the foundation of the neo-Solomonic state. Yet it was his external borderlands which dominated his reign. He perished on one of these, the northwest frontier against Mahdist Sudan; but perhaps more importantly in the longer term, while Yohannes was relatively successful in managing his restless polity, he singularly failed to resolve the issue of his external frontiers. Yohannes' legacy was two-fold: first, a Tigrayan renaissance which rested on the idea of rightful inheritance and self-realization; and, second, a failure to bring stability and security to the Eritrean frontier zone, a failure in which several other actors—Egyptians, Italians, British—were also complicit. Both legacies would mature into full-blown crises for the Ethiopian state in the century after Yohannes' death.

Frontiers (1): the Mereb River zone

In the middle decades of the nineteenth century, the idea that 'Ethiopia' had the right of direct access to the coast first emerged in its modern form. It was an idea which would loom increasingly large in the highland imagination; it would become extraordinarily destructive in the twentieth century, and to all intents and purposes remains unresolved at the time of writing. But that is for later in our story: suffice to say here that the basic idea is rather more novel than is sometimes assumed, and only takes on the properties of a political issue in the course of the nineteenth century. Prior to the nineteenth century, and certainly the *zemene mesafint*, Christian polities in the highlands had neither the ability nor the desire, on available evidence, to in any way administer the escarpment and coastal lowlands beyond periodic, tenuous, and frequently contested suzerainty over the *kebessa*. Conversely, there is much anecdotal evidence that the average highlander heartily despised the coastal zone as an alien and ghastly environment, and the peoples there as 'Arabs', *shifta*, wild and lawless 'tribes'. However, it became an article of faith from the late nineteenth century onwards among foreign scholars and observers as well as the Ethiopian political elite that some amorphous, ancient Ethiopian state had 'always' held the coast, until being kicked out by the 'Turks'. It has become one of the most curiously stubborn misapprehensions in the modern history of the region—and, again, one of the most dangerous.[10] In many respects, to be sure, it is a key tenet of the 'Greater Ethiopia' thesis. Yet this is not to adhere to some wrongheaded endorsement of an extrapolative Eritrean nationalism. The situation in the nineteenth century was much more fluid and ambiguous than this. Due recognition needs to be given to the very distinct political ecologies between the central and northern Ethiopian Highlands and the shores around Massawa port,[11] including those between the *kebessa*, the escarpment, and the hot coastal plains. For Erlich, Yohannes' commander in the north, *Ras Alula*, 'fortified Eritrea as Ethiopia's gate';[12] Alula himself reportedly declared with appropriate bombast that 'Ethiopia goes up to the sea; Egypt begins there'.[13] Yet the reality was that 'the north'—the Mereb River zone, the *kebessa,* and the adjacent coast—was seen in the course of the nineteenth century, and beyond, to present no end of trouble to the highland interior. Eritrea was *Mereb Melash* to Tigrayans, *Kemerab Wedya* to the Amhara—the land beyond the Mereb, a zone of conflict in which recalcitrant locals and external enemies alike were to be confronted and overcome. If Ethiopia was indeed, as Consul Portal had it, 'a Christian island set in the midst of a stormy Moslem sea',[14] then Eritrea was the place where the waves broke on the rocks. Simply put, it was an extraordinarily dangerous fault line, arguably the single most important zone of conflict in the region.

The Egyptian presence in Massawa was an increasing affront to the Solomonic state-builders, Tewodros and Yohannes, who were only too aware of the increasing value of the Red Sea—and fearful of the growing power of Islam around it. An annual lease was granted by Ottoman Sultan Abd al-Majid to Muhammad Ali on the Red Sea ports of Suakin and Massawa in 1846, although it was not until 1865 that *Khedive* Ismail permanently annexed them to the Egyptian Sudan. Tewodros was watchful on the northern frontier in the 1850s and early 1860s, although ultimately he lost control in the north in the face of repeated rebellion. Under Ismail from the mid-1860s, Egypt embarked on an altogether more aggressive approach to Ethiopia, and during the reigns of he and Yohannes the Mereb River zone became one of the key frontiers of violence, with a number of minor skirmishes and two major clashes with Egyptian forces in the mid-1870s.

Contemporary European accounts, again, must always be treated with caution, not least in terms of their crude racial stereotyping, but the commentary they contain on the Mereb frontier are nonetheless important. In the early years of the nineteenth century, Henry Salt considered that Tigray 'proper' was 'bounded on the north by the river Mareb', and reported that the inhabitants of Hamasien 'are said to bear a very distinct character from the rest of the Abyssinians'; the Danakil peoples, meanwhile, were 'completely ungovernable'.[15] In 1811, *Ras* Welde Selassie of Tigray lamented in a letter to King George III of Great Britain that 'before me are infidels and behind me are infidels, on my right hand and on my left are infidels, and in the midst of those that are all infidels; and all that is on the shore of the [Red Sea] is infidel'.[16] In the 1830s, Hamasien province—on this occasion rather misleadingly described as stretching to 'the territory of the wild and uncultivated Shankallas'—was judged to be inhabited by people 'barbarous in their manners, cruel in their tempers'.[17] The region was divided into numerous chieftaincies, each 'entirely independent of the Ras of Tigre'.[18] Sebagadis had succeeded in temporarily imposing tribute on the Saho, but they remained troublesome: the missionary Gobat recorded that on hearing of Sebagadis' death in 1831, the Saho revolted and refused to pay the tribute.[19] Likewise Plowden, in the 1840s, reported that the people of the *kebessa* were 'a fierce and turbulent race', paying only periodic tribute to their Tigrayan neighbours, while the Saho and Afar constituted 'a wicked and treacherous race...at enmity with all men'.[20] While the communities of Hamasien and Serae clearly spoke Tigrinya, they were 'scarcely considered by the people of Teegray as a portion of that country, whose governors since [the time of *Ras* Mikael], have made war on them to enforce payments of an irregular tribute'.[21] Violence, indeed, defined trans-Mereb relations. 'The frontier provinces of Teegray toward the sea, Kalagooza [=Akele Guzay] and Hamazain', wrote Plowden,

> are now disorderly republics, save a tribute forced on them by the arms and the fortune of Oobeay, and will probably soon entirely detach themselves from the shaking fabric of Abyssinian society; and here there is no law or protection for the trader, save such moderation as self-interest may teach the villagers on the road...[22]

This gives some indication of the extent to which the violence of the *zemene mesafint* was reflected north of the Mereb. Certainly, swathes of the *kebessa*, and Tigray too, were devastated by cyclical violence: one account refers to the 'devastation and ruin' in Hamasien in the mid-1840s, and also to the 'deserted, uncultivated' district of Shire in Tigray, formerly heavily peopled and agriculturally productive.[23] *Ras* Wube periodically raided the Bogos area, too: '[b]eing plains, and richly cultivated with Indian corn, they are the favourite field for the incursions of Oobeay's troops, affording the most spoil with the least fighting'.[24] This was the familiar pattern of large-scale organized military expeditions against small agricultural settlements located in vulnerable and contested borderlands.

This region may indeed have been a happy hunting ground for Tigrayan soldiers, but it was the violent insecurity of the frontier that was both the cause and the symptom of the militarized polity further south. Notably, for all the later claims of ownership of the coast, the littoral itself was an alien, hostile environment, containing diseases, according to Salt, 'which produce in the minds of the Abyssinians that great dread and horror of the coast which they generally entertain'.[25] Just south of Massawa, Tigrayan expeditions mined salt under heavy armed guard, and relations between the Tigrinya-speaking uplands and the communities of the coast were episodically violent.[26] The same was true in the Tigrayan lowlands, where salt-mining operations took the form of military expeditions owing to the fact that the area was 'infested by a cruel race of Galla, who make it a practice to lie in wait for the individuals engaged in cutting it'.[27] Welde Selassie himself highlighted the fundamental tension at the heart of Tigrayan territorial aspirations when he told Salt that 'he could easily drive [the Muslims] from Arkeeko or any other point...but of what advantage could it be to possess a barren coast, which at all times the Abyssinians are averse to visit'.[28] On a separate occasion, the *Ras* declared to Salt: ' "You will know that my people are very averse to go down to the coast for a day"'.[29] Wube's later claim to be 'king from Gondar to the sea of Massawa' was thus hyperbole indeed;[30] nonetheless, he wrote to Louis-Napoleon Bonaparte in 1849: 'All the land on the coast is mine'.[31]

While Tigray's geopolitical importance was growing in the late eighteenth and early nineteenth centuries, the province was also wracked by internal strife, conflict which spilled over into the *kebessa* and which further rendered the plateau volatile. When Welde Selassie was confronted with Sebagadis' revolt in 1809, his forces penetrated as far as Debarwa in pursuit of the rebels but were at length compelled to withdraw, leaving the region of Akele Guzay and Serae in some upheaval.[32] Similarly, the violence with which Tewodros had to contend in parts of Tigray, as well as north of the Mereb, prevented him from even coming close to his declared ambition of a permanent presence on the coast.[33] In the late 1850s, notably, the rebel leader

Neguse was active in the Agame district in Tigray, and in Akele Guzay, where he managed to establish some form of popular support; from there he raided across Hamasien, forcing Tewodros' representative there, Hailu Tewelde Medhin, to flee into Serae.[34] Neguse's assaults on political strongholds in the *kebessa* reflected his own territorial claims across the region, including the coast.[35] One source from 1860 refers to 'the anarchy which again reigns in all Tigray',[36] and there can be little doubt that this had repercussions north of the Mereb, too. In the course of the 1860s, Tewodros was continually defied in Tigray and the *kebessa*—despite his description of the *na'ib* of Massawa as his 'vassal'[37]—and the northern region was a patchwork of garrison-based military occupation and zones of active hostility.[38] One of Tewodros' key garrisons in the north in the mid-1860s was at Keren, comprising 'villainous-looking scoundrels', according to Blanc, evidence that Tewodros 'was not very particular as to whom he selected for such distant outposts'.[39] In 1866, as Tewodros' reign entered its final bloody phase, the north was in turmoil, with the effects of famine across Tigray and the *kebessa* exacerbated by the armed incursions of Gobaze (the future Tekle Giyorgis) of Lasta, who likewise sought to impose order in the north, and whose troops clashed with those of Tewodros in Akele Guzay.[40] Detailed evidence is sometimes lacking, but it seems clear that food shortages drove a great deal of the violence of this period, as armies and beleaguered farming communities alike sought to secure new agricultural supplies or protect what they already had. It is clear, moreover, that the culture of violent confrontation which characterized Ethiopian politics in the nineteenth century had a dramatic impact on the Eritrean region; but the troubled frontier in turn served to destabilize *habesha* politics and heighten levels of violent insecurity south of the Mereb.

With the fall of Tewodros and the rise to pre-eminence of Yohannes, the history of the northern zone entered a new phase, with the northward shift in the balance of power to Tigray having major implications for politics north of the Mereb. Propagandist rhetoric for *Dejjazmach* Kassa in 1869 had it that he was ruler from 'Tekkeze to Massawa... All the land is pacified and well provided for';[41] but the reality was that the convulsions which followed Tewodros' death rendered Yohannes' power base even in Tigray unstable. Yet his gaze was indeed fixed on the Eritrean frontier. From the early 1870s, his chief tormentor was Egypt, which not only sought 'to prevent me from having any outlet on the Red Sea',[42] but actively pushed the frontier southward and challenged his jurisdiction at every opportunity. Like Tewodros before him, Yohannes interpreted the struggle unfolding before him in religious terms, perceiving a single pan-Islamic threat across a broad arc of territory from Massawa, through Keren and Kassala, to the modern Ethiopian–Sudanese borderland.

Egypt, wrote Yohannes in 1872, had 'seized all the country on the other side of the Mereb where are white (lit. red) and black Barea (slaves), Bogos, Hebarb [?], Mensa, Ailat, Asgade Bakla, Zoulla, Tora, Sanhali, Amfela, all the soil below the Afaf [?], which properly belongs to Hamasien'. Moreover, Yohannes was the lawful master of the 'Shankelas'.[43] Yohannes' counsellor and confidante General Kirkham suggested that while the 'Turks' might possess Massawa, 'all the other Bays, Inlets and Ports' belonged to Yohannes.[44] This broad zone of conflict would come to define Yohannes' reign, and his state, with long-term implications. Yohannes asserted that Egypt had aggressively entered Abyssinian territory, seizing 'the whole of the [coastal] lowlands' and the Bogos region in the north-central highlands.[45] He complained to Ismail in mid-1872 that an Egyptian army had occupied Mensa, Halhal, and Hamasien: 'Hamasen', he asserted, 'is the original capital of Abyssinia . . . [and] from these countries my kingdom extends as far as the coasts of the Red Sea'.[46] Yohannes' distress at his inability to control this territory is evident in his anger at Munzinger's appointment as ruler 'over Mereb Melash—half of Tigray—[and] all the borderlands'.[47] Similarly, his assertion in 1873 that the lands of the Danakil and Arafali south of Massawa belonged to him, as they did to his predecessors, has a ring of desperation to it, for the Turks had recently pillaged the area, and with apparent impunity.[48] The Egyptians had occupied Bogos, seized Ailet, and built a sawmill at Sabaguma; Metemma—which Yohannes acknowledged as being 'half to Egypt & half to Ethiopia'—had been fully occupied by the Egyptians; in sum, '[b]etween Massawa and Metemma, the whole of the low lands have been invaded, and on the other side of Massawa, Mennsa, Ailet, Zula, Semhari, Dankali, and the province of Amphilea, have been occupied'. In so doing, 'the Egyptians have completely isolated Abyssinia from the rest of the world'.[49] Yohannes begged the British to acquire for him 'an outlet on the seacoast', for 'Anfila and Zula have been my districts since early times'.[50] Much of this, of course, was couched in religious terms: Egyptian advances represented the encroachment of Islam on Christian Ethiopia, and thus was Eritrea a cultural and religious frontier, as well as a political one, where Ethiopia's very existence was at stake.[51]

It was not *simply* that Yohannes believed in the historic right of Ethiopia to the coast, however important this was; it was also the fact that Ethiopia's image in the world, its structures, cohesion, and prestige, were being tested and defined in Hamasien, Akele Guzay, and Serae. Thus did the land across the Mereb loom large in Yohannes' imagination. By September 1875, Yohannes had dispatched up to 30,000 troops down the escarpment onto the coastal plain, occupying the key roads which linked Massawa to the highlands.[52] The Egyptians complained that this force was pressing in on their territory, sending parties of marauders to within sight of Massawa itself.[53] And yet, when in November the Egyptians responded, advancing up the escarpment and onto the plateau, little resistance was encountered. They reached the Mereb unmolested.[54] In a brilliant tactical manoeuvre, Yohannes' army had drawn the Egyptians 'into a most difficult and intricate country', and it now pounced at Gundet, attacking from several directions *en masse* and wiped out the bulk of the Egyptian force.[55] Only weeks later, the Egyptians suffered a second major defeat, at nearby Gura.[56] Not for the last time in the nineteenth century, however, a *habesha* victory in the Mereb zone was not followed up by any significant advance north of it, although Gundet and Gura facilitated Alula's temporary occupation of swathes of Hamasien and the escarpment.

One of Yohannes' major difficulties—as it was for his predecessors—was the ambiguity of loyalties and identities across the central Eritrean plateau, an ambivalence which further contributed to the instability of the frontier. Tewodros had attempted to use sporadic influence over Hamasien to launch attacks on Egypt by co-opting local elites,[57] but by 1867, Tewodros' formerly 'loyal' appointee in Hamasien, Hailu Tewelde Medhin, had begun to make overtures to Egypt, no doubt realizing that political realities were changing and that conflict in Tigray threatened to engulf the area. 'The frontiers of Egypt are near ours', he wrote to Khedive Ismail in November 1867. 'Therefore friendship and treaty terms ought to exist between us and the ruler of Egypt'.[58] Munzinger, moreover, described a complex array of shifting alliances across the *kebessa*, with communities either under the sway of the 'King's Governor' in Hamasien, or owing allegiance to Egypt, or seeking succour from alternative sources of power—notably in Tigray—in opposition to central authority further south.[59] Yohannes found himself having to deal with exactly the same problem. Welde Mikael of Hamasien was qualified in his assessment of his own relationship with Kassa in 1869: 'Although I am under [the authority of] *Dejjazmach* Kassa, I am of old the legitimate ruler of my country Hamasen from my father and my grandfather and my great-grandfather'.[60] Kassa himself was compelled to intervene in a plot to overthrow his authority, imprisoning Welde Mikael who aspired to 'rule beyond the Mereb'.[61] The frontier zone was fractured and complex, witness the shifting policy of the Saho, for example. At the end of the 1860s it was reported that several Saho communities were 'banded together in order to hold their own against the Tigre people of the plateau, who are Christians, and consequently their bitter foes. For this frontier service they receive the protection of the Egyptian Government'.[62] Yet in 1873 a group of Saho chiefs complained bitterly that the Egyptians were now attempting to impose taxes on them, prompting them to declare: 'Our ruler and our lord is the king of Ethiopia ... We protect the caravans when they descend from Ethiopia, and we escort them to the capital of the kingdom'.[63]

Such ambiguity and/or outright rebellion continued to undermine Yohannes' imperial project through the 1870s; confronted with violence from different directions, Hamasien elites frequently opted for a strategy of playing larger powers off one another in order to maintain some degree of autonomy.[64] More 'popular' feelings are clearly difficult to assess, though one source asserted at the beginning of 1876 that the people of Hamasien, which had been evacuated by Yohannes' forces, 'are reported to be friendly to the Egyptians'.[65] There was certainly much Egyptian propaganda to this effect. The *Moniteur Egyptien* of December 1875, while omitting to mention the defeat at Gundet, emphasized that 'the Egyptian soldiers were welcomed with great joy by the inhabitants of Hamasien'. At the Mereb itself, the people of Gundet had warned the Egyptian force of the Ethiopian advance and begged protection from the 'invaders'.[66] Whatever the case, it is clear that Yohannes' largely unprofitable victories over the Egyptians at Gundet and Gura in 1875–6 exposed the fragility of his position in the *kebessa*. Welde Mikael fled to Massawa to join the Egyptians, and the *khedive* proposed placing him in charge of Hamasien as a vassal, creating a territory which 'would be a good barrier between Abyssinia and our territory'.[67]

Yohannes himself surely recognized the futility of his victories: he immediately sought a reconciliation, though not before reminding the Egyptians that the war started because 'the frontiers have not been respected and because you have listened to the rebels in the kingdom of Abyssinia',[68] an admission that the frontiers of the *kebessa* were in fact riddled with 'rebels'. Yohannes lamented that Welde Mikael, whom he had appointed as governor of Hamasien, 'has betrayed us and joined you', while '[y]ou have given the reins of government to the inhabitants of Akkele Guzay in order to rouse them against us'.[69] Matters were further complicated, of course, by the fact that the great rivals of Hamasien, Tsazegga and Hazzega, were themselves engaged in escalating conflict through the mid-1870s.[70] This aspect of nine-teenth-century *kebessa* history requires much more research; but it is cer-tainly clear that Welde Mikael himself, having sided with the Egyptians, found the latter less than enthusiastic about responding to his requests for assistance against Yohannes' 'pillaging'.[71] Across the Eritrean plateau, vio-lence escalated from the late 1870s onward, between rival groups whose loyalties—or at least requests for protection—were directed toward either the Egyptians or the Tigrayans.[72]

Much of Eritrea in the nineteenth century was defined in terms of crimi-nality, banditry, and 'illegitimate' violence. A great deal of this was racial or 'tribal' stereotyping, of course; but it is indeed the case that war spawns new forms and cultures of violence and definitions of 'criminality', particularly in the context of the frontier. 'Banditry'—*shifta* activity—went hand-in-hand with social displacement and the mobile military frontier. From early in his career, for example, Yohannes was keen to project the image of legitimacy in his use of violence: as Kassa, he declared in 1869: 'all brigands [and] predators (lit. lions) have been subdued in the country I rule'.[73] He was the legitimate state, and thus his use of force was righteous; his enemies were criminals and, indeed, little better than wild animals. At the level of the state, it was crucial to project ideas about order and rectitude, and there can be little doubt that the situation on the troubled frontier contributed in no small way to Yohannes' need to create such imagery. In the last two years of Tewodros' reign, as his state descended into chaos, so too did the northern frontier, as we have noted: in mid-1866 it was reported that the route to the coast through Akele Guzay was virtually closed because of bandits, with merchants instead attempting to use the Serae road. Moreover, '[r]obbers and bandits have become very numerous in Tigray'.[74] Again, there can be little doubt that much of this criminalized and paramilitary activity was driven in large part by food shortage across the north. Such supposedly 'illegitimate' violence proliferated on the frontier, perpetuated by the excluded and the disaffected, the criminal and the 'ungovernable'. Around Massawa, for exam-ple, southbound caravans were plundered with impunity throughout the nineteenth century,[75] and references abound to an endemic predatory war-fare on the roads from Massawa into the highlands, with travellers depicting a no-man's-land where 'wild' groups preyed on unsuspecting merchants.[76] Littoral and escarpment Eritrea was a zone of 'illegitimate' and stateless violence. The much-maligned Saho, again, had gained a reputation for rob-bery by the 1860s,[77] while according to Portal they inhabited a country 'notorious for its breed of robbers and professional brigands'.[78] By the 1880s, indeed, 'murder and brigandage' had become so common 'as almost to put a stop to all trade'. Between the Italian position at Sahati and Alula's base in Hamasien was 'disputed territory... said to be infested by wandering bands of brigands and evil-disposed Arab tribes'.[79] While some bandits were thus held to be genetically 'evil', others were exiles and renegades from the high-lands, one source identifying a ringleader of attacks on Abyssinian caravans as Debbeb, no less than a cousin of Yohannes himself. According to the source, moreover, '[t]he Governor of [Massawa] and other officials winked at (if they did not actively encourage) the raids on the Abyssinian caravans, and allowed the proceeds of the robberies to be sold openly in the bazaar'. Debbeb, indeed, recruited his 'robber-band' in Massawa itself.[80] The authorities at Massawa saw this, no doubt, as war by other means: it was clearly in their interests to encourage such 'lawlessness', particularly in respect of caravans carrying firearms to Yohannes.[81]

Above all, Yohannes undoubtedly articulated *habesha* territorial claims more clearly and more powerfully than anyone before him. Gerald Portal wrote in the late 1880s that Yohannes

> consistently denied the right of the Italian or of any other foreign Government to be at Massowah at all. He maintained that by right of descent Massowah and all the south-western coast of the Red Sea had for centuries belonged to Abyssinia. Tradition lives long in Abyssinia; as far back as the sixteenth century, the superior armament and discipline of the Turks had driven the Abyssinians from Zeyla, and later from Massowah... [D]uring all these 300 years, argued King Johannis, Abyssinia had never given up its claim to the sea-coast; the Turks, and subsequently the Egyptians, had only held these places as they had acquired them—by the power of the sword.[82]

Yohannes himself, of course, understood very well the power of the sword: his own advances north, across the plateau and down onto the coastal plain, were exercises in military adventurism.

Frontiers (2): Sudan and the north-west

Egyptian expansion between the 1820s and the 1840s from their newly established base at Khartoum encroached into lands either traditionally claimed by Christian highlanders, or which at least had been regarded as

carefully maintained buffer zones along the northern and western escarp-
ments and lowlands.[83] In particular, the Egyptians—having occupied much
of the Nile valley—moved into the area of what is now the western lowland
of Eritrea and north-east Sudan, abutting the north-west approaches of
Ethiopia. The Gash-Barka zone was thus emerging as another key borderland in the making of the modern region—and would remain key for
Ethiopia, Sudan, and later Eritrea itself. Yet the advance of the Egyptians
into this area by the early 1840s was ambiguous. For while this development
unfolded as a territorial (and indeed religious) threat, at the same time the
revival of Red Sea commerce which it prompted, again, was of enormous
benefit to Ethiopian territories in the northern and western highlands.
Tigray in particular was well-positioned to take advantage of the trade; so
too were the territories abutting Sudan, especially Shoa, whose rulers were
increasingly able to enrich themselves to the detriment of the imperial
court at Gondar.

From the 1820s, increasingly aggressive Egyptian commercial, military,
and religious expansion proceeded apace into southern Sudan, including the
upper Nile basin and equatorial regions, and the area of Bahr al-Ghazal and
Darfur, which had been reached by the mid-1870s.[84] The Ethiopian–Sudanese
borderlands had long been zones of conflict and ambiguity, and in many
respects Egyptian imperialism 'merely' breathed new life into these, much as
Mahdism would along the Christians' north-west frontier. In particular, the
Ethiopian–Sudanese marches had long been a destination for the displaced
and the discontented, thus rendering this zone politically volatile. Groups in
political or religious opposition to successive regimes in the Ethiopian
Highlands and in the upper Nile basin took to these borderlands, where they
merged with refugees from the slaving expeditions so common throughout
the nineteenth century. With the expansion of Turco-Egyptian administration from Khartoum, a number of groups took to the marches, and Ali
Khurshid Agha, Muhammad Ali's administrator in Sudan from 1826, spent
much of his lengthy tenure seeking both their return and the stabilization of
the frontier. In terms of the former, he was moderately successful from the
late 1820s—Sheikh Ahmad al-Rayyah al-Araki submitted, for example,
bringing with him thousands of his Arakiyyin followers—but his success on
the borderlands themselves was somewhat limited. Campaigns against the
Hadendowa in Taka in the early 1830s were at best inconclusive, while frontier wars further south against Kanfu—governor of Kwara and the paternal
uncle of the future Tewodros—rumbled on for several years during the 1830s

with mixed results. In the later part of the decade, fearful that Kanfu was seeking the annexation of Gallabat—which would have rendered that province a haven for anti-Egyptian resistance—Khurshid prepared a major assault on the Ethiopian marches, only for Muhammad Ali to be warned by the British not to attempt any serious incursions into *habesha* territory. Khurshid's successor was Abu Widn, and he too was confronted with the ongoing problem of rebels fleeing to the marches. He was rather more successful than his predecessors in campaigning against the Hadendowa and into the western Eritrean lowlands: under him, what would become the province of Taka became somewhat more firmly established in the 1840s, and Kassala expanded as a key strategic settlement on the site of a military camp.

Between the 1840s and the 1860s, an increasingly aggressive Egyptian presence was established in southern Sudan and the western lowlands of present-day Eritrea, and was creeping into the Christian highlands around Agordat and Keren. The latter area became, in the course of the nineteenth century, a decidedly ambiguous frontier, and would evolve into an even more explosive one in the twentieth; it was inhabited by a range of pastoral and semi-nomadic groups which at best had shifting and multiple relationships with surrounding expanding statehoods, and which would take advantage of the eventual 'formalization' of international boundaries in the area by using them as frontlines in ongoing localized animosities, and as markers in the evolution of larger (and politically expedient) regional identities. The creation of the Egyptian administrative province of Taka—to the east of Khartoum, encompassing Kassala and the Gash-Barka plains, and stretching into the foothills of the *kebessa*—with a fortified outpost at Keren constituted a direct threat to Amhara and Tigrayan control to the south. The same was true of the consolidation of Egyptian control of Massawa on the Eritrean coast, leased from the Ottoman authorities. Thus was a northern arc formed which effectively constituted a new and aggressive front blocking the highlanders' view of the Red Sea and Mediterranean worlds which would become ever more important to them. This was the *habesha* dilemma: those who were necessary as trading partners for the highlanders were also, ultimately, political and religious antagonists. It contributed powerfully to the *habesha* sense of encirclement, while Ethiopian highlanders were increasingly frustrated by the seeming lack of interest of the European powers who were supposed to be their natural spiritual allies.

New political and indeed religious communities were emerging elsewhere, too, in the course of the nineteenth century, notably on the Ethiopian–Sudanese borderlands.[85] On the Ethiopian side of the frontier,[86] the sheikhdoms of Aqoldi (or Asosa), Beni Shangul, Gubba, and Khomosha were the result of a larger aristocratic network—that of the Watawit, of Sudanese origin—over the Berta and Gumuz. These would be increasingly squeezed between two expanding imperialisms, much like the peoples of the Gash-Barka region, namely the Egyptian (later Anglo-Egyptian) Sudan and Solomonic Ethiopia—although neither would be in a position to exert control over the lands between them, which indeed came to define the fractures and fissures of those empires themselves. If it is broadly accepted that across north-east Africa states and societies have only ever been as 'strong' as their weakest and most volatile borderlands, and were indeed ultimately defined by the dynamics of those borderlands, then what we do know about the Ethiopian-Sudanese frontier territories tells us a great deal about the nature of the political missions on either side of them throughout the nineteenth and twentieth centuries. For the *habesha*, of course, these were the lands of the *shangalla* or *baria* further north—savages and slaves, usually with some derogatory inference concerning darker skin colour— and these territories were indeed key hunting grounds for the predatory highland state. This was politically motivated, and racially justified, slaving violence. In many respects the western frontier was the one by which high-landers judged their own cultural and genetic supremacy.

We have already observed that Yohannes perceived one continuous 'frontier' from the coast to the interior lowland plains, but for our purposes it is important to look briefly at the region now known as the western lowlands of Eritrea, as in some ways it constituted a distinct geopolitical sphere. As with the central Eritrean highlands, this was a frontier which reflected anxieties at the very heart of the *habesha* state, and which had troubled highland rulers throughout the nineteenth century, particularly since the conquest of the area by Muhammad Ali. The advance of the 'Turks' into the vicinity of Sennar and Metemma in the late 1830s led Sahle Dingil to reflect ruefully that 'a conqueror recognizes no boundaries', and that they had seized territories which 'were the dominions of our king'.[87] The lowland zone immediately north of Tigray was an ambiguous no-man's-land, known in Tigrinya, according to one source from the mid-1840s, as 'Addy Barea', country of the slaves.[88] To the Amhara, this formed part of the vast *shangalla* frontier district between *habesha* and Arabic civi-lization.[89] The area was another of Wube's hunting grounds, if not always as fruitful as the Bogos region. In one prolonged campaign in 1844, Wube's troops were repeatedly harassed by the 'Baria'—presumably Nara or related

groups—and at length became lost and ran out of water, owing to 'ignorance of the country'. Some did, however, succeed in returning with slaves
and cattle, despite fierce resistance.[90] So wide ranging was Wube's campaign
on this occasion that his troops inadvertently or otherwise attacked several
groups on the Egyptian side of the frontier zone.[91] In the then thickly for-
ested Takkaze River valley, moreover, renegade 'Arabs' established military
camps away from the encroaching Egyptian authorities in Taka.[92] The lowland area swiftly gives way to the rugged spur of mountains north of
Agordat and Keren, the Halhal district, which reached Nakfa further north
still—the area, as we see in Part IV, of such significance in the history of the
Eritrean nationalist struggle. In the mid-nineteenth century, Halhal was
likewise a contested zone, prone, as Plowden observed, to attacks 'alternately by the troops of Oobeay, and the Turks of Sennaar, from the quarter
of Taka or Gasch'. The pastoral and semi-pastoral communities of these
hills periodically paid tribute to whoever was perceived as the greater
threat, whereupon, as Plowden memorably described it,

> these districts are…left to govern themselves as they please, and to replace
> their losses by plundering their neighbours. As may be supposed, the only law
> is that of the strongest; and wars and blood-feuds, betwixt man and man, vil-
> lage and village, tribe and tribe, as each may find that exciting pastime agree-
> able, are the only occupations that vary the monotony of driving their flocks
> and herds to pasture.[93]

The Egyptian position in the mid-1870s was that 'Abyssinian' raids across
the plains of present-day Gash-Barka province had compelled them to
secure their frontier with reinforcements. But the alleged raiders were no
'Abyssinians', and this misreading—whether deliberate or otherwise—of
particular groups' loyalties and motives only served to underline the ambiguity of the frontier zone. One source suggested that

> the marauders belonged to the Bari tribe, who inhabit the country immedi-
> ately south of Kassala, and are notorious for their predatory and lawless habits,
> and who have probably a very indistinct idea of the nature of a frontier
> between two States, and have not been as yet brought under subjection to
> Prince Kassai's Government.[94]

But the Egyptians held Yohannes responsible for any 'incursions' into Taka,
and certainly rejected the idea that Bogos belonged in any way to 'Abyssinia'.
The district was supposedly non-negotiable as a part of Egyptian-Sudanese
administration, although one Egyptian source conceded that 'the peoples

and barbarous tribes placed in this condition have naturally very little stability; they are very restless and very mobile'. Moreover, certain acts by the
government—the punishment of insurrection, or the reinforcement of the
border against potential enemies by moving troops into the area—inevitably
caused such peoples to flee towards 'Abyssinia'. However, this, asserted the
source, was no indication of sovereignty: the people of Bogos, in any case,
had come to accept Egyptian overlordship. Now Yohannes had destabilized
the region by positioning some 15,000 troops, deployed under five commanders, in a broad front stretching from Hamasien to north-west Tigray.[95]

Yohannes needed to maintain relations with whatever power occupied
the north-west frontier. In early 1884, Yohannes received 'with great distinction' a Beni Amer embassy which had come 'to ask his aid against the
Mahdi'.[96] The emperor's response is unrecorded—although in July 1884 he
moved with a large force into the Barka area, effecting a rendezvous with
Alula's army moving down from Hamasien, ostensibly to collect his annual
tribute[97]—but it is clear that he had wider concerns when dealing with the
communities of the north-west frontier. Yohannes was confronted with a
substantial Muslim population in his domains, and his ongoing conflict
with Egypt heightened tensions in this regard, even more so with the rise of
the Mahdist state. Yohannes had reason to fear that a direct clash with the
Mahdists would prompt a general Muslim uprising across the region.[98] The
Mahdist state, of course, had its own ambitions in the region, with a bloody
clash between the Mahdists and *Ras* Alula's forces taking place near Kassala
in 1885;[99] and when the first major Mahdist invasion came, in 1887, *habesha*
military capacity was extremely stretched, as Wylde explained:

> ...some [forces] were in the north watching the northern frontier both against
> the Italians in the east and the Dervishes in the north-west, others were at their
> homes cultivating, and some in the south-east watching the Danakils and
> Gallas, who had also been incited to attack Abyssinia. King [Takle Haymanot]
> of Godjam had only his badly armed population and few soldiery...The
> Dervishes gained, after severe fighting, a complete victory...[100]

A few years later, the Italians themselves halted a Mahdist expedition into
Eritrea at Agordat[101]—although that is a different stage in the story of this
frontier, and one which we will pick up in due course.

Yohannes had in fact sent placatory messages to Khartoum in this period,
suggesting among other things that they had a common enemy to fight—
namely, European imperialism. Such offers of peace were haughtily rebuffed,
however, and the Ethiopians prepared for war. When in 1889 Yohannes went

forth to give battle, near Metemma, his forces were initially successful, until an apparently stray bullet ended the emperor's life and the Ethiopian force fell into disarray. Never the most loyal of Yohannes' servants, Menelik none-theless held off from outright rebellion until the emperor had been thus felled. Throughout the 1890s, there was something of an uneasy truce between Abdullahi's state in Sudan and Menelik's Ethiopia; to all intents and purposes, the Mahdist *jihad* against the Christian empire was abandoned. The Mahdists would, in any case, soon have their own wars to fight: the Italian advance into the Eritrean highlands, and then down into the low-lands, in the course of the 1890s was achieved by a military victory at Agordat and then the seizure of Kassala. Ultimately the Mahdist state would be conquered by the British, from the north, and between them—on paper—Britain, Italy, and Ethiopia would now delineate their territories with clearly marked boundaries, even if, in Rome, it was imagined that Ethiopia was but a temporary actor and Eritrea only a springboard for much more dramatic advances. In reality, those borderlands remained insecure, and would become the breeding grounds for ever more militant, if moveable, identities.

Pax Solomonia? The restless militarism of Menelik's empire

While Menelik may have briefly considered making his grab for the rein-vigorated imperial throne in the aftermath of Tewodros' destruction in the late 1860s, when he was still only in his mid-20s, he was dissuaded from this; never wholly reconciled to Yohannes' accession, however, his was, again, an ambivalent loyalty. In the late 1860s, he commanded between 40,000 and 50,000 men, of whom only a relatively small number were armed with muskets; this number would increase dramatically over the next twenty years, and thus was Shoa able to expand through both firepower, manpower, and clever political agreements at the local level.[102] A skilled political strate-gist, Menelik spent much of the 1870s and 1880s creating the political and material groundwork for an Amhara imperial renaissance, consolidating his own position, expanding the borders of Shoa, and doing a brisk trade with European traders via Zeila and Djibouti. In that way was he able to stockpile large amounts of modern firearms, one of the largest such arsenals anywhere in nineteenth-century Africa, at least under a single ruler. Yohannes' mounting problems with the Egyptians, then with the Italians, provided Menelik with his opportunity; and even as Yohannes had been preparing to make war on the Mahdists, the issue of internal disunity was once again rearing its head—as the emperor sought to assemble an army on the north-west frontier, rumours abounded that both Takla Haymanot in Gojjam and Menelik in Shoa were plotting revolt. It was ironic indeed that Yohannes was undermined in his dealings with both the Italians and the Mahdists—representing two of the gravest threats to the *habesha* polity for some considerable time—by his own internal enemies;[103] but Menelik's achievement in subsequently stabilizing his fractured inheritance, if only temporarily, was nonetheless remarkable.

When Yohannes was killed in the fighting in 1889, Menelik swiftly proclaimed himself *negus negast*, and in truth there was little significant opposition.[104] There were few serious alternatives, especially following Menelik's military success in the south; the imperial army under Yohannes was in some disarray following the debacle at Metemma, and—perhaps most critically of all—Menelik's aggressive action came against the backdrop of one of the region's worst famines in living memory. Famine, or at least severe food shortage, had had a major impact on the intensity and flow of violence earlier, notably in the late 1860s. While those shortages may have been man-made in the mid-nineteenth century, at least in large part, the 'Great Famine' of the late 1880s and early 1890s was caused first and foremost by a failure of the rains. Nonetheless the catastrophe intersected with political and military developments. The effects of famine were exacerbated by the cumulative militarism of the nineteenth century which placed massive strains on northern resources; in many respects, this junction of phenomena provided a newly aggressive and increasingly urgent impetus to southward expansion on the part of the *habesha* state from the early 1890s onward.

It was to Menelik's advantage, particularly across swathes of the north and north-east where potential opposition was dissipated by hunger and disease—the cattle epidemic, rinderpest, would make its appearance at the same time—and his preparedness to act decisively in the event of Yohannes' death was crucial. However, he did find it necessary to tour the north in some force to ensure obedience and acceptance; he was well aware that there were many irreconcilables in Tigray who still waved the flag of Yohannes, not least the redoubtable *Ras* Alula and Yohannes' son Mangasha. He was met there with a great deal of hostility—to him personally, as a Shoan and an Amhara, and also to the state structure he represented. Nonetheless it was not sufficient to divert him from his path; he also enjoyed the support of the Italians, who accordingly supplied him (somewhat myopically) with arms and ammunition.[105] In late 1889, Menelik was formally crowned at Entoto, on a hill which today lies on the outskirts of Addis Ababa—the capital which Menelik and his wife Taitu (whose idea it largely was) would establish shortly afterwards. Once again, the centre of political gravity had swung decisively away from Tigray and back south to the Amhara.

Ethiopia was also fanning out below the central plateau along an expanding economic frontier, deep into the south toward Lake Turkana, and to either side, south-west toward the foothills of the Blue Nile and the river Akobo, and into the hot plains of the Afar and the Somali to the east. Again, to a very real extent this process of southern expansion was driven by the need for food and a range of other exportable commodities to both offset the effects of chronic famine in the north, and also to pay for the greatly swollen and massively expensive militarism which was now the defining feature of Ethiopian political culture. The Amhara genius was the ability to achieve these remarkable imperial feats in the age of European hegemony, and while the Amhara themselves were simultaneously the target of European aggression. Shoan conquests in the south and west, and also to the east into Somali territory, were as dynamic and ultimately as successful as any European imperial partition in the region. In fact, to a very real extent Menelik was merely continuing the work begun by his grandfather, Sahle Selassie, who was already expanding the southern and western borders of Shoa into Oromo territory in the 1830s.[106] Yet initially, Menelik was confronted with the dominance of Gojjam, both in the Gibe River area and among the western Oromo groups: by the beginning of the 1880s, Takle Haymanot had established himself as *negus* of Kaffa in the south-west, and had had his overlordship recognized among the Oromo states of the Blue Nile region. A brief but intense Shoan–Gojjami rivalry ensued, culminating in Menelik's triumph at the battle of Embabo in early 1882, which essentially broke Gojjam's hegemony in the west and south-west. In the course of the 1880s, Menelik extended his control over a swathe of Oromo territory—including Leqa Nekemte and Jimma—over which he instituted a new form of control in the conquered areas, not merely extracting but creating a form of indirect rule through tributary relationships with Gurage and Oromo chieftaincies. There was economic benefit to be had for elites on both sides of the arrangement, and indeed Menelik was also able to recruit Oromo into his own forces for further expansion.[107]

Yet there could be little doubting the extreme violence that had accompanied this new dispensation of power in what would become southern Ethiopia. First-hand testimony provided by the Russian military attaché Alexander Bulatovich is worth quoting:

> The Abyssinians pursue two goals in the governing of the region: fiscal and political security of the region and prevention of an uprising. All families are assessed a tax. This is very small... In addition, families are attached to the land. Part of the population is obliged to cultivate land for the main ruler of the country, and part is divided among the soldiers and military leaders. The whole region is divided among separate military leaders who live off their district and feed their soldiers.

At the same time, this had been a destructive and violent imperialism:

> The dreadful annihilation of more than half of the population during the conquest took away from the Galla all possibility of thinking about any sort of uprising. And the freedom-loving Galla who didn't recognise any authority other than the speed of his horse, the strength of his hand, and the accuracy of his spear, now goes through the hard school of obedience.[108]

These were clearly districts which had been conquered directly, having originally resisted; others submitted willingly, and Bulatovich names Jimma, Wellaga, and Leqa Nekemte, where 'the former order has been preserved... The Abyssinians obtain taxes from them and do not interfere in their self-government. Aside from the payment of taxes, they also feed the troops stationed there'.[109] In part, then, the military hegemony of the mid- and late 1890s rested partly on sheer force of conquest, partly on cultural assimilation, partly on loose tributary and tax-based levels of suzerainty. Garrisons of troops, sometimes several thousand strong, were stationed across the conquered zone; these often became substantial urban settlements, such as Bareilu, described by Bulatovich, which also had the advantage of lying on the main commercial route between Shoa and Wellega.[110] Meanwhile, Amhara settlers were increasingly to be seen across the south.[111] In sum, a more stable, permanent, and economically driven administrative system had been created on the expanding frontier. Bulatovich wrote approvingly that in participating so decisively in the scramble for the region, Menelik was 'only carrying out the traditional mission of Ethiopia as the propagator of culture and the unifier of all the inhabitants of the Ethiopian Mountains and of the related tribes in the neighbourhood'.[112]

Considerable bloodshed also attended the subjugation of the Arsi, south-east of Shoa, who put up several years of dogged resistance until their internal divisions and Shoa's superior firepower put it to an end, in 1886. Harar was Menelik's next eastward target: the emirate had been evacuated by the Egyptian garrison in 1885, and under Abdullahi was threatening something of a resurgence—here, Menelik was able to argue to his British and Italian counterparts in Somali territory further east that this was a dangerously unstable borderland that he was best placed to subdue. They agreed, and after initial setbacks the Shoans seized Harar in early 1887. Shoan expansion entered a hiatus owing in large part to Menelik's concern with domestic politics, and also to the awful famine which now raged; but from the early 1890s there were prolonged wars of conquest against the key southern kingdoms of Welayta and Kaffa, while several chiefdoms on the Ethiopian-Sudanese borders—including Illubabor, Aqoldi, and Bela Shangul—were incorporated.[113] Some of this imperial expansion was piecemeal, however. Famine and disease in the late 1880s had caused much hardship across a wide area, prompting local *habesha* administrations to raid into neighbouring areas less severely hit, in search of resources. For example, *Ras* Mekonnen, newly appointed governor of Harar and father of Haile Selassie, organized a series of raids into the Ogaden and seized livestock from the Somali; such limited-objective raiding swiftly became conquest. Ethiopian commanders sought local allies, and easily prized open fissures between Somali clans, thus establishing another form of indirect rule, like that in the south-west, in which more permanent governance was achieved through particular Somali clan heads. Ethiopian military garrisons were founded across the Ogaden, as they were across the south and west, a heavily armed presence which ensured that—certainly following Menelik's victory over Italy at Adwa, examined in the next chapter—Ethiopia needed to be treated with respect as a 'player' in the region's international politics. Menelik was surrounded by some gifted commanders—among them *Ras* Mekonnen and *Ras* Gobana—and that military establishment had proven itself easily the equal of the European colonial militaries in adjacent territories. This was a military expansion which also brought about a major economic shift from north to south, as Shoa became the treasury into which the riches of the southern territories were poured: the profits of gold, ivory, coffee, and indeed slaves were reaped by the Shoan elite, who also embarked on a process of land alienation across the south, with estates of land and commercial concessions distributed by Menelik to a loyal soldier-administrator-settler class which would form the socio-political backbone of the Ethiopian state for decades to come. Local communities were reduced to what amounted to serfdom, a state of servitude on the land now owned by armed settlers from the north. *Gabbar*, the term for farmer with serf-like connotations in southern Ethiopia, now laboured under a class of *neftennya*, which literally means 'one who owns a gun', referring to the soldier-settlers across the south to whom Addis Ababa granted rights over both people and land.[114]

Menelik's kingship was a curious amalgam of the old and the new, founded on violence but in many respects maintained through negotiation—and spectacular Italian failure. In the course of the campaigns of military and political expansion of the 1880s and 1890s, the new Ethiopia was born, and a series of new frontiers—in physical terms, as well as in the contexts of ethnicity, culture, belief—came into being, this time enclosed within a shared sovereign space. Again, however, perhaps the most remarkable characteristic about the empire founded by Menelik in the years either side of 1900—a characteristic which would be inherited by Haile Selassie—is that it was founded upon both violence and co-option. It was not his post office, his banking system, his railways, and the various other attempts at the stuff of modernity, but his ability—in the short to medium-term, at least—to manage the vast and fractious territory he had helped bring into being. *Habesha* culture was both hegemonic and assimilationist—perhaps all successful cultures are—and the reasons behind the attractiveness of the Amhara–Tigrayan cultural complex to a host of incorporated peoples are doubtless manifold. Many Oromo had been similarly drawn to it since the sixteenth and seventeenth centuries. Christianity held its own attractions, and certainly its monotheism explains much; above all, it was the richly historic, articulate, and literate expression of *habesha* culture which no doubt drew many to it, even grudgingly. All that said, however, many more would come, in the course of the twentieth century, to reject it violently. Although Menelik's military machine had, for the time being, imposed a *pax* on particularly hostile frontier zones, he had created deepening pools of hostility for the longer term. Menelik would have been only too aware of this, as his army was continually attacked by Tigrayan, Azebo, and Oromo peasants alike on its march back from Adwa, the scene of the emperor's greatest triumph.[115] The Azebo and Afar in the north-east, for example, may have been temporarily becalmed in the face of modern weaponry;[116] but their resentment at *habesha* cattle-raiding would only increase over time. Likewise, Tigray was subordinate but simmered with

bitterness at the impositions of 'southern Abyssinians' who had impoverished vast districts in the run-up to the battle of Adwa, and at the apparent
greed of Menelik who kept the compensation paid by the Italians for himself, even though Tigrayan leaders 'were the chief sufferers by the war, and
bore the brunt of the fighting'. As Wylde observed, 'it is not at all unlikely,
that it will bear fruit in the future, and make the northerners more eager
to improve their present condition'.[117] As another contemporary source
noted, 'everywhere [Menelik] found his Shoans received with hatred and
contempt by the inhabitants of Tigre. The latter had not yet forgotten that
they were the true leaders of the Ethiopian race'.[118]

The 'modern' Ethiopia that came into being in the last twenty years of the
nineteenth century was the product of a restless, cumulative militarism. The
political system rested heavily on the effective deployment of armed force;
this was a political culture, and a social system more broadly, that was the
outcome of prolonged violence. It was, in turn, a fragile, volatile polity in
which arms had come to play a dangerously inflated role in political and
indeed economic development. In terms of the latter, notably, the military
burden would prove huge. This was a system open to abuse by ambitious
state-building elites, and which clearly facilitated authoritarianism; yet it was
also characterized by a degree of social mobility, and an access to the means
of socio-political change, which meant the empowerment of a military class
capable of inducing such change, should the opportunity and the will arise.

A large number and range of sources through the nineteenth century
point toward the increasing size and significance of both soldiery and militarism in the *habesha* socio-political order.[119] Young men—and not a few
older men—were drawn increasingly to military service, and a vastly swollen
military establishment was the cumulative effect of cyclical violence as well
as economic insecurity. From the village level upwards, men had long been
eligible to follow their local leaders to war for a defined period of time;[120]
but the nineteenth century saw a widening and a 'professionalizing' of such
service, and an apparent increase in the numbers of camp followers.[121]
Moreover, firearms—and modern ones, at that—were common, and a veritable gun culture had emerged across the highlands by the 1880s and 1890s.
It was a reasonably recent creation, for while during Tewodros' reign only
imperial troops were generally able to acquire guns,[122] the expansion of
trade and a dramatic increase in supply meant, in Wylde's words, that:

> The peasant is no longer miserably armed with spear and shield, or sword and
> shield, but is generally the owner of a fairly modern breech-loading rifle, and

has a good store of cartridges, and can always procure more on next local market day, where they are openly sold or bartered and count as coin.[123]

Firearms became the instruments of political power from the 1870s onward, although always in conjunction with cavalry, down to the 1930s. New technologies were one thing, but cultures of violence predated these. Beginning during the *zemene mesafint* and continuing under Tewodros, Yohannes, and Menelik, large armies and their attendant cultures would prove difficult if not impossible to demobilize once brought into being: military cultures require regular feeding. As Portal observed at the time of Yohannes' mobilization against the Italians,

> [t]he great probability is that, if the present object, i.e. war with the Italians, were to be take away, these... armies, some of them from the country of the Gallas, from Shoa, and from the extreme outskirts of Abyssinian dependencies, would refuse to return empty-handed to their own countries, and Abyssinia would soon be torn by a series of internecine struggles between the different Chiefs and Kings...[124]

A typically glum European prognosis, no doubt, but containing more than an element of truth. Wylde was equally gloomy:

> [The nobility's] only chance of employment is if war breaks out, or they are sent on an expedition to annex further territory or punish some border tribe... The final settlement of the southern portion of the Abyssinian kingdom will leave King Menelek face to face with the question of what he will have to do with his fighting feudal barons and his large army, as he will have no enemies to conquer... The military may settle down and turn their arms into reaping hooks and ploughshares, but most likely civil war will break out... The soldiery were called into existence by Abyssinia being surrounded by their Mahomedan enemies, and little by little they increased and multiplied till they have got out of all proportion to the wants of a peaceful country. To keep these soldiers quiet they either have to be paid or allowed to loot... Paying all of them... is out of the question... so looting has to be allowed or expeditions started into country that never belonged to Abyssinia.[125]

This was misleadingly stark; the empire would diversify sufficiently to provide alternative, or at least additional, activities for socio-political elites. Nonetheless the central point holds true, namely that a dangerously potent militarism had been created which would not easily be undone. It seems possible to suggest that the region has hardly demobilized since the early nineteenth century.

Enormous levies were possible from the mid-1870s onward in the defence of the region against outside aggression—and indeed such mass mobilization became the mainstay of Ethiopia's military success in the last quarter of the nineteenth century. In many ways the epitome and apex of that success was against the Italians at Adwa in 1896, examined in the next chapter. Suffice to observe here that victory at Adwa was as much as anything else the culmination of a restless militarism which Menelik succeeded in harnessing, if briefly. The common assertion, increasingly made in European sources as the nineteenth century progressed, that every Ethiopian man was born a 'warrior' was doubtless racial cliché; but it did reflect the reality of the well-armed and readily mobilized community as the basic building-block of the *habesha* polity. At the same time, in the half-century or so between Tewodros' accession and Menelik's apogee *c.*1900, the perfect fusion of political and military establishments had been achieved; the key offices of state were held by soldiers, and no separation existed—although some would open up in the early decades of the twentieth century—between political and military authority.[126] Menelik's Ethiopia was the product of armed force and a culture of violence a century or more in the making; this was a century in which warfare had been honed as an effective tool for bringing about political change. Further, the polity was defined by its conquered and volatile frontiers—political, ethnic, faith-based—whose evolution can only be appreciated over *la longue durée*. The modern state was now precariously balanced, stilt-like, on a series of frontier zones both internal and external, zones to which Western boundary-making legality was now being applied but which were in different ways of considerable antiquity. The last word, perhaps, should go to Bulatovich. '[T]he history of Ethiopia', he wrote, 'is one of continual war with both internal and external enemies. The basis of imperial power can only be actual military strength, and on the army as on a foundation, has been built all the rest of the edifice of the Ethiopian Empire'.[127] The militarization of political culture was the experience of many other states and societies in Africa in the nineteenth century; but whereas it was generally arrested, temporarily at least, by the onset of colonial rule, this would not be the case in Ethiopia. The implications of this massive military complex and the resultant primacy of armed force, for Ethiopia and for the region as a whole, would become clear in the decades that followed.

PART III

Colonialisms, Old and New

5
Demarcating Identity
The European Colonial Experience,
*c.*1890–*c.*1950

A great deal of transformative power is attributed to colonial modernity across Africa, and so it is in our region which had the unique experience of both European and African imperialisms in operation over a remarkably large area. This chapter is concerned with the territories of European administration. It will be suggested here that, of course, European colonial rule was important in certain respects, as particular identities became rather more sharply demarcated. And yet the tendency of historians for a generation or more has been to contribute to the concept—whether inadvertently or explicitly—of a transformative colonial modernity which, in north-east Africa at least, amounts to a distortion of historical realities. I argue here that in many respects European colonialism was nowhere near as significant as has been suggested, and that a range of conflicts and core aspects of political culture far pre-dated the European administrative presence, which merely provided new elements in struggles of antiquity. It might be suggested, indeed, that in the case of Eritrea and Ethiopia, the Italians were inadvertent actors in ancient borderlands; ultimately, in many respects it was the Italians who were co-opted into a larger, more ancient struggle, while their contribution was the introduction of superficial modernity.

Blood on the tracks: Italians on the Mereb

From the humblest of beginnings—a foothold at Assab at the southern end of the Red Sea, purchased by the Rubattino Shipping Company in 1869 and taken over by the Italian government in 1882—Italy extended their

control to the more centrally located Massawa in 1885, and thence crept up
the escarpment and onto the *kebessa*. It was not a straightforward process: in
1887, a company of Italian soldiers was destroyed at Dogali in the coastal
foothills by Alula's frontier force, and the Italians were compelled to remain
clustered around Massawa until 1889, when crises in the interior facilitated
their rapid push inland. Menelik, of course, had courted Rome for some
time when still *negus* of Shoa, with a view to access to modern weaponry,
international recognition, and support for his eventual claim to the
Solomonic inheritance. In the fragile aftermath of Yohannes' death at
Metemma, Menelik sought Italian support as part of a larger strategy of
rapid consolidation, and in the middle of 1889 signed the Treaty of Wichale
with the Italians.[1] Essentially a treaty of friendship and commerce, in the
Amharic version Article 17 stated that the Ethiopians *might, if they so chose,
ask for the assistance of the Italian government* in conducting foreign relations.
The Italian version, however, expressly stated that the Ethiopian government *was obliged to go through the Italian government* in conducting foreign
relations. In effect, as far as Rome was concerned, Italy had secured a protectorate over Ethiopia.[2] Menelik spent the early 1890s demanding that the
treaty be withdrawn, and preparing for war. Further clarifications in 1890
had established in greater detail the Italo-Ethiopian border of the infant
colony of Eritrea; but the Italians subsequently made incursions into Tigray,
which were themselves in violation of the treaty, and although they withdrew, the first half of the 1890s witnessed a build-up of both troops and
tensions along the northern frontier. At the same time, Italian forces were in
action (with rather more success) against the Mahdists in the western lowlands; the latter were defeated at a key engagement at Agordat in late 1893
by an Italian force that was greatly bolstered by local levies.[3]

Much of this took place against a backdrop of crisis on the Ethiopian
side.[4] In the middle of 1888, the epidemic of rinderpest, carried by infected
cattle through Massawa, swept into the highlands, devastating the Hamasien
region and then moving into Tigray before proceeding south into Lasta,
Gojjam, and Shoa, and destroying the livelihoods of large numbers of Somali.
Livestock mortality was huge across a wide region, with herds exterminated
with extraordinary speed; it is no coincidence that the Italians were able to
move into the *kebessa* with some ease through 1889, establishing a base at
Asmara in the midst of a province devastated and weakened by the epidemic. In the same period, 1888–9 witnessed a severe and prolonged drought
across the Sahel belt, which crippled agriculture across north-east Africa

and compounded the effects of rinderpest; it led to a severe shortage of meat and grain, and in their weakened state people succumbed to a range of other epidemics in the early 1890s, including smallpox, dysentery, typhus, and cholera. It took several years for Menelik's fragile polity to approach recovery, and it was only through the creation of extensive granaries and the postponement of direct, full-scale military engagements with the Italians that Menelik was able to manoeuvre himself into a position from which he could address the growing threat in the northern borderland. Once again, climatic instability had a profound influence on the nature of military affairs—as it had earlier in the nineteenth century, and as it would in the later twentieth.

In September 1895, however, Menelik was able to declare a general mobilization, seeking to harness the restless militarism which had built up across the Ethiopian region since the 1860s, and indeed throughout the nineteenth century. From this perspective, the great clash between the Italians and the Ethiopians represented, among other things, a critical release of pressure for Menelik. In Eritrea, General Baratieri—commanding some 35,000 men, mostly Eritrean *ascari*—made the fatal error of regarding Menelik as a mere savage at the head of an unruly rabble that would surely be unable to withstand a modern European army. Italian intelligence and planning were deeply flawed. In the second half of the nineteenth century, *habesha* armies had proven themselves remarkably adept at dealing with external threats, usually through mass levies vastly outnumbering opponents.[5] A military confederation of upwards of 100,000 men assembled in central and eastern Tigray in late 1895, skilled in the use of both terrain and reinforcements, and better armed than most contemporary African armies, with perhaps four in five men possessing a firearm of one form or another.[6] The late nineteenth century, indeed, had heralded the coming of age of the firearm in Ethiopia as an instrument of real political and military power.[7] Yet the outcome could still have been very different—indeed, there might have been no battle at all. In January 1896, one important advantage lay with the Italians, in that they could afford to wait, whereas Menelik's army was on the point of starvation. With food supplies in Tigray dwindling, sectors of the army becoming restless, and tensions developing between troops and locals—tensions which would endure long after the battle—Menelik was considering disbanding by mid-February. He was saved, however, by the intervention of Italian domestic politics. With the government pressuring Baratieri to resolve the standoff and conjure up some much needed national glory, the Italians decided to march into Tigray, which they did on 1 March. The details of the ensuing battle, fought in the hills around Adwa, are well-known:[8] the Italians' comparatively tiny force of 14,500 men was outflanked and outgunned by a huge Ethiopian force, and was quickly in disarray. By noon, when the retreat was sounded, 4000 Italians and 2000 Eritreans had been killed, as against the much smaller proportion of between 4000 and 7000 Ethiopians, and the Italian imperial dream in north-east Africa—at least as it had first been conceived—was dead. Rome sued for peace, offering the abrogation of the Treaty of Wichale, and unconditional recognition of Ethiopian sovereignty. A new treaty in October 1896 recognized the Eritrean frontier—although Eritrean prisoners of war were mutilated in the standard fashion on Menelik's orders, effectively as 'traitors' and rebels. Menelik's victory at Adwa—not to mention his own campaigns of territorial expansion in the south and east— confirmed him and his state as a fully sovereign actor in the region's affairs, and indeed a *bona fide* participant in its partition. Adwa itself would become a reference point of remarkable power.

Much has been made of Menelik's decision to 'sell off' Ethiopia's supposed northernmost province—i.e. Eritrea—to the Italians at this time. It would become a *shibboleth* of much twentieth-century scholarship that somehow 'Eritrea', in some curiously timeless form, belonged immutably to 'Ethiopia', in a similarly timeless, imagined manifestation, and that Menelik had for one reason or another 'given it away'. At best, it was an ugly distortion of a much more complex set of realities; at worst, it was simply an untruth.[9] Certainly, Menelik was nowhere near strong enough, either in economic or in purely military terms, to contemplate some kind of grand campaign to drive the Italians into the Red Sea. Menelik was confronted with serious unrest in Tigray, and had rather larger territorial issues to deal with in the south and east. Tigrayan ill-feeling toward the restored Shoan political establishment rendered Menelik vulnerable and diffident in the north; an assault into the *kebessa* and beyond would have exposed his aching flanks to all manner of hostility (never mind a presumably regrouped Italian opponent). As it was, the army was subject to attacks by Tigrayan and Oromo communities in the period after Adwa. Groups of Oromo and Tigrayan *shifta* and armed peasants harassed Menelik's troops as they wound their way home along southward roads. More broadly, as an Amhara, his view of the region was rather different from that of his Tigrayan predecessor. He had less of an interest in the north, for the riches of the south now absorbed him, as well as access to Djibouti, which port he had always used. Above all, the long frontier that eventually would be drawn up between the new imperial Ethiopia and Italian Eritrea was, in the main, a recognition and formal delimitation, whether unwitting or otherwise, of a pre-existing set of borderlands. The Danakil depression, and in particular the Mereb valley and the Gash-Takkaze lowland zone, had all constituted contested borderlands since long before Italy was even unified as a nation-state. The fact that several historical fault lines were now contained within a territory named 'Eritrea' scarcely altered the fact of their antiquity, nor indeed the fact that they remained active.

Raising the first born: Italian Eritrea, to 1941

It has become axiomatic that Italian colonial rule was crucial to the creation of 'modern Eritrea'—axiomatic, that is, among scholars of Eritrea, and absolutely fundamental to the nationalist interpretation of the region's history. The Italian creation of Eritrea, it is argued, set the territory on its own distinctive path, contributed significantly to a discrete sense of identity—separate, crucially, from that of Ethiopia—and fundamentally laid the foundations for the modern nation.[10] Italian colonialism is the *sine qua non* of Eritrean nationalism. No doubt; but it is important to note that much of the literature produced on Eritrea from the late 1980s and through the 1990s was concerned, explicitly or otherwise, to explain (and quite often laud) the nationalist cause, and so it was history written backwards, characterized by an earnest search for the first shoots of the nationalist liberation movement, broadly defined. However, if we remove the desire to account for an explicitly *modern nationalism* from the equation, we might have a rather different view of the region's development over *la longue durée*. This interpretation suggests that the nationalist thesis in fact prevents us from seeing what is most interesting about the history of the Eritrean region and its adjacent territories, and argues for the 'de-modernization' of the Eritrean liberation struggle, which is—for one reason or another—viewed exclusively in modernist terms, both by students of it and of course by the protagonists themselves. In fact, the nationalist movement grew out of a conjunction of dynamics, and was the product of a series of conflicts and tensions, which had their roots in the nineteenth century and arguably earlier, not in any transformative European colonial experience. This is not to dismiss the very real impacts resulting from Italian colonialism, but to place them in context.

The Tigrinya of central Eritrea, over the course of several centuries, had been gradually cut adrift from the Tigray-Amhara political and cultural system—and the inheritance it implied—further south. They increasingly inhabited a fault line, a frontier which was international as well as 'internal', according to the Kopytoff thesis. Like Tigrayans themselves, they had a history of producing mavericks, defying orthodoxy, and struggling against southern domination of a Christian tradition supposedly northern in provenance; over the long term, they had come to see themselves as *different*, the product of the volatile northern borderland. Italian colonial rule underpinned and indeed exacerbated that sense of difference, and opened up new schisms in terms of group perception. Of course, throughout Eritrea's story, 'Abyssinia' lurks in the background of the nationalist narrative, like an elderly and sinister relative with suspect designs. But the actions of the Italians through the 1890s were in pursuit of one major goal—namely, the creation of an east African empire that included Ethiopia—and the aim was clearly that Eritrea would only form part of a much larger imperial territory. Eritrea itself was born of the failure to carry this grand scheme to fruition, created essentially out of military and political failure; and the subsequent relationship with the first-born was as that of a parent hoping for a larger family but thwarted by a certain infertility. With the aggressive advances of the Italians repulsed at Adwa—a notably unsuccessful attempt at penetration—Eritrea was briefly assigned the role of only child, and after Somalia and Libya were added, Eritrea was the eldest child in a dysfunctional family, separated from its siblings by considerable time and distance; the significance of using Eritrean soldiers in campaigns in both Somalia and Libya is clear enough. Above all, however, Italian failure compounded the unstable frontier, and served to compound the *kebessa*'s historic insecurity and sense of political ambiguity.

Italy had initially conceived of Eritrea as a settler colony: swathes of the highlands were alienated for the purpose between 1893 and 1895, while the first experiments in commercial agriculture were attempted in the early 1890s, at Asmara, Mendefera, and Gura.[11] But with the rebellion of Bahta Hagos in 1894—examined below—as well as smaller-scale incidents of resistance, and the defeat at Adwa, the project was mostly abandoned in favour of developing Eritrea as a commercial and industrial centre. Two large farms were established at Asmara in 1899, and from 1901 further concessions in the cultivation of coffee, cotton, and tobacco were made to both Eritrean and European farmers.[12] Alongside the ongoing refinement and consolidation of a system of colonial governance, the Italian period therefore witnessed the development of a light industrial economy, significant transport infrastructure, and some measure of commercial agriculture. Combined, these dynamics brought about socio-economic transformation across the territory, whose peoples' relations with one another were thus fundamentally recast. Hamasien province was arguably the most industrialized zone in north-east Africa by the 1930s. This fuelled urban growth, most notably in Asmara and Massawa; in Asmara, manufacturing and a vibrant service sector served the needs of an expanding Italian community.[13] In terms of agriculture, while the *kebessa* was intended to produce food for local consumption, the 1920s and 1930s witnessed the creation of land concessions in the western lowlands through which capital-backed farms would produce for export, for example coffee. The territory was bound together by an extensive road and rail network, connecting the central areas with the northern highlands and western lowlands, and with the southern Afar region. The growth of a wage labour economy absorbed many young men from across the region;[14] it would be the failure to sustain economic growth, however, that would propel a large number of them back into the 'bush' to become *shifta*.

   The colony was initially under a military administration, but in 1898, following the relocation of the capital from Massawa to Asmara, the appointment of Martini as Governor marked the shift to a civil administration.[15] Between 1897 and 1907, boundaries with Sudan, Ethiopia, and French Somaliland were delimited, although it was not until mid-1908 that the question of the Danakil boundary between Ethiopia and the Italian authorities was resolved. While Eritrea was divided into *commissariati*, or districts, each headed by an Italian bureaucracy, administration was in other ways conducted through fairly classical indirect rule, with particular chieftaincies and local aristocracies being co-opted for the purposes of stable governance. At the same time, the provision of education was extremely limited—no Eritrean could advance beyond the fourth grade—and thus created something of an indigenous underclass of unskilled labourers and soldiers, similar to socio-economic systems in Kenya and across southern Africa. A system of racial segregation had been in place since the beginning, but it became rather more rigid and codified with the introduction of Fascist laws in the early 1930s.[16] Nonetheless through mission education and the rare appearance of opportunity, a small class of Eritrean functionaries did work their way into the colonial administration as clerks and translators, while at the same time, in Asmara, an Eritrean lower middle class of entrepreneurs was also beginning to appear by the 1930s. In many respects these would be critical in the political developments of the 1940s.[17] Otherwise, a common, and not unattractive, career for tens of thousands of Eritrean men was as *ascari*, soldiers in the colonial army: on the eve of the Second World War, there may have been a remarkable 300,000 Eritrean *ascari* in the colonial army. Such troops were critical, indeed, to the Italian imperial mission, and were deployed in Libya and Somalia down to the early 1930s, in the invasion of Ethiopia in 1935–6, and against the British in 1940–1. The early 1930s witnessed a dramatic build up of men and material in Eritrea: the impact was mainly experienced in Asmara and its environs, long the major destination for Italian traders and craftsmen, and by the end of the decade the population of the city was some 120,000, half of them Italian. Preparation for war against Ethiopia fuelled a short-term economic boom. The huge influx of settlers and soldiers drove the racial segregation policies noted above, and a marked increase in the recruitment of *ascari*.

Eritrea's total population in the mid-1930s was some 600,000. Around half of these were Christian farmers in the highlands, and the standard historiographical position has been that they retained 'a sense of continuing attachment to Ethiopia' which was 'kept alive both by Orthodox clergy and by European missions'. There were also obviously close ties to Tigray, across the Mereb.[18] Meanwhile, in terms of local landownership and authority, there was both continuity and discontinuity. While some nineteenth-century chiefly families in the *kebessa* retained their positions throughout the period of Italian rule, and indeed beyond, others were displaced by rivals who won Italian support, and also by *ascari* who were rewarded with land for service.[19] Caulk has argued, at any rate, that there was rather more disruption among pastoralists, among whom patron–client relations were increasingly severed— the colonial legal system increasingly favoured serfs who were 'freed' from obligations to their feudal masters in the western lowlands.[20] In the 1910s and 1920s, this opened up a new cash crop economy, and perhaps more socio-economic upheaval as a result—and it might be possible to argue that such growing commercial competitiveness, as well as inequities in wealth, laid the foundations for the emergence of new forms of violence (*shifta*) in the western lowlands toward the mid-twentieth century. More broadly, this became a new economic borderland in the course of the twentieth century, one replete with opportunities for adventuring entrepreneurs but one fraught with risk as a result of political volatility—as well as being vulnerable to environmental and climatic instability.

Eritrea continued to struggle economically through most of the era of Italian colonial rule—and in this sense one must be careful to critique the later Eritrean nationalist conceptualization of the colony as some kind of light-manufacturing idyll, its economic prosperity in stark contrast to the feudal misery of anachronistic Ethiopia. Certainly the territory's economic importance in many ways lay in transit trade, with products from Sudan and Ethiopia imported and sold for re-export; while this was officially up to 25 per cent of total trade in 1915, for example, it was reckoned in reality to be much higher.[21] Through the early twentieth century, colonial Eritrea depended on imported grain from northern Ethiopia. Although the railway was extended impressively—toward Keren and Agordat in the course of the 1920s—hopes that it would spark a dramatic expansion in the cash economy proved unfounded, as did the hope that thousands of Italian settlers would be attracted to the place. Eritrea continued to rely heavily on Italian government subsidy;[22] the Italian government itself, indeed, often appeared uncertain as to what to do with Eritrea, or unsure as to what the 'grand plan' actually was. The permanent settlers did not arrive, although again there was a considerable influx of Italians during the build-up to war with Ethiopia. In many respects Eritrea, as a colonial entity, remained one in curious limbo, in a more or less permanent state of anticipation of something which never came. Its modern history has been defined by this state of expectation.

This has to be understood as the backdrop for one other major phenomenon of the era, and that of a later era, too, namely the migration of Eritreans southward, especially to Addis Ababa. This has frequently been understood as the manifestation of some kind of primordial longing, with the image of *kebessa* Eritreans drawn moth-like to the great and ancient beacon of Ethiopia, fluttering hopefully around the Emperor like prodigal moths. But the fact is that thousands of Eritreans migrated to Ethiopia in the early decades of the twentieth century for socio-economic reasons. In 1931, for example, the Italian government—enacting new Fascist legislation—barred Africans from government secondary schools, while from the following year Swedish and American missionaries were prevented from entering Eritrea.[23] Through the 1930s, therefore, Eritreans increasingly had to move to Ethiopia in order to continue their education, or achieve any meaningful level of education. The migration intensified during the economic downturn in the north during the 1940s and 1950s—although of course paradoxically there was also a brisk northward, partially seasonal migration of Tigrayans into Eritrea in search of casual work. But the important point here is that Eritrean highlanders moving to Addis Ababa did not signify some great wave of unionists voting, as it were, with their feet: it was a question of economic opportunity, even if many Eritreans did indeed become more or less absorbed into Amhara society and culture. Moreover, these demographic shifts opened up new frontiers, uneasy borderlands, within the urban environment itself—both in Addis Ababa and in Asmara.

Elsewhere, boundaries and frontiers were more remote from the concentrated urban centres, but no less important in shaping the lives of communities and in demonstrating the weakness of the colonial state—for these were frontier communities which in many ways represented the unstable foundations on which colonial systems (and later nation-states) rested. Nowhere was this more in evidence than the northern Eritrean border with Anglo-Egyptian Sudan, where the Rashaida frequently skipped across the frontier to escape Italian taxes, or defied attempted Anglo-Italian policies of separation by crisscrossing the border to trade and visit kin with impunity. In that sense colonial borders were used when it was convenient—tax avoidance, notably, or using legal boundaries as springboards for raiding patterns which actually pre-dated them—and ignored likewise, again when it suited local communities to do so.[24] The borders between Eritrea and Sudan in the 1920s and 1930s were effectively uncontrollable, or at least represented zones where the power of the colonial state was much diminished, where the hum of colonial authority was so faint as to be almost inaudible. In 1922, for example, the British encountered fierce Rashaida opposition to their attempts to register arms which were increasingly being used in local raids, and the following year Sudanese Hadendowa and Beni Amer drove their cattle into Eritrea in order to avoid having it registered by the British, who ultimately had to abandon the project and settle for the payment of token tribute. Moreover, as Young has pointed out, the Rashaida were able to simply take their camels away from watering holes for long periods at a time, thus avoiding the police units who necessarily gravitated toward them.[25] The British also found themselves unable to prevent the thriving cross-border grain trade in the late 1930s and early 1940s, with Sudanese merchants—including some Rashaida, in all probability—taking advantage of

Italian demand in the war years especially. Police units were easily avoided.[26] Again, this was the archetypal trading-and-raiding zone, an economic borderland which was unstable, but potentially lucrative.

Throughout the 1890s, the Italians were faced with resistance, particularly against the early expropriation of land on the plateau, and from chiefs—'elite resistance', as Tekeste Negash has referred to it—who discerned a loss of status and privilege in the European occupation. *Dejazmach* Aberra, a chief from Hamasien, clashed with the Italians in 1892, went into hiding, and ultimately succeeded in fleeing to Ethiopia, where Menelik famously uttered, 'Rather than a thousand Amhara, a single Aberra'. He even took part in the battle of Adwa, and eventually lived out his days in Shoa.[27] Bahta Hagos, based primarily in Akele Guzay, had worked with the Italians since the late 1880s—indeed by all accounts was considered the model 'collaborator', having also converted to Roman Catholicism—but in the course of the early 1890s he was increasingly restive, and communicated his fears regarding Italian expansion to Menelik. In late 1894, he rebelled, leading some 1600 men against the Italian district headquarters at Segeneiti and promising to liberate the people from Italian oppression. He was defeated after only three days, by Italian reinforcements which attacked him in his rear after he had abandoned Segeneiti and moved against a small Italian fort at Halay. But the uprising arguably ushered in a period of chronic instability for the Italians, culminating in the defeat at Adwa.[28] In fact, in many respects, the story of Bahta Hagos—formerly a *shifta*, from the mid-1870s through much of the 1880s, following a family dispute with an uncle of Emperor Yohannes—exemplifies the vagaries of frontier life in the Mereb zone.[29] Bahta's son escaped into Tigray after the defeat in 1894, and ultimately joined forces with the *shifta* Muhammad Nuri in the area of Senafe, and fought a low-level campaign against the Italians,[30] mostly hit-and-run attacks on Italian garrisons, plantations, and isolated settlements. There was a shift in Italian policy, as the naked expropriation of land was moderated and some degree of cohabitation with the wary 'natives' was achieved in the years that followed, certainly by the time of the First World War.[31] Chiefly titles on the plateau were protected, particularly in terms of land ownership, while a lowland aristocracy was maintained.[32] Arguably the Italians also feared the growth of Islam in Eritrea, and were keen to nullify any potential threat from that direction; a British report from 1920 suggested that 'Italian authorities are agreed that Mohammedanism is making rapid progress in Eritrea'.[33] In some areas, perhaps, Islam offered an appealing form of quiet defiance.

According to Tekeste Negash, while the peoples of the western lowlands very broadly welcomed Italian overrule—which pacified the area and provided them with protection from the *habesha* raiding parties that periodically stole cattle and seized slaves, as they had throughout the nineteenth century—the Eritrean highlanders eschewed direct military confrontation with colonial authority, indeed often actively collaborated with it, but also in the 1920s and 1930s developed irredentist resistance networks.[34] This was not Eritrean nationalism *per se*, and therefore not even organic Eritrean protest, but was motivated by a desire to rejoin the Ethiopian motherland, actively encouraged by Ethiopia itself. Both highland and lowland models seem somewhat simplistic. The real capacity of the Italian administration to 'pacify' the west, especially the borders with both Ethiopia and Sudan, must be questioned; cross-border violence continued, largely immune to the periodic patrols by both British and Italian police forces, even if the overt threat from Ethiopia had been somewhat nullified. With regard to the highlands, Tekeste's self-appointed mission to denigrate any kind of 'nationalist' achievement, and simultaneously to depict any kind of Eritrean political consciousness as essentially *Ethiopian* is not difficult to spot. For sure, Eritreans were in some ways caught in a standoff between Rome and Addis Ababa, to the point at which, from the mid-1920s, the Italians had sought to break the links once and for all that existed between the *kebessa* and the Ethiopian population.[35] But it is wholly understandable that the authorities in Asmara, in the years following humiliation at Adwa, would have been careful to prevent a wider African resistance developing from across the border, into which Eritrean protest might tap. It is also wholly credible that Eritreans would indeed have tapped into it, not because of any grand design to 'rejoin' Ethiopia necessarily—although clearly some did aspire to this, witness the various strands of unionism which came to the fore in the 1940s—but because Ethiopia represented the most natural reservoir and facilitator of resistance in the area. A trans-Mereb resistance network was the natural recourse of Eritreans who would defy Italian rule. For their part, it is clearly the case that many Ethiopians—beginning with the Amhara political establishment of Haile Selassie—sought the incorporation of Eritrea and the acquisition of a coastline which this would entail, and that the encouragement of irredentism inside Eritrea was part of a strategy aimed at the achievement of this goal. It was also, of course, an anti-Italian strategy. Just as unionism was anti-colonial resistance for some Eritreans, for many Ethiopians the encouragement of irredentism and unionism was a matter of regional security.

Along the Mereb borderlands, existing patterns of *shifta* activity became instrumental in resisting Italian administration from the 1900s onward, although to describe this as explicitly anti-colonial resistance would be misleading. Often, armed action against the Italians was the by-product of local disputes and even organized criminal activity—banditry, in other words. As Alemseged Tesfai has made clear, *shiftanet* was common throughout the Italian period, but this was mostly motivated by local personal grievance, and was not driven by any larger political programme.[36] Again, typical tactics included limited raids on neighbours' villages and livestock, and the ambushing of traffic on the highways. Often such activities were driven by personal vendetta. Nonetheless it is clear—the example of Bahta Hagos' son illustrates the point—that *shifta* could be co-opted into larger causes, witness the emergence of the Ethiopian Patriots in the late 1930s during the Italian occupation, examined in the next chapter. *Shiftanet* represented a long-established culture of defiance against established authority, in the nineteenth as in the early twentieth century, and was the product of the volatile, fertile borderland. In the 1940s and 1950s, *shifta* would indeed be increasingly co-opted into causes being championed beyond their immediate vicinities, first in terms of unionist militancy, and later in the context of the nascent nationalist struggle. The roots of the modern phenomenon lie in the late nineteenth and early twentieth centuries, although disgruntled and disenchanted armed men had long been utilized for larger political causes across Ethiopia, Eritrea, and Somalia; the borderland had long been pressed into service in order to effect change at the centre. In a sense, contested frontier zones represented reservoirs of disengagement and defiance which might be harnessed—which in essence is the story of our region's twentieth century, or at least a very large part of it.

In the final analysis, Italian rule in Eritrea was demolished not by mass resistance or revolt, but by a British-led Allied invasion force—although they were aided by both Ethiopian 'Patriots' and Eritrean deserters from the Italian colonial army. But the Allied 'liberation' in fact took the familiar form of borderland advancing on metropolitan centre, albeit mechanized. In the middle of 1940, a few weeks after they entered the war, the Italians had made advances into the frontiers of neighbouring British territories, capturing Kassala in Sudan and Moyale in Kenya. But by early 1941, they were obliged to repair to more secure positions: in Eritrea, they pulled back toward Barentu and Agordat, and were able to construct a fearsome defensive position around Keren.[37] There, the fortified scene of much nineteenth-century contest, was

fought one of the bitterest battles of the African campaign, in February and
March 1941. Only with the Italian defeat at Keren was the way open to
Asmara and, ultimately, Ethiopia. The British, meanwhile, sought to exploit
the flagging loyalty and confidence of the Eritrean *ascari*, who had begun to
desert, although numbers are difficult to establish.[38] The British also launched
a concerted propaganda campaign, dropping leaflets on the colonial troops
containing promises of what would happen if they deserted and helped crush
the Fascists:

> Eritrean soldiers, listen!
> Desert from the Italians and join us. [...]
> We know the reason you would not fight against us was that you did not wish
> to be ruled by the Italians; you will receive your full reward.
> You people who wish to live under the flag of His Imperial Majesty, Haile
> Selassie I, and to have your own flag, we give you our word that you shall be
> allowed to choose what government you desire.

Haile Selassie had his own, rather less equivocal statement prepared, likewise
deposited from the air by the RAF, in which he appeals to *both* Eritreans and
Somali:

> Eritrean people and people of the Benadir! You were separated from your
> Mother, Ethiopia, and were put under the yoke of the enemy...
> But now the day has come when you will be saved from all this ignominy and
> hardship.
>   I have come to restore the independence of my country, including Eritrea
> and the Benadir, whose people will henceforth dwell under the shade of the
> Ethiopian flag...[39]

The British, famously, did not liberate Eritrea for Eritreans, as the popular anecdote goes,[40] but as part of a much larger regional effort to secure
East Africa, the Nile valley, and the Red Sea from Axis control. Nonetheless,
their arrival did usher in a turbulent new era in the territory's history, at
least in part because they showed themselves unwilling or unable to live up
to the promises that had fluttered from the sky.

Somalia divided

The Somali had close linguistic and cultural links to a range of groups across
the eastern and southern zones of our region, notably the Afar on the

eastern side of the Rift Valley, and the Oromo, including the Boran.[41] In part these links were enhanced by the common profession of Sunni Islam; and so by the late nineteenth century, there was a potential network of action across a wide area, without the need for overarching centralized leadership. As far as resistance to infidel colonial rule is concerned, Islam provided coherence and a relative unity of purpose—as it had, sporadically, in conflicts with the Christian highlanders to the north and west in earlier periods. However, as we shall see, Somali unity was continually undermined by clan-based and territorial factionalism, which often took precedence over the authority of common law—*heer*—or Islamic law, *shari'a*, both episodically evoked to resolve conflict.

In many respects the renewed aggression on the part of the Solomonic state in the late nineteenth century represented a renewal of the titanic struggle between Christian *habesha* and Muslim Somali which had been played out between the early fifteenth and mid-sixteenth centuries. Yet the struggle was greatly complicated by the presence of foreign powers, nibbling at the edges of the Somali region. Zanzibari suzerainty over the southern littoral, including Mogadishu, was rather less threatening than the appearance of an Egyptian presence in the north in the 1870s. *Khedive* Ismail, with British encouragement, took control of the Berbera coast, and went as far as sacking Harar, but with the evacuation of the Egyptians in 1885 came new and more dangerous developments. Menelik's Shoan forces defeated Harar in 1887, while the British established their Somaliland Protectorate with a view, primarily, to securing food supplies for their base at Aden. The British, meanwhile, also assisted the Italians in the attempt to fulfil their ambitions further south: in the course of the 1890s, the Italians established a presence along the Benaadir coast between Kismayu and Mogadishu, and although they initially posed as 'protectors' of the Somali against increasingly aggressive Ethiopian campaigns, they could do little to prevent these in reality.[42] Indeed, less than a year after Adwa, Italy suffered another disastrous defeat at Lafoole, just inland from Mogadishu, in which a group of Somali clansmen crushed a small force comprising mostly Arab *ascari*.[43] It set the Italian project back several years, but this did proceed in time—and when it did, massive Ethiopian territorial expansion was also taking place from the north and west, into the Ogaden and the Haud plateau. Both the Ogaden and the Haud were of fundamental importance to the seasonal migrations of Somali pastoralists, and in the era of high imperialism they became the focus of rising tensions. In the years before Adwa, the British were prepared to concede the Ogaden and Harar regions to the Italians;[44] but with Ethiopia soon establishing dominance in the area, it was necessary to deal with Menelik instead, with whom Britain negotiated seasonal access to the Haud for Somali pastoralists. However, they formally ceded the area to Ethiopia in 1897 in a treaty which only came to light for most Somalis in 1954, when it was fully implemented. Not unlike the Eritrean western lowlands, this also became a volatile economic frontier zone, across which a commerce in livestock thrived, and into which adjacent states attempted to extend political as well as economic control. The meeting of local and external dynamics made for an unstable environment; it was a land of opportunity, but a dangerous one with it.

As Menelik's armies thrust into, and built military garrisons across, the lands of the Somali, Oromo, and Afar, the French asserted themselves over their little stretch of Somali and Afar territory, in Djibouti; and the British were advancing from yet another direction—the south, from their East African Protectorate (Kenya). As they reached the hot grasslands east of Lake Turkana, they encountered both Oromo (Boran) and Somali, as well as a vaguely defined Ethiopian jurisdiction, in the late 1890s and early 1900s. This was the zone which would come in time to be known as the Northern Frontier District of Kenya, abutting the southernmost reaches of the Amhara empire in the hills north of Turkana.[45] It would become the archetypal colonial backwater, of little value and even less interest to administrators in Nairobi, and yet in time it would become one of the key zones of transition in the development of a putative pan-Somali identity, and interstate relations between Kenya, Ethiopia, and Somalia. Thus, between the 1880s and the First World War, were the far-flung Somali divided into no less than five imperial territories. From Djibouti, through British and Italian Somaliland, eastern Ethiopia, and into northern Kenya, was an enormous, crescent-shaped, cultural, and ethnic frontier—arguably one of the largest on the continent. This vast borderland would become a major zone of violent conflict in the course of the twentieth century, drawing neighbouring metropoles into it and profoundly influencing regional ideologies, as Somali nationalists came to embrace the notion of a pan-Somali identity, fired by the image of the nation split asunder. Somali irredentism and the struggle for union would become one of the rallying calls of the twentieth century history of the region. Nevertheless, visions of Somali unity were habitually undermined by the fractiousness of the clan system, which was to prove rather more robust than the nationalist project; there was often mistrust and not infrequently violent clashes, for example, between the Ogadeni groups and the Isaq in what would become British Somaliland. Clan rivalries—manifest in clashes between mobile bands of armed men, engaged in conflict over access to land and water—would become sharper with the rise of the Somali nationalist project.[46]

Much earlier, meanwhile, Somali violence had erupted on a more localized scale—though still spreading across a considerable area, on a scale similar to the kind of resistance put up by the Sanusiyya against the Italians in Libya. The Somali region had been devastated by the economic catastrophes of the late nineteenth century, with rinderpest decimating herds and drought piling misery on misery. But while these crises rendered many communities incapable of sustained resistance, desperation pushed many Somali toward violent struggle against the forces amassing on their horizons. The key figure was Muhammad Abdille Hassan, born in 1864 in the area which would become British Somaliland, and by the 1890s a leading religious scholar in the region with several thousand followers.[47] He spent much of the 1890s warning about the perils of expanding European influence and in 1899 he declared a *jihad* against the infidel, proclaiming himself to be the Mahdi, the chosen one, who would unify all Muslims and expel the Europeans. In early 1900, his army of 'dervishes' launched attacks across British Somaliland and into the Ogaden; between 1901 and 1904, the British organized four major campaigns against him.[48] Most of his support came from the Ogaden and Dhulbahante clans. Although an uneasy armistice was maintained between 1904 and 1908, periodic raids were carried out by Muhammad Abdille's men on British garrisons, until in September 1908 he launched a new and sweeping offensive across both British and Italian territories, and against the Ethiopians in the Ogaden. For a time, the insurgency represented one of the most successful anti-colonial rebellions of its time, forcing the British to evacuate the interior in late 1909 and retreat to their coastal bases; only the Anglo-Italian strategy of developing local resistance to the dervish forces and exploiting divisions in the Somali community—tried and tested elsewhere in the colonial world—brought the uprising under control. A pact between the Warsangeli and Majeerteen Somali of the Darod clan—in the British and Italian territories respectively—led to joint military operations against Muhammad Abdille, who was at length driven out of Italian Somaliland; between 1913 and 1920 he remained active in the British territory.

Muhammad Abdille's forces kept the British occupied throughout the First World War, and when rumours circulated concerning a possible alliance between him and the new emperor in Addis Ababa, *Lij* Iyasu, there was genuine concern in British military and intelligence circles at the prospect of a region-wide insurgency. Iyasu, as we see in the next chapter, was of Muslim ancestry and had clear Islamic sympathies, even if he had not yet actually converted; his Islamic dalliances, the success of the Somali insurgency, and proclamations coming out of Istanbul about the need for a holy war against the British infidel all fuelled growing fears of a mass uprising of east African Muslims.[49] Such fears would gradually dissipate: Iyasu was summarily removed from office in 1916, although he remained at large in the Ogaden for several years, and the call to universal *jihad* was largely ignored. But the potential for religious violence remained real, anticipating events in the early twenty-first century. The British threw all available resources at Muhammad Abdille in late 1919 and early 1920, and the ageing leader was now decisively defeated—although importantly, he again evaded capture, fleeing into the Ogaden. The British pursued him, but never caught him, and he died in either late 1920 or early 1921. He was a remarkable personality, and even if his influence and standing had waned somewhat among Somali in his last years, he became something of a nationalist figurehead in the years after his death.[50] Never mind that certain aspects of the story were decidedly ambiguous in terms of his role as nationalist hero—many Somali had indeed remained 'loyal' to the British, the Italians, and the Amhara and had fought against him—he held a natural attraction for the next generation of Somali political activists, and in particular the emerging pan-Somali movement of the 1940s, which deployed his memory to good effect in the ill-fated struggle for Somali unity.

In truth, actual Italian administration in Somalia was limited; swathes of the territory remained beyond colonial control, periodic armed patrols in rural areas notwithstanding, down to the 1930s. Likewise, Ethiopia maintained little more than a light presence in the eastern part of its empire in the 1930s, and the Ogaden was frontier country through which *habesha* caravans and patrols travelled nervously.[51] When they swept up from Kismayu, through Mogadishu, and into Ethiopia across its southern frontier in early 1941, the British found a dangerously restless, and heavily armed, society: unrest was endemic in Mogadishu itself—the British were confronted by something of a crime wave in the early 1940s—while in the deeper interior and across the Ogaden 'border' clan feuds erupted in 1942–3, most clearly visible in the form of livestock raids by armed militias, requiring the rushing into active service of a hastily-assembled Somali gendarmerie. The British attempted to disarm the 'lawless tribes' of the interior, with limited success.[52] The situation was brittle and tense at best, and beyond the control of the authorities at worst: as one official wrote despairingly,

> [i]n the areas within immediate reach of authority some slight abatement of lawlessness is discernible, but elsewhere the country is in a state of wild and uproarious disorder in which it is bound to remain till adequate numbers of political officers and gendarmerie can arrive on the scene.[53]

It was against this turbulent background that Somali nationalism emerged in its 'modern' form, initially through the Somali Youth Club, established in Mogadishu in 1943. As it expanded its operations through the mid-1940s—becoming the Somali Youth League (SYL) in the process—the movement became the major vehicle for Somali nationalists, who became increasingly fixated with the idea of a 'greater Somali' unity. The SYL's central message was the unification of all Somali within a single nation, including (perhaps even especially) their brothers in the Ogaden and what were now known as the Reserved Areas, the latter comprising the Haud and the key market town of Jijiga, administered discretely by the British from the early 1940s.[54] Doubtless prompted by international discussions over the future of the former Italian territories, and in particular over the status of the Ogaden and the Reserved Areas and Ethiopia's increasingly aggressive claims over those areas, the SYL became ever more active, and the eastern Horn once more became a frontier of political contest which would define the future of the wider region.

In the end, however, the goal of Somali 'reunification'—in any case something of a misnomer—was unrealized, or at least only partially achieved. While the SYL swept the board in elections held in Italian Somaliland in 1959, in the British territory in 1960 an alliance between the Somali National League—whose stated aim had also been Somali unity—and the United Somali Party dominated the new parliament.[55] Within days of both territories becoming independent, they united to become Somalia, but large numbers of Somali—many, though by no means all, of irredentist persuasion—remained 'stranded' in northern Kenya, and in eastern Ethiopia. Once again, international machinations meant that Ethiopian imperial ambitions in the Somali lands of the Ogaden were fulfilled; but the force of nationalism among sovereign Somalis, combined with that of irredentism in the Ogaden, would reignite old tensions and conflicts between the *habesha* state stretching into the eastern plains, and the Somali state beyond.

Choices: Eritrea, 1941–52

The clearest chance of acquiring Eritrea, as well as the Somali Ogaden, and thus completing the process of Ethiopianization of the region begun in the 1880s, arrived in the 1940s. It was a crucial decade for Eritrea, for many different reasons, and also for Ethiopia. Many opinions were expressed, and arguments made, and identities manifest; there were bitter machinations on both sides of the contested border. 'Nationalism'—or perhaps more appropriately 'patriotism'—meant different things to different people, and in many respects the divisions which opened up in terms of regionalism, ethnicity, and faith remain entrenched. Crucially, the question of Eritrea's status and future was one of the first major African issues to be handled by the post-war international community at large and the UN in particular, and the strategy adopted failed: this too was critical, and would not be forgotten in Eritrea. Meanwhile, the political dynamics of the decade were played out against the background of escalating violence in Eritrea and Tigray. *Shifta* activity, a key element in central and northern Ethiopian political discourse throughout the nineteenth and early twentieth centuries, increased dramatically in the 1940s and 1950s, and destabilized the Mereb zone; the insurgency was a serious concern to the outgoing British administration by the beginning of the 1950s, and many of the insurgents would later contribute their manpower to movements of armed 'liberation' which would transform the politics of the region. In the western lowlands, too, a resurgence of borderland conflict would later connect with the violence of the wider region, as it had in the nineteenth century.

In contrast to the Italian era, according to the popular Tigrinya saying, during which one could 'eat but not think', during the British period it was possible to 'think but not eat'—alluding to the relative political freedom but economic recession associated with the British Military Administration (BMA).[56] The general view is that while Eritrea had become materially more integrated by the beginning of the 1940s, it lacked a sense of common identity; but during the 1940s, the BMA facilitated the emergence of a new Eritrean political culture, with Tigrinya and Arabic coming to the fore as literary languages, and several political parties contesting Eritrea's future; these were frequently led by members of an emergent urban middle class who had served as functionaries of the Italian and now the British bureaucracies. The BMA promoted a vibrant press, facilitating in turn political consciousness, at least in the urban centres. Labour unions flourished in Asmara and Massawa. Primary and secondary education were introduced, in contrast to the restrictions of the Italian period.[57] Self-conscious nationalisms emerged, but there were deep cultural, ethnic, and religious divides between these, and fiercely contested visions of the Eritrean future—contests which frequently exploded into open violence. The escalating insurgency, as well as the failure of Eritrean leaders to unite, contributed in no small way to the decision of the UN to federate the territory with Ethiopia, which was implemented in 1952. Nonetheless, an optimistic interpretation would be that by the early 1950s, a liberal, democratic culture had begun to take shape in Eritrea—only to be crushed within a decade by Ethiopian, or more specifically Amhara, autocracy. Much of this political activity took place against a background of severe economic problems. The short-term economic boom experienced during the late 1930s and early 1940s rapidly dissipated from the middle of the decade, and serious decline, particularly in the industrial sector, continued into the 1950s. The British had dismantled industrial capital in the course of the 1940s, while the Ethiopians would starve the territory of investment from the 1950s onward, and thus Eritrea entered a spiral of economic depression that would span several decades. That sense of economic disaster—combined with political and cultural subjugation and marginalization—unquestionably fuelled an upsurge in the politics of violence by the end of the 1950s and beginning of the 1960s.

The history of the political parties and the key debates of the 1940s are relatively well-known, even if the interpretation of that decade will remain— as it should—a matter of heated debate.[58] In crude summary, the 1940s was, depending on one's ideological positioning, either the period in which Eritreans finally won the right to rejoin the Ethiopian motherland, and in which unionism was the natural expression of Eritrean identity; or the era in which nationalist consciousness was finally awakened, manifest in the coalescence of several pro-independence parties. Neither pole is correct, but likewise neither position is wholly invalid; the reality, however, is rather more interesting, and can only really be understood by taking a long-term view of the Eritrean region as a contested borderland, the fertile frontier where the spaces within which groups define themselves are continually made and remade. Moreover, the period highlighted not only conflict between the Tigrinya frontier and the Amhara heartland, but fierce contests *within* the Eritrean borderland, and, notably, between Tigrinya with different visions of the nature of the territory; Eritrea was a contested space among its inhabitants, and this would have far-reaching consequences, with which Eritreans are still living.

Political views ranged across a spectrum from unconditional union, to conditional union, to conditional independence, to unconditional independence.[59] Some—many, indeed—shifted their positions over time, and certainly a number of these belonged to the first umbrella organization, known as *Mahber Fikri Hager Ertra* (MFHE), or Society for the Love of the Land of Eritrea, set up in May 1941. The MFHE started out as little more than a coalition of various opinions-in-the-making—its members shared a basic anti-colonial sentiment, and the organization might be considered at least proto-nationalist—but it was increasingly dominated by a faction which favoured some form of union between Eritrea and Ethiopia. Another key faction came to disagree, and this was the point of departure: for them, union—at least unconditional union—was unacceptable, and independence for the territory, perhaps following a European trusteeship, was the way forward. The fundamental point is that with the split in the MFHE, the key battle lines were drawn, however much the precise position of the trenches might alter one way or the other. Both unionist and separatist wings— broadly defined—can be considered 'nationalist', again loosely interpreted. Resisting the temptations of presentism, it is clear that those who advocated union with imperial Ethiopia regarded themselves as patriots no less than did those who envisaged an independent Eritrea. While it is clearly tempting to see the independence factions as somehow 'more nationalist', this is essentially to see the history of the 1940s from the perspective of the 1990s, when the independence movement had seemingly—for the time being— won the argument. Modern distaste for contemporary references to Mother Ethiopia should not blind us to the fact that the unionist position often reads as stridently nationalist and patriotic, and that 'union' meant liberation from European domination or the threat of it.[60] It should further be noted that the idea of 'union' has been variously defined since the 1940s and 1950s, and in fact has been referred to positively in Eritrean political discourse down to fairly recently.

This was, then, the era of competing nationalisms. Out of the MFHE sprang what would eventually become known as the Unionist Party (UP) in 1944, complete with its aggressive and militant youth wing, known as *Andinet*, and its wholehearted backing from Addis Ababa, chiefly from the direction of the Society for the Unification of Ethiopia and Eritrea, founded in Addis Ababa in early 1944. The UP would also enjoy the active support of the Coptic Church, and the shrilly vocal support of a pro-Ethiopian lobby back in Britain.[61] The independence faction, meanwhile, broke off from the MFHE to found the *Ertra n'Ertrawian*—Eritrea for Eritreans— organization in 1945. The latter movement would eventually evolve into the Eritrean Liberal Progressive Party (ELPP), formed in February 1947. One notable idea with which some members briefly flirted in the mid-1940s was that of 'Greater Eritrea', or *Tigray-Tigrinya*, as it was also known. As a politi- cal principle it appears to have fizzled out fairly quickly, but behind it was the central notion that all Tigrinya-speaking peoples should be united against 'Ethiopia', defined in this context in terms of Amhara hegemony. In part, it has been supposed that certain *kebessa* elites were sympathetic both to the oppression and decay suffered by the Tigrayan aristocracy, and the plight of their brothers during the *Woyane* revolt of 1943, examined in the next chapter. Certainly some scholars, notably Alemseged Abbay, have become rather excited by the presence of the idea; at the very least its exist- ence does indeed suggest a certain ambiguity on the part of some highland Eritrean elites regarding their trans-Mereb identity.[62] The Mereb frontier was cross-cut by shared Tigrayan-*kebessa* loyalties and ties, very largely in opposition to Amhara power.[63] But certainly antagonisms between the ELPP and the UP increased sharply over 1946–7—especially after an attempt at reconciliation between the two factions collapsed in acrimony—with key unionist Tedla Bairu highlighting the fact that leading pro-independence leader Woldeab Woldemariam was of Tigrayan parentage, and therefore could not legitimately participate in any discussions on Eritrea's future. This was clear evidence of major difference between two Tigrinya-speaking blocs, difference—whether real or imagined, or both—which would become all the sharper and more violent in the later part of the century.

In the meantime, while the Tigrinya highlanders were organizing them- selves, the Muslim community formed the Muslim League (ML) at the end of 1946, like the ELPP opposed to the union and indeed to the partition of Eritrea between Ethiopia and Sudan.[64] This was followed, in early 1947, by the National Muslim Party of Massawa, and in September of that year by the New Eritrea Pro-Italy Party which was also supported by a number of Muslims who considered that some form of European 'protection' or trusteeship might just be preferable to Ethiopian rule. Indeed, in many respects, Eritrean Muslims were in the forefront of the early growth of anti-Ethiopian nationalism, and remained so through the 1950s; the Muslims of the western lowlands, in particular, had distinct historical reasons for rejecting the emperor's authority, just as they had reasons to feel hostile toward the idea of joining Sudan. There can be little doubt that Muslims across the territory had much clearer cause to champion an independent Eritrea than did Christian highlanders.[65] While the Tigrinya might share certain basic tenets of faith and culture with the Amhara, agro-pastoral peoples in the west had lived along a contested fault line since the early nineteenth century and had been subjected to violence from the direction of Sudan and Ethiopia alike. In simplified form, this was the sentiment to which such organizations as the ML appealed. Yet faith was only one frontier of competition, and one which interconnected with a network of other conflicts—a scarified political landscape in which a set of intertwined borders were beginning to open up dramatically by the late 1940s and early 1950s. There were tensions between the urban and the rural, between highland and lowland, and between provinces even within those broad divisions; there were economic and religious frontlines, some of ancient standing, others more recent creations. In the course of the late 1940s, especially after the official British ban on political parties was lifted in 1946, a stream of organizations bubbled to the surface, out of the fissures in the political landscape; a network of overlapping concerns and loyalties was manifest in the continual formation and reformation, splitting and sub-dividing, of political organisms. While the UP remained fairly constant and continued to enjoy the support of—indeed was in some respects an appendage of—the Ethiopian government, a host of other groups espoused various versions of oppositional stances. There were tensions and ultimately splits among Muslim lowlanders, largely as the result of the fact that the leading figure in the ML, Ibrahim Sultan, was increasingly associated with Italian interests. The ML now spawned other broadly Islamic groupings, such as the Independent Muslim League—which now became basically unionist—and the Muslim League of the Western Province, which held that union with Ethiopia might be acceptable until such times as Eritreans voted to have independence.

A broad church organization, the Independence Bloc, had come into being in 1948 under Ibrahim Sultan, in part in order to petition the UN Commission of Investigation dispatched to find out 'the wishes of the Eritrean people'.[66] But by the beginning of the 1950s, there were tensions within this coalition of pro-independence movements over the precise meaning of 'independence', and how this might best be achieved;[67] the Liberal Unionist Party, for example, involving some former members of the

ELPP, came to advocate *conditional* union, presumably involving a form of the federation which was eventually decided upon. Another group, the somewhat ambivalently titled 'Independent Eritrea United to Ethiopia Party', essentially came to espouse union. Other parties still, advocating various forms of autonomy and trusteeship, but resisting both wholesale Ethiopian takeover and the partition of Eritrea between Ethiopia and Sudan, represented the interests of former *ascari*, or of the sizeable Italian and Afro-European community. As of 1950–1, the Independence Bloc—which would reform as the Eritrean Democratic Front in the middle of 1951—comprised the Muslim League, the Liberal Progressive Party, the New Eritrea Party, the Independent Eritrea Party, the Veterans Association, the National Party of Massawa, the Intellectual Association, and the Italo-Eritrean Association. It was a amalgam of interests, faiths, and cultures, loosely 'united' by the notion that full annexation to Ethiopia would not be in most Eritreans' best interests. It was an idea that cut across regional and ethnic lines, shared by groups of highlanders and lowlanders, Christians and Muslims, urban-dwellers and rural communities. Nonetheless, there remained, among a number of parties and associations, a belief that 'union' might be variously interpreted, even within the Independence Bloc, and that the concept *per se* was not necessarily 'a bad thing', as long as it could be negotiated and was both conditional and contingent. This is crucial, and is oft forgotten in the smoke and noise of the battle that followed between the 1950s and the 1990s: conditional union *might* have worked, had it been nurtured appropriately, and it certainly was not inevitably doomed to fail.

The unionist cause, meanwhile, gathered pace, fuelled by Ethiopian propaganda and funds. Violence was deployed, both by the *Andinet* youth militants and in the form of the co-opting of *shifta* along the Eritrean–Tigrayan borderlands. Such violence took the form of beatings administered to, and assassinations of, known separatists and those sympathetic to the separatist cause, as well as the kinds of banditry common throughout the colonial period aimed at keeping the borderlands unstable. The Coptic Church played an integral role, too, threatening excommunication for anyone who espoused the separatist cause; this had a significant impact among God-fearing communities across the *kebessa*, although in fact it is striking that so many highlanders continued nonetheless to support the independence cause. Whatever the case, the Church was part of the socio-political establishment seeking full restoration in an Ethiopian future. Indeed, the social context of the political debate needs to be noted. Many of the early leaders of the various political groupings—Ibrahim Sultan, Woldeab Woldemariam, Tedla Bairu—were part of a newly educated class, a group which may have been rural in provenance but which had been exposed to 'Western' education and which was increasingly urbanized. Many of them represented what Jordan Gebre-Medhin has described as 'the first-generation Eritrean intelligentsia', part of 'a restless new class'[68] which might be considered in some respects displaced from its roots. In some respects, they had emerged to stand alongside an older, 'traditional' elite, which, in Ruth Iyob's view, sought the restoration of pre-colonial status in the early 1940s,[69] and herein was an early fault line: while some of the new elite perceived that independence was the only way in which to sustain social development and mobility, others, along with a late nineteenth-century elite, saw union with Ethiopia as the guarantee of cementing their places in the socio-political order. The frequently Byzantine nature of the political debate and the fragmentation of Eritrean politics, ultimately, reflected two things. First, it reflected the network of political tectonics across the northern region which could be dated to the eighteenth and nineteenth centuries; it represented a perpetuation of extant conflicts, borderlands across which were contested faith, ethnicity, culture, province. Second, it reflected a deep level of uncertainty about what 'Eritrea' actually meant. The splits within an otherwise confident, talented new elite—from Tedla Bairu to Woldeab Woldemariam—were symptomatic of an inherent diffidence about what it meant to be 'Eritrean', and therefore represented the updating of a series of more ancient struggles across the territory. A rather more militant, assertive sense of *Eritreanness* would only emerge at the end of the 1950s and the beginning of the 1960s.

Against these continuing political debates was the violence of the period. Through much of the 1940s and 1950s, Eritrea was a violent place—in terms of low-level, though episodically explosive, insurgency, as well as more common forms of opportunistic armed criminality. Too often the activities of *shifta* in this period are subordinated in importance in scholarly analyses to the political debates taking place in Asmara, Massawa, Keren, Tessenei; in fact they are central to understanding the 1940s and 1950s, and certainly emblematic of the frontier zone in *la longue durée*. As we have seen, *shiftanet* was one of the most important socio-political mechanisms available to individuals and groups with grievances, facilitating personal vendetta, political resistance, and organized criminality—sometimes all three simultaneously. It was a constant in *habesha* life, stretching back into the nineteenth century and further back still; certainly, as we have noted, *shifta* activity persisted, albeit perhaps on a lower level, through much of the Italian period, even if it may not be described as explicitly political.[70] Nonetheless it seems safe to suggest that the 1940s witnessed the rise of new forms of *shiftanet*, in addition to those older patterns of armed defiance: whereas in the nineteenth century the term often had noble connotations, by the mid-twentieth century *shiftanet* also embraced the rural dispossessed and economically and politically marginalized, and came to be associated with common 'banditry' and criminality as well as larger 'noble' causes.

From the beginning of the 1940s, violence escalated dramatically in some parts of the territory. The history of modern Eritrea—the history of the northern borderland—is the history of the transition from *shifta* to *sha'abiya*, from patterns of banditry played out on the frontiers of culture and polity to the 'revolutionary' guerrilla organization which attempts to seize control of the borderland. Further, the escalating violence in the territory by the early 1950s—when a general amnesty in the twilight of the British administration brought about a temporary lull—hastened the transfer of Eritrea to Ethiopian overlordship; while unionist violence forced the issue in the late 1940s, the insurgency dissuaded interested foreign parties from considering any other option than the incorporation of Eritrea into Ethiopia, albeit within a federal framework. It is arguably the first instance in the making of modern Eritrea of violence being deployed—successfully—in the pursuit of a particular political issue. At any rate, the lessons for later nationalists were there for the learning.

With the defeat of the Italians, *shifta* activity increased, for several reasons. Jordan Gebre-Medhin's work is important in highlighting the importance of a dispossessed nobility leading to an upsurge in politically motivated violence across the *kebessa* in the mid-1940s.[71] In particular, a great deal of *shifta* violence has been understood as the armed wing of unionism, with various bands of malcontents utilized for the purpose of terrorizing known or suspected pro-independence figures and their supporters.[72] The campaign of bombing, assassinations, and more general tactics of intimidation—as well as the destabilization of rural highways, for example, which bore the hallmarks of rather more straightforward criminality—apparently intensified during the periods when the Four Powers Commission, and later the UN Commission, was deliberating over Eritrea's future. The aim, it seems, was to persuade foreign observers that Eritrea would never be pacified unless its rightful status—a province of the Ethiopian motherland—was achieved. In fact, of course, there were several factors fuelling *shifta* violence in this period. The last British governor of the territory, Sir Duncan Cumming, considered banditry simply as something which 'usually emerges in Eritrea and Ethiopia in times of stress'[73]—as good a summation as any, perhaps—but Trevaskis provided rather more in the way of analysis.[74]

At the general level, there was the idea—not without merit, even though it conforms to a standard colonial stereotype about the prominence of the military in African life—that across the Eritrean and Ethiopian highlands, a life spent at arms was covered in glory and associated with both honour and enhanced social status. Military activity, very loosely defined, was an important way of achieving social mobility, as well as effecting political change—and there is indeed much evidence to suggest that this was the case, in the nineteenth century as in the twentieth. In the 1940s, Trevaskis opined, the only means by which this 'spirit of military adventure' could be sated was to become *shifta*. There was no other outlet for it, and again—although we need to exercise caution here, as in dealing with European sources for the nineteenth century—it might be argued that there was a basic truth in Trevaskis' assessment. Combined with the large scale demobilization of thousands of Eritrean *ascari* from the Italian colonial army, and the availability of weaponry scattered across the territory in the early 1940s, it went some way to explaining the significant upsurge in *shifta* activity throughout this period. Eritrea was awash, for example, with an array of machine guns, rifles, pistols, and hand grenades in the years following the overthrow of the Italians, and thousands of Eritreans knew how to use them. Two further factors were important. One was the economic depression, noted earlier; unemployment and increasingly desperate living conditions, especially from 1946 to 1947 (coinciding with international deliberations on the territory's future), drove many young (and old) Eritreans with access to a few rifles into a life of *shiftanet*. Second, there was political uncertainty, and there is no doubt that this intersected with the prevailing economic conditions and fuelled the existing culture of political violence from the mid-1940s onward. Trevaskis noted that *shifta* often acted with impunity, calculating that the BMA was not destined to remain in place for long, and that there was a general lack of belief that the British could do much about banditry with the limited means at their disposal, and given their evident lack of long-term commitment to Eritrea.

Certainly, much *shifta* activity was rooted in personal grievance and feud, even if larger communities often took up arms for a particular local cause. A century earlier, indeed, Walter Plowden appears to have been describing much the same phenomenon across the northern mountains.[75] But local disturbances frequently became politicized, just as they did in the mid-and late nineteenth century; 'liberation struggle' as it emerged in the 1960s and 1970s was rooted in the complex intersection between local and 'national' issues in the 1940s. Violent struggles between ruling families in the *kebessa*—notably in Hamasien and Serae in the early and mid-1940s, for example—which stretched back into the nineteenth century became complicated by the identification of one or other group with larger political causes, namely unionism or separatism, broadly understood.[76] Local *shifta* were brought into these struggles and deployed accordingly, although much of the overt violence—which ranged from beatings to destruction of property—was associated with unionist-employed *shifta* against those who had identified themselves with the pro-independence camp. A further issue involved the continued Italian presence. In the minds of many unionists, pro-independence activists were preparing to 'do business' with the Italians, who might therefore return to power in some shape or form; thus were Italian land-owners, who had been the beneficiaries of land concessions at the expense of local communities, targeted relentlessly through the 1940s. Many of the *shifta* involved saw themselves as 'patriots', in this respect, attempting to drive out the hated colonial occupier. Thus we can identify, at the most basic level, two broad strands of the 'new' *shiftanet* of the period, namely that which was rooted in local causes and disputes, and that which was tied to larger political causes affecting the territory as a whole, and developing into a full-scale insurgency. Both strands escalated as the 1940s progressed, notwithstanding a temporary lull of sorts in the 1944–6 period, and each increasingly intersected with the other.

Immediately following the British occupation of Eritrea, there was a certain calm across the territory, but by 1942 this was beginning to be threatened by low-level activity.[77] Raiding across the Tigray–Serae frontier seems to have been related to the deposition of the ruler of the Adi Quala district, *Dejazmach* Haile Tesfamariam, who had links with Tigray; this violence continued into 1943. At the same time, Tigrayan *shifta* were beginning to resume raids on the Kunama around Barentu. Again, the years 1944–6 were reportedly relatively quiet—quiet enough, indeed, for the British 'Frontier Striking Force' to be disbanded and the number of police to be slightly reduced—while the British used the opportunity to remove a number of troublesome Hamasien chiefs. But in 1947 *shifta* violence increased sharply across the *kebessa*, and included attacks on pro-independence figures and Italians, while Tigrayan bands increased the incidence of their attacks on the Barentu area.[78]

By 1949, the violence had amounted to something approaching a unionist *shifta* insurgency, especially on the plateau, although this was compounded by ongoing conflict between various groups around Barentu and across the western lowlands. The British increased their military presence as the UN Commission began their deliberations; it was no mere coincidence that *shifta* activity increased so sharply as the UN delegates arrived. In the course of 1950 and 1951 the British security forces struggled to deal with the *shifta* violence: their deployment of locally recruited armed counter-gangs along-side regular forces (which included British troops as well as the Sudan Defence Force) foreshadowed similar tactics in Kenya just a few years later, but it was met with limited success in Eritrea, where by 1950 the conserva-tive estimate was that some 2000 *shifta* were active across the territory. Even the Eritrean Police needed to be watched carefully, as many of them were suspected of being sympathetic to the unionist cause, and a number deserted in the final years of the British administration.

As for the *shifta* themselves, these were fighters who might easily melt into their local communities, or into the hills, or—particularly irksome for the British—across the border into Tigray. In addition to patrolling the highly porous border areas and vulnerable main roads, and creating mili-tary 'special areas' where *shifta* were especially active, the British adopted the soon-to-be-common tactic in counter-insurgency warfare of collec-tive punishment, imposing fines, confiscating property, and arresting key figures in communities suspected of harbouring or otherwise supporting *shifta*.[79] Ethiopian support—tacit or overt—presented a rather more deli-cate problem, involving as it did the need to place pressure on an ostensibly sovereign state. Just how much direct imperial involvement there was in 'terrorism' is perhaps debatable; but numerous *shifta* did operate out of Tigray—many were indeed Tigrayan—and it was felt that the Ethiopian government could have an impact by publicly condemning *shiftanet* and naming those receiving succour in the north. Addis Ababa was initially loath to do so; unionist *shifta* were not terrorists but patriots, cut from the same cloth as those who had taken to the bush to fight the Italian occupi-ers of Ethiopia in the late 1930s. In the 'official mind' of *habesha* imperial-ism in the late 1940s and early 1950s, there was a direct line of continuity between anti-Italian guerrillas of 1936–41, and the fighters now taking up the cause in the 'occupied north'. However, by 1951–2, the Ethiopians were cooperating on the Tigrayan side of the Mereb frontier zone, dispatching 'anti-*shifta*' missions to consult with the British and attempting to patrol the border with rather greater intent;[80] a cynical interpretation, however, might have it that this was—by the early 1950s—an empty gesture, as by this time the insurgency had largely achieved its goal of some form of unification with Ethiopia.

At the same time, conflict of a somewhat different kind had been unfolding in the western lowlands. The war between the Beni Amer and the Hadendowa dated to the early 1940s, and stemmed from Hadendowa claims over pastureland between the Eritrean frontier and the Barka river, although in fact it appears to have been both instigated—and pursued with much greater ferocity—by the Beni Amer.[81] It quickly brought about major insecurity in the area of both Agordat and Barentu, and provided something of a western lowland vortex within which other localized conflicts erupted—similarly over access to land—involving the Kunama, other groups of Beni Amer and the Nara. At the same time, Tigrayan *shifta* conducted raids on the Kunama, and from the BMA's viewpoint were harder to apprehend, owing to their ability to shrink back into the Adi Abo area of north-west Tigray. There were also ongoing skirmishes, over land and cattle-theft, between the Beni Amer and groups of farmers on the western Hamasien plateau; and a similarly land-related feud between the Tsenadegle in Akele Guzai and the adjacent Teroa, associated with the Saho of the eastern escarpment. While the Tsenadegle were Christian and the Teroa Muslim, this seems to have mattered less than rights over particular tracts of grazing land; importantly, it was a dispute which dated to the early Italian period, if not earlier, as many such disputes did. The contest between the Beni Amer and the Tigrinya of Hamasien, for example, was not a novel one in the late 1940s. The Beni Amer-Hadendowa war was negotiated to an end by late 1945, but it had created a great deal of upset across the area; it had also intersected with an initially isolated peasant revolt among the Tigre in the north against their 'aristocratic' rulers, which by the mid-1940s had spread into the Barka area. The hard-pressed BMA had managed to bring about some form of 'serf emancipation' by the end of the decade, but it had been a traumatic decade for the communities involved, characterized by a fair degree of reinvention and creativity on the part of the people themselves as well as the British authorities.[82] Importantly, the socio-economic disruption and dislocation occasioned by the various conflicts in the west and north bred new patterns of violence, enhanced existing ones, and produced an armed 'class'—for example, Hamed Idris Awate, later the putative pioneer leader of the Eritrean liberation struggle—willing to turn their guns on whatever system they perceived as the enemy, and willing to be mobilized for larger political causes. In this group were situated the progenitors of the nationalist liberation struggle, the armed pioneers of the early Eritrean Liberation Front. Importantly, there emerged a large, if far from coherent, pool of Muslim consciousness across this swathe of Eritrea into which early Muslim nationalists might tap—particularly in terms of fears of Christian domi-nance, from whichever side of the Mereb.

In the end, although it had some success in resolving the more localized disputes over land, the BMA was unable to bring the *shifta* under control by military means. In 1951, they declared a general amnesty, and over several months several hundred fighters took advantage. Others were continually reported as being anxious to do so, including Hamed Idris Awate, although it seems that many, including Awate, regarded the offer of an Amnesty merely as an opportunity to 'rest up' and prolong negotiation. The larger picture sug-gests that the British had been soundly beaten. With the passing of the UN resolution federating Eritrea with Ethiopia at the end of 1950, the main aim of the outgoing BMA was the most basic management of Eritrea's affairs so that the territory could be handed over, under the uncomfortable glare of the UN itself, on time and in reasonably good order with Britain's reputation for governance more or less intact.[83]

Above all, the insurgency of the late 1940s and early 1950s presaged the violence both of the liberation struggle, and of the civil war that would rage at its centre. The *shifta* crisis was of course the outcome of the unstable, contested borderland of some antiquity, as well as representing the tried and tested mechanism of political and socio-economic protest in the region. In that sense there was a great deal of continuity from the pre-1900 era; there is certainly something in the pattern of events in the 1940s and 1950s which is redolent of the 1860s–80s period across the *kebessa*, in terms of divided loyalties, the ambiguities of the frontier zone, and opportunistic and low-level but pervasive violence. At the same time, however, mid-twentieth-century *shiftanet* was also the symptom of very particular grievances and circum-stances: unemployment and economic anxiety more broadly were particu-larly important. We have seen how in earlier periods such economic stresses were crucial determinants of violence, driving forward the militarization of communities and the propulsion into the bush of disaffected and heavily armed young men. Militarization was what occurred when such communi-ties were denied access to critical resources; groups took up arms in the absence of industry, and political causes flourished in these fertile frontiers.

It was so at key points in the nineteenth century; and in the mid-twentieth century, economic trauma provided a fertile seedbed indeed for political radicalization—a process of radicalization which continues to reverberate across the region. In the 1940s and 1950s, economic uncertainty intersected with political uncertainty and upheaval, the proliferation of guns across the region as well as ex-servicemen well-versed in their use in the wake of the Second World War. At the same time, more specifically, many *shifta* were heroes to some, insofar as they represented new forms of political con-sciousness, pro-union or anti-Italian—either way, essentially, anti-colonial. More generally, *shifta* themselves represented an early example of the armed frontier marching on a contested centre: it would be repeated in the decades that followed, and provided some early, but salutary, lessons for those who would later take to the bush in ever more sophisticated ways in order to engineer political change.

It was against this background, then, that decisions were taken by foreign powers regarding Eritrea's future.[84] In December 1950, the UN passed Resolution 390A(v) which proposed that Eritrea would be feder-ated with Ethiopia, as a constitutionally autonomous unit, under the Ethiopian crown. The Ethiopian government regarded it as a less than total triumph—it was not, after all, full incorporation. But it was a start. As provided for by the Federal Act, Eritrea was to have a Constitution which would safeguard the rights and freedoms of its citizens, and which would in turn, in theory, be guaranteed by the UN itself. That Constitution,[85] adopted by the first Eritrean Constituent Assembly in July 1952, was representative of an ill-disguised tension between the suppos-edly budding democratic culture in Eritrea and the 'feudal' omnipotence of the Emperor in Ethiopia. In political and legal terms, it was profoundly problematic. Even more significant for the medium term future was the fact that around the same time the Constitution was being adopted, the US signed a mutual defence pact with the Ethiopian government. In return for military assistance and development aid, Haile Selassie leased Kagnew base in Asmara to the US for twenty-five years. It was to become, for a time, the US's largest communications base outside the US itself. This secret agreement was to prove of rather greater significance—and indeed permanence—than the 1952 Constitution. The Federation for-mally came into being in September 1952, when the British withdrew and the Eritrean Constitution came into force. At that point, there was, by most accounts, a reasonable level of optimism that the system might work, given the appropriate safeguards and degree of good faith on the part of Ethiopians and Eritreans. Its swift failure—engendered by both international duplicity and Ethiopian imperial aggression, according to a later generation of radical Eritrean nationalists—would provide the latter with a foundation stone around which the architecture of grievance would come to be created. It would prove a robust structure indeed.

6

The Empire of Haile Selassie, *c.*1900–74

The anomalous empire

Haile Selassie inherited an intrinsically unstable, restlessly violent state. Yet Haile Selassie himself occupied a curious position: a 'modernizer' to some, arousing opposition accordingly, and the arch-conservative to others, with fierce critics in close attendance. In truth, in the end, he was the latter rather more profoundly than he was the former, but those who overthrew him would prove themselves no more capable of revolutionary change than he was; they themselves were products of the system, and ultimately proved themselves not revolutionaries, but legatees with occasional flashes of creativity. That is for later in our story. For now, suffice to say that our concern in this chapter is with how Haile Selassie inherited both the restless centrifugal militarism of the nineteenth century and the unstable frontiers of the Menelik state. Our concern is also how he and the Amhara political establishment spectacularly misunderstood—wilfully and otherwise—what it was they had inherited, and in particular its inherent flaws, and how this spelt a level of destruction with which the region is still dealing. The outcome of Haile Selassie's reign was the exacerbation of a number of extant wars, with some bitter new twists added.

Nonetheless, the young son of *Ras* Mekonnen was not the initial choice to succeed the old emperor; rather, it was Iyasu—known as *Lij* Iyasu, owing to his youth, the son of *Ras* Mikhail of Wollo and Menelik's daughter—who was his chosen heir.[1] Menelik had designated his successor in 1909 while also exhorting his ministers to ensure a peaceful succession and to avoid the political upheavals of the previous century. Yet the situation thus created involved a fragile balance of power. Owing to Iyasu's minority, a regent was appointed in the person of the Shoan noble *Ras* Tesemma Nadaw; meanwhile the young Iyasu had already been married to the daughter of *Ras* Mangesha Yohannes of Tigray in an attempt to consolidate the alliance between Shoa and that province. Hovering over all these proceedings, while her husband's life slowly ebbed away, was Empress Taitu, who belonged to a long tradition of powerful women in *habesha* political life. Her continual interference—and her Gondari background—drew fierce opposition from the Shoan political establishment, which turned to the increasingly politically important *mahal safari*, the units of the imperial army attached to the palace. They moved against Taitu in 1910, and she was sidelined to Entotto on the outskirts of Addis Ababa—though in a final dignified act, she appealed to her brother, *Ras* Wale of Yajju, and Mikhail, Iyasu's father, to avoid bloodshed as they squared up to one another on the contested borderlands between Yajju and Wollo in the north. Iyasu's regent Tesemma died in early 1911, and thus began the young man's *de facto* reign, even though Menelik clung on to life until 1913.

Iyasu is deserving of much greater attention than for a long time he received.[2] He appears a complex character, capable of administrative reform yet a slave-dealer whose reign was characterized by a system of personalized rule. His much-discussed hedonism was in stark contrast to the abstemiousness of an older generation. But this was unimportant alongside the larger issues of politics and faith which combined to be his undoing. He moved increasingly against his grandfather's generation of advisors and indeed against the Shoan heartland, favouring his father's province of Wollo instead; indeed, his father Mikhail became *negus* of Wollo and Tigray in a remarkable move which saw Wollo rival Shoa as the political centre of the empire. Iyasu (who was never actually crowned, either as *negus* or as *negus negast*) was contemptuous of the Shoan nobility, and spent much of his time outside Addis Ababa. The political concerns of the Shoan elite were paramount, but they were easily disguised in religious garb, for Iyasu's tolerance toward Islam and indeed abiding interest in the rehabilitation of Muslims in Ethiopian society and polity led to (inaccurate) rumours that his own conversion was imminent. His father had been a Muslim, converting to Christianity in the late 1870s, and to the Shoan nobility it all added up: a residual Islamic influence, both in the family and within his retinue, his building of mosques, his marriages to the daughters of important Muslim families, his wanderings in the (predominantly Muslim) Ogaden. Indeed his interest in the Ogaden was another striking feature of his short reign; he spent a great deal of time there, opened up a new level of engagement with local Somali elites, and provided support to Muhammad Abdille Hassan in his war against the British and Italians.

Of course, he had also married into prominent Christian families, and provided funds for the building or expansion of churches and monasteries—but no matter. By 1916, the Shoan Christian elite, with the support of neighbouring European administrations, were ready to move against him; European colonial officials were persuaded by talk of Iyasu's imminent apostasy, and further fuelled the rumours. He was formally deposed in September 1916 by an alliance headed by Zewditu, Menelik's daughter by a previous marriage. Iyasu himself was defeated in a pitched confrontation in the nineteenth-century fashion some way east of Addis Ababa, and retreated to Afar country; *Negus* Mikhail mobilized indignantly, assembling a force of some 100,000 men. The new regime in Addis Ababa was soon able to mobilize a sizeable force of its own, from Shoa and from the south and west. While the coalition troops assembled on the northern frontier of Shoa, Mikhail advanced, and battle was joined at Sagale, a few miles to the northeast of Addis Ababa in October 1916. Mikhail's army was comprehensively defeated by that of *Fitaurari* Habte Giorgis, a decisive moment in modern Ethiopian history, in what would prove to be, in essence, a victory for the forces of conservatism. Menelik's order would be preserved. The whole episode was also a sharp reminder of the deep-seated religious tensions at the heart of the Ethiopian state, regardless of the lack of evidence for Iyasu's imminent apostasy: Islam was feared and despised, and the early-twentieth-century polity was founded upon Christian intolerance which was itself rooted in a history of religious antagonism. Ethiopia was to be a Christian state, and although Muslims might serve even in high office, they were in effect co-opted by the Solomonic polity. The Amhara political establishment, no less than the European colonial authorities in neighbouring territories and indeed probably more so, was keenly aware of its being surrounded by several million Muslims, and of the perils of a radical, political Islam becoming active across northeast Africa. Iyasu himself remained a fugitive until his capture and imprisonment in 1921, although even in detention he remained a figure of considerable allure to many, especially as pools of opposition emerged against *Ras* Tafari.

Tafari himself—formerly governor of Harar, and moved by Iyasu to Kaffa—may have been an influential figure in the alliance that led the coup against Iyasu, but he was very much a junior member of that alliance, and subject to greater authorities than himself, including Empress Zawditu; his elevation to Zawditu's regent was precarious.[3] Tafari found himself conducting the day-to-day administrative business of the empire, but very much under the shadows of the powerful Zewditu herself, the great general Habte Giorgis, and various provincial governors. The soldiers at his own disposal represented a paltry force, and his military force remained for many years greatly overshadowed by the larger, more impressive provincial forces, under much more experienced military commanders; Tafari himself had no military experience to speak of. He slowly bolstered his position in a number of ways. He concentrated on foreign affairs, effectively becoming Ethiopia's foreign minister, and sought to project a favourable image of Ethiopia abroad. Recognizing the importance of Shoa at the centre of the empire, he formed an alliance with *Ras* Kassa Hailu, the province's most important political figure. He thus focused on Shoa throughout his career, and on Addis Ababa, which very much became his own creation and the arena in which so many political battles would be fought. From the early 1920s onward, Addis Ababa became an increasingly important socio-political environment, a swelling and politicized urban jungle which represented many of the stresses and strains in the Ethiopian polity. The restless city would, in the longer term, become an incendiary device at the heart of the imperial regime.

The early months of the regency were defined by a military crisis, developing in the aftermath of the defeat of Mikhail of Wollo. In the course of 1918, thousands of soldiers protested that they had failed to receive pay and food, and blamed their venal officers, who in turn accused the council of ministers (itself something of a recent innovation) of incompetence. A military committee was formed and demanded the dismissal of the council, and its replacement by a regency council comprising Tafari, Zewditu, and Habte Giorgis. They had their way, and in the aftermath of the dramatic reshuffle, Tafari began to appoint 'new' men to key government posts; this modernizing reorganization of the Ethiopian government through the 1920s brought about enhanced centralized control and a much greater flow of information from the provinces to Addis Ababa. It was a policy which gave rise to a new generation of *habesha* officialdom, the Young Ethiopians, who would be, in Marcus' definition, 'efficient, modern, and patriotic'— but the transition to this new breed of government bureaucrat would be a gradual one.[4]

Slavery had long been endemic in highland society, and with the increasing attractions of commercial agriculture—for example coffee in the south—landlords sought to strengthen their control over both land and labour. Indeed Menelik's expansion of the empire in the late nineteenth century provided a fillip to the slave trade in the early decades of the twentieth: these new frontier regions in the south and west were fertile hunting grounds for the acquisition of slaves by the nobility, for whom the ownership of people remained an indicator of social status. Slaving campaigns, involving, as in the nineteenth century, the large-scale organization of men and firepower targeting dispersed agro-pastoral communities, regularly resulted in massive dislocation in the deep south, in newly acquired regions such as Maji and Kaffa; *Lij* Iyasu himself led one such campaign, in 1912. The slave trade continued to thrive on the western border with Sudan, too.[5] In short, these new commercial frontiers in southern and western Ethiopia would greatly alter the context within which the political battles of the twentieth century would be fought. In the wake of Menelik's imperialism, a new set of provincial governorships became available—highly lucrative, in terms of both trade and production, and politically weighty—while the state's organizational capacity for local exploitation was greatly enhanced. The expansion of the highland ruling class to the south and west created, over the longer term, reservoirs of resentment and collective experiences of brutality at the hands of an Amhara ruling class. In 1918, Haile Selassie had issued an edict abolishing the slave trade, but had added the strong caveat that this was only the first step toward the abolition of slavery itself. He was, in sum, having to address the whole system of violence which underpinned Ethiopian political economy.[6]

His cunning, patience, and inscrutability became proverbial; but he was also opportunistic, and needed to be, given the stubborn forces ranged against him. Notably, his camp was associated (in the minds of Zewditu's followers) with the dilution of Ethiopia's hard-won independence through the increasing foreign involvement necessary to achieve political and material progress; but in fact, for many of the western-educated reformers attached to Tafari, his professed reformism was, in the end, limited in its ambition and indeed at times disingenuous. These reformers—in many cases inspired by the model offered by Japan—advocated 'modernization' in various spheres, including the economy, the constitution, the civil service, and education;[7] but although Tafari was indeed enthusiastic about many of the accoutrements of European modernity, notably in the technological realm, his primary concern was the consolidation of Solomonic centralism and autocracy, and whatever 'modernity' could offer him in the achievement of this. Following the death of Zewditu's key ally Habte Giorgis in 1926, Tafari went about undermining Zewditu's authority and enhancing his own power base. He dismissed *Dejazmach* Balcha, influential governor of coffee-rich Sidamo and a key conservative opponent, in 1927; crushed an attempted mutiny by the formidable *Dejazmach* Abba Weqaw Berru, head of the palace guards, in 1928; and utilized his supporters' unrest in Addis Ababa to forward his claims to the imperial throne. Elevated to *Negus* in 1928, and crowned as Emperor Haile Selassie I in 1930, his accession was not universally welcomed, and his position was far from secure. Arguably his most dangerous challenge came from *Ras* Gugsa, governor of Begemeder and Zewditu's former husband. Importantly, Gugsa was supported by the Italians in Eritrea, and by his neighbouring governors in Gojjam and Tigray, although they, in the end, held back from outright rebellion. Gugsa's refusal to acknowledge several orders from Addis Ababa was tantamount to rebellion, and his defiance culminated in the battle of Anchem, in March 1930, in which Gugsa was killed and the insurrection crushed.[8]

At Haile Selassie's coronation, Wilfred Thesiger opined that the newly crowned emperor was unpopular, and described how '[s]trange rumours are afloat that *Lij* Yasu is coming back in the role of a saviour of the country', and how a number of the key governors had been biding their time during Gugsa's revolt to see the outcome.[9] No doubt Thesiger was referring to Gojjam and Tigray. Yet the 1931 constitution formalized absolutism, and laid the framework for its expansion. By the mid-1930s—the eve of the Italian war—it was widely acknowledged that Haile Selassie had gone some way toward 'modernizing' his administration, which in effect meant a heightened level of monarchical authoritarianism, in particular through the placement of 'loyal' governors over formerly troublesome provinces. Such appointments, moreover, were increasingly based on merit rather than inheritance. The ghosts of the *mesafint*—at least some of them—appeared, for the time being, to have been laid to rest. In the Christian, Semitic heartlands, Shoa, Amhara, and Gojjam appeared pacified and stable—or at least those who distrusted Haile Selassie were temporarily in abeyance; a greater sense of stability was discernible even in the west and south-west, too, notwithstanding the increasingly troubled autonomy of Jimma, granted by Menelik following Abba Jifar II's peaceful submission in 1882. The incorporation of Jimma in 1932—doubtless motivated by economics but justified by Abba Jifa's grandson's failure to cooperate with central government[10]—arguably sparked a renewed *habesha* imperial land grab, interrupted by the Italian occupation but culminating in the securing of the Ogaden and Eritrea in the 1950s. There had also been the successful incorporation of some southern and western aristocracies into the *habesha* ruling elite, such as that of Wellega, for example; these often proved themselves adept at imposing systems of taxation on the new territories, establishing more efficient forms of economic and political dominance, and simultaneously reinforcing both their own positions and that of their Amhara overlords in the process. Clearly, as Bahru Zewde points out, 'the class basis of exploitation and oppression was as important as the ethnic one',[11] and such systems of co-option were particularly effective in the south and west.

In the north, and on the eastern side of the Rift Valley, the picture was rather different from that presented in the central highlands. Haile Selassie may have secured himself at the centre, but his authority diminished by degrees further out. Tigray under *Ras* Kassa was equivocal, as would be evident during the Italian invasion of 1935–6, and in the early 1940s. In the north-east, 'Ethiopia' scarcely existed, no more than did Italian Eritrea or French Somaliland. Neither the Aussa sultanate—even more autonomous than Jimma, based largely on ignorance that Haile Selassie even laid claim to it—nor the Afar federation recognized the authority of Addis Ababa. Thesiger's lively descriptions of hunting in Danakil country in the early 1930s indicate the extent to which this was territory which was hardly under the control of Addis Ababa—or even Harar—in any meaningful way.[12] These were the proverbial 'wild tribes of the frontier areas', according to contemporary scholarship.[13] In the late 1920s, there was serious unrest in eastern Tigray and Wollo, regions struck by drought and locusts, as the highlanders descended into the Afar lowlands on raiding expeditions; indeed it was *Ras* Gugsa's unenthusiastic response to an order to restore order here that led to the *denouement* between him and Haile Selassie.[14] The pro-Italian Evelyn Waugh would write dismissively of 'Ethiopian unity' in the mid-1930s, and of restive and resentful subject peoples groaning under 'the dead weight of the Abyssinian occupation'.[15] These, he asserted in his bombastically inimical way, were only too glad to see the end of 'Abyssinian' rule—as in Harar, where Italian 'liberation' was eagerly received. Haile Selassie's state collapsed easily enough, owing to sullen subject peoples, rampant disloyalty within the composite Ethiopian army, and the 'ungovernable' places into which Haile Selassie's rule barely reached.[16] Much the same was true of the Ogaden, which was a vast, dangerous borderland in the 1930s; south of Harar or Jijiga *habesha* power scarcely extended beyond the well-armed caravans necessary to conduct trade with the European-governed Somali.[17] Notably, '[t]he Ogaden—the chief Somali tribe of the south', wrote Jones and Monroe in the mid-1930s,

> are equally primitive and lacking in consciousness of a nation to which, offi-cially, they belong....Whatever the progress made in Addis Ababa, it will for years to come be idle to mention the word modernisation in the same breath as these wild lowland tribes. It is they who, bent on blood feuds and quarrels over wells and grazing grounds, are responsible for the frequent raids into British, French, and Italian territory. The modern frontier lines are as little known to them as is a national feeling for Abyssinia.[18]

Moreover, borderlands to the south and west of the empire inherited by *Ras* Tafari had been impossible to govern since the partition of the region in the late nineteenth and early twentieth centuries. They represented zones of alternate realities, alternate, that is, to the various exercises in modernity and putative civilizing missions unfolding in distant metropoles—whether British or Amhara or Italian. The complexities of local interaction are cap-tured in Almagor's studies of the Dassanetch, notably.[19] The Northern Frontier District (NFD) of Kenya abutting southern Ethiopia was the scene of ongoing skirmishes in the years either side of the First World War between the King's African Rifles and Amhara, Oromo and Tigrayan 'raiders' and 'poachers'; it was a volatile and violent zone of interaction, requiring a con-tinual military presence on the part of the British, toward whom Amhara forces and renegade *shifta* were apparently equally hostile. Sir Philip Mitchell, senior British colonial official in east Africa, would write ruefully of 'the everlasting murderous raids from across the Abyssinian frontier' which would render life and service in the NFD so intolerable.[20] As the KAR historian Lt-Col Moyse-Bartlett put it, describing the situation between 1908 and 1914:

> ...the role of the KAR became increasingly that of a frontier force. The pres-ence of unadministered tribes near Lake Rudolf, in country where illicit ivory-hunting and gun-running still flourished, and of intractable Abyssinian neighbours beyond the Northern Frontier District, who rendered scant obe-dience to the control even of their own government, punctuated the monot-ony of service in those barren and little-known areas with unexpected incidents.[21]

Ethiopian raiding incursions, targeting scattered agro-pastoral settlements across the region, were frequent, however, and the situation in this archetypal frontier zone was complicated by local patterns of resistance—from the Turkana, notably—and by the influx of Somali herdsmen toward the Moyale–Marsabit area in search of water, especially in times of drought, as in 1909. Communities were caught in the crossfire of militarized societies, for example the Samburu and Rendile, regularly squeezed between the raids of the Turkana and armed *habesha* bands in search of ivory and livestock. For Ethiopians, these were natural hunting grounds; they were also places of commercial opportunity, with a large belt either side of Lake Turkana representing a burgeoning market for intrepid highland peddlers of the tools of destruction. The reach of the armed Ethiopian frontier was felt elsewhere, too: in northern Uganda, the first British units in 1911–12 encountered well-armed Acholi who had enthusiastically purchased guns from Ethiopian traders as security in uncertain times. Early British operations were thus against both Acholi and Ethiopian gun-runners who were operating in the territory west of Lake Turkana.[22]

Across northern Kenya, the British struggled to maintain order in a vast area with relatively few resources, although in the years after the Anglo-Ethiopian boundary delimitation of 1907 they expanded their military posts from Moyale to Marsabit and other key points.[23] Major operations in 1919 were followed by further incidents in the course of the early and mid-1920s. In 1925, for example, a group of several hundred 'raiders', including Oromo and Amhara, launched a major attack near Moite and took off with some 4000 camels.[24] The success of this operation is noteworthy, given that the frontier herdsmen who were the victims were by now long accustomed to the sudden ambushes of highlanders from the north. They were, however, vulnerable in their need to gravitate toward wells, and when they periodically clustered around markets. The situation in the area was exacerbated further in the mid-1930s with the Italian invasion of Ethiopia, whereupon thousands of refugees, armed opportunists, deserters, and assorted desperadoes flooded into the NFD from southern Ethiopia and Somalia.[25] In this zone, too—as on the Nilotic frontier—was group cohesion contingent on local circumstance and external intrusion, and was political creativity heightened as a result.[26] The dynamism of the frontier—often fuelled, at least in the first instance, by survival strategies—in turn drove creativity at the centres of the state-building exercises, which (consciously or otherwise) defined themselves increasingly by what was happening at their peripheries.

Gun-running was an expanding business in the early years of the twentieth century in other areas, too, and highland Ethiopians were again the pioneers. In the Upper Nile districts along the Sudanese-Ethiopian border, a continual flow of firearms was facilitated by Ethiopian entrepreneurs into the hands of the Nuer and Anuak, among others, in exchange for ivory.[27] Indeed, as Douglas Johnson has demonstrated, Ethiopian–Nilotic relations along the border between the 1890s and the 1930s were nuanced and finely balanced, though also continually shifting; the Ethiopian 'presence' in the area was mediated by local power structures, and indeed limited by the 'highland distaste for the unruled and unruly lowlands, whether forest, swamp or desert'.[28] There was flexibility in terms of administration, and continual 'reinvention' in terms of which side of the border particular groups inhabited at a particular point in time, to whom they owed allegiance, and in terms of assimilating outsiders and outside influences. Cyclical conflict between a range of groups in the area, moreover—not least between Amhara and Oromo—meant that Nuer and Anuak could squeeze between the cracks thus left in administration and carve out their own spaces along the borderland.[29] From the early 1900s, in other words, local groups along the Ethiopian–Sudan border were already utilizing external intrusions and adjacent state-building projects to their own advantage; thus were identities continually made and remade in this especially fertile frontier.

At the same time, Ethiopian raids into Sudan remained a feature of frontier life throughout the colonial period. In the northern border areas, around Gedaref and Sennar, raids on Sudanese communities by Ethiopian renegades and generically termed *shifta* west and north of Lake Tana were not infrequent, and reflected perhaps even older patterns in that area of essentially privatised violence; and further south, on the Nilotic frontier, while some Ethiopians traded guns, others attacked those same Sudanese communities for slaves and ivory.[30] In 1923–4, for example, Ethiopian attacks (as well as those by Swahili poachers) along the Daga valley, across south-eastern Sudan, and as far as northern Uganda from the direction of Maji and the Boma plateau, prompted the convening of a conference in Kitgum to discuss increased security in the region.[31] Maji inside Ethiopia, and the adjacent Mongalla province in the far south of Sudan, bordering Kenya and Uganda, were regarded as beyond the reaches of any administration. Despite the highlanders' hatred for the lowland swamps and forests of the Nilotic frontier, this was nonetheless a borderland of great opportunity for traders and *shifta* alike. Violence and commerce went hand-in-hand in the places where imperial projects, whether of the British or the Amhara, could scarcely reach, or at least where hegemonies were transient. Further north, in the Funj borderland west of Lake Tana, and in the Kassala district abutting the Eritrean western lowlands, the activities of armed Ethiopian adventurers were restricted by mobile border security units; but even here, throughout the 1920s such activities persisted. Of particular concern to the British was the highly organized slave trade which operated across the Funj–Lake-Tana borderland, in which slaves were exchanged for firearms. Even in the early 1930s Haile Selassie's officials were—or at least claimed to be—powerless to prevent it.[32] The victims included the Berta, part of a large swathe of population in the eastern Sudan long known to be contemptible to the *habesha* as *shangalla*. Along the entire stretch of the border, while there were many local communities which were victims, others were able to take advantage of frontier flux and grow wealthy on the proceeds of a commercial system which was rather older than the colonial administrations which now tried to suppress it. The western and southern economic borderlands were therefore lucrative but unstable, and have remained volatile frontier zones to the present day. They have long sucked states into them: this has further destabilized the frontier zones themselves, while the latter have served to pare down state power to its essence, namely a restless, mobile militarism with none of the accoutrements or even the rhetoric of civilizing modernity. Vulnerable to predation and drought in equal measure, these were vortices in which economic desperation and political opportunity interconnected.

From Wal Wal to Kagnew: war, reconstruction, and reinvention

It was in this context, then, that the Italians moved to avenge Adwa; once again the northern frontier was a source of national crisis. Ethiopia was much weakened in military terms; opportunities for military development had become rather fewer in the early twentieth century than in the second half of the nineteenth, and the Ethiopian army was now scarcely a match for Italian tanks and mustard gas. Western governments were prepared to do precisely nothing, save for some half-hearted and ineffectual sanctions on Italy imposed via the increasingly redundant League of Nations. Nonetheless, it is the case that Haile Selassie and the Shoan political establishment were

able to use the painful experience of Fascist aggression to lend moral force
to their claims for recompense and protected sovereignty in the course of
the 1940s. Between the mid-1930s and the early 1950s, Ethiopia experienced both trauma and triumph, however short-lived the latter would prove
to be; and after the nadir of foreign occupation came an aggressive repositioning and reinvention which constituted, in hindsight, something of a last
throw for the Solomonic state. The journey from Wal Wal—a remote watering hole on the Ethiopian–Somali frontier, a name thrust into the notepads
of foreign correspondents as the point at which the Ethiopian–Italian war
began—to Kagnew, the US base on the northern plateau and thus a guarantee of Ethiopia's place in the new world order, was a remarkable one
indeed.

It is not our purpose to describe in detail here the course of the war
itself.[33] Suffice to say that tensions between Ethiopia and Italy had been
building since the late 1920s, notably over aggressive Italian plans for economic concessions in Ethiopia; and in truth war was inevitable from the
beginning of the 1930s, when *Il Duce* set his sights on Ethiopia as vengeance
for Adwa and as part of his grandiose plans for the putative 'new Roman
empire'. Predictably, perhaps, it was the undemarcated and volatile eastern
frontier zone which provided the Italians with the justification they required
for invasion: in late 1934, matters came to a head at Wal Wal, a small settlement around some wells in the eastern stretches of the Ogaden, and an area
which was the point of heightening tension between Ethiopian and Italian
forces. The Italians believed firmly that Wal Wal was in Italian Somaliland;
they had been there several years, and the legality of their occupation of it
was—they said—beyond dispute. But the Ethiopians did indeed dispute it,
asserting that Wal Wal was very clearly in Ethiopia, in fact was some way
from the Italian Somaliland border. In December 1934, a clash between
Ethiopian and Italian troops there[34] led inexorably toward a major conflagration—some futile attempts at negotiation notwithstanding—and in
October 1935 the Italians invaded Ethiopia in force. They crossed from both
Eritrea, where there had been a massive build-up of men and materiel, and
Somaliland. There would be no reprise of Adwa. With control of the air, and
massive superiority in terms of armour and firepower, and indeed often of
manpower, and despite several points of serious resistance by individual
Ethiopian commanders, the Italians swept through the north in late 1935
and early 1936. Campaigns in the south and in the Ogaden at times were
slower going and involved more Italian casualties, but the end result rarely

seemed in doubt. Winning key engagements, and then bombing and gassing Ethiopian troops as they dispersed, the Italian forces exacted revenge for the 'stain' on Italy's reputation inflicted forty years earlier. They entered Addis Ababa in May 1936; but the emperor had already fled, heading to Europe to admonish the League of Nations in a speech full of foreboding, and finally settling in somewhat reduced circumstances in England. His decision to leave Ethiopia was contentious; a number of senior figures had counselled him to remain and lead the resistance burgeoning across parts of Ethiopia beyond the lines of the Italian advance, resistance to which we return below. Many would not forgive him for rejecting the advice, and for departing with his entourage and his imperial dignity intact.

Various factors explain the Ethiopians' swift defeat, weaponry and logistics foremost among them. Menelik had enjoyed a great deal of parity with the Italians in this respect; he was also the beneficiary of a restless and potent militarism built up over several decades, and of armed forces with some experience of repulsing foreign incursions. Haile Selassie's Ethiopia, however, was a profoundly disunited polity, much weakened in political as well as military terms; since Adwa, Ethiopian political culture had become no less militarized, but it was a more insular, intensely localized militarism which had grown up because of the Shoan regime's aggressively centralizing tendencies. For all his 'modernizing' centralism—and indeed because of it—the centrifugal forces which had long dogged highland state-building exercises were once again rampant, and old fissures opened up across the empire. The Italian invasion had exposed the fundamental fragility of Menelik's empire. The Italians were able to develop alliances or at least tacit cooperation among a range of groups in *habesha* society. While the 'patriotism' of many resisters to Italian rule has been much celebrated,[35] the fact remains that, as in other parts of Africa, foreign invasion and occupation was characterized by complexity and ambiguity and above all pragmatism. The Italians were assisted by political discontent within the unstable empire. Corrado Zoli, former governor of Eritrea, wrote: 'Some of [the feudal chiefs]—e.g. the principal feudatory of eastern Tigre—not only spontaneously submitted to the Italians but faithfully fought throughout the campaign under the Italian flag at the head of their troops'.[36] It is certainly the case that Zoli's own policy from Asmara had been the winning of influence among particular disgruntled figures within the *habesha*, and especially in the Tigrayan, political establishment—a policy known as the *politica periferica*, which clearly made some sense in the Tigrayan context at least.[37] More specifically, then, the Italian authorities in Eritrea pursued a *politica tigrina*—encouraging provincialism in Tigray and luring key figures away from the emperor—as opposed to the Italian Foreign Ministry's prior *politica scioana*, namely coexisting with Ethiopian centralization.[38]

On the face of it, at least, Haile Selassie's increased centralized control over key provinces had greatly strengthened the military capacity of the centre; but in fact political and regional fissures swiftly re-emerged with the Italian invasion, and the attendant military weakness of the state was exposed, especially in the north. Chiefs and their troops in Begemeder, Gojjam, Tigray, and Semien either jumped ship and joined the Italians—and were often rewarded with political appointments—or fought half-heartedly for a regime they scarcely trusted.[39] Swathes of the Somali and Oromo populations had actively welcomed the Italian occupation.[40] 'The great majority of the inhabitants in Western Tigre', observed Zoli, 'received the Italian troops with sympathy, often with manifestations of joy, heralding them as liberators from the dreaded yoke of Shoa'.[41] Tigray is indeed an important case in point.[42] Politically marginalized since the 1890s, but still a crucial bulwark between the Shoan state and the Eritrean frontier, Tigrayan elites—the ruling families were essentially unchanged from the nineteenth century—were always potentially problematic. Tigrayan leaders had been at least ambivalent if not actively hostile to Tafari's accession, watching the rebellion in Begemeder in early 1930 with interest; following his enthronement, Haile Selassie had sought to pacify the north by marrying his children to those of the two key figures in Tigray, Seyoum and Gugsa, in western and eastern Tigray respectively. The Tigrayan nobility remained bitterly opposed to Shoa's centralism, but the political marriages produced an uneasy balance of power, both between Shoa and Tigray, and between Seyoum and Gugsa; but the death in 1933 of both Gugsa and Haile Selassie's daughter who had been married to his son, Haile Selassie Gugsa, destroyed this delicately poised arrangement. Haile Selassie Gugsa now sought to mount a challenge against Seyoum by communicating with the Italians in Asmara, who were also in contact with an array of more minor chiefs along the frontier. With the invasion underway, Haile Selassie Gugsa crossed to the Italians in October 1935, following the fall of Adigrat. Seyoum opted for loyalty, and continued fighting into the early months of 1936; but the potential role of Tigray as a barrier against the Italian advance—both geographically and politically—had been fatally undermined, and opened a crucial highway into the heart of Ethiopia. In early 1936, moreover, in the wake of the repulsion of the long-awaited Ethiopian counterattack, bedraggled and retreating Ethiopian soldiers were attacked by the Raya and Azebo Oromo groups in the south-east lowlands of Tigray, as revenge for punitive raids carried out on them a few years earlier. As for Seyoum, after his surrender in July 1936, he spent some time in prison, and in Italy, before returning in 1939 to collaborate with the Italians. This forms the crucial prelude to the Tigrayan uprising against the restored Haile Selassie in 1943, to which we return a little later.

The bulk of the studies of the Italian invasion and occupation of Ethiopia have situated themselves very much in the context of interwar European history—international relations, appeasement, and the rise of Fascism—and have had little to say about the actual impact on Ethiopian society. Alessandro Triulzi's review article from almost thirty years ago, indeed, remains essentially valid,[43] although the work of Alberto Sbacchi and Haile Larebo's exhaustive study, for example, have gone some way to addressing the imbalance.[44] In terms of territorial reorganization, the Italians redrew the boundaries of the key ethnic regions, which reflected a massively simplified Italian ethnographic wisdom, and which for a few short years (until 1941) provided a glimpse of 'what might have been' had the battle of Adwa produced a different result. Eritrea was swollen dramatically to include Tigray and the bulk of Afar territory; the Amhara and Harar zones formed the central districts, along with Addis Ababa itself; the 'Galla and Sidama' territory broadly occupied the present-day area of the Southern Peoples' district; and 'Somalia' was extended into the Ogaden. In a predictably pro-Italian assessment of the new arrangement, Corrado Zoli described how the Italian victory had 'liberated' the peoples of Ethiopia 'not only from slavery but from all sorts of servitudes and barbarous tyrannies', and how a system of 'direct rule' was necessary to avoid bolstering the feudal organization of the old Ethiopian empire through the retention of 'hordes of chieftains, great and small, who used to attach themselves like leeches to the bodies and goods of the miserable native populations'.[45] Indeed Zoli, after a fashion, paid tribute to the modernizing and centralizing programme of the deposed Haile Selassie, and to some extent his predecessor Menelik. The Italians, it seemed, were merely finishing the job—albeit, of course, in a rather more efficient manner. But Italy's civilizing mission was otherwise attended by much the same rhetoric as that of the age of high imperialism half a century earlier. The new administration was confronted by dramatic depopulation across swathes of formerly fertile land, the 'direct result of the barbarous Shoan domination'. Moreover, '[t]he abuses of the Shoan overlord—the continual wars, the

punitive expeditions and the large scale slave raids—have reduced this people from prosperity to a primitive state of barbarism'.[46]

The violence of the new political order was inherent, of course; resistance continued, as Zoli acknowledged, although he was predictably sanguine about the ability of the Italian administration to crush it.[47] In large
part, this was down to the new military restructuring put in place in the
months after Italian 'victory' in mid-1936, with the 'colonial detachments'
composed of African soldiers under Italian officers (in addition to the
'African detachments', which were composed entirely of Italians). The system was building on the success of earlier recruitment programmes among
Eritreans, Somali, and Libyans, native battalions of *ascari* who, 'in addition to
their military value, form effective instruments of political penetration and
of civilization among the local populations'. Regional recruitment was
partly responsible for the evident success of these battalions, as was the
'family-camp' system, 'in which the soldiers live with their families while on
service'.[48] The Italians undoubtedly reinforced the notion of soldiery as
representatives of the state, billeted on and among local populations, and
enjoyed a higher status as a result. It was the latest development in the concept of military service as denoting a distinctive class—defined politically as
well as socio-economically and indeed culturally—and of its representing a
politico-military establishment which was ultimately about the provision of
authority and leadership and the inculcation of certain 'values'. In the analysis provided by Zoli, in fact, the numbers we are dealing with are actually
relatively modest, namely 40,000 'native' troops in a total force of 65,000 for
'imperial defence'.[49] This would increase quite dramatically by the time
Italy entered the Second World War in June 1940.

The Italian presence unleashed a new wave of violence and unrest, a
significant proportion of which can be considered to have been continued
resistance in the wake of the emperor's flight. Even Addis Ababa itself was
prone to sudden attack by marauding bands in the weeks that followed; it
was an edgy, nervous environment.[50] Resistance was doubtless stimulated
over the longer term by the bloody reprisals carried out by the Italian
authorities following an assassination attempt on Viceroy Graziani in
February 1937; in Addis Ababa, the Fascist Blackshirts embarked on a frenzy
of killing, mutilation, and destruction.[51] A great many intellectuals were
eliminated, and a number of nobles were also deported to Italy as a result.
In the provinces, *shifta* activity erupted in earnest, and very often, again, this
was opportunistic violence driven by largely criminal elements set loose by

the collapse of the political order. They were well-armed, highly mobile, and an indication that—in many rural areas, at any rate—the Italians had little prospect of establishing anything approaching military or administrative control.[52] Alongside this—and probably frequently overlapping with it—there emerged the 'Patriots', groups of guerrilla fighters. Initial resistance can basically be seen as an extension of the war itself, with conventional tactics deployed under the leadership of the last few senior Shoan figures still at large. One such was *Ras* Emeru Haile Selassie, who became the focal point of resistance in 1936 in the west and south-west, inspiring the newly formed Black Lion organization[53] to follow his (increasingly diffident) leadership. He surrendered to the Italians after failing to create a stronghold in the south-west, and after his forces were confronted with local Oromo hostility. But after the awful reprisals following the attempt on Graziani's life, resistance increasingly took the form of a guerrilla insurgency, especially in the northern provinces of Gojjam, Begemeder, and Shoa, although groups of fighters were present across the empire. Shoa boasted one of the most charismatic and significant resistance leaders in Abeba Aregai, later confirmed as *ras* and Minister of War by the emperor in the 1940s as a reward. The guerrillas attacked transport infrastructure and government installations, developed an extensive network of intelligence with regard to Italian strengths and weaknesses, and established cells in Addis Ababa and the provincial towns, under the Italians' very noses. In many respects the Patriots' resistance represented the harnessing of older patterns of *shiftanet*, enlarged in scale and scope in order to confront the foreign occupation, and across Ethiopia the Italian administration was both destabilized and perpetually challenged.

Armed resistance, and the existence of such groups as the Black Lions in exile, has contributed in some quarters to the notion that in times of national crisis—the 1890s, the 1930s—Ethiopians were able to tap into an ancient patriotism with which to confront external threats. It is, as we have seen in the context of Adwa, a key component of national mythology and self-image. The reality is rather more complicated. There were deep-seated and frequently violent rivalries between guerrilla groups; conflict between them, as well as with the Italians, was a defining characteristic of the armed resistance of the mid- and late 1930s. A chronic lack of unity was reflected in the absence of any overarching political programme or ideological direction, moreover. This was parochial violence, concerned with local issues, and the 'nation' was notably absent from the discourse of the resistance. The fact remains, too, that the Italians were able to create locally recruited counter-insurgency forces—known as *banda*, a term which became synonymous with collaboration—which were often more successful in their engagements with the Patriots than the Italians themselves. Large numbers of Ethiopians—Amhara and Tigrayan, as well as groups historically hostile to the Shoan polity such as the Oromo—did indeed actively 'cooperate' with the Italians whether politically or militarily, or at least reconciled themselves to the new order as their emperor fled. Come 'liberation', there would be room for both Patriots and *banda* in the restored political order, producing a new set of tensions between those who had been on opposite sides during the Italian occupation, but who now jostled for privilege and position in the early 1940s. Most obviously, again, *Ras* Seyoum Mangesha of Tigray worked closely with the Italians—in 1940 they made him 'Prince of Shoa and King of Tigray'—although he swiftly threw his support behind the British in 1941; he was confirmed as governor of Tigray by Haile Selassie. *Blatta* Ayela Gabre, for example, was placed in charge of the native courts under the Italians; after 1941 he served as Minister of Justice. Tsahafi Taezaz served the Italians in the administration of Addis Ababa from 1938 to 1941; in 1942 he became vice-governor of Shoa. Other more minor figures served both the Italians and then the restored emperor, Balachaw Yadate and Dawit Ogbazghi (an Eritrean) among them.[54]

Haile Selassie and his entourage had been close behind the Allied advance from Sudan, stepping onto Ethiopian soil in April and returning in great pomp to Addis Ababa in May 1941. But it was a highly volatile situation, with several dynamics interacting dangerously. The British were nervous about the entry of a multitude of armed guerrillas into Addis Ababa, and tried to limit numbers following the emperor (and, more importantly perhaps, Abeba Aregai) into the city. Their fears were often well-grounded,—witness the violent disorder which broke out when the Patriot leader Garasu Duki was placed in charge of Jimma in 1941. Haile Selassie was only too aware of the empire's fragility. Nonetheless the emperor, recalled the British colonial official Sir Philip Mitchell, 'became suspicious of our intentions and resentful of what he—sincerely, no doubt, but mistakenly—supposed to be our designs on his full sovereignty'.[55] While Haile Selassie was relieved to have been restored, Ethiopia's sovereignty was a compromised one, for the British remained in control of key aspects of political administration and military affairs.[56] Eritrea could be treated straightforwardly as occupied enemy territory, but Ethiopia was a rather odder case; nonetheless, one

European occupation had in effect been replaced by another one, and British hegemony was a undeniable fact. Haile Selassie's chagrin was palpable: for the second time in less than a century, British troops stood in the central highlands. The emperor had cause to be suspicious not only of British intentions, but also of his own nobility who had shown themselves fragmented and in a great many cases less than faithful to him over the preceding five years. Many Ethiopians, indeed, believed he had abandoned them by going into exile and that he should have remained to lead the resistance. Meanwhile, the Amhara not only had the British to worry about; the 'empire' itself was in trouble. Eritreans, Tigrayans, and Somali were potentially problem peoples who resolutely did not share Haile Selassie's vision of the beneficent *imperium*—although once again the ambiguity of some of these relationships was underlined by the fact that in the course of the 1940s and 1950s thousands of Eritreans flooded to Addis Ababa in search of socio-economic opportunities. The emperor would make good use of some of them. The Oromo question would become ever more urgent, meanwhile; but in fact it was Tigray which would be the first to explode into open revolt, in the *Woyane* of 1943. It was the shape of things to come. All in all, the Italian interlude had led to an escalation of the conflict between centralizing autocracy, on the one hand, and restless centrifugal forces and rebellious borderlands, on the other. Having said all this, the 1940s was also a time of great opportunity for the restored Solomonic state. Haile Selassie's twin objectives in this period were the establishment of his authority over a turbulent, fractious empire, and the pursuit of an aggressive foreign policy and renewed programme of imperial expansion. Here was a chance to embark on the first major imperial expansion since the late nineteenth century: using a combination of wile, guile, threat, and manipulation, the Ethiopian government went about laying claim to both Eritrea and the Ogaden in what would amount to a second partition for the region.

The British initially made clear to Haile Selassie—in the first Anglo–Ethiopian Agreement in 1942—that Ethiopia's full sovereignty was very much pending, and for the time being subordinate to the requirements of the war effort. In mid-1941, notably, it was by no means certain—as Ethiopian officials must have been well aware—that the Axis powers were never returning to the region; after all, the battle for North Africa and the Suez Canal was still in full flow, and Britain's ability to hold Egypt was far from clear. However, the second agreement, in 1944, gave Ethiopia rather more independence, and the privileged position enjoyed by the British was largely dismantled. The British Military Mission to Ethiopia was now answerable to the Haile Selassie's Ministry of War, and mandated to provide training for the Ethiopian army.[57] It was an awkward and ambiguous relationship, characterized by mutual mistrust, but also mutual need. The success of the British Mission in Ethiopia—which aimed at the stabilization of the region, and resolutions for the issues of Eritrea, the Ogaden, and Tigray—very much depended on Ethiopian cooperation; Haile Selassie still needed British assistance in re-imposing himself on his fractious empire—not least in putting down the revolt which erupted in Tigray in 1943.

The Tigrayan revolt, known as *Woyane*, had both deep roots and immediate causes—the former related to the province's long-term neglect and marginalization, and simmering discontent with Haile Selassie's rule, the latter connected to the turmoil of the late 1930s and early 1940s.[58] It is, of course, dangerous to search for the deeper roots of some form of distinct Tigrayan *nationalism*, however tempting various actors find this exercise in political modernity; it is clear, for example, that many early fighters in the TPLF in the 1970s regarded themselves self-consciously as politically descended from the 'first' *Woyane*.[59] But the quest for nationalism and ultimately nations, again, often distracts us from appreciating the real dynamism of particular frontier zones—and this is as true of Tigray as it is, say, of Eritrea or 'Oromia'. The 'first' *Woyane* had its deeper roots in the shifting political sands of the late nineteenth century—in Yohannes' failure to resolve the issue of the northern frontier, and in the emergence of Shoa as the successor to Tigray at the apex of the remade Ethiopian empire. We have noted the willingness of key leaders to work with the Italians in the late 1930s. The events of the early 1940s, therefore, must be seen in terms of continuity from those years of fragility; the revolt represented, in a sense, unfinished business. The *Woyane* of 1943 was the product—to borrow a phrase once used of the French Revolution—of a 'concatenation of events', a 'relatively restricted, localized uprising with strong provincialist or ethnic overtones', as Gebru Tareke has summarized it.[60] A disillusioned and embittered local nobility, acutely aware of the gradual erosion of its local powers at the hands of the Shoan-led monarchical state, was critical in providing a leadership role to a peasantry weary of the exactions of the state, in terms of brutal taxation and administrative inefficiency. Tigray had also long suffered from environmental degradation and thus reduced resources in terms of land and economic opportunity, further increasing the potential for popular insurgency. As in Eritrea in the same period, once again environmental and

economic pressures drove violence—in different ways in different communities—while in Tigray the ghosts of remembered greatness and a supposed
imperial inheritance rendered those material traumas all the more intense.
A third element—the lowland groups in the south-east of Tigray, the Azebo
and Raya, Oromo in origin—likewise feared the encroachment of the state
on their egalitarian socio-economic system. As Gebru has pointed out,
although some common threads linking these groups are discernible, in
many respects the revolt was profoundly divided in terms of objective and
certainly lacked ideological coherence.[61]

The violent adhesive binding the disaffected together was the *shifta* activity which greatly heightened the potential for physical action. A number of
the key leaders of the rebellion were *shifta*, including Haile Mariam Redda;
and while these had long been active in Tigray, as elsewhere, in the early
1940s *shifta* activity increased dramatically—due to transitional weakness
between regimes, availability of weaponry in the wake of the Italian defeat,
and economic turmoil. As in Eritrea in the same period, *shifta* were co-opted
into political action and also took advantage of widespread turbulence. They
were from a range of backgrounds, again as in Eritrea: many were displaced
and landless peasants; others were demobilized *banda* or had deserted; others
still were a motley collection of socio-political malcontents. Haile Mariam
Redda provided inspirational leadership for a time, tapping into widespread
grievances using the language of political radicalism, and in May 1943 the
uprising began in earnest, with initial successes against small garrisons
around Mekele. Taken by surprise, it was several months before the Ethiopian
state reasserted itself—and only then by calling on the support of the British.
In the major counter-offensives of September and October, the rebel bases
were decimated by artillery fire and bombed from the air by British aircraft,[62]
with inevitably large numbers of civilian casualties. The uprising was crushed,
with heavy loss of life; in the end, only the nobility could claim much in the
way of success, as many were reinstated in the regional administration and
guaranteed certain local privileges. The Raya and Azebo arguably suffered
most in terms of the brutal suppression of the peasantry, enduring large-
scale land alienation and the quashing of their autonomy. Yet even the
Tigrayan nobility could hardly claim 'victory'; in truth, the monarchical
state had—for the time being—asserted itself in the clearest possible manner, and had in reality greatly curbed regional autonomy, that of both local
notables and the province of Tigray more generally. While the *Woyane*
was itself the reflection of several decades of accumulated and multifaceted

bitterness, the 'second' *Woyane* of the TPLF from the mid-1970s was made possible by, and drew inspiration from, the widespread political violence and its brutal suppression in the 1940s.

The involvement of *shifta* in the disturbances of 1943 was symptomatic of the unstable borderland; bandit-rebels in Tigray were the product of political disenchantment and anxiety, of economic marginality and upheaval, just as they were in Eritrea. It is most likely, moreover, that in the wake of the *Woyane*, many of the same *shifta* were involved in both periodic disturbances in Tigray, and in the insurgency in Eritrea; the continual complaint from British officials in Asmara was that many of the *shifta* in Eritrea were in fact Tigrayan, and frequently skipped back and forth across the border out of reach of Ethiopian and British security personnel alike. The Ethiopian government was either unable or unwilling to compel local notables and their communities in Tigray to surrender *shifta* or refuse them succour. Ethiopian forces lacked the reach to coerce in this way; but almost certainly Ethiopian officials were unwilling to provoke local communities or the *shifta* they were concealing in the wake of the *Woyane* of 1943, for fear of igniting another. After all, Tigrayan *shifta* were pursuing an agenda broadly in line with that of the Addis Ababa government—namely, the unification of Eritrea with Ethiopia—which is of course striking, given the goals of their own uprising; but for many Tigrayans it was never actually about the *illegitimacy* of the emperor's rule, but about the status and condition of Tigray and its various constituent parts, and the unwelcome intrusions by the monarchical state into Tigrayan political and economic life. It is not, therefore, wholly incompatible—indeed far from it—for many *shifta* to subsequently fight for the 'return' of their Tigrinya brothers across the Mereb, thus both enlarging Tigrinya power in the north and removing the possibility of a hostile situation in a foreign-ruled or independent Eritrea. Besides which, in rather more practical terms, Eritrea offered some easy pickings for an opportunistic and well-armed band of warriors.

Having 'pacified' Tigray, Haile Selassie now moved ever more aggressively to secure the Ogaden and Eritrea. In the meantime, he also manoeuvred Ethiopia increasingly toward the US at the expense of the British. This was in part motivated by the fact that from an early stage in the war, the latter were at least sceptical about Haile Selassie's claim on Eritrea.[63] He was indeed adept at utilizing shifts in the global balance of power, sensing that the US, not Britain, was his guarantor of future regional security.[64] Thus he projected himself a key ally of the West in terms of his hostility to both

communism and militant Islam, and offered his services—or more specifically, a crucial military base on the outskirts of Asmara, Kagnew station—in
return for military and other assistance. He sent a contingent of troops to
fight alongside the US in Korea to show his commitment to the cause.
Washington swiftly recognized that an independent Eritrea was a risky
unknown, a potentially destabilizing element in a volatile region rendered
vulnerable—in Cold War terms—by the imminent withdrawal of British
colonial rule and the rise of militant nationalisms across a broad arc of territory from Kenya and Uganda to Egypt and the Middle East. No unneces-
sary gambles were to be taken with the Red Sea zone, and Ethiopia was the
perfect strategic ally. And so began a partnership—enduring until the
Marxist seizure of power in Ethiopia in the mid-1970s, and even that would
prove to be a mere interruption—which represented one of the US's first
and enduring forays into African geopolitics. While Eritrea had been an
issue of international concern, however, the Ogaden was a question purely
for Addis Ababa and London, the British proving resistant to an Ethiopian
takeover of the Ogaden down to the late 1940s; however, after prolonged
discussion,[65] and perceiving both long-term security issues and long-term
costs, the British handed over the bulk of the Ogaden to Ethiopian administration in 1948. The Haud and Reserved Areas followed in 1954. In many
respects, the process of expansion and partition begun by Menelik in the
1880s and 1890s was complete, or at least by the early 1950s, it had gone as
far as it was going to go, in territorial terms. Both Eritrean and Ogadeni
chalices were laced with toxin, however.

     In the meantime, Haile Selassie created a veritable cult of personality and
built a coercive, repressive, and at times brutally violent regime as he sought
political consolidation, for the first time since the early 1930s. He created a
nominal 'council' of ministers—a continuation of the ministerial system
initiated in the early decades of the century—made up, by and large, of men
of low birth who were used to counterbalance the power of the provincial
nobility, the bane of centralizing monarchs over many centuries. As the
emperor became ever more concerned with foreign affairs, some ministers
did have authority in domestic matters, but never beyond the reach of the
royal prerogative. There was a creeping fear throughout the 1950s among the
educated elite and would-be reformers that Ethiopia was ossifying, and that
its political system appeared profoundly anachronistic alongside the momen-
tous political changes sweeping across Africa as decolonization proceeded
apace. The new Ethiopian constitution of 1955 certainly confirmed the

Emperor's absolute power of decree, and appeared to sound the death knell of liberal reform.[66] Yet opposition continued to foment,[67] and among its early leaders, in fact, were implacable Patriot leaders from the late 1930s, some of whom had long-standing grievances against Haile Selassie, not least of which was the fact that the emperor had fled in 1936, and many of whom resented the fact that *banda* were offered key positions after 1941. Among these oppositional figures were *Dejazmach* Belay Zellaqa, in Gojjam, who staged his own small-scale revolt in 1943; and *Blatta* Tekle Walda-Hawariat, who made the journey from loyal servant to the emperor to one of his most relentless antagonists between the late 1930s and the late 1960s. He was involved in two plots against Haile Selassie in the early and mid-1940s; released in 1954, he was brought into the administration, but rebelled again many years later, in 1969, and was killed. More generally, across the empire of the 1940s, *shifta* activity was widespread, and localized pools of anti-Shoan opposition periodically appeared in regions hardly reconciled to the 'new order', such as in Wollo and Harar—disturbances in the latter involving Muslim activists perhaps taking inspiration from the activities of the Somali Youth League further south.[68] In the late 1940s, there was escalating *shifta* violence in Tigray (as well as Eritrea), anti-taxation disturbances on the part of Oromo communities north of Addis Ababa, and Somali raids on Ethiopian military outposts in the Ogaden.[69]

More broadly, it is worth noting that between the major periods of drought and famine in the 1880s–90s and 1970s–80s, environmental insecurity also drove low-level violent instability, doubtless thrusting communities into desperate straits and often outlawry. This was provincial volatility that required a muscular state response; coercion, again, was critical to the functioning of the modern Ethiopian empire-state owing to the episodic fragility of the political system's environmental and economic foundations. Famines appeared across the central and northern highlands in the middle decades of the twentieth century—in 1927–8 (at a delicate point in the internal balance of power in Ethiopia), 1934–5 (on the eve of the Italian invasion), 1947–50 (as the Eritrean crisis was mounting), and in the late 1950s.[70] In each of these periods, economic trauma was one of the key drivers of entrepreneurial violence at the local level; and those entrepreneurs either had political causes readily to hand, or did not have to search long to find them.

Yet while storms of political violence were gathering on Ethiopia's borderlands, the main forces for change from within the country's socio-political system came from the ranks of the army and the young educated elite—apparently disparate groups, but in the course of the 1960s coalescing into a broad front for radical change. Ironically, as it turned out, one of the regime's 'modernizing' policies concerned the army and the security forces from the early 1940s onward. Although clearly one of the purposes of the reorganized military apparatus—more so in Ethiopia than in many other African states—was external defence, it is also clear that internal control was high on the agenda of the military modernizers. The imperial bodyguard constituted an elite force, while the British- and US-trained army formed the main fortification around the state; the police force was organized along British lines, while the potentially troublesome patriots and *shifta* were reformed into a territorial militia. Yet tutored in the use of violence to achieve political goals, and increasingly self-conscious in its role as guarantor of order and defender of the state, the army in the 1950s and 1960s contained the seeds of the regime's own destruction. While rank-and-file soldiers inevitably shared the concerns of the broad mass of the citizenry as socio-economic and political conditions deteriorated in the 1960s, senior officers were drawn into debates—increasingly radicalized—about Ethiopia's political future.[71] This was parallel to developments in the higher education sector, where students who were expected to benefit the imperial system in the long run came to embrace radical change and challenge that same system.[72] In this context, the first clear cracks in the Solomonic edifice appeared in the latter half of 1960.[73] While University students embarked on a series of public protests, in December 1960 a small but fiercely motivated group of army officers in the Imperial Guard organized a *coup d'etat* while Haile Selassie was in Brazil on a state visit. It was disorganized, and lacked the full support of the military; in subtle but important ways the US intervened to ensure the Emperor's survival, refusing to endorse the *coup* and bringing pressure to bear on senior Ethiopian officers. The attempted *putsch* was swiftly crushed, and many senior people were killed, including members of the large corps of middle-ranking officials in government and a number of army officers; yet it was only the beginning, and indeed it changed the very nature of opposition to the imperial regime, ushering in a new era of broad-based and overt protest.[74]

In terms of Haile Selassie's twin objectives of domestic consolidation on the one hand, and external expansionism and reinvention on the other, it may be argued that in the short term he succeeded on both counts. He overcame a series of internal challenges, including that of the reformers and modernizers and an uprising in Tigray, and oversaw the 1955 constitution; he acquired Eritrea and the Ogaden, and his alliance with the US brought an unprecedented degree of international security. As we see below, he also saw off the Somali threat during the 1963–4 war. Yet all these triumphs were both hollow and short term. Over the longer term, forces of violent change would prove too powerful for the Solomonic state to subdue, and were already reasserting themselves in the course of the 1960s. There was growing political radicalism in government circles, in the army, among students and workers; there were ethnic, national, and class-based rebellions breaking out across the empire, in Bale, Gojjam, and Eritrea, and the makings of revolt in Tigray and among the Oromo. But arguably the greatest long-term force for change across the region—and Haile Selassie's greatest mistake—was in Eritrea, the frontier zone with transformative power on a regional scale.

Fatal federation

A decade of scheming, cajoling and threatening had paid off, for now at least. The UN-brokered compromise was a problematic one, however, as was the entire unification project. The Orthodox Church had played a significant role in effecting the 'return' of Eritrea to the 'motherland', yet there were several hundred thousand Muslims in Eritrea who were at best ambivalent about the empire to which they were now attached—not to mention the hundreds of thousands of Christians who were likewise unsure about just how much they shared in the way of language, culture, and outlook with the Amhara and even Tigrayans to the south. This was the ambivalence of the frontier writ large. Nonetheless, the Amhara acquisition of Eritrea in the early 1950s was one of the great sleights of hand in modern African history, and one which would have long-term consequences. Decisions made in the early 1950s regarding Eritrea would destabilize the region for the next half-century, and continue to do so at the time of writing. The history of the 1950s remains an area of considerable research potential, but the basics of the story are well-known: Haile Selassie's representatives in Eritrea presided over the steady erosion of the territory's federal autonomy, and Eritrean rights and freedoms, in the course of the 1950s, and ever more militant movements swiftly emerged in response. Eritrean nationalism took a decisive turn toward expounding unconditional independence, and many who had tacitly or otherwise supported the federal compromise withdrew their support for it once it became clear that Ethiopia had no intention of honouring the arrangement. By the time the Eritrean Assembly was forcibly abolished in 1962—under armed threat it voted itself out of existence—the war had already begun. In the late 1950s, the Eritrean Liberation Movement (ELM) had gone into exile and had begun the campaign for Eritrean independence; it was soon supplanted by the Eritrean Liberation Front (ELF), which in the early 1960s was beginning to organize violence against the Ethiopian state. It did so initially by harnessing the *shifta* tradition in the western lowlands; in the course of the 1960s *shifta* became guerrillas, and the Eritrean war escalated rapidly.

From the point when Haile Selassie symbolically crossed the Mereb in October 1952 on his first tour of the new province, it was clear that the Eritrean federal apparatus was to be entirely subordinate to the imperial executive.[75] Eritrea had an elected assembly and a chief executive, the latter position held initially by unionist leader Tedla Bairu. However, real power lay in the person of the *enderasse*, the emperor's representative, who was in theory merely the link between the Eritrean assembly and the imperial government but who by 1955 was making clear to the former that, as far as Addis Ababa was concerned, there was to be no distinction between Ethiopian and Eritrean affairs. Increasing interference led to Tedla's resignation as chief executive in 1955, an important turning point in that it marked the rapid disillusionment of those Christian highlanders who had been 'unionist' over the preceding decade but not, it seems, wholly unconditionally. Tedla's successor, notably, was *Dejazmach* Asfeha Woldemichael—no less a person than the deputy to the emperor's representative—and under him the assembly became ever less 'autonomous' from the imperial government. Political parties were abolished, and assembly members could only 'petition' the emperor as individuals; troublesome members were publicly vilified and subject to the close scrutiny of state security. In the meantime, Ethiopian army units were stationed across Eritrea, even if the police remained Eritrean.

By 1955-6, organized, if often necessarily covert, opposition was beginning to crystallize.[76] Eritrean Muslims were already in the vanguard of nascent nationalism, notably. In the course of the 1940s, an urban Muslim middle class had tapped into the Tigre revolt in the rural west and north to create a large umbrella of political activism which was, at the very least, sceptical about the benefits of absorption into Ethiopia.[77] Such scepticism was also present among some Tigrinya highlanders, but it took repressive imperial policies to galvanize a wider highland nationalism. As Ethiopia dismantled political parties, outlawed independent associations, and suppressed labour unions, it became clear, by the mid-1950s, that the Ethiopian state actively sought the destruction of the autonomy supposedly guaranteed to Eritrea by the federal arrangement. Eritreans came to behold Haile Selassie very differently from those outside the region who perceived a benign, indeed heroic figure who was a champion of African unity and the incarnation of ancient African civilization and dignity. Eritrea's vibrant press was soon muzzled; Arabic and Tigrinya were replaced by Amharic as the language of government and public affairs. Eritrea's flag was replaced by the Ethiopian flag; its criminal code by the Ethiopian version; and imperial signs and symbols appeared in Asmara and other towns across the territory, while the influence of the Emperor's representative over the Assembly became pervasive and aggressive.[78] Significantly, such influence led to the resignation of the president of the assembly, Idris Muhammad Adam, in 1957; Idris Adam, an influential champion of autonomy and (significantly) a key Beni Amer leader, had long clashed with chief executive Asfeha, and his departure was as important a moment as Tedla Bairu's resignation. Shortly afterwards, he went into exile in Cairo.

Heightening Ethiopian repression was playing out against a backdrop of severe economic problems across Eritrea—both urban and rural—which had their roots in the slow economic decline of the 1940s. It is clearly no coincidence that—just as in Tigray, where various forms of protest were fuelled by economic marginalization—in Eritrea the foundational decades of political activism were the 1940s to the 1970s, a period of chronic material decline and seriously limited opportunities for the bulk of the population, especially the young. This clearly connects with the broader point already made that economic conditions frequently fuelled violence, in the mid-twentieth century as at various junctures in the nineteenth. In 1958, for example, the Eritrean highlands suffered a very poor harvest, and hardship was acute in the months which followed. Violent, popular insurgency grew up within a framework provided by economic deterioration. Nationalist politics, arguably, had their roots in these economic challenges; certainly, as Tom Killion has suggested, the Eritrean labour movement was in the vanguard of protest in the mid- and late 1950s.[79] Workers' protests culminated in the general strike of 1958 which was violently crushed by the Ethiopian security forces; and although ostensibly the strike was concerned with workers' rights, in reality it represented the crystallization of political protest against the undermining of Eritrean autonomy and civil rights more broadly. As Markakis has pointed out, the crushing of the labour movement effectively alienated a nascent Eritrean working class, the majority of whom were Christian, thus pushing swathes of the latter into the anti-Ethiopia camp.[80] In the aftermath of the strike's brutal suppression, all labour and other associations were banned, and political protest began to take new directions, under new forms of leadership. Although there was some overlap between the labour and nationalist movements, political activism from the late 1950s onward was led by nationalist figures in exile and members of the student movement within Eritrea itself.

Eritrea itself was by now a dangerous place for open protest, and by 1957–8 Cairo was becoming the assembly point of Eritrean nationalism.[81] In addition to Idris Adam, nationalist leaders such as Ibrahim Sultan and Woldeab Woldemariam had fled into exile there, and were using radio broadcasts to promote the cause. Eritrean leaders were able to take advantage of the pan-Arabism sweeping the region, and Muslim leaders in particular were keen to tap the reservoir of sympathy for the Eritrean cause across North Africa and the Middle East.[82] This in itself would later cause tensions between Christian and Muslim elements within the Eritrean struggle; but in the absence of alternative audiences, certainly in Europe, Arab nationalism represented a natural source of succour. This made sense, too, given that the nationalist struggle was to begin in the Muslim western lowlands of Eritrea, with the Christian highlands following later. Nonetheless, there can be little doubt that Eritrean nationalism as a modern phenomenon was the product of two converging streams, namely deep-seated Muslim hostility to the Ethiopian state, now encouraged by pan-Arabist agendas across the wider region, and Christian disengagement and disillusionment from the Ethiopian state following the latter's betrayal of the federal arrangement. Meanwhile, in Asmara, the Ethiopian state moved ever more aggressively toward total incorporation as a means to 'resolving' that instability. In mid-1960 the Eritrean assembly was renamed the Eritrean 'administration', explicitly under imperial authority; harassment of disruptive members was intensified, and the full weight of the coercive security apparatus developed in Ethiopia since the early 1940s was brought to bear on the territory. Ultimately, under threat of armed intervention—the assembly buildings were surrounded by Ethiopian army units—the assembly voted itself out of existence in November 1962, whereupon Eritrea became the fourteenth province of the Ethiopian empire. Federation was finally exposed as fiction; and although, as Erlich makes clear, there is legalistic debate over the 'right' of the Eritrean assembly to vote itself out of existence,[83] the fact remains that Ethiopia's abrogation of the Federal Act was an explicitly and unabashedly political manoeuvre, clearly signposted since 1941.

The thoughts of some nationalists had already begun to turn to armed struggle in the late 1950s. In this context models and inspirations were on hand in neighbouring Sudan, where a serious conflagration was in the making which would have a major influence on events in Ethiopia and Eritrea. Tensions had been building in southern Sudan in the first half of the 1950s; a mutiny at Torit in 1955 was followed by some very low-level military campaigns against those rebels still at large, but by the end of the decade the oppressive and aggressive political and military strategies adopted by Khartoum toward the south were pushing southern elements toward armed struggle.[84] Southern opposition either went into exile to form the Sudan African Nationalist Union (SANU)—modelled on eastern and central African nationalist movements—or joined the *Anyanya*, the name given to the emerging guerrilla forces in the bush. Both SANU and *Anyanya*, and events in southern Sudan more broadly between the mid-1950s and the mid-1960s, were closely monitored by Eritrean nationalists.

Violence seemed now to present itself as the only alternative in combating Amhara incursions; but from the outset, the Eritrean struggle was characterized by sectarian rivalries and divisions.[85] In 1958, a group of young Eritrean Muslims in Port Sudan formed the ELM. Inspired by Sudanese independence a couple of years earlier, and by the organization and activity of the Sudanese Communist Party, the ELM espoused religious unity as well as armed struggle in the pursuit of independence from Ethiopia, and began to organize clandestine cells across Eritrea. In the *kebessa*, the ELM became known as the *Mahber Shewate* ('association of seven'), as each cell contained seven activists. Its appearance, however, was denounced by the exiled leaders in Cairo, who had established the ELF; they rejected the ELM as communist and (they claimed) a cover for the Ethiopian security forces. As the ELM attempted political mobilization, it was outflanked by the somewhat better-organized and better-funded ELF, which now tapped into the growing unrest in the western lowlands—even if its claims to be leading that unrest were far-fetched. By 1961, it had succeeded in recruiting a motley collection of *shifta* and former *ascari* in the western lowlands for the purpose. Eritrean nationalist mythology has it that the first shots of the thirty-year campaign were fired by the well-known Nara *shifta* Hamed Idris Awate on 1 September 1961, when he and a small band of men attacked a remote Ethiopian police post in the area of Haicota in Gash-Barka. While it is clearly crucial for those involved in nationalist struggle to establish clear chronological markers for the purpose of memorialization and celebration—poignant punctuation in the narrative arc—the reality is that the armed struggle had been fizzling into life since the late 1950s, and that by 1961–2 two distinct streams of activity had converged, namely *shiftanet* and nationalist ideology.

Like most armed insurgencies, it began inauspiciously, and almost imperceptibly; initially, at least, the Ethiopian security forces would scarcely have distinguished early attacks on remote outstations from the episodic actions of ever-restless *shifta* in the Gash-Barka zone. But it was quickly clear that there was more to this, and indeed the public squabbles between the ELM and ELF drew attention to the emerging struggle itself. The ELF was soon recruiting across a wide area, and the insurgency may even have prompted the Ethiopian authorities to finally abolish the federation in late 1962 and send forces into the territory in considerable strength. They were swiftly emulating their British predecessors in patrolling the streets of Asmara, targeting suspect rural communities across the territory, establishing intelligence networks in zones of rebel activity, and chasing *shifta* wherever they could be espied. Certainly, the Ethiopian authorities could hardly be in any doubt that a serious revolt was brewing, even as the official line from Addis Ababa was that these ruffians were mere *shifta*, perennial malcontents without programme or higher aims. Most of them were indeed *shifta* but they were also rather more than that: these bedraggled bandits on horse- and camel-back with Second World War rifles, ranging across the hot plains in the west and the turbulent mountains in the north, were the harbingers of one of the bloodiest upheavals in the region's modern history.

Crises impending

The empire that Menelik had built, and which Haile Selassie had striven to maintain, was beset by a series of crises from 1960 onwards. While the Emperor struggled to defend autocracy, notwithstanding some extremely limited and half-hearted reforms, in the wake of the attempted *coup d'etat* in 1960, the decade saw increasing political radicalization among Amhara students, workers, and army officers. Rebellion in the countryside—notably in Bale, in 1968—and the escalating violence in Eritrea was sharply redolent of the situation a century earlier, in the 1860s, although Haile Selassie was no Tewodros. Meanwhile, while many Tigrinya continued to join the assault on the imperial state—indeed some of them would aspire to lead the attack—a complex relationship was suggested by the fact that many other Tigrinya lived prosperous lives in Addis Ababa, and even served in the imperial government. It is true that some of these would become politically active in support of their Eritrean compatriots' armed insurgency; but the status of tens of thousands of Eritreans at the heart of the Ethiopian empire was always ambiguous, and politically troubled, if economically secure. There were heightened ethnic tensions elsewhere, too, in particular among the Oromo whose political consciousness was beginning to stir in the early and mid-1960s. The sum of these events was that by the early 1970s, Ethiopia was crippled by ethnic, religious, and nationalist conflict—each of which was driven by economic exclusion—and even if Eritreans (who were not, in any case, an 'ethnic' group) and Oromo (who were) struggled to find internal unity, there was enough in the way of militant identity to launch serious assaults on the Solomonic state. Moreover, the war with Somalia in 1964 was a reminder of the violence that lay waiting just beyond the border to the south; and all the while, radicalized Amhara in Addis Ababa and beyond began to ponder whether Solomonism had not outlived its usefulness, and came to the conclusion that the problem lay not with provincial violence *per se*, but in the structures of the Ethiopian empire itself, and in the ideologies which underpinned them.

It was in Eritrea that the violent contradictions of the Ethiopian state were writ large. Many of the early fighters in the ELF were recruited from among the predominantly Muslim Tigre, seasonal farmers and herdsmen inhabiting that vast arc of territory from the western lowlands, across the northern mountains, and onto the northern coastal plains; in particular, many were from the Beni Amer, Marya, and Mensa sub-groups of Tigre speakers. Other early ELF fighters were Bilen, from the Bogos area around Keren, and Nara, from the far western plains.[86] Recruitment, or the lack of it, elsewhere in Eritrea was often shaped by older, more local rivalries. Among the Afar of the northern Danakil, for example, loyalties were divided between Massawa and the Aussa sultanate in Ethiopia; only those of the former persuasion provided recruits to both the ELF and, later, the EPLF. The Kunama around Barentu had long been ambivalent, at the very least, toward highland centres of power on both sides of the Mereb, and locally had long been hostile toward the Nara and the Beni Amer; it meant that the Kunama largely stayed aloof from the unfolding struggle, and some even worked alongside Ethiopian authorities against the armed movements—and, more recently, against the independent Eritrean state, which has consequently come to regard them with deep suspicion.

Meanwhile the Eritrean nationalist cause was leant critical early support from Khartoum, peeved at Ethiopia's pro-Israeli stance and Addis Ababa's own tacit sympathy for the southern Sudanese rebels. In the course of the 1960s, strains between Sudan and Ethiopia created vital space—physically as well as politically—within which Eritrean guerrillas could operate and continue to consolidate.[87] Throughout the 1960s, the ELF expanded rapidly, its recruits predominantly Muslim but increasingly from the *kebessa*, too; by the mid-1960s it tapped into the radicalized and politicized youth of the Christian highlands, mostly—though not exclusively—from the land- and property-owning *petit bourgeoisie* of Asmara and the major towns, whose children were politically active at school and even Haile Selassie I University in Addis Ababa. The student movement, indeed, was increasingly important in Asmara, especially, in terms of expressing dissent—more important, for a time, than either the ELF or ELM themselves.[88] Continued harsh economic conditions in Eritrea throughout the 1960s pushed recruits into the ranks of the guerrillas, although in truth the liberation forces themselves were responsible for a fair amount of rural hardship as they not infrequently preyed off rural communities' food supplies. More common *shifta* strategies of survival were adopted, too, including highway robbery and raids on plantations and factories.[89] Clearly, 'civilians'—insofar as such a category had ever existed in the region—were being caught up in this war, and certainly the Ethiopian security forces' response drew ever fewer distinctions between combatant and non-combatant, especially in the rural areas.

Yet just as the armed liberation movement was growing, it was riddled with internal tension and dissension. By 1965, notably, the ELF had effectively crushed the attempts of the ELM to establish itself as an armed movement in the north of Eritrea. Some inside the ELF ranks—especially young Christian recruits—quickly came to despise its overly hierarchical, aristocratic leadership structure, while Christians were frequently persecuted and increasingly felt themselves at grave risk for questioning the direction and organization of the movement.[90] The ELF leadership also had a natural leaning toward the Arab world: it sought succour from Egypt, Syria, and Iraq, and took inspiration from—and to some extent modelled itself on—the FLN in Algeria. This created a distinct unease among Christian recruits who considered that they had not embraced revolutionary secularism—or at least espoused it—only to see their leaders associating themselves with Arabism or even Islamism. More specifically, there was disquiet among Christian highlanders at the obvious connections being emphasized by the ELF leadership between northern Eritrea and northern Sudan, connections which again underpinned a set of Arabist, Islamic identities and loyalties. The ELF was, for young radicals both Christian and Muslim, nowhere near revolutionary enough for the demands of the age and in fact seemed to be too much rooted in the feudal structures of northern and western Eritrea. Many young 'commissars' returning from training in China or Syria, as well as the young, educated, politically sophisticated class joining up from across the *kebessa*, became highly critical of the supposedly 'reactionary' nature of the organization—particularly as its showing against the first major Ethiopian offensive in 1967 was poor.

The ELF has been much maligned in recent decades, the EPLF having established—for the time being—a monopoly on 'public truth' with regard to the story of the struggle. But the ELF was indeed a flawed and largely ineffective organization in the late 1960s.[91] Its leadership was almost wholly in exile, with the revolutionary command based in Kassala; it was structured according to territorial zones, with initially four divisional commands treated as personal fiefdoms by absentee commanders, with a fifth zone subsequently added covering the Christian highlands. The movement was thus fragmented and ill-led, and fault lines swiftly opened up. Christian recruits were prone to be made scapegoats for both military failure and internal dissent, as in the aftermath of the 1967 offensive, when more than two dozen Christians were executed at the orders of the Muslim deputy commander of the highland zone for failing to adequately perform their duty. The commander himself was in Kassala at the time. Other incidents—for example the killing of Christian fighters on suspicion of their being Ethiopian agents—produced profound levels of disenchantment and mistrust within the rank-and-file. A reform movement, known as the *eslah*, gathered momentum, and culminated in 1968 in the abolition of the zonal structure and the revolutionary command in Kassala. The changes—notably the dismissal of the existing leadership structure—would themselves engender long-standing rivalries and factionalism within the ELF, even though the reforms represented the beginning of a wholesale restructuring and indeed reinvention of the movement over the following decade. But it was already too late. By 1970, the Eritrean struggle had splintered into several groupings, a process of violent fragmentation that has come to define Eritrean political discourse and the culture of 'liberation'. Out of a cluster of small bands emerged the EPLF, which would in time come to challenge the ELF itself, as well as the Ethiopian state; the great northern borderland was erupting in spectacular fashion, and it would wreak havoc on both Ethiopia and its own inhabitants alike.

Nonetheless, despite these deep cleavages across the liberation movement, Eritrean guerrilla forces had by the late 1960s and early 1970s begun to carve out loosely defined 'liberated' zones. Operating largely on foot, while using such supplementary transport as donkeys and camels, guerrilla units were between twenty and sixty strong, according to contemporary British reports,[92] and thus highly mobile. They conducted hit-and-run attacks on Ethiopian security targets and on selected non-military targets—foreign-owned farms and factories, notably—and then sought to evade the inevitable Ethiopian military response, all the while feeding off local communities which were thus brought into the conflict whether they were sympathetic or not. In many respects these were the classic tactics of the long-established *shifta*. As the 1970s unfolded, they were increasingly effective tactics, too, not least because of the disarray and demoralization experienced by the Ethiopian forces in light of political and economic upheavals further south.

Of course in reality, Eritrea's political instability—of which fractious modern nationalism was the latest manifestation—can be dated back rather further than the 1940s and 1950s. The modern liberation movement, broadly defined, had grown out of the practice of *shiftanet* in Eritrea and the region at large; the fronts themselves were essentially *shifta* in a modern setting, enhanced by manifestos as well as military hardware, and their modern divisions reflected the cultural and political and geographical fissures which traversed the northern landscape in antiquity. Eritrea's was a curious nationalism, therefore, rooted in the violent instability of the borderland, and riddled with discord from the outset. In terms of splintered and brutally internecine nature of the struggle, there is nothing in Eritrea's past which bodes particularly well for the future, which is precisely why the EPLF would later become deeply wary of the past itself. As the 'old' encountered the 'new'—*shifta* morphing into guerrillas and revolutionaries—violent

chauvinisms would be born, and indeed certain forms of these were comparatively novel, notably the nationalist militancy of the EPLF itself.

Violent insurgency was fermenting elsewhere, too. Heightened Oromo
activism needs to be understood in the context of the ongoing Somali
problem for the imperial regime, for the two intersected at crucial fault lines
in the south and south-east. Notably, the problem of the Somali frontier in
the Ogaden was intensified with the independence of Somalia in 1960.[93]
The pan-Somali lobby of the 1940s and 1950s had sought the unification of
all Somali peoples scattered across northern Kenya, eastern Ethiopia, and
Italian, British, and French Somalilands. The project failed, although the
Republic of Somalia was an amalgamation—itself an unwieldy one—of the
British and Italian territories. The pan-Somali failure, and continued
Ethiopian occupation of the Ogaden—not to mention the 'stranded' Somalis
in northern Kenya—led to a reigniting of one of the region's most ancient
zones of conflict. The Somali government provided support to insurgencies
in both eastern Ethiopia and northern Kenya. In the Ogaden, a low-level
guerrilla insurgency began after the Ethiopian state attempted to impose a
new tax on Somali pastoralists, and by the middle of 1963—mirroring events
in Eritrea to the north—Somali fighters were attacking police posts and
making gains against a poorly organized Ethiopian army. Confronted with
guerrillas armed by Mogadishu, Haile Selassie appealed to his American
benefactors for assistance, and at the beginning of 1964 Ethiopia moved a
US-equipped division into the Ogaden and launched a series of more vigorous counter-attacks. The insurgency swiftly disintegrated, and within
weeks Ethiopian troops had advanced to the Somali border, threatening
Mogadishu to cease its support for the rebels. Somalia negotiated a ceasefire
in March 1964, and although a standoff ensued, the Ethiopians had at least
won what they believed to be a measure of security on their eastern
flank.[94]

It would prove short-lived. Indeed just across the border in northern
Kenya, a Somali insurgency had also begun in the course of 1963. The so-
called 'Shifta War' was fought from 1963 to 1968 between Somali fighters
and the rather better equipped and trained Kenyan security forces.[95] Recent
research suggests that many Somali shifta in northern Kenya were not particularly concerned about irredentist, Somali nationalist agendas, and that
much of the violence had a specifically local flavour and motivation;[96]
either way, again Mogadishu was compelled to retreat from its position of
support for the insurgency by 1967–8, and indeed the Somali government

appears to have lost some interest in the issue. But its retreat was doubtless compelled in large part by the united front displayed by Jomo Kenyatta and Haile Selassie, who had much to gain from cooperation on the issue of frontier insurgencies. Ethiopia and Kenya had signed a defence pact in July 1963, while Haile Selassie later showed a great deal of interest in the situation in northern Kenya itself. On a state visit to Kenya, the Emperor visited victims of the *Shifta* War and donated funds to their recovery. Notably, he declared—in a somewhat backhanded expression of solidarity with Kenyatta—that if anyone had a territorial claim to Kenya's Northern Frontier District, it was not Somalia but Ethiopia: after all, it was the natural home of the Boran of southern Ethiopia.[97] Certainly Addis Ababa had long viewed the Kenyan border as a potential weak spot in fortress Ethiopia's defences—the empire's 'soft underbelly', as Mburu has it[98]—although of course, as noted earlier, it was also a zone of opportunity for bands of violent entrepreneurs from the highlands. But above all, both the Somali issue and indeed the Eritrean problem compelled a tough line from Addis Ababa on the whole question of irredentism and secessionism—as it did from Nairobi, and many others. While the Somali insurgencies were erupting in the Ogaden and the NFD, and the Eritrean war was escalating, Haile Selassie was one of the key architects of the OAU charter, adopted at the inaugural conference (in Addis Ababa) in 1963, which stated that colonial boundaries were inalienable and sacrosanct, and that resultant African sovereign territories were inalterable. The somewhat awkward questions of the Somali and the Eritreans (among other issues then emerging) were swept aside, one of the hallmarks of the OAU's conduct of business in the decades to come; but while most of those present applauded the principle, the Emperor, sitting astride a patchwork of violent fault lines, had more to lose than most.

Meanwhile, in the province of Bale neighbouring the Ogaden, an Oromo and Somali peasantry had become increasingly politicized as the result of an array of impositions since the early 1950s.[99] Land shortages owing to changes in the tenure system, heavy taxation, the settlement of highlanders, and a venal administration combined to create an explosive situation by the early 1960s, not dissimilar to that witnessed in Tigray a few years earlier, with some important differences. In Bale, exploitation of the peasantry was much more clearly the central cause of the revolt which erupted in 1963, while Islam provided an ideological framework within which violence against the state and its representatives could be carried out. The Somali, moreover, could tap into the irredentist agenda then in currency, and indeed Somali nationalists perceived Bale as part of the putative greater Somalia. As in Tigray and Eritrea, the rebellion was at least initially driven by *shifta* who had taken to the bush as economic outlaws as much as political bandits, and it spread rapidly across the district in the mid-1960s. Initially, indeed, the Ethiopian government attempted placation, but in 1966–7 launched a massive offensive—just as they were counterattacking the Eritrean rebels, indeed—and the uprising was gradually, and bloodily, suppressed over the ensuing three years. The tactics were similar to those employed in Eritrea, too, with Ethiopian forces attacking rebel encampments and civilian targets indiscriminately: as in the nineteenth century, and most markedly under Tewodros, the key to the 'winning' of such wars was held to be in the visitation of violence upon the entire community, not simply pitched combat against men-at-arms. The uprising was finally crushed in early 1970, but not before another revolt—this time in Gojjam—had begun, in 1968.[100] Gojjam was a rather different proposition, as a largely autonomous province through the 1940s and 1950s, violently resistant to impositions from the direction of central Shoan government. Indeed it was a newly aggressive Shoan administration (headed by the brother, in fact, of the governor of Bale) attempting to bring various *shifta* groups to heel and impose a new tax regime that sparked the uprising in 1968. It was crushed by the end of the year with a brutality that was by now becoming characteristic of the imperial response to such challenges—again, there was fairly indiscriminate killing of rebels and their suspected but often unarmed supporters, as well as a dose of scorched earth tactics—although in fact the government did subsequently offer tax concessions and restructured the local administration to render it more palatable.

Bale and Gojjam were the most prominent of the peasant revolts of the period, but there were others—in Gedeo, in the south-west, and in Yajju in Wollo. It is clear that such revolts were often class-based and economic at root, but they also contained powerful ethnic and/or regionalist elements, and the latter would become ever more prominent in the years to follow. It is also the case that, just as in Eritrea and the Ogaden, they exploded along fault lines of varying degrees of antiquity, zones of contest between 'centre' and 'periphery' which produced ever more militant and militarized identities. Yet whatever was lost or gained in the course of these uprisings, worse was to follow for the peasantries themselves: the 1973 famine ravaged the northern parts of Ethiopia in particular, and was an apocalyptic backdrop to—and indeed a catalyst for—seismic shifts in the higher reaches of the polity in the early and mid-1970s. Once again, major environmental change—in this case compounded by chronic state neglect—drove an upsurge in the direction and quality of violence; prolonged drought and resultant hunger across the region from the early 1970s and into the 1980s changed the very nature of the wars themselves. While hundreds of thousands starved to death in the worst famine since the beginning of Menelik's reign, the body politic itself swayed feverishly, weakened by chronic malnourishment of a more abstract kind; only massive ingestions of political radicalism could save it, argued a younger generation of soldiers, students, and workers. But while Marx might provide food for thought, it remained to be seen whether revolutionary ideology would be sufficient to revive the weakened corpus.

The abortive *coup* of 1960 represented the opening shots in the reassertion of overt military power at the centre of Ethiopian politics. While the novelty of an increasingly radicalized military in Ethiopia by the late 1960s and early 1970s lay in its adoption of an array of modernist revolutionary agendas, its readiness to intervene in politics in fact belonged to a rather older tradition. Ceremony and symbol notwithstanding, Haile Selassie had never been a soldier, and thus the bulk of his reign may be seen as somewhat anomalous *vis-à-vis* the previous two centuries of *habesha* political development. In the nineteenth century the business of government and military activity were never distinct, and political leadership usually came about through military command; rulers had proven themselves in battle, and power was achieved and wielded through command of men and (increasingly) guns. The state was no secluded concept to be protected by some monolithic, 'professional' military establishment; it was, rather, a living resource over which influence might be exerted and which might ultimately be captured for particular ends. In other words, simply put, there was a deep tradition of military involvement in politics in the Ethiopian region. The 1960 *coup* attempt had been the first indication of the resurrection of this tradition. The Ethiopian military from the late nineteenth century onward, moreover, had been concerned with *both* internal control *and* external adventurism, and indeed often the two were indelibly interlinked. Soldiers were thus predisposed to intervention in political affairs, notwithstanding the fact that a core component of Haile Selassie's modernization programme had been the creation of what we might loosely term a 'Western' military model of professional, apolitical detachment. The tensions between this model and the Patriots of the 1930s, or the *shifta* in harness in Eritrea in the 1940s, are clear enough; but in any case the professionalized Ethiopian military establishment had an inbuilt propensity for action against elements within state structures seen as detrimental to particular interests—whether soldiers' own, or those of a range of regional or ethnic groups, or indeed those of the empire as a whole. And to be sure, several of the multiple crises unfolding in the early 1970s, it was believed, required more decisive military action. The move against Haile Selassie must be seen at least partly in this context.

Meanwhile, in the Eritrean context, what is clear is the rejection by a generation coming of age in the late 1950s and early 1960s of the unionist sentiments of the generation preceding it. In what would become, in the fullness of time, something of a generational conflict, the 'new nationalism' of the pivotal *c.*1958–*c.*1962 period was expounded by many whose parents had been unionists, for one reason or another; the struggle for Eritrea now took new forms. Even if the new nationalist struggle would carry along with it many older Eritreans, men and women of the 1940s and 1950s, it was the young who led them, and frequently the radicalized, idealistic young, of the kind likewise discernible in the Ethiopia of the 1960s and early 1970s.[101] In Eritrea, it was a process of radicalization which was made possible, at least in part, by the brutal mishandling of the territory by an apparently ill-informed and hubristic Amhara elite who had been offered an opportunity to 'secure' the north but who failed to seize it. An institutional myopia prevented the Emperor and his court from perceiving the political and cultural gorges opening up which would come to swallow armies and state structures alike; driven by a desire to possess those lands, the state itself was already being shaped by its frontiers. It would prove to be one of the most significant political failures in the modern history of northeast Africa, and it has given rise to a great many crises in its turn.

Ultimately, then, a more strident, more sharply defined Eritrean nationalism came into being in the late 1950s; it was the product of several converging dynamics, some of which can be traced to the nineteenth century, and others which were rather more recent creations, i.e. dating to between the 1900s and the 1950s. Quite how much 'political awakening' there was in the 1940s and 1950s is questionable, however, for the roads which led to the ELM and the ELF have their starting points long before the BMA permitted newspapers and lifted the ban on political parties. Moreover, the Eritrean nationalist interpretation of the last fifty years has made much of external intervention and betrayal; Eritreans have laid great emphasis on the victim-hood underpinning their experience. To be sure, it is a thesis which contains some compelling arguments. But a great deal of caution needs to be exercised here. The federation was not a catastrophe simply because the international community sacrificed little Eritrea on the altar of Cold War expediency; it was a catastrophe because Ethiopia abused the federal constitution recklessly, and because Eritrean unionists appear to have wholly misunderstood the intentions of the Haile Selassie government. The ambiguous nationalism of Tigrinya unionism, in particular, was to prove a flimsy defence against Shoan ambition. Unionism, broadly defined, has had a long and robust history in the Eritrean highlands, down to the mid-1990s; but it has always been conditional in one way or another, and successive Ethiopian political establishments have consistently misread this, wilfully or otherwise. In any case, the 1960s witnessed the maturation and the co-option of some long-standing patterns of violence across the region; and around that violence there now formed militant identities represented by groups whose modernist programmes made stentorian claims for revolutionary change. The symbiotic relationship between 'centre' and 'periphery' was never clearer than in the latter decades of the twentieth century, and it is to that which we turn, now, in the final part of the book.

PART
IV

Revolutions, Liberations, and the Ghosts of the *Mesafint*

7
Revolution, 'Liberation', and Militant Identity, 1974–91

The violent state renewed: the *Derg*

The regime that would become known in popular parlance as the *Derg*—the deceptively innocuous Amharic word for 'committee'—had its roots deeply embedded in the violence and political settlements of the late nineteenth and early twentieth centuries, for all the revolutionary and modernist language and symbol which surrounded it. Mengistu Haile Mariam, who would quickly emerge as the head of state, bore some resemblance to Tewodros a century earlier, at least superficially. In some respects, certainly, the period between the mid-1970s and early 1990s represented the latest stage in the deployment of overt brute force in the name of a larger, centralized Ethiopian unity, a process which had begun under Tewodros in the 1850s and 1860s. And yet it looked, if only for a brief moment, as though it might have been very different. The revolution which began the process of demolishing *l'ancien regime* came on the back of a new radicalized sense of outrage across several walks of life in Ethiopia, and held out the promise, for some, of the application of some measure of political idealism to Ethiopian government and society in a rapidly changing world. That promise came to nothing—at least in part because of the failure of Ethiopia's own intellectuals to develop creative (and 'authentic') solutions to the country's crises.[1] Within a few years, the regime had become one of the bloodiest and most authoritarian anywhere in the world.[2]

By 1973–4, imperial Ethiopia was confronted with the worst concatenation of crises since the period following Menelik's accession. Against a background of escalating provincial rebellion and a devastating famine, a series of strikes, demonstrations, and mutinies paralysed Ethiopia in the course of 1974. Students, civil servants, and members of the security forces formed unlikely—indeed often unwitting—collaborators in the revolutionary surge; but it was representatives of the military and police forces, who formed the leadership of the committees, who were in the vanguard of political change. In September, the emperor was deposed, and died a few months later; Mengistu's faction won through, and the *Derg* embarked on a programme of Soviet-style socialism—or at least that was the stated intention. Opposition, whether within political circles in Addis Ababa, in the rural areas, or in the form of the rebel movements in the north, was not tolerated.

The *Derg* was an example—not uncommon across the continent in the 1970s and 1980s—of the so-called 'radical military regime' created in the wake of army takeovers.[3] The violence of the Mengistu state was overt, and that heightened level of violence was a response to the crises confronting the Ethiopian state—yet both the crises and the response had deep and intertwined genealogies, and each fed off the other, militarizing political culture and discourse to a dramatic degree, redolent of the nineteenth century. Certainly, again, Mengistu had much in common with Tewodros, in terms of his apparent belief in the primacy of armed force, and in his conviction that all enemies of Ethiopia could, and should, be violently crushed. His roots—apparently in a Konso slave family in the south—were somewhat more obscure than those of Tewodros, who at least could claim some kind of noble blood; but they shared a continual anxiety concerning questions over their legitimacy. Both came from the edges of highland Semitic civilization—physically, in the case of Tewodros, and also culturally and ethnically in Mengistu's case. The latter's contemporaries sneered quietly that he was not even 'Ethiopian'—his Konso roots meant he was not truly *habesha*—and that he was *baria*. In some respects, both might be held up as exemplars of how the armed frontier produced those who aspired to the capture and transformation of the centre. The hostile frontier was their undoing in turn.

It is important to place the *Derg* in global context, too, for in this period the region became the borderland in another, somewhat farther flung set of contests.[4] During the Haile Selassie era, and indeed for the first few months of the new regime, the US had invested heavily in Ethiopia. From the early 1950s until the mid-1970s, the Americans had supported the Ethiopian army, which became the largest and best-equipped in sub-Saharan Africa as a result, and regarded Haile Selassie as a key regional ally in the Cold War. The USSR, meanwhile, saw Siad Barre's Somalia as representing an African foothold, and offered some measure of support and ideological encouragement to a regime which presented itself as one of the most revolutionary in the continent, and which was grateful for the material assistance. Yet within a few months in the middle of the decade, the situation changed dramatically, a process of transformation which also involved another major war between Ethiopia and Somalia, in 1977–8. With the ascension of the *Derg* and the ideological realignment which resulted, the US was no longer welcome in Ethiopia, and its facilities in Asmara were abandoned as the Carter administration took office; the Soviet Union, meanwhile, irritated by Siad Barre's conduct toward Ethiopia in the run-up to the war and rather more impressed by the Mengistu regime, withdrew its favour summarily from Mogadishu and redirected it toward Addis Ababa.[5] American policy toward the Horn was now characterized by 'wait-and-see'; the Carter administration was inclined to become involved in neither the affairs of the major states in the region nor in those of the rebel movements. It would come to regret this.

The interjection of the Soviet Union had important consequences, as did the rather less dramatic support provided by Castro's Cuba. It greatly strengthened the Ethiopian military and served to prolong the struggle in the north, in particular; the EPLF, as we see below, was compelled to withdraw from its dominant position across the territory in the face of concerted new attacks, and it arguably prolonged the war in Eritrea by a decade. Yet it needs to be kept in mind that those wars were already being fought; the exigencies of the Cold War sometimes *exacerbated*, and *complicated*, but did not *manufacture*, patterns of violence across the region. Eritrean nationalists would condemn—understandably—Soviet imperialism, and make much political capital out of the failures of the international community; but it is perhaps worth remembering that the Eritrean civil war did as much as the intrusions of Moscow into the region to prolong the war in the north. In any case, from 1974–5, it was clear that the new government was absolutely intolerant of any suggestion that armed enemies might be negotiated with rather than conquered. When Somalia invaded in 1977, Mengistu appealed to 'ancient Ethiopian patriotism' in exhorting the populace to resist and work for the victory of the motherland—with some success, it must be said; and when the Somalis were indeed thwarted, it was promised that 'victory in the east shall be repeated in the north'.[6] The murder of General Aman Andom in late 1974, the one senior figure arguably capable of bringing about a negotiated settlement in Eritrea, meant that the war—with or without external assistance—would not simply continue, but increase in intensity.

The militarization and sovietization of Ethiopia continued apace through the late 1970s and beyond.[7] Against a backdrop of escalating war in the north, and inter-state war in the Ogaden with Somalia, the *Derg* arrested, tortured, and killed thousands of suspected internal enemies in 1977 and 1978, in what became known as the 'Red Terror'. Extreme violence was deployed against 'enemies of the revolution';[8] hundreds were killed or injured when security forces fired at anti-government rallies in Addis Ababa in April and May 1977, for example, and torture in detention camps and extralegal killings were commonplace.[9] As the *Derg* violently consolidated its power, meanwhile, it developed a philosophy of self-consciously 'indigenous' or 'organic' Marxism aimed at mass mobilization; the philosophy, it seems, was at least in part designed as a rebuttal to the 'foreign' Marxism espoused by the student movement as well as a range of political parties, while the mobilization it entailed was to be used to address a number of crises, from rural development to foreign invasion. Underpinning it all was the principle of *Ethiopia Tikdem*, or 'Ethiopia First'.[10] The Mengistu state sought control through 'revolution', not the other way around. Moscow, moreover, may have had some influence in the introduction of further constitutional reforms through the 1980s, culminating in the proclamation of Mengistu as President of the renamed People's Democratic Republic of Ethiopia in 1987. Yet it was the striking conjunction of political hubris and environmental catastrophe that rendered comparisons of the Marxist-Leninist regime with the imperial one that had preceded it most compelling. Drought and famine were the defining phenomena of the 1970s and 1980s across the Sahel belt from Mauritania to the Ethiopian Highlands, natural in provenance but indubitably exacerbated—and indeed utilized—by human agency. Just as in the late 1880s and early 1890s, environmental catastrophe was politicized: it galvanized liberation violence and indeed compelled various 'peoples' fronts' to search for ever more innovative organizational principles and embrace ever less compromising military strategies. By the same token, it drove centralizing, imperial violence and enabled the regime to extend new levels of control over troublesome areas and population groups, at least in the short term; entire communities were relocated from the north to the south of Ethiopia in order to 'protect' them from the ravages of famine, but clearly such strategies were aimed at stripping rebel movements of their support base. From the mid-1980s, moreover, food aid—generated by well-meaning governments and other agencies in the West—was routinely diverted from insurgent areas and was used by the Ethiopian army itself.[11] However in the longer term, arguably, such human tragedy was the undoing of the *Derg* itself.

Reports of actual food shortages or of impending famine had begun to filter in months earlier, but they were largely ignored; and when the full force of the famine hit through 1984 and early 1985, shocking in its proportions, the government was virtually powerless, owing to a lack of resources and initiative within the system.[12] Almost eight million people were affected; around one million died. In eventual response to this crippling economic and social failure, the government embarked on relocation and villagization programmes which were bitterly resented by the millions of people involved. Perhaps half a million people were forcibly moved from the drought-affected and drought-prone areas in the north and centre to the comparatively more fertile regions of the south and south-west. As a policy it contributed as much as anything else to the massive human suffering experienced by swathes of Eritrean and Ethiopian populations in what was a dreadful decade for the region; violent radicalism increased markedly as a result, moreover. It was, at the very least, controversial, and highly unpopular—as was the decision to create new villages by uprooting and grouping communities together, relocating them in such a way (so went the official rhetoric) as to make the provision of aid and assistance easier to rural areas. This policy began in the east and south-east, for example in Bale and Hararge, and was thereafter spread across the country in the course of the 1980s. The state had effectively used catastrophe for political ends, and it rendered millions of ordinary Ethiopians bitterly opposed to central government, and susceptible to the suggestions of advancing guerrilla organizations. Potential energy on so many borderlands would soon become kinetic, and in many respects the events of the 1980s heightened resistance to and suspicion of central government with which the current Ethiopian government is still confronted, for all its supposed devolution of power.

Inter-state front lines

Before turning to the 'internal' frontiers which would ultimately consume the Marxist state, it is important to note the inter-state borderlands most important to the Ethiopian state in the 1970s and 1980s—those of Sudan and Somalia. First, tensions were rife throughout the period between the governments in Khartoum and Addis Ababa, thus involving the movements which flitted across their frontiers. Open war was avoided, but proxy war was ongoing.[13] The escalation of the Sudanese civil war in the latter half of the 1960s had major implications for the wider region, not least because both Khartoum and Addis Ababa used the other's internal wars to enhance their own position as well as their regional standing—lessons in brutal *realpolitik* which would not be lost on the liberation movements who were alternately the victims and the beneficiaries of shifts in regional politics.

From the mid- and late 1960s there was a marked degree of Sudanese support and sympathy for the Eritrean struggle, and indeed—at least initially—a measure of Sudanese influence in the early ELF. When relations between Sudan and Ethiopia were difficult, Khartoum offered support for the ELF—which could also draw on left-wing Sudanese political opinion, as well as various Beja groups along the frontier with whom many members of the movement shared familial and ethnic links. In this way, too, were frontiers fertile, producing new forces or variations of old ones to challenge the state. Meanwhile, Haile Selassie provided succour to Sudanese dissidents, in the form of the *Anyanya* from the mid-1960s until 1972. In early 1972, the signing of the Addis Ababa Agreement between the Sudanese Government and the Southern Sudan Liberation Movement brought the first civil war to an end; but the regimes in Addis Ababa and Khartoum remained alert to opportunities to undermine one another. With the coming to power in Khartoum of Jaafar Nimeiri in 1969, and then Mengistu in Addis Ababa in 1974, the situation escalated.[14] While in the late 1960s and early 1970s the level of support which the respective Eritrean and Sudanese rebel movements enjoyed was very much contingent on the degree of frost in inter-state relations between Khartoum and Addis Ababa, the hardening of political loyalties and positions in the 1970s firmed up that support. With Nimeiri increasingly anxious about Ethiopia's (and Libya's) pro-Moscow leanings, he increased the flow of arms and support to the Eritrean movements—though particularly the ELF, which was more evidently Muslim, and drawn, at least in origin, from among the groups which straddled the Eritrean–Sudanese borderlands. He was a little less friendly toward the EPLF—highland, and Christian, and Marxist after a fashion—but nonetheless both groups enjoyed access to Port Sudan, and to offices in Khartoum itself.

In retaliation, meanwhile, Mengistu increased Ethiopian support for the SPLM in southern Sudan from 1983, especially as Nimeiri moved ever closer into a US sphere of influence. The collapse of the Addis Ababa Agreement and the beginning of the new phase of north–south Sudanese violence created new opportunities for Sudanese–Ethiopian antagonism. Again, escalating civil war in both countries in the early to mid-1980s rendered states themselves incapable of extending firm control over their frontiers—and in those frontiers, therefore, both the brutalities and weaknesses of the those states were exposed, while the political cultures of emergent guerrilla movements were hardened in battles against internal and external enemies alike. The internal wars of Sudan and Ethiopia became indelibly intertwined. Mengistu permitted the SPLM a base in Gambella region, as well as weapons, training, and other equipment. The SPLM's ability to move in and out of south Sudan was greatly aided by the (falsified) documentation supplied by the Ethiopian government. It is clear, however, that Mengistu was in no position to encourage secessionist movements in Sudan while attempting to crush those within Ethiopia, and so Addis Ababa was allegedly instrumental in the formation within the SPLM of a commitment to a New Sudan—i.e. a united one— with John Garang emerging as the leader willing to pursue this.[15]

Other Ethiopian resistance movements—including the TPLF, the Ethiopian People's Revolutionary Party (EPRP), and the Ethiopian Democratic Union (EDU)—also operated out of Sudan to a large extent, often mobilizing local groups along ethnic lines on the Ethiopian–Sudanese border, and thus creating, for Khartoum, a buffer zone between the two regimes. The EDU, for example, preyed on the rootless groups in the borderlands west of Lake Tana, making use of the *shifta* activities characteristic of the region for much of the 1980s; in that sense, the EDU was the classic regional political movement with distinctive historical characteristics, operating in the frontier zone and harnessing local patterns of resistance and defiance. While the EPRP was largely vanquished by the TPLF in the early 1980s, a faction evolved into the Ethiopian People's Democratic Movement (EPDM) which likewise operated in the Ethiopian–Sudanese borderlands in alliance with the TPLF, particularly the area of modern-day Benishangul-Gumuz.[16] On and behind the borderlands themselves, there was the swelling population of Eritrean, as well as Tigrayan, refugees who in the course of the 1970s and 1980s fled the fighting inside the territory and became long-term residents of eastern Sudan, notably around Kassala and south toward Gedaref.[17]

These 'people in between' found themselves squeezed between the competing power blocs in north-east Africa whose own borderlands became all the more violently volatile as a result. These regions had long been zones of contest between political systems either side of the Blue Nile; in the 1970s and 1980s, the level of politicized violence increased sharply, during which time the military complexity on the ground likewise heightened considerably.[18] Khartoum lent some support—albeit limited, given the enormity of its struggle with the SPLM—to a range of groups in the southern Blue Nile and Upper Nile borderlands who were broadly in arms against the Mengistu state; the EPRP, in particular, was at least tacitly encouraged in its attempts to mobilize the Berta and Anuak (or Anywaa) peoples against the *Derg*. In an ominous portent, meanwhile, the EPLF and the TPLF also involved themselves in the affairs of the western frontier in the course of the 1980s, attempting to coordinate patterns of local resistance and mould these into cogent movements for armed liberation on the model of the Eritrean and Tigrayan organizations. The outcome of these combined efforts—not to mention the extant wellspring of centrifugal hostility—was the Berta and Gambella liberation movements, notably the Gambella People's Liberation Movement, largely Anuak in composition. For its part, the *Derg*, in conjunction with the SPLM, likewise armed groups of local militia, including the Anuak in Gambella and the Berta in Benishangul; and thus were new armed front lines opened up along the Ethiopian–Sudanese borderland, front lines which were arguably critical in the region's Cold War struggle.[19] The arming of local communities undoubtedly fuelled extant patterns of violence and retaliation, hardened causes for which people were willing to fight, and contributed to the destabilization of an already-complex and volatile frontier zone. In a pattern dating to the nineteenth century, and intensifying in the course of the twentieth, lines between the 'civilian' and the 'military' were blurred and recognized by neither guerrilla nor government.

In particular, these regions were transformed from being important zones of commercial and cultural interaction, notwithstanding the periodic instability associated with the eastern Sudanese marches, to being armed frontiers into which the Ethiopian state now aggressively involved itself. Communities were pulled this way and that, caught in the crossfire of a multifaceted struggle between Addis Ababa and Khartoum, and between those regimes and a range of 'internal' enemies.[20] An additional protagonist in the area—though not an especially effective one—was the

Oromo Liberation Front (OLF), which briefly captured the Benishangul town of Asosa in 1989, but which was more interested in the eastern theatre of operations, as we see below. Between the mid-1980s and early 1990s, shifts in the Addis-Ababa–Khartoum axis were dramatic, and had equally dramatic consequences for the wider region. These are more closely examined in the last chapter; suffice to say here that the collapse of Nimeiri's government in 1985, and the overthrow of Sadiq al-Mahdi's coalition in 1989 by Omar al-Beshir and the National Islamic Front, spelt new directions in Sudanese foreign policy, while in 1991 the demolition of the *Derg* signalled a new stage in Ethio–Sudanese relations. Sudan lurched through a series of foreign policy disasters in the early 1990s, finding itself at odds with Egypt, Eritrea, and Uganda; only with Ethiopia, reconfiguring itself under the EPRDF, did relations improve markedly,[21] thrusting independent Eritrea into the role of regional spoiler. The change would have a major impact on the armed borderlands between these states.

Along the frontier zones between Ethiopia and Somalia, meanwhile, violence was episodically explosive, and in between, there was watchfulness and tension. Inter-state war in our region was confined to these two countries until the Eritrean–Ethiopian war in 1998; the immediate prelude to renewed conflict was the emergence of the pan-Somali movement in the 1940s and 1950s, and the clash in the Ogaden between Somali and Ethiopian forces in 1963–4, which had ended with Ethiopian advances to the border forcing Mogadishu into a ceasefire. By the mid-1970s, tensions were once again mounting, this time between Mengistu and Siad Barre.[22] The latter, receiving military aid and other assistance from the Soviet Union, had been steadily building up Somali forces and continued to agitate for the unification of all Somali peoples; he was greatly emboldened by the fact that in the mid-1970s, Ethiopia appeared in disarray, with the turbulence of the revolution and the escalating war in Eritrea sapping Addis Ababa's traditional military hegemony in the east and south-east. The Ogaden seemed ripe for the taking, and even the transfer of the Soviet Union's favour to Ethiopia was not sufficient to dent Siad Barre's confidence. He launched his invasion in May and June 1977, the Somali army advancing in conjunction with the Western Somali Liberation Front (WSLF) which was active across the Ogaden.[23] For the first few weeks, Siad Barre appeared vindicated in his policy of aggression, as the Somali army swiftly overran much of the Ogaden and the Ethiopians fell back in disarray.

The triumph was short-lived, however, and ultimately Somalia was undone by both resurgent Ethiopian military might and diplomatic failure.[24] The USSR massively stepped up its military assistance to the Mengistu state, while the latter itself embarked on a dramatic mobilization and recruitment campaign at home which sought to inspire Ethiopian patriotism against naked foreign aggression. Once again, the Ethiopian state's ability to historicize the violence on its frontiers was a clear political advantage. Further assistance and support came from Cuba and South Yemen—an injection of military hardware and counsel that was to have massive implications for the war in the north, too. Somalia itself, meanwhile, was increasingly isolated. Siad Barre had sought to win over the US to its cause, but the Americans were not interested; Mogadishu also desperately sought international recognition of its rights to the Ogaden, and had somewhat naive hopes of persuading the OAU in particular. But the OAU—headquartered in Addis Ababa, a clear disadvantage for the Somalis, as the Eritreans were also learning—was wholly unwilling to recognize Somali claims, and clung, with a doggedness born of terror, to the notion of the inviolability of colonial boundaries. It was a notion, of course, which was written into the OAU Charter in the year that the Somalis had last attempted to raise the issue of the Ogaden before the August assembly, in 1963.

The Somali position, politically and militarily, quickly collapsed. The Ethiopian re-conquest was launched in early 1978, with the army making such rapid headway that by March the Ogaden had been largely recaptured. The situation remained tense and highly volatile along the scarcely demarcated Somali–Ethiopian boundary.[25] Siad Barre had attempted to resolve, once and for all, the explosive question of identity and territory in the eastern Horn—a question which dated to at least the late nineteenth century, and which had escalated slowly but surely from the middle decades of the twentieth. Not only did he fail to resolve it, however—and it seems unlikely, in any case, that it could be resolved by force alone—but the 1977–8 war raised tensions even among the Somali themselves. Refugees fleeing into northern Somalia from the Ogaden brought with them clan loyalties which were hardly welcome among the Isaq of the north. Ogaden–Isaq rivalries had long been a feature of trans-Somali relations; and in the rush to fulfil the promise indicated by the five-pointed star of the Somali flag, extant tensions *within* the wider Somali community had been heightened substantially. The full implications of these tensions would become clear a little over a decade later. In the meantime, the Ethiopians continued to monitor the situation across the contested frontier, and were able to turn their attentions fully to the north, where they anticipated similar results. Addis Ababa and Mogadishu reverted to the more familiar pattern of supporting one another's dissidents and armed rebels on either side of the Ogaden frontier, a pattern only (in theory) ended by the peace accord signed between the two governments in early 1988. But the collapse of Somalia by the beginning of the 1990s only introduced new stresses into the contested zone.

Emerging markets of violence: ethnic and nationalist borderlands

Wars of nationalist independence and ethnic regionalism escalated dramatically in the course of the 1970s and 1980s. These wars were mainly in Eritrea and Tigray in the north, and among the Oromo in the south and centre; there was also a growing, if comparatively low-level, insurgency along the western frontier with Sudan and in the southern marches of Ethiopia, as well as political violence in the Ogaden which was part of a package of tensions with Somalia across the border. The liberationist violence of the 1980s was the historical Ethiopian state writ large: unable to control regionalism or to channel emerging nationalisms, or to prevent the political radicalization of the liberation movements themselves and swathes of the populations these purported to represent, the Ethiopia built by Menelik and Haile Selassie was being ripped apart.[26] While the patterns of violence stretched back to the eighteenth century, it was the centralizing brutality of the state of the late nineteenth and early twentieth centuries that had sown the seeds of the violence of the 1970s and 1980s. The *Derg*'s response was increasingly brutal, its uncompromising stance manifest in the targeting of entire civilian populations among which guerrillas moved. The Ethiopian security apparatus routinely arrested and 'disappeared' thousands of individuals suspected of activities sympathetic toward a range of nationalist guerrilla movements, or engaging in activities otherwise judged hostile to the state and its goals. Urban populations and rural communities alike were targeted. Mary Dines, one of the most assiduous chroniclers of war crimes in Eritrea, identified numerous attacks by the military on civilian targets: MiG fighters bombing the village of Dekidashim in August 1986, and then villages near the Barka province in November; villages set alight by Ethiopian soldiers near Keren in May and June 1986; the use of napalm on civilian targets.[27] In Eritrea, indeed, Mengistu and his lieutenants declared that they wanted 'the land, not the people'—the latter were expendable, indeed were actively loathed for the troubled and ambiguous landscape which they inhabited. In a variation on a theme, Mengistu was wont to utter that he would 'poison the sea to kill the fish'—that he would visit total war on the Eritrean population in order to rid Ethiopia of the despised *shifta*. It was a formula repeated across the Ethiopian empire in the 1980s, as jails and torture instruments were as important in the war against recalcitrant populations as AK-47s, tanks, rocket launchers, and Russian fighter-bombers. Ethiopian centralism, meanwhile, had ultimately rendered these conflicts unavoidable. The peoples' wars that represented the response on the part of the liberation movements became ever more sophisticated and articulate, and ever better organized. The northern frontier, in particular, would ultimately advance on Addis Ababa. This violence was attended by a political and a scholarly redefinition of the Ethiopian empire-state, both within and beyond the region itself; and while the ghosts of the past returned to haunt the body politic, the new 'marginal' struggles of persecuted minorities became ever more visible, and the frontiers of the nineteenth century closed in on the centre.

Across east and north-east Africa in this period, the state was under attack from increasingly well-armed guerrilla forces, representing what we might consider a 'new wave' of military intervention in African politics.[28] The latter aimed not simply at the capture of the extant system—as previous *coups d'etat* had done, for example—but often the complete destruction and radical remaking of that system, or at least this is what the rhetoric suggested. In this sphere, if in no other, the influences and irruptions of the Cold War were relevant, owing to the massive influx into the region of automatic weapons and a range of other equipment; the continent more broadly was swiftly awash with the ubiquitous AK-47. Such weaponry fuelled emerging markets of violence, and enabled a range of populist movements to challenge the state to much greater effect than previously. Marginalized and disaffected groups which in the 1950s and 1960s might resist the state using Second World War rifles had access in the 1970s and 1980s to machine guns and rocket launchers. The state-level monopoly on military might and the exercise of 'legitimate' violence—in place in Africa since the 1890s and jealously guarded by colonial and post-colonial governments alike—was gone. While there may be no direct correlation between the increase in access to modern firepower and the coalescence of individuals and communities into peoples' liberation fronts, there is little doubt that the latter—born of identities and grievances crystallizing in various ways since the nineteenth century—now sought to dominate increasingly lucrative (politically speaking) markets of violence for larger political ends. Therefore, guerrilla movements sought, first, the firepower necessary to challenge the extant order; second, the moral high ground, in terms of ideas about social revolution inspired by ideologies which were as important a part of these movements' armoury as guns themselves; and, third, political power itself.

These movements were organized in different ways, and motivated by a range of local factors and dynamics. Guerrilla themselves were ever more professional fighters, even if they did not always look it, and their commanders were increasingly skilled in the military arts, both defence and offence. Most organizations combined mobile guerrilla warfare, in which by the 1980s fighters were well-versed—the writings of Mao Zedong in particular were closely studied—with conventional pitched battle, although some, notably the EPLF, were rather keener on the latter than others. Most organizations made extensive use of auxiliary units and cells, notably 'civilian' militias and cells of organizers and intelligence agents in the towns and cities. Some were structured more explicitly than others in terms of ethno-national identity, such as those in Tigray and among the Oromo, or at least one ethnic group was dominant; others were overtly anti-colonial and nationalist, as in Eritrea. Others still were, or became, tactical alliances of an array of groups with a common goal. In terms of organization and ideological orientation, many evoked and developed Leftist doctrine and extolled the virtues of 'people's war', which it was claimed was necessary in order to accomplish true 'liberation', i.e. through popular social revolution. Guerrilla leaders, with varying degrees of sincerity and pragmatism, utilized Marxist rhetoric (and indeed Stalinist practice, in terms of internal control) in exhorting populations to revolt; certainly, they needed to mobilize and 'educate' the peasantry and win their support, for no guerrilla movement could survive, as Mao had asserted, without the sustenance of the people.

One dramatic manifestation of ethno-nationalism was among the Oromo population across southern and central Ethiopia. Various Oromo communities have historically had markedly diverse experiences in the course of their settlement in the area of present-day Ethiopia from the sixteenth century onward, and their interaction with a range of different hosts has likewise been complex. It is this very diversity and complexity which has led to questions being asked about the validity of the 'Oromo struggle', and it was certainly argued by the *Derg* that the whole concept of some kind of ethnic 'homeland' named Oromia was a nonsense.[29] Clearly, Oromo history is not straightforward—although few such large-scale migratory histories are. Part of the problem was the sheer geographical spread of the Oromo themselves, who therefore lacked the compact space within which struggle proceeded in Eritrea or Tigray. However, it is clear that, in the most overarching manner, the story in the twentieth century was of conquest, subordination, and marginalization. This in itself fuelled Oromo consciousness, as did the long history of racist derogation of the Oromo past and culture at the hands of the Amhara (and indeed Tigrinya) political establishment.[30] While an Oromo identity was certainly emerging in the 1950s, as was a low-level resentment of *habesha* domination, it was during the following decade that political consciousness became rather more radicalized, owing to an increase (ironically, no doubt) in educational opportunities for Oromo students, and the attendant increased entry of Oromo into the workforce.[31] Heightened levels of education exposed Oromo youth to both casual Amhara disdain toward them, and the means of redress—namely revolutionary nationalism—in much the same way that a host of students of other 'nationalities' were being radicalized in the same period. Increasingly aggressive 'Amharization' also had its effect, with the Oromo language sidelined, cultural and political institutions abolished or undermined, and history denigrated or simply ignored.[32] The fruits of the policy—in the form of a disillusioned and politically angry younger generation of Oromo—were clear by the 1960s. The 'new' Oromo nationalism first gained cogent expression through the Macha-Tulama Self-Help Association, founded in 1963–4 with a view to improving welfare for the Oromo population and in so doing mobilizing it.[33]

Following some initial optimism that the *Derg* would begin to address Oromo grievances, Oromo activists turned their fire on the new regime with the realization that, if anything, the Mengistu state would surpass the old regime in brutality. The Oromo armed struggle was galvanized by a newly aggressive approach toward the Oromo population. There was the massacre at Chercher in eastern Ethiopia in August 1974, which was carried out under the pretext of hunting down Oromo armed dissidents. A thousand soldiers backed up by a tank company entered the area and killed a local guerrilla leader and a number of women and children too. Then there was the murder of two prominent Oromo, Colonel Hailu Regassa and General Taddesse Birru, in early 1975, both men symbols of emergent Oromo nationalism. A further massacre of Oromo civilians by Ethiopian security forces took place in April 1976 in several provinces, including Kaffa, Illubabor, Arsi, Bale, and Hararge. The killing of several thousand peasant farmers was a signal of intent on the part of the new regime that—as in Eritrea—the state was prepared to take the war to the whole community, not simply a handful of armed dissidents. It was a style of war which was rooted in the nineteenth century. During the early part of the 1977–8 war with Somalia, Oromo farmers in Hararge were made the scapegoats for initial Ethiopian setbacks, while hundreds of thousands of Oromo were caught up in the villagization programme of the Mengistu government. The internal displacement of Oromo was on a massive scale, while swathes of Oromo land were in fact cleared to make way for northern settlers in the course of the 1980s. Urban Oromo suspected of the crime of 'narrow nationalism', meanwhile, were targeted by the security forces.[34] Altogether, as in Eritrea and Tigray, *Derg* strategies of control and containment merely served to further radicalize significant proportions of the Oromo population, and spurred recruitment into the OLF. While such abstract ideas as Oromo unity and a singular Oromo nationhood might invite debate, as they continue to, there could be little doubt about the commitment and passion of a newly persecuted generation of outraged activists, nor the violent brutality which had pushed it forward. In a sense, the Oromo struggle has been all the greater considering the widespread ignorance of their history and the hostility to their cause by those who argued for the cohesiveness and unity of Ethiopia—both within and outside Ethiopia itself[35]—and considering the relative lack, again, of a neatly bordered arena of action.[36] The notion of the borderland is less straightforward for the Oromo than for many other groups, owing to the ambiguity of the Oromo position in the Ethiopian socio-political order. While many Oromo did indeed inhabit the southern frontier zones, notably the Boran groups along the Ethiopian–Kenyan border,[37] a great many others, as we have seen earlier in this book, had become integrated into highland society and culture. This has proven singularly problematic for those who would espouse a unified Oromo 'nationalist' cause, no less than the difficulties facing those who had sought a singular, united Somali identity.

As for the OLF itself, success in the actual field of combat was limited—although, according to Asafa Jalata, its mere survival was a matter for celebration, given the challenges confronting it.[38] Initially confined to the eastern provinces, by the early 1980s the OLF had been divided into four commands, namely eastern, south-eastern, central, and western 'Oromia'.

Guerrillas operated in small units within those vast zones, and had some success—Eritrean- and Tigrayan-style—in setting up local, elected administrative councils in the 'controlled areas'. Also corresponding to the Eritrean and Tigrayan models, the guerrilla forces themselves were offered succour by the Oromo Relief Association, headquartered largely in Sudan, which was in the main concerned with the massive refugee problem.[39] But despite some limited successes, the OLF list of military accomplishments is not a lengthy one alongside those of the TPLF and EPLF—from whom the movement periodically received assistance, moral and material—and in part, no doubt, this reflects the fact that even for much of the 1980s Oromo nationalism was not a mass movement.[40] Arguably, the struggle to raise awareness and mobilize was necessarily given precedence over the armed struggle, which was somewhat more restricted as a result.

Tigray: revolution and renaissance

The lingering bitterness experienced in Tigray following the crushing of the 1943 revolt hardened during the 1950s and 1960s as the province suffered from political and economic marginalization. It gave rise to a process of radicalization which would culminate in the emergence of the TPLF in the mid-1970s. Tigrayan nationalists occupied a curious, traumatizing space in the Ethiopian body politic from the early twentieth century: Tigray was an ancient historical centre, and yet was now a periphery, neglected, abused, and even despised by both Amhara and the 'other Tigrinya' on the Eritrean side of the Mereb River. The heat of the issue is demonstrated by the writings of some early twentieth-century Ethiopian intellectuals, one of whom, Afework Gebreyesus, in his biography of Menelik, represented a certain element of Amhara opinion in heaping contempt on Tigray for their lawlessness and treachery at the time of Adwa. The Tigrayan writer Gebrehiwot Baykadan had responded by condemning the impoverishment of the province and the tragic migration of its people.[41] The debates were no mere academic trifle: they represented the very real tensions between Tigray and the Amhara-centric empire, tensions which would become ever more explosive as Haile Selassie's reign progressed. These shifts in marginality had a profound impact on local populations in real terms, as well as on aspirant new political elites—such as that evident in the Tigrayan student movement of the late 1960s and early 1970s, and subsequently in the leadership of the TPLF itself. The usurpation of Tigray's leadership of Ethiopia in 1889–90 by the Shoan Menelik was within living memory in the 1960s and 1970s, and clearly Yohannes IV—the last Tigrayan emperor—had iconic status even among the radicalized younger generation of Tigrayan nationalists.[42] Tigray had been of crucial importance throughout the nineteenth century; in the twentieth, it represented the classic fertile frontier, producing in time a level of restorative militant violence which was quite distinct from that further north in Eritrea, or among the Somali or Oromo further south.

At the same time, Tigrayan nationalism emerged against the backdrop of—and indeed was in many ways closely linked to—another socio-economic frontier, namely the migration of Tigrayans out of the province in search of both work and education. The increasing poverty and neglect of Tigray—both urban and rural—had compelled the brightest students to travel to either Asmara University for their higher education, or southward to Addis Ababa, to Haile Selassie I University. The political radicalism of the student body in the latter campus is well-known; but Asmara University, too, was something of a seedbed for Tigrayan student activism in the late 1960s and early 1970s, and would be instrumental in the formation of the early nationalist movement.[43] Meanwhile, poor rural Tigrayans travelled increasingly to Eritrea to find work, and a Tigrayan labouring class became a key feature of the mid-twentieth century Eritrean economy, just as an Eritrean merchant class became a highly visible aspect of the urban socio-economy of Addis Ababa in the same period. In Eritrea, these Tigrayans acquired a reputation for thrift—money earned was sent back to villages in Tigray—and in time for uncouthness and ignorance, as immigrant labourers usually do. Eritreans came to regard them with contempt, and to haughtily describe them as *Agame*—a reference to the impoverished eastern district of Tigray from whence many (though by no means all) of the immigrants hailed. Many also travelled to Addis Ababa.[44] What may have begun as a joking relationship was an increasing affront to Tigrayan sensibilities. Tigrayans believed—with some justification, it must be said—that Eritreans looked down on them, even despised them, and regarded themselves as vastly superior in every respect. It would come to the surface as the rivalry between the EPLF and the TPLF developed in intensity—and would return to haunt both communities with renewed war in 1998.

Almost everyone in north-east Africa in this period was always fighting more than one war. The intensity of the rivalry between various movements and organizations, the continual ideological positioning and repositioning, the need for vigilance against the shifting agendas of neighbouring guerrilla movements and distant states alike, meant that each political community was compelled to fight on several fronts simultaneously. Tigray was certainly caught between two fierce militancies—namely, the most immediate enemy to the south in the form of the *Derg*, and the less overt but no less natural antagonist in the form of the Eritrean nationalist movement to the north. The challenge facing the Tigrayan nationalist front, broadly defined, was to manage these surrounding threats and simultaneously to bring about the social revolution headed, crucially, by the revolutionary party, that would facilitate Tigray's political resurgence. This sense of betrayal, marginalization, and righteous, militant anger was no less keen in Tigray than it was in Eritrea, although there were indeed significant differences between the two in provenance and articulation; and those seeking the roots of the present-day political *impasse* in Ethiopia, engendered by a recalcitrant TPLF ruling class, might do no better than to appreciate the position of Tigray in the early 1970s and the effort required to right perceived historic wrongs.

The TPLF was founded in February 1975 in western Tigray, in a barren lowland borderland with, appropriately, a tradition of *shiftanet*.[45] It quickly developed a political programme, and sent recruits for training to the EPLF, from whom it drew inspiration and support in its early years—although only after it accepted the Eritrean case for secession. Even so relations with the Eritrean fronts were strained from the outset, as we see in greater detail below, not least because of the support given to the TPLF's early, and initially rather more powerful, rivals: the Marxist EPRP, which was the key movement for revolutionary change in Ethiopia and particularly prominent in eastern Tigray, received support from the EPLF in the late 1970s, while the EDU, dominant in western Tigray, was favoured by the ELF. The political environment was a dangerous one, as it was in Eritrea; the early TPLF was ill-equipped, badly trained, and vulnerable to the predations of its better-supplied and more prominent rivals. Its fighters were repeatedly worsted in pitched battle with the Ethiopian army and the EPRP and EDU alike. Yet it learnt quickly from its mistakes, and assiduously cultivated peasant support. It also benefited, in time, from the weaknesses and failings of the EPRP and EDU. The TPLF programme of land reform contrasted favourably with that of the EDU, which was led by the Tigrayan nobility; while its espousal of Tigrayan nationalism was highly popular, the EDU suffered from organization problems and by the beginning of the 1980s it was largely

sidelined, inhabiting the borderlands outside Gondar. The EPRP, too, suffered from divisions within the leadership, while the TPLF was again able to
outflank the EPRP in mobilizing the peasantry, and benefited from *Derg*
alienation of the priesthood, with many parish clergy becoming TPLF sym-
pathizers and activists. Increasingly confident militarily, the TPLF inflicted
serious defeats on the EPRP which was soon dispatched out of Tigray and,
effectively, out of the contest to dominant resistance to the *Derg*. Some elements later returned to participate in the EPRDF coalition.

Thus the TPLF grew up in a tough neighbourhood, and grew in stature
as a result.[46] The movement tapped into both Tigrayan nationalist sensibilities, and the need for social reform, especially in the realm of land
tenure. As in Eritrea, *Derg* policy fuelled sympathy for and recruitment
into the TPLF: increasing levels of taxation, the purchase of food at less
than market prices, and the forced resettlement of thousands of peasants
to the south (many were seized during the 1984-5 famine when they
came to feeding centres for help) all served to alienate Tigray from the
regime in the course of the 1980s and strengthen the TPLF's hand. The
Relief Society of Tigray (REST) was the movement's wing for humanitarian assistance and development; and in the early 1980s, recruitment into
the TPLF increased sharply from among the peasantry. Indeed, during the
1984 famine, the TPLF was able to project itself onto a global stage, and it
won significant attention for the first time. In terms of political organization, the movement was arguably even more successful than the EPLF in
preventing the emergence of a personality cult by revolving the chair-
manship between two early leaders, Aregowie Berhe and Sebhat Nega; a
third key leader from the outset was Meles Zenawi. Collective decision
making was encouraged, although like the EPLF an elite party at the core
of the movement—the Marxist-Leninist League of Tigray—enhanced the
authoritarian centre and sought to ensure the ideological purity of the
movement. Nonetheless, it was pragmatic, and would later discard its
Marxist programme in favour of a markedly more liberal-capitalist manifesto; in a similar vein, early on it had moved away from expounding
Tigrayan secession to regarding itself as in the vanguard in the wider
Ethiopian struggle for democratic unity. But the TPLF's policy positions
frequently brought it into sharp conflict with the EPLF.

By the late 1980s, the TPLF was a well-organized, battle-hardened
organization with mass support and a clear sense of political direction.[47]
In the course of 1988-9, it launched a series of new offensives across

Tigray—at Adwa, Axum, Endaselassie, Shire—against a backdrop of some horrendous civilian casualties as the *Derg* brought its airpower to bear on the province.[48] But the momentum was now with the liberation forces, and a unity agreement with the EPLF greatly enhanced their combined military capacity in the north. In early 1989, the *Derg* forces in Tigray were all but crushed, precipitating an abortive *coup* against Mengistu by several of his senior commanders, but also raising a new problem in terms of the prosecution of the war. Several thousand TPLF soldiers now returned to their homes, believing that with the liberation of Tigray the job was done, and unconvinced as to the need to carry the war further south. The EPLF strongly disapproved, and so too did the TPLF leadership, which now argued that only the total destruction of the *Derg* and the liberation of all of Ethiopia (and Eritrea) would bring lasting peace and security to Tigray itself.

In early 1991, the newly-formed EPRDF forces—including the TPLF, the OLF, and some smaller groupings, and assisted by mechanized units from the EPLF—launched the somewhat self-consciously and ironically named 'Operation Tewodros' which cleared Gojjam and Gondar of *Derg* forces. Although there had been some confusion in the respective Eritrean and Tigrayan ranks as to the kind of war this had now become—namely, the drive for the absolute destruction of the *Derg* and/or its unconditional surrender—the final grand operation was an indication of how far the process of military maturation had come as far as the EPLF, the TPLF and their various allies were concerned. This was now full-fledged conventional war, with head-on pitched battles against Ethiopian forces and mopping-up exercises in the rear. As the *Derg* retreated, civilian casualties continued to mount, for as ever non-combatants were caught up in a war which was now spread across a broad front; but as the 1980s drew to a close and the 1990s dawned, in some areas at least there was something approaching a respite for the broader population, for as the *Derg* collapsed, the war swept on into the Ethiopian heartlands, leaving exhausted communities in the north to enjoy a brief peace and ponder the uncertainties of the future. Meanwhile, the advance on Addis Ababa continued, and as it did, the TPLF finally abandoned its Marxist-Leninist rhetoric for the language of liberal democracy altogether more comforting to the US, now watching events with close interest. Meles Zenawi, who was now the future, was courted by the US as Mengistu prepared to flee, which he did on 21 May; a week later, the EPRDF and the EPLF entered Addis Ababa.

Eritrean epicentre

The Eritrean frontier was the epicentre for much of the violent conflict across the region, fundamentally destabilizing the Ethiopian edifice in the late twentieth century. The Eritrean region had been, in one way or another, the crucial borderland zone since the early nineteenth century; now, the armed liberation movement to which the frontier had given birth both led the way in terms of ideology, nature of the struggle and organization—many movements would model themselves on, or take inspiration from, the EPLF, ultimately—and reached out beyond the Eritrean mountains into others' struggles, into Tigray and across southern and eastern Ethiopia, and into the Ethiopian–Sudanese borderlands. The EPLF saw its war as anti-colonial, defining Eritrea in terms of its colonial boundaries (a matter not quite as straightforward as it was evidently believed to be, as future events would show), and claiming for the territory a distinctive history.[49] While the movement looked and talked like an Eritrean nationalist organization, the EPLF was also a manifestation of specifically Tigrinya militancy, and the remarkable expression of a radicalized Tigrinya identity—notwithstanding the fact that several other groups, including the Tigre and Saho, had a presence within the organization. Nonetheless the Tigrinya claimed to speak for the whole territory and laid out a very clear nationalist position. Such separatism could never be quite as unambiguous in Tigray, but the TPLF also toyed with Tigrayan separateness from Ethiopia, representing a new militant but awkwardly positioned nationalism. Even so, the TPLF could appeal to a much deeper sense of Tigrinya/Tigrayan identity than was possible in Eritrea, and it is certainly the case that those differing visions—essentially an intra-Tigrinya contest—were the source of major tensions between the two movements from the outset. The EPLF and the TPLF had a troubled relationship which would spill out beyond the immediate region, and beyond the 1980s; ultimately, the EPLF went its nationalist way and the TPLF positioned the destiny of Tigray in an Ethiopian context. It would need to do so in conjunction with a number of other movements. But in fact it was the EPLF which would take on the role of regional revolutionary vanguard, attempting to shape others' agendas and control the region-wide struggle.

It was at the Eritrean epicentre, moreover, that the violent contradictions of the modern Ethiopian state were most clearly exposed: debates about nationalism and nationhood, ethnicity and belonging, the past and the future, were cacophonous and virulent in the Eritrean context, and have continued to resonate. The contradictions would be inherited by the independent Eritrean state. It was, and is, the frontier society writ large, with all its implications for political and military culture, social cohesion, and individual rights and obligations. In such an environment it was not possible for cooperation between movements to ever be more than short term and purely functional; and in this respect two broad themes are important to note. The first is that whatever 'liberal' political culture there had briefly been in the late 1940s and early 1950s in Eritrea—or more precisely, Asmara—was dead within twenty years, and has yet to be revived. By c.1970, political culture in Eritrea was mercantilist and exclusive, and increasingly violently so; antagonisms were between organizations and individuals, and were both ideological and personal. Increasingly, it was a political culture characterized by simultaneous and successive attempts to monopolize 'truth', and while the purest of the goals espoused by Eritrean nationalists of various hues—the creation of a free, coherent, pluralistic nationhood—might be laudable, the struggle would accrue such cost that some might wonder whether the fight had, after all, been worth it. Certainly, the violence necessary to seize control of the frontier and reconfigure the centre was ultimately inimical to the achievement of those other goals—popular participation in politics, social justice, basic liberties—in pursuit of which so many lent their labour to the struggle in the 1970s and 1980s. The second theme is the lack of capacity for genuine, long-term collaboration and partnership between the EPLF and the TPLF. From the early 1960s onward, the respective nationalisms of Eritrea and Tigray were fundamentally on a collision course with one another; the forms they would ultimately take rendered a deep-rooted alliance not simply impossible, but actually inherently contradictory *vis-à-vis* Eritrean aims. The best that could be hoped for—and for a time it was achieved—was arm's-length, tactical, short-term cooperation in pursuit of the defeat of the common enemy, without the removal of whom neither Eritrea's nor Tigray's aspirations could be realized. This is true even taking into account early EPLF nurturing of the TPLF—in any case held by Tigrayan leaders to have been grossly exaggerated by the former. For a time, too, that cooperation appeared to offer some genuine hope, for it accomplished a cease-fire in the long frontier war, between 1991 and 1998; but war did indeed resume, and the question should not be—as it often has been—*why did the two countries go to war?*, but rather *why did they not go to war sooner?*

The 1970s was the decade in which the Eritrean liberation movement came close to tearing itself apart, and certainly the territory witnessed a civil war—as well as a pronounced degree of brutality within the movements themselves—which remains a dark basement in the political structure of independence.[50] It has certainly had serious implications for plurality and inclusivity in independent Eritrea. Nonetheless, given the frictions of the 1940s and 1950s, it was entirely predictable that the ELF would fragment. With its roots in the *shifta* tradition of the Muslim western lowlands, and in the pan-Arab oriented and largely aristocratic leadership in exile, the ELF faced challenges from within, and fissures soon opened up between lowland and highland; but these were rather less to do with Muslim-Christian tensions—even if these were important at times—than with the distinct historical experiences of *metahit* and *kebessa*, regions which in some respects were fighting rather different wars for much of the 1970s and 1980s.[51] These were frontiers within the frontier, and although, for example, Nara and Tigrinya might at length find common cause against the Ethiopian enemy, their local visions of the violent frontier were informed by very distinct historical experience. Fragmentation was also about the very nature of the 'revolution'—as it often is—and was brought about by new recruits imbued with the Marxist-Leninist leanings of the age confronting what they saw as the reactionary or counter-revolutionary leadership and agenda of the ELF. In a sense, the struggles within the Eritrean nationalist movement, culminating in the hegemony of the EPLF, thus represented the early *Derg* in miniature.

The EPLF was essentially the product of the coming together of two splinter groups which had broken away from the ELF in 1970.[52] The first was largely Muslim from the Massawa area but also comprised some Christians, and gathered in the Danakil where the dissident ELF leader Othman Saleh Sabbe arranged for them to be supplied with weaponry; the group became known as the Popular Liberation Forces (PLF). The second group was Christian Tigrinya, and fled from the ELF following the killing of some Christians by an ELF commander. Gathering at Ala in Akele Guzay province—it was known as the 'Ala Group'—this small band was centred on the young Isaias Afeworki, and in its statement, *Our Struggle and its Goals*, it accused the ELF of Islamic sectarianism and failure to develop revolutionary leadership. Between 1970 and 1972, Ala Group and the PLF conducted negotiations and slowly integrated; it was a process of unification which culminated in a joint plan of action in October 1972, and the following year in the creation of an integrated fighting force. For a time the 'Obel Group' of some Beni Amer fighters was also involved, but they later withdrew. The fractious and violent political environment within which the EPLF was born is crucial to understanding its subsequent development, ethos, and nature. Even regardless of the Ethiopian military, the movement was immediately confronted with the external threat of the ELF, and by internal dissent. Civil war between the dissident movements and the ELF had erupted by 1972, and continued sporadically throughout the 1970s, notwithstanding a period of quasi-reconciliation in the mid-1970s.[53] Most of the clashes between the ELF and the EPLF took place in the mountainous Sahel region in the north of Eritrea, and took various forms, from minor skirmishes between small bands of fighters, to rather longer, pitched battles over several days, in which fighters dug trenches and exchanged prolonged fire. Civil war can be considered to have ceased by 1981, when an increasingly powerful EPLF finally succeeded in expelling the ELF from the field of combat, into Sudan; thereafter, it became a beacon of opposition to EPLF hegemony, both among the Eritrean refugee community in Sudan and among the portions of the Eritrean diaspora in Europe and North America, although the ELF itself would continue to splinter and reform in the years that followed. The eventual triumph of the EPLF in the internecine struggle has come to be understood by many—certainly many within Eritrea itself—as somehow inevitable, as Eritrea's unassailable destiny; it was not, for the ELF continued to recruit even from among Tigrinya highlanders throughout the 1970s, and the movement subjected itself to a fair amount of self-criticism and consequently underwent significant internal reform. Clearly, however, the EPLF was both politically and military more efficient—clinically so, indeed— more disciplined, and ultimately more successful in terms of recruitment, dissemination of propaganda, and social programmes. Nonetheless the Eritrean civil war was a conflict that ripped communities apart and undoubtedly set the independence struggle itself back several years; the experience of Eritrean killing Eritrean, moreover, an apparently bloodier sequel to the violent divisions of the 1940s, confirmed the EPLF leadership in its belief that absolute loyalty and commitment to a single political line was necessary to the successful pursuit of sovereignty. The movement would kill to achieve it; only through killing, and through the application of the severest discipline, could the volatile frontier be brought under control. The experience of the civil war further contributed to the idea that open debate was ultimately a fruitless distraction, and that disagreement or divergence in opinion was tantamount to betrayal, a tendency that has persisted in Eritrean political culture to the present day.

If conflict with the ELF persuaded the EPLF leadership of the need to take Eritrea by force, likewise the internal crisis in 1973 convinced it of the need for brutal discipline. A dissident group comprising a number of new recruits, nicknamed *manqa* or 'bat' as it convened at night, emerged to criticize the leadership for what it perceived as worryingly authoritarian tendencies, as well as flaws in military strategy and organization more broadly.[54] Isaias Afeworki himself was singled out for particular criticism. The leadership moved decisively against its critics, with a number of people summarily executed and others forced to publicly recant. The *manqa* crisis, like the experience of civil war, was a formative episode in the EPLF's development: thereafter, debate was strictly controlled, and while it might occasionally be initiated by the leadership itself, fighters were otherwise expected to obey unquestioningly the decisions emanating from the central committee. By the time of the First Congress in 1977, the structure and ethos of the EPLF was largely in place, although political maturation was to attend the withdrawal of the movement to its rear base in Sahel for much of the 1980s.

While the overthrow of the imperial regime in September 1974 gave pause for thought—as it did among Oromo nationalists—it was swiftly clear that the *Derg* was no more disposed toward a negotiated solution to the Eritrean question than was Haile Selassie. Any hopes that Aman Andom might have achieved a settlement were quickly dashed; his brief attempt at winning hearts and minds in Asmara was followed by the violent retrenchment of the Mengistu regime.[55] It is perhaps an open question whether the Eritrean fronts would indeed have negotiated with Addis Ababa had they been given the opportunity to do so; in any event, for Mengistu it was beyond question. Yet in the mid-1970s the EPLF was more concerned with the ELF than with the Ethiopian threat *per se*; political disarray at the centre weakened the Ethiopian army, while the Somali invasion of the Ogaden in 1977 was a further boon to the liberation fronts. By the end of 1974, an armistice between the ELF and the EPLF was followed by a series of attacks on Asmara, and between them the two fronts controlled up to ninety per cent of Eritrean territory, with the Ethiopian army beleaguered in the major towns. The Ethiopian response was fierce, targeting Asmara, rounding up civilians, and instigating something of a reign of terror in those parts of Eritrea which it could still reach;[56] Ethiopian security forces routinely carried out extra-legal executions in order to instil fear in urban and rural communities alike; thousands languished in prison, where torture was common and where women were exposed to the additional torment of sexual assault.[57] *Derg* policy drove recruits into the ranks of both fronts, while military successes involved the capture of equipment from the Ethiopians— arguably, captured ammunition, guns, and tanks constituted the EPLF's single most important supply of hardware throughout its struggle. The balance of military power shifted in 1977–8, however, and the period proved debatably the most decisive in the history of the Eritrean armed struggle— both in the prolongation of the war itself, and in the political implications.[58] Having defeated Somalia, and now receiving massive military assistance from the Soviet Union, the Ethiopian army turned its full and replenished attention to the north, launching a series of offensives which threatened to extinguish the nationalist movement altogether.

Inspired by Maoist teaching and recent Vietnamese experience in the arts of prolonged liberation struggle, the EPLF put into action its long-planned strategy of staged retreat to the rear base in Sahel.[59] In what became known as the 'strategic withdrawal', the EPLF pulled out of its positions across the territory and converged on the mountainous Nakfa area in the north.[60] It was a watershed: militarily, the movement survived, and consolidated; politically, it enabled the EPLF to refine its organization and further develop its visions and programme for government. While many at the time began to write the movement off, in fact the struggle had entered a new phase; what marred an otherwise brilliant military manoeuvre was a new outbreak of fighting with the ELF at the end of the 1970s and early 1980s which resulted in the expulsion of the latter into Sudan. In the Nakfa area, the EPLF constructed an elaborate and impregnable defensive structure, and withstood repeated Ethiopian assaults.[61]

The EPLF was a remarkable organization, certainly among the most remarkable movements for popular liberation anywhere in the world since the Second World War.[62] It prided itself on its revolutionary progressiveness, its self-sufficiency, and its highly disciplined membership; it stood for the unity in diversity of the various Eritrean peoples and cultures, and argued— relatively simply—that the Eritrean nation, forged through the bitter experience of colonial rule (Italian, British, and Ethiopian), must wage an anti-colonial war against Ethiopian occupation which was illegal and historically unjustified. It was an argument, of course, which was summarily and violently rejected by the *Derg*, which dismissed the northern rebels— often lumping the TPLF in with the EPLF, much to the chagrin of the former—as mere bandits without a cause, or as bankrupt secessionists.[63] But even as the Mengistu state poured contempt on the very notion of Eritrean secession, it was proving singularly difficult—and by the mid-1980s impossible—to defeat the movement. Again, its major source of weaponry was *materiel* seized from the Ethiopians themselves, although in their early period the movement was supported by the People's Democratic Republic of Yemen; subsequently, however, the movement made much of its independence, and certainly from its entrenched position in Sahel it was free of reliance on a host state. The EPLF's strength lay in several key areas. Vigorous recruitment programmes from the early and mid-1970s made the EPLF a serious fighting force, notwithstanding the vast numerical supremacy confronting it: estimates of frontline fighters through the late 1970s and early 1980s ranged between 30,000 and 50,000, but certainly by the eve of liberation in 1991 there were some 100,000 men and women under arms. Ruthless authoritarian leadership was scarcely challenged after the 1973 crisis, and an unquestionably highly gifted group of people remained at the helm of the movement politically and military until the achievement of independence.

The EPLF instigated ambitious and generally successful health and education programmes in the liberated rural areas, and in the rear base around Nakfa.[64] The movement campaigned for political awareness—itself of limited scope, as events would prove—but more importantly for literacy and rural development, for women's rights and land reform. The rear base itself was a striking achievement, comprising an underground world—hidden from the daily predations of Ethiopian fighter bombers—of hospitals, schools, and factories. A new generation was born and raised in the Sahel rear base—the 'Zero School' children—who were either orphans or the offspring of fighters. It was a veritable revolution in the mountains, and one which subsequent mythologizing should not diminish. Cults of personality were avoided—although everyone knew who was who—and much was made of egalitarianism within the movement, and of relationships between fighters based on respect and total loyalty. Meanwhile, the Eritrean Relief Association (ERA) channelled aid to refugees and the rural poor, and became a vibrant and impressive agency for humanitarian assistance; it was especially important when Eritrea was struck by the famine of 1984-5.[65] The EPLF was also adept at mobilizing the considerable Eritrean population abroad, raising funds and awareness, and contributing to the diplomatic lobby in Europe and North America. Although, increasingly, the ranks of Eritrean fighters in the actual field of combat would come to regard themselves as something of a distinct, exclusive class—fiercely proud of a bond forged in mortal danger—it is doubtful that the struggle would have succeeded in quite the way it did without the efforts of the Eritrean diaspora.[66]

Above all, the EPLF was a state in waiting, and a remarkably tightly run, disciplinarian state at that.[67] The strategic withdrawal, necessitated by a wave of new Soviet-backed Ethiopian offensives, arguably prolonged the armed struggle by a decade; but it also facilitated the creation of the EPLF's model society around Nakfa, and enabled the movement to prepare, in effect, for government—things would have been rather more chaotic, bloody, and perhaps liberal had victory been achieved in the late 1970s. As it was, the 1980s witnessed the EPLF honing its political structure, eliminating its enemies, and preparing to administer the Eritrean people: the political machine built in Nakfa would then be transposed onto Asmara and Eritrean society at large. The First Congress of the EPLF in 1977 had witnessed the completion of the unification process—Ramadan Muhammad Nur and Isaias Afeworki were the key figures—as well as the publication of the Front's first 'national democratic programme';[68] in the years that followed, the movement's structure was further developed. It comprised, in summary, a clandestine party—the Eritrean People's Revolutionary Party (EPRP), which sat, concealed, at the centre of the movement, and whose existence was unknown to the vast majority of fighters—the political cadres, and the security apparatus. The Revolutionary Party developed strategy, disseminated policy from the leadership downward, and monitored the movement as a whole; its activities were obscured from view until relatively recently.[69] The cadres were highly trained activists, deployed throughout the movement as commissars, organizers, and political education officers; the cadres were responsible for the obligatory programmes of political 'awareness' through which all Eritreans who became involved with the Front were passed. Internal security was concerned with internal and external threats: in terms of the latter, it was concerned with the Ethiopians and the ELF, but in terms of the former it maintained strict discipline within the Front and essentially functioned as a military police force. In addition to these core elements, there were popular organizations of women, workers, and students, rural militias, secret urban cells in the major towns and cities, and elected committees in the liberated areas.[70]

In the meantime, however, the Front's other major conflict—and one which would have long-term consequences—was with the TPLF across the border. I have argued elsewhere that the disputes between the two movements in the late 1970s and sporadically through the 1980s sowed the seeds for future violence;[71] here, suffice to say that the multiple disagreements were both old and new, and represented a series of political tremors which presaged a catastrophic tectonic event which continues to destabilize the wider region. Arguably the single most remarkable aspect of this story is the degree to which it was overlooked in the literature for much of the 1980s and 1990s.[72] Even seasoned observers of either movement apparently failed to pick it up, or if they did, regarded it as fairly unimportant.[73] After the outbreak of war in 1998, naturally enough, there was a rush to press of various analyses highlighting one or other of a series of 'causes' and dynamics. Some began to 'notice' the strained relations between the EPLF and the TPLF during the armed struggle itself, and more generally the history of tensions—as well as intimacy—which characterized Tigray–Tigrinya cross-border relations.[74] Others began to 'remember' those tensions rather more clearly, both publicly and privately, and to recall incidents which now took on the characteristics of portents.[75] This was not merely a matter of journalistic and scholarly oversight; it is in fact part of the story, for the ability of the two fronts to suppress their deep-rooted conflicts from the late 1980s onward was remarkable, as was the apparent pact of forgetting which was as important to the stability of Eritrea (and of course Ethiopia) in the early 1990s as was silence over the civil war with the ELF. In a very real sense, the drama of the two fronts' respective triumphs in 1991 served—for a time—to conceal *both* the true nature of the bloody civil wars which defined their formative years, *and* the deep-seated conflicts between them once they were hegemonic in their respective fields of combat.

The violent instability of the northern frontier zone, dating back to the nineteenth century, would serve ultimately to produce militarized cultures and identities, the 'modern' manifestation of which was the EPLF and the TPLF. Violence, in sum, had become customary within political organizations seeking to inherit power across the region, in terms of both 'internal' affairs—the treatment of dissidence, notably, and the ordering of society—and 'external' matters, in dealing with outside threats, whether real or imagined. A robust, muscular approach to issues of import had become characteristic of the region's political culture, which itself had long been shaped by force of arms. Broader populations, too, became, if not impervious to, then certainly intimately familiar with, violence as an indelible aspect of public life and therefore in some senses tolerated and accepted it to a marked degree. Nor was this merely a matter of violence or the threat of it as a top–down imposition: wider communities had long been willing to be galvanized into supporting and participating in violence against enemies old and new, and, again, both real and imagined. Violent conflict, in other words, had long become part and parcel of public political discourse, the most natural part of basic human relations. This, therefore, is the broader psychosocial and cultural context within which intense inter-organizational and inter-community (and later international) violence in the Horn of Africa in the later twentieth century must be understood.

But there was also a range of rather more novel dynamics which settled on top of earlier layers of issues, converting the latter into the kind of human fossil fuels which would continue to drive forward conflict as well as political and cultural creativity. Broadly, we are concerned with the themes of *identity* and *territory*. The EPLF did provide the early TPLF with military assistance, but this has perhaps been exaggerated by the former and downplayed by the latter.[76] More important was the issue of the TPLF's objectives—and its definition of 'Tigray'. Initially, the movement appeared to lean toward a secessionist stance, which would involve the creation of a 'people's republic of Tigray'—later a source of some embarrassment—and in 1975 it defined a Tigrayan as anyone who spoke Tigrinya, as well as such border communities as the Irob and Afar.[77] At the same time, however, it claimed to support the Eritrean case, and prided itself on having changed the 'negative mindset' of the Tigrayan people toward the Eritrean question.[78] This glaring ambiguity notwithstanding, it is clear that the EPLF leadership regarded with suspicion the TPLF's definition of 'Tigrayan', incorporating as it did the highlands of Eritrea; it expressed concern over this aggressive new form of Tigrayan nationalism with its reliance on such alien (to Eritreans) historical reference points as Yohannes IV and *Ras* Alula. The EPLF position had been that the TPLF must abandon talk of an independent Tigray, and fight for a democratic, multi-national Ethiopia. The EPLF argued, in essence, that Tigray had always been part of the 'Ethiopian empire', dismissing the idea of an independent Tigrayan nationhood as economically, socially, and historically ungrounded.[79] In an apparent rebuttal, the TPLF had declared that theirs (Tigray's) was a truly 'national' struggle, as all peoples within the territory were Tigrayan, but that that of the EPLF was multi-national—for there were many nationalities in Eritrea, and the EPLF should cooperate with other liberation movements within Eritrea.[80]

Ultimately, the various nationalities of Eritrea—which was, after all, a wholly artificial colonial creation—should have the right of secession.

The EPLF found this hypocritical and provocative. The EPLF position was that while the right of secession might be granted to oppressed groups, democratic unity would effectively remove the need for secession; the EPLF was determined to put paid to any notion of Eritrean disunity, and to place clear ideological distance between their struggle and that of Tigray, which again should proceed in the pan-Ethiopian context. The Tigrayan leadership saw this as a violation of the fundamental right of peoples to self-determination.[81] In sum, the TPLF was, at the very least, raising questions about the very legitimacy of the Eritrean struggle, as defined and led by the EPLF; the EPLF was dismissive of Tigrayan nationalism, and was only prepared to support the TPLF struggle should they become part of the larger war for Ethiopian democratic unity. Each side was telling the other to do much the same thing, and each resented it. Of course, the TPLF did soon abandon its secessionist position and widen its vision to the liberation of Ethiopia; but tensions over the nationality and identity questions remained, while the perceived arrogance and aloofness of the EPLF merely further offended Tigrayan sensibilities and fuelled resentment toward their would-be partners north of the Mereb. The close linguistic and cultural—and, often, even familial—links between the two Tigrinya communities notwithstanding, there were sharp differences on either side of the Mereb.

Some of these more recent differences were manifest in border disputes, which can be dated to at least the mid-1970s. Early instances include the claim by the ELF—then dominant in the west and south-west of Eritrea—that the region up to Sheraro in lowland north-west Tigray was part of Eritrea, with armed clashes with the TPLF breaking out in the Adiabo area in 1976.[82] Nevertheless the TPLF—then weak—'permitted' the ELF to establish militias in the area and administer it for the time being, recognizing that there were many 'Eritreans' in the region, itself a significant problem when it came to aligning boundary with nationality.[83] With the destruction of the ELF by 1981, the TPLF brought much of the disputed region back under its control, but in the early 1980s the question of borders was once more high on the agenda—at least on the agenda of the TPLF, for the Eritreans were apparently rather less interested in the issue, again much to the annoyance of the TPLF. At the core of the issue, it seems, was the TPLF's desire for Tigray's borders to be fully demarcated, which the EPLF interpreted as Tigrayan territorial expansionism. In the mid-1980s, the EPLF issued a statement:

> In the period between 1979 and 1983, at different times the TPLF had caused many serious problems and tensions on the question of boundaries. The EPLF stated then that it was not the right time to raise such questions and that the colonial boundary was clear. However, the TPLF [continued to raise] the boundary issue by claiming the territory of the district of Badme, in the centre Tsorona, and in the south Bada, while the TPLF inhibited the EPLF's movement in and administration of those areas. Moreover, the TPLF [claimed that] Tigray had an outlet to the outside world through Dankalia.[84]

The TPLF felt that clarification and demarcation was indeed needed, not least as they felt that Tigrayan territory had been eroded during the reigns of both Menelik and Haile Selassie. The Eritreans were dismissive: 'Eritrea's legal boundary', they declared, 'is its colonial boundary', and there could be no talk of 'any other fabricated boundary'.[85]

Frustrated, the TPLF shelved the issue, and indicated that 'such problems can be solved in the spirit of negotiation', but warned that

> [t]his does not mean that there is no need for negotiation concerning the Eritrean–Ethiopian boundary...The TPLF's viewpoint is that Eritrea as a nation was created during Italian colonial rule. Therefore, by official agreement between the Ethiopian king Menelik II and the Italian government, the boundary between Eritrea and Ethiopia was clearly demarcated...However, we cannot say that there will be no problems in implementing this Agreement between Menelik II and the Italian government, because (1) for instance, some places are clearly demarcated on the map but not clearly demarcated on the ground, and (2) moreover, in the agreement...some places are recognized as belonging to either Eritrea or Ethiopia, but again the area may not be found in the respective country as it is stated in the agreement.[86]

The EPLF's silence on questions which the Tigrayans considered of vital importance was taken as further evidence of Eritrean arrogance, and ultimately of the EPLF refusal to treat the TPLF as an equal.[87] What is certainly clear from the exchanges between the late 1970s and early 1980s is that both sides were very well aware of the serious problems over border demarcation. That nothing was done is an indictment of both sets of leaders.

There were other problems, too, of course; again, we have already noted the somewhat less tangible issue of Tigrayan sensitivity toward a perceived Eritrean sense of superiority and hubris—which certainly could not have been more clearly manifest than it was in the leadership of the EPLF.

Tigrayans, maligned and marginalized, had much to be righteously indignant about; the nationalism of the TPLF tapped into that wellspring of
resentment, and when they looked north they perceived a movement that
had disengaged from their immediate environment with a haughty brutality
which quietly angered many in the TPLF. The EPLF, of course, had its own
worries, and distrusted the Tigrayan front, its programme and (initially, at
least) its military weakness. Famously, moreover, the EPLF cut the TPLF's
supply link through Eritrea to Kassala in Sudan at the height of their disagreements; the TPLF responded by organizing 100,000 peasants in the construction of a new route linking western Tigray to Gedaref. The episode
would leave a lasting bitterness. The movements also disagreed over military
strategy. The TPLF prided itself on fighting a genuine 'people's war', operating within the peasant communities whose liberation they sought, while
the EPLF—especially following the withdrawal to Sahel at the end of the
1970s—was accused of fighting a conventional, 'bourgeois' military campaign, distant from 'the people'. (Nonetheless, the TPLF did commit several
brigades to the EPLF's defence of Sahel in the early 1980s, contributing to
the thwarting of the Red Star campaign.) Between 1985 and 1988 there was
a more or less total break in relations between the two fronts;[88] but in 1988
tactical cooperation resumed, with both sides displaying their pragmatism in
the face of a faltering regime. Successes for the EPLF at Afabet in March
1988, and at Shire for the TPLF in February 1989, cleared the way, effectively, for a final joint push toward Addis Ababa. But the problems which
had dogged relations between the two movements over the preceding decade were not forgotten, merely set aside, and close to hand.

Politically, the EPLF demonstrated its essential pragmatism at the 1987
Congress, at which Marxism-Leninism was largely abandoned in favour of
democratic institutions, pluralism, and market principles.[89] Militarily, the
movement at first staunchly defended its position in Sahel, and then increasingly took the war to the *Derg*, through a combination of guerrilla activity
behind enemy lines and conventional attacks from the north. Mengistu's
1982 'Red Star' offensive—the sixth major effort by the Ethiopian army—
came close to overwhelming the Eritrean positions, but they held firm;
from this point, gradually, the military momentum began to seep back to
the EPLF.[90] In 1988, EPLF forces won a major battle at Afabet, south of
Nakfa, and finally broke out of their defensive ring, destroying a sizeable
Ethiopian force in the process.[91] Famously, it was described by the scholar
and commentator Basil Davidson as the most significant defeat of a national

army by a guerrilla force since the French loss at Dien Bien Phu in 1954.[92] Afabet was indeed crucial, as it effectively split the forces of the *Derg* in Eritrea in two—those concentrated in the *kebessa*, and those now cut adrift in the western lowlands. In the course of the following year, the EPLF attacked through the eastern side of the territory, and captured Massawa in early 1990, though at considerable cost.[93] The armed frontier was now on the march toward the centre.

In the late 1980s, recruitment into the EPLF increased dramatically— including contingents of former ELF personnel who now detected the unmistakable whiff of inevitable victory in the air, and who could not but be impressed by the EPLF's extraordinary achievement. Indeed, the political capital of the movement at this time was inestimable, and that of Isaias Afeworki particularly so; to his supporters and neutrals alike, there was something of the quiet visionary about him, and certainly genius in the core leadership. Even if some, with rather longer memories and first-hand experience of the Front's attitude toward dissent, had reservations about the imminent victory of the EPLF, they were, for a time, silenced by the sheer magnitude of the accomplishment and the general exuberance which would follow liberation from Ethiopia. The end came swiftly: with pockets of demoralized Ethiopian forces encircled across Eritrea, and surrendering in their droves, the EPLF finally made its entry into Asmara on 24 May 1991, while Eritrean units were seconded to the EPRDF forces simultaneously advancing on Addis Ababa, seized several days later. The EPLF had seized control of the frontier; the politics of the borderland now loomed large in the north.

Just as the TPLF was the product of a century of violent struggle, political upheaval, and ultimately marginalization in the north, so the EPLF had similarly deep roots, and was the outcome of a troubled, turbulent, and ultimately extraordinarily fertile frontier. Yet what was remarkable about the EPLF itself was the manner in which it sought to impose order on the frontier, a military solution to the problems of provincial and cultural complexity, and political ambiguity—although, as we shall see, the full implications of that order, the nature of the solution, would only become clear in the years after independence. Besides the importance of the decade or so in which the EPLF was able to prepare for government, two other long-term issues need to be reiterated here. The first is that Eritrea became, in the 1970s and 1980s, an extraordinarily brutal and violent political environment, characterized by violence and counter-violence between a militarized state and its militarized frontier. Lessons in control and force would be learnt by the leadership of the EPLF. The political culture of the rear base, of the siege and the fortress, would continue to develop into the 1990s and beyond. There were high hopes in the early 1990s that a new kind of politics would prevail; but the war of liberation had taken rather more of a toll than was immediately apparent. Second, the prolonged and deep-rooted disputes with the TPLF, and the subsequent propulsion of the latter into power in Addis Ababa, meant that it was not a matter of *if*, but *when*, Ethiopia and Eritrea would return to arms against one another; the bitterness and suspicion between the two movements, while often unspoken and low-level, were nonetheless poisonous.

In many respects, the deposition of Mengistu's regime signalled the end of an era in which professional soldiers—the descendants of colonial armies elsewhere in Africa, though not in Ethiopia itself—had both a monopoly on physical force, as well as on available weaponry, and also a monopoly on moral rectitude. The army barracks of the 1960s and 1970s had been the sole repositories of the moral and certainly the physical order—however wrongly, it had been believed that the barracks were the wellsprings of political and social change and development. But a new wave of armed force had broken both monopolies, and the movements involved had demonstrated themselves more than equal to the task of challenging the state-level purveyors of violence. These represented aggressive new markets of violence, fuelled by heady levels of material and ideological investment, spurred by emergent nationalisms and ethnocentrisms. And those marketplaces were crowded indeed: both the EPLF and the TPLF were as much the products of prolonged and bitter civil wars as they were the victors over some 'external' force. The internecine dimension of their violent formative experiences cannot be underestimated, although it often is, owing to the drama of their victories over the *Derg*. Yet in other ways, the events of 1991 were merely the latest—albeit arguably the most dramatic—manifestation of a pattern of long standing in regional history, namely the advance of the armed borderland on the centre. In 1991, the armed frontier seized the centre, both in Eritrea and in Ethiopia; it remained to be seen, however, whether the politics of the frontier might be left behind as easily as the frontier itself.

8

New States, Old Wars

Violence, Frontier, and Destiny in the Modern Era

The dead governing: liberation and federation

By the middle of 1991, the armed frontier had recaptured the centre, both in Eritrea and Ethiopia. The fact of prolonged armed struggle had important implications for the nature of state and society across the region. To varying degrees, these movements exhibited a belief in the absolute primacy of armed force in the resolution of 'problems', whether internal—in the suppression of opposition—or external, in the confronting of adjacent enemies. Violence, simply put, produced violence exponentially—as the very existence of the movements in question demonstrated. The success of armed force in the achievement of political power persuaded a new generation of leaders that it might be deployed in other arenas; and there would be the arming of new frontiers to confront those new centres in their turn. Moreover, despite the various claims made for democratic, social revolution by movements of liberation, the latter were organized necessarily around unquestioning obedience; guerrillas, in sum, would prove unenthusiastic democrats, as wars fought by vanguard movements on behalf of broader populaces invariably produced cultures of authoritarianism. Closely connected to this, blood sacrifice was often translated into a moral right to rule, which in turn was reconfigured into the fulfilment of some kind of national destiny. No 'civilian'—that is to say, non-combatant—could possibly be justified in challenging this, and if they did, it might be interpreted as a new form of treason. The exclusivity of participation in the armed struggle bred new political elites. Eritrea provides the best example. Here, the memory of the martyrs—those who fell in action during the armed struggle—would become sacred, and increasingly, though almost imperceptibly, political. The struggle itself—'the field'—would become the stuff of legend, and ex-fighters themselves constituted a new elite, save the permanently disabled, who were provided with accommodation and basic sustenance but who lived on the periphery of society. Ethiopian martyrs likewise joined the great pantheon of the fallen in defence of the Ethiopian motherland, and became part of the great military tradition—even if veterans might be seen begging in the streets of Addis Ababa. In both Eritrea and Ethiopia, these new elites became the righteous, battle-scarred guardians of national destiny, and possessors of arcane knowledge.

Initially, however, there was a fair amount of political creativity in both countries.[1] First, they had to separate: that had been the arrangement reluctantly accepted by the TPLF several years earlier, even if they had periodically questioned the entire basis on which the EPLF was pursuing and organizing the struggle itself. While the new Ethiopian government might regard itself as magnanimously setting the Eritreans free, and paternally supporting the latter in their bid for international recognition, for its part the Eritrean government saw itself as having long since won the argument through its own achievements in 'the field', and as the guarantor of order and stability in *Ethiopia* (never mind Eritrea) during this difficult period of transition. The EPLF, some suggest, agreed to wait two years before holding its referendum on independence, while the EPRDF government stabilized itself in Addis Ababa. Meles Zenawi, meanwhile, made it absolutely clear that he would support the Eritrean bid for independence from the outset. It must be borne in mind, of course, that what made these outwardly efficient, cooperative arrangements especially impressive was the stark contrast they offered with events further south, in Somalia. There, with the overthrow of Siad Barre, the state had ceased to exist by the early 1990s; alongside such chronic disintegration, Ethiopia and Eritrea appeared the resolute harbingers of a new order in north-east Africa. The situation in Somalia, of course, would eventually come to consume both Eritreans and Ethiopians—while relations with Sudan likewise augured ill for the future.

Nonetheless, for now, there was indeed collaboration between Addis Ababa and Asmara in the lengthy operation to separate the two countries. In the end, it was something of a hatchet job, but it appeared to work: both countries survived the procedure, although no-one had noticed the massive internal damage inflicted. The Eritreans probably did contribute to the stabilization of the EPRDF regime by holding off from an immediate referendum; it is also the case that Ethiopia, bluntly, had little choice in Eritrea's 'secession', because militarily the argument was indeed won. The facts on the ground were such that no Ethiopian force could have prevented the creation of an independent Eritrea. Nonetheless, Asmara would probably not have been able to make good its bid for international recognition of its sovereign status had it not been for the strong support offered by senior EPRDF personnel, and Meles in particular; it is also the case that a stunned Amhara and Tigrayan population, in particular, within Ethiopia needed to be persuaded of the righteousness of the Eritrean cause by TPLF cadres. The lingering doubts over whether the Eritreans would *really*, in the final analysis, become independent were removed in the course of 1992 and early 1993, even if many Ethiopians—including a great number of people within the TPLF and the EPRDF more broadly—never actually accepted it. But they, like the new government in Addis Ababa itself, had little choice. Eritrea's departure dramatically and apparently permanently altered the balance of power in north-east Africa.

The referendum itself, however, took some organizing, and by the time the moment arrived in April 1993—attended by hundreds of UN and other observers—Eritreans had long been primed as to the issue at stake, or at least the issue on the ballot paper.[2] They were being asked to approve or disapprove of Eritrean independence; the EPLF case was clear, and was deeply appreciated by many Eritreans, based on a history of forcible incorporation, violent persecution, and the fundamental right of self-determination. The vote was 99.8 per cent in favour of independence, and had been, on the whole, well-organized and was declared free and fair by the UN reporters, notwithstanding some chaotic anomalies around the country. Eritrea was *de jure* independent, after two years of *de facto*. The rejoicing and justified self-congratulations were marred by the events of 20 May 1993, when a group of fighters, annoyed by the unilateral announcement by the government that EPLF personnel would effectively continue unpaid for the foreseeable future, seized control of government offices and the airport in protest.[3] They met with Isaias, and later disbanded peacefully; but if they had fears about a newly-detected highhandedness in the government's attitude, it was only the beginning. A few days later, the protest forgiven if not forgotten, Eritrea celebrated its formal independence. In a ceremony in Asmara, the key figure at the feast Meles Zenawi, now Ethiopian president—neither wicked stepmother nor

Banquo, just yet—declared his hope that 'the wounds of the past will be healed'.[4] This was the EPLF's moment.

The first few years of Eritrean independence were dominated by three broad and intimately interrelated themes, namely the struggle for economic development, the difficulties encountered in the quest for a stable political system, and a problematic and complex relationship with neighbouring states, particularly Ethiopia. While in the immediate term these need to be understood, naturally, in the context of new-found independence, in fact each of these challenges was rooted in the deeper past. The rhetoric of the 'new beginning', and the bullish and indeed naive optimism of the early 1990s, would soon evaporate. Nonetheless, expectations in 1993 were indeed high.[5] On the face of it, at least, the EPLF possessed an enormous amount of political capital; few questioned (publicly, at any rate) the EPLF's assumption that overwhelming popular support for independence in fact meant a popular mandate for the movement itself, even though that was *not* the issue at stake during the referendum. The sheer scale of the EPLF's military success, and the euphoria which attended the achievement of independence, was sufficient to enable the movement to contemplate the enormous task of reconstruction with some confidence. The EPLF initially went about this task with the same vigour and commitment that had characterized its armed struggle, and Eritrea won plaudits from the donor community for its determination to avoid excessive national indebtedness, and to ensure that all much-needed international aid would go directly to the people who needed it. The government's much-publicized stubbornness when dealing with NGOs and donor countries—notably, it demanded absolute control of aid money[6]—won it admiration from foreign observers, some of whom became enthusiastic supporters for a time, although aid workers and would-be investors increasingly found Eritrean institutions and bureaucracy impossible to deal with. The relationship had already begun to sour in 1996 and 1997, when several major NGOs were compelled to leave the country as the government decided it could do certain things better by itself. This was rash, and would come back to haunt it.

In political terms, too, initial prospects had seemed good. Shortly after EPLF forces entered Asmara in May 1991, a senior figure in the movement, Sebhat Efrem, later Minister of Defence, remarked in an interview with the journalist Dan Connell that a time would come for the EPLF to 'disappear', its mandate fulfilled.[7] Others, including Isaias Afeworki himself, would intimate something similar in the months before the independence referendum. Nominally, of course, the EPLF did indeed 'disappear' soon afterwards: at the movement's Third Congress, held at Nakfa in February 1994, the EPLF abolished itself and was replaced by the People's Front for Democracy and Justice (PFDJ). A National Assembly was created as the core forum for political debate. In reality, the PFDJ was—and remains—the EPLF in everything but name, and would continue to dominate Eritrean politics and society, while liberation-era figures continued to occupy the vast majority of key government posts from the presidency downwards. Meanwhile, the constitution-making process received a great deal of attention down to 1997, when a comprehensive draft was produced; but it was never ratified, still less applied. The constitution itself, under the overall direction of Bereket Habte Selassie, was a remarkable achievement, and involved much consultation and input from Eritreans from many walks of life, as well as some outside specialist counsel;[8] but it was doomed. The war that broke out a year later was used as the excuse for its abeyance, and it has collected dust ever since.

The natural authoritarianism of the EPLF's leadership, as well as attitudes toward rivals and dissidents alike during the struggle, meant that there had been, in all likelihood, no genuine commitment to the constitution.[9] From the early 1990s, the government was similarly intolerant of perceived nonconformers and dissidents—notably certain Protestant denominations and Jehovah's Witnesses—and it was clear early on that 'human rights' were not a particular priority for the Eritrean state.[10] All this said, in the period immediately following independence, many suspended their natural scepticism; human rights abuses were *relatively* limited and did not, on the whole, tarnish the reputation of what was still seen as an essentially progressive, principled and well-intentioned political movement. Meanwhile, a measure of amnesty had been granted to members of the ELF, for example, some of whom returned to Eritrea to participate in the nation-building exercise. Many of these worked with refugees, in the rebuilding of social and economic infrastructure, and in the education sector. Troubled relations with Sudan and Yemen notwithstanding, there was enough positivity to engender a degree of optimism that the great northern war was indeed over. It was to prove an illusion.

Nonetheless, while the process of temporary disarmament—or at least standing down—of the northern frontier was taking place, plans were being developed within Ethiopia for novel political arrangements, for there were other frontiers to be mollified and indeed incorporated. In essence, the

ethnic federalism which the EPRDF government initiated had its roots in
the *zemene mesafint*, and in many respects was the logical response to a century and a half of centrifugal violence, even if this was not the explicit
justification for it—the deep past rarely makes its way into mainstream
political discourse. More directly, it represented an attempt to address the
chronic problem of the multi-ethnic nature of the Ethiopian empire-state—
and more expressly, the emergence of militarized ethnicity—which had
become clear since the 1960s and 1970s.[11] A federal system based on an
equitable distribution of power among ethnic groupings was the only means,
it was argued, by which Ethiopia could survive at all—especially in the light
of Eritrea's departure—and it was no historical accident that the political
experiment now unfolding was spearheaded by a Tigrayan elite representing a group which accounted only for some ten per cent of the total population of Ethiopia.

   Some foreign observers of long standing predictably embraced the new
regime with gusto, and proclaimed the 'resurgence' of Ethiopia;[12] for many
Ethiopians, however, the question of the government's intentions was not
long in the answering. There was an initial welcome given to the Transitional
Government of Ethiopia's announcement in mid-1991 that it would recognize the country's ethnic diversity by reorganizing Ethiopia as a federal state
divided into ethnically-defined regions. It quickly became clear, however,
that regional administrations were to be politically and ideologically affiliated with the EPRDF. By the end of 1992, the OLF had already withdrawn
from the coalition, followed early the next year by members of the Southern
Ethiopia People's Democratic Coalition. The events of 1992–3, indeed,
were salutary.[13] Confused and deeply flawed elections were held in June
1992, in which the OLF and the All-Amhara People's Organisation (AAPO)
refused to take part, and during which opposition was routinely intimi-
dated. Disorganization at the local level meant that extraordinary authority
was enjoyed by EPRDF officials during the polls themselves. Nonetheless,
although it was difficult for anyone to say whether the result really was an
endorsement of the EPRDF—it seems safe to suggest that it was not—
Meles declared that he had won a popular mandate as president. Within a
few months, various groups had withdrawn from the coalition; and then, at
the beginning of 1993, the police violently suppressed a demonstration by
students in Addis Ababa, marching in protest against the imminent independence of Eritrea. Meles brooked no dissent on this issue—and swiftly
moved to purge Addis Ababa University of dozens of academics who were

accused of inciting student violence.[14] These were mostly Amhara—some were active members of the AAPO—and it was not difficult for many to reach the conclusion that the government had now embarked on a form of ethnic cleansing made possible by an increasingly authoritarian regime. Notably, of course, the perception grew that Meles Zenawi himself—with Eritrean heritage—was suspiciously 'close' to the Asmara government, and appeared to Amhara critics to be Isaias' stooge in Addis Ababa; with the TPLF in power, Ethiopia was losing its coastline, and a 'natural' part of 'ancient Ethiopia'. It was one part of the bitter ethnic *melange* of Ethiopian political culture in the 1990s and into the new millennium, characterized by shifting and multi-dimensional enemies, positioned along different borderlines at the same time, straddling issues and overlapping loyalties.

The government pushed ahead with its constitutional programme. In 1994, the new federal constitution was unveiled, of which Article 39.1 stipulated the right of regions to self-determination *up to and including secession*. The events of the early 1990s in Ethiopia contained more than a touch of irony: a strictly applied constitution along the lines of the 1994 version, forty or even thirty years earlier, might have kept Eritrea inside Ethiopia; it took several decades of violence, including that in Tigray itself, to arrive at this constitutional reality. Ultimately it was an attempt on the part of the TPLF at the constitutional disarmament of the frontier, of which the TPLF itself was a product. Even then, of course, it has not been at all clear that the EPRDF government truly accepts the spirit of the new constitution; the TPLF leadership is more aware than any regime previously of unfeasibility of centralism, covert or otherwise, and yet it still needs to remain in power—and so it has tended to embrace the political strategies of its predecessors, with some novel elements thrown in. But as Prendergast and Duffield put it, the 'brilliance' of the federal system lay in the fact that 'it regionalised conflict that might have been expressed at the national level'.[15] Ethnic regionalism, according to this view, represents the attempt by the EPRDF to quarantine violence which might spill over onto the national arena; if so, it represents a chronic misunderstanding of Ethiopian history, beyond a recognition that regional conflict has been extremely destabilizing. Ethnicity, in this context, has been used at the level of the state to devolve violence to the regions to which it properly belongs. As Donald Donham suggests, the ethno-federalism of the EPRDF 'was a form of "indirect rule" based on official definitions of ethnicity'.[16] Above all, of course, this was a system brought into being by a militant Tigrayan leadership acutely aware of its vulnerability at the centre of the Ethiopian polity; if Tigray was to maintain its rediscovered dominance, or even simply survive, the TPLF would need a deft combination of armed force and political guile—and some degree of cooperation with the Amhara and the Oromo.

In recent years, there has been increasing interest in the relationship between both ethnicity and power in contemporary Ethiopia, and between violence against particular groups by the state and ethnic identity, whether claimed or imposed.[17] Furthermore, in the case of both Ethiopia and Eritrea, there has been an examination of the manipulation of ethnic imagery in the development of group cohesion—particularly in the context of state-formation from the early 1990s onward—and the flexibility and indeed ambiguity of ethnic belonging.[18] There is little need to recover the ground traversed by much of this excellent scholarship, constituting as it does an unprecedented level of scrutiny of the role of ethnic identity in Ethiopian political life, notably from the perspective of democracy and human rights.[19] This relatively new focus is to be warmly welcomed, because this *is* scholarly research which involves holding political systems both to account and up to close scrutiny. I argue, however, for the need to avoid foreshortening the analysis of ethnicity, identity, and conflict across our region, and to lengthen as well as deepen our understanding of some key phenomena and processes in north-east African political culture. Again, the region is crosscut with a series of interlocking fault lines and borders, which sometimes follow what we can loosely call 'ethnic' fractures, and at other times run across ethnicity and involve the boundaries of the state and of state-formation. There can be little doubt that the modern Ethiopian government has used ethnicity to manipulate public opinion and discourse, and that ethnicity itself is frequently characterized by ambiguity: the most obvious example in our region is the Tigrinya bloc straddling Tigray and highland Eritrea, the 'trans-Mereb' zone. But this does not mean that therefore ethnicity itself is a deliberate creation, a product of the instrumentalism at the heart of modern human relations and power structures. Rather, such episodic appeals (or reversions) to ethnicity co-exist with deeper-rooted, primordial senses of what it is to belong to a particular group, state, or 'community', while the latter have themselves often been forged through violent struggle over the longer term. It is also clear that ethnicity is a political weapon, as we have noted earlier, and that particular ethnic groups are ostracized or persecuted because of their perceived propensity for opposition—although clearly 'political groups' might also be ethnically ostracized, i.e. labelled as belonging

to a particular ethnicity which has always 'caused trouble', or which is per-
ennially 'lawless'. Either way, the end result is invariably the formation of
kinds of armed borderlands described through this book. We return to these
issues below.

The new constitution was approved by the Ethiopian parliament in mid-
1995, with Meles becoming prime minister and Negasso Gidada, an Oromo
activist, becoming a largely ceremonial president, a post he held until falling
foul of the leadership in 2001. Indeed efforts were made to create the
appearance of inter-ethnic cooperation in government, with Amhara,
Oromo, Somali, and Gurage, among others, being represented in the council of ministers; but few close observers could doubt that the key ministers
and assistant ministers were Tigrayans. The army was reorganized, too, under
the direction of Tsadkan Gebretensae and Yemane ('Jamaica') Kidane, both
central figures in the military and political wings of the TPLF. Again, senior
officers from other ethnic groups were appointed, including Oromo and
Amhara; clearly, however, these were carefully vetted, ideologically reconciled individuals, and favour was still given to Tigrayan officers.[20]

In the immediate aftermath of the war with Eritrea, there was the first
major split within the TPLF over its prosecution. In 2001, there was a purge
of the politburo and cabinet in which Meles effectively removed those who
accused him of failing to finish the job, of pulling his punches in dealing
with the Eritreans, who had been, it was supposed, on the ropes in the middle of 2000 when Meles agreed to a ceasefire.[21] It was an indication—or a
reminder, to those rather better acquainted with the movement's history—
of the Meles faction's brutality and intolerance of dissent at the centre of the
organization. Indeed, in the early twenty-first century, new opposition
movements appeared within Tigray itself, bitterly opposed to the hegemony
of the TPLF and its cronyism, and serving as a stark reminder of how the
TPLF itself had risen to prominence through the destruction of rivals within
the province. But the TPLF found it increasingly difficult to engineer the
failure of those which would challenge it, whether within Tigray or elsewhere in Ethiopia. Certainly, in the early years of the twenty-first century,
the TPLF appeared increasingly besieged, with a mentality to match, at the
heart of the Ethiopian polity; for that reason, too, many Tigrayans rejected
the movement, for they saw it as ultimately jeopardising Tigray itself, and
exposing it to some violent future backlash, as had befallen the Amhara in
the 1980s. It was increasingly common to hear mutterings that Tigray was
in effect being 'held hostage' by the TPLF; born aloft on a new wave of

Tigrayan nationalism, the TPLF was now placing Tigray in grave danger. In the years following the Eritrean war, the EPRDF government became ever more authoritarian—or at least, ever less willing to conceal it, much to the annoyance of those foreign governments which had backed Meles Zenawi with such enthusiasm. It was increasingly clear that the TPLF-led state had no intention of surrendering power for the foreseeable future.

The Ethiopian government also took advantage of the US interest in the region as part of the war on Islamic extremism. Under this kind of cover the Ethiopian security forces could certainly pursue the growing number of armed insurgencies across Ethiopia with relative impunity. Below, we look briefly at the Ethiopian intervention in Somalia; here, it is important to note the allegations made concerning the existence of detention centres in eastern Ethiopia for Muslim 'terror' suspects.[22] There was novelty here in the context, and in the international climate, and arguably in the degree to which state apparatus could be deployed to political ends; but there was precedent in the nineteenth century and earlier in the treatment by the highland polity of Muslim threats. Tewodros and Yohannes alike would have recognized the 'mission' embarked upon by the EPRDF state to quash the radical Islamic threat looming to the south and east, and indeed within *habesha* society itself. Elements of Somali Islam were indeed more markedly radical—there were foreign models to provide inspiration in motive and organization, notably in Iraq and Afghanistan[23]—but this was only the latest stage in a long and ambiguous religious war in the Horn. As elsewhere, it would prove self-perpetuating: Ethiopia would become an even more vulnerable target for the region's Islamists as a result of its close association (however misconstrued) with the US in the latter's 'war on terror', and its own bloody adventures in Somalia. None of this prevented the Ethiopian government from blaming the Eritreans for ultimately being behind occasional bomb blasts in Addis Ababa and elsewhere.

The great unexpected war

There is an expanding body of literature on the causes and nature of the 1998–2000 war between Eritrea and Ethiopia. At various times and in various contexts, writers have been struck by the apparent futility of the conflict, and have broadly lent support to the 'bald men fighting over the comb'

notion which has undermined comprehension of events from the beginning. It is a characterization, indeed, which has warped understanding of
African warfare more generally for a very long time, as I have argued elsewhere.[24] Others have dwelt on the 'family feud' concept, resting on the idea
that the EPLF and the TPLF, or Eritrean Tigrinya and Tigrayans, or even
Eritreans and Ethiopians generally, are somehow 'brothers' who then spectacularly fell out.[25] Some of the more nuanced literature has highlighted the
shocking humanitarian as well as wider political and historical implications.[26] Of course, in the post-Cold-War world, this curiously inexplicable
conflict—reminiscent, so many journalists could not resist informing us, of
the Western Front in the First World War—was supposedly a reminder of
the simmering barbarism and atavism of politics in the Horn. In that sense
it was easier to draw out the peculiarly *African* nature of the war. Nonetheless,
while the initial rush of scholarly and journalistic analysis was characterized
by a fair amount of bias for one side or the other, and certainly routine
accusations and counter-accusations of subjectivity, the academic treatment
of the war—while somewhat in abeyance at present—is growing steadily
more sophisticated and less overtly subjective.

This was, then, the great unexpected war; no-one, or very few, saw it
coming. Perhaps this is the most singularly remarkable aspect of the entire
conflict. It became less 'unexpected' as time went on, naturally enough; certainly, within a short space of time, there could be scarcely any doubt about
the degree of mutual hostility, nor about the existence of in-built cultural
and political mechanisms to facilitate such animosity. It is also clear that our
understanding of the war has been hampered by geographical reductionism
and temporal foreshortening, misrepresentation in terms of both time and
space. It was not *simply* about who owned Badme, but concerned the competition for hegemony across the wider region, as well as access to the Red
Sea coast, in itself an issue of some antiquity. Nor was it *simply* about the
stupidly dangerous disagreements between two men, or even two organizations, but rather the *resumption* of the war in mid-1998 after a brief armistice
was the latest—and arguably the most violent, to date—manifestation of a
pattern of violence both within and around the contested Eritrean zone
dating to at least the middle of the nineteenth century. The borders between
Eritrea and Ethiopia mattered; but what was more important, now, was the
fact of Eritrea as frontier nation, built on a fault line, and of the militaristic
and chauvinistic EPLF as the product of that volatile environment. The
Ethiopia of the TPLF-EPRDF, too, was the product of a concatenation of

frontier wars; but once again it was Eritrea which became the epicentre of a regional network of violence.

The 1991–8 period was a mere armistice in a very long war. Initially, however, as in other spheres, the signs were positive. The Ethiopian government accepted and blessed the outcome of the 1993 referendum; this was quickly followed in September 1993 by a series of agreements between the two states encompassing trade, banking, defence, and nationality.[27] Indeed through the mid-1990s, a form of neo-unionism had emerged, espoused by senior Eritrean figures who spoke warmly of the intimacy between the two countries. Economic ties appeared particularly close, not least because Ethiopia represented Eritrea's commercial hinterland; the agreement of September 1993, followed by another as late as January 1997, demonstrated an official expectation, at least, that this economic interdependency was to continue, indeed grow stronger.[28] Whether wishful thinking on both sides, or the clever deployment of rhetoric in advance of betrayal, or simply political naivety, this public language masked deep problems, and there was a fair amount of protesting too much doubtless willed on by the need for a period of recuperation and consolidation. This element, indeed, is clearly critical, and often overlooked; neither the TPLF nor the EPLF was in a position to adopt an aggressive stance toward one another in the early 1990s, and even if—as is likely—leaders on both sides anticipated some future trial of arms, a little breathing space was necessary given the massive military effort of recent years. Legitimacy, moreover, both internal and external, would have been less forthcoming had a clash come sooner. Whether either side expected a war on *quite* the scale of 1998–2000 is another matter; it seems, on balance, they did not.

Eritrea's introduction of a national currency, the *nakfa*, in 1997—previously it had used the Ethiopian *birr*—led to a trade war which escalated rapidly in the months prior to the outbreak of war in mid-1998.[29] This was surprising, on the face of it, as a separate Eritrean currency had been anticipated in the 1993 agreement. Ethiopia boycotted the port of Assab, in effect an Ethiopian port in any case, for it hardly served the Eritrean economy in any meaningful manner, and accused the Eritreans of imposing hefty duties; the Eritreans denied this. Trade between the two countries swiftly withered. It was the beginning of an economic war which Eritrea could not win. Meanwhile there were problems at the border, too, along the ancient fault line which ran across the northern region. Border problems, as we have seen, existed during the liberation struggle, and were manifest in clashes over administrative zones between the Ethiopian and Eritrean movements. They continued through the 1990s, approaching crisis point by 1997–8.[30] In July and August 1997, Ethiopian incursions in two areas—Badme in the west, and Adi Murug in the centre—prompted an exchange of letters between Isaias and Meles concerning the need for restraint and eventual demarcation,[31] something in which the TPLF leadership had been interested since the early 1980s. Indeed a joint border commission had met sporadically through the 1990s, but in time each side would accuse the other of failing to take this seriously. These were no mere teething troubles: the real issue was the very nature and indeed existence of Eritrean statehood, however important were other, more specific, issues at the local level. The question remains how much the Ethiopian government, increasingly self-confident and secure, genuinely accepted Eritrean independence, involving as it did the loss of Ethiopia's entire coastline and a substantial population held by most outside Ethiopia itself to be 'Ethiopian'. Similarly, the question remains how much the Eritrean government actually had faith in the viability of its new nation, and certainly in its regional security. Nonetheless it would adhere doggedly to the argument that the border question was 'straightforward': it was a matter of colonial boundaries, no more and no less. Ethiopia argued that these boundaries had never been demarcated on the ground, and that therefore the question was one of *actual* occupation and administration. As the war unfolded, depths of antagonism between the two states were rapidly revealed which were clearly related to a much wider range of issues. This is not to suggest that borders did not matter; on a certain level, they did, of course. But border demarcation was only part of a much more complex historical and geopolitical equation. What happened at the frontier between these two states was symptomatic of tensions at their respective centres.

The events of the war itself are well known and require only a summary here.[32] In May 1998, an exchange of fire took place at the hamlet of Badme in which several Eritreans were killed, and the Eritrean army moved in force to retake the disputed area. The Eritreans appear to have been rather better prepared for this eventuality; the Ethiopian army, for all the evidence of armed militia in the area, remained under strength for several weeks.[33] Fighting erupted along the central portion of the border, too, and by early June the conflict had begun in earnest, complete with Ethiopian air-raids on Eritrea and retaliation by Eritrea on the Tigrayan town of Mekele. Early attempts at mediation, through both a US-Rwanda peace plan and the

OAU, failed, and although the war entered a quiescent phase for several months the conflict itself was increasingly disastrous for Eritrea, not least because of the mass mobilization which took place, placing enormous strains on a fragile society and economy. Moreover, a new 'front' opened up in the form of deportations: beginning in June 1998, Ethiopia deported tens of thousands of 'ethnic Eritreans' and Ethiopians of Eritrean descent, and the vitriolic language which characterized the Ethiopian government's pronouncements spoke of a deep well of resentment and bitterness regarding the new state to the north, and its people, broadly defined. The Eritrean government did not immediately respond in kind and generally showed restraint in its press releases, as well as something close to over-compensation in terms of its protective treatment of Ethiopians living in Eritrea.[34] Only later did the Eritrean government initiate an extensive and at times brutal programme of 'repatriation' of Ethiopians, especially Tigrayans, from the country.

In February 1999, a major Ethiopian offensive recaptured Badme, and the Eritrean government indicated a willingness to accept the OAU peace plan in what was widely interpreted as an embarrassing climb down. It should have signalled the end of the war; but the war continued, with some of the worst fighting taking place along the central front between April and June 1999. Once again, the war entered a lull, and diplomatic activity on the part of the OAU, the UN, and various individual interested parties was frenzied. However, in May 2000, Ethiopia launched its most overwhelming offensive to date, breaking the Eritrean lines in the west and advancing deep into Eritrean territory. The Eritrean army was compelled to abandon the west of the country, and withdrew into the mountain plateau from which they managed to halt the Ethiopians, at great cost to the latter. Even so, for a country which had prided itself on its military capacity and ability to withstand any external threat, the offensive of May and June 2000 was shocking to the Eritrean populace.[35] In addition to the material and economic disaster which it brought, these setbacks also had considerable political fallout which would only become clear after the war, when deep rifts inside party and government over the prosecution of the war would come to light. In reality, the two sides had fought each other to a standstill; it was a war neither could hope to 'win', at least in the unconditional sense. Eritrea could not have withstood further assaults, certainly not in economic terms, while strains were already telling on broader society as well as within political structures and relationships. The Eritrean government could claim to have withstood Ethiopian aggression, and thwarted Ethiopia's expansionist plans; and certainly the implicit Ethiopian aim of removing Isaias Afeworki had not been realized, however much the latter's position had been shaken by the events of the war. But Eritrea was exhausted, and large swathes of the population were weary and disillusioned—although not as much so as they would become. When the ceasefire of June was followed by the formal agreement of December 2000, it was greeted in Eritrea with a marked blend of relief and tired sadness. Many would wonder, after all, what the conflict had been about; at least Eritrea itself was intact after an experience as bruising in its own way as the decades of liberation struggle, but as the political cost of the war became clear, many would begin to question even this.

Until 2008, a demilitarized zone patrolled by the UN divided the two countries, and the border remained undemarcated, while two of the largest armies in Africa faced one another down, in places only metres apart. In early 2002, a border commission produced the document to which it was hoped both sides would adhere, outlining how the border would be delimited and demarcated.[36] While it was accepted by Eritrea, the Ethiopian government rejected key parts of it—notably the awarding of Badme to Eritrea—and in the years that followed requested further negotiation on the matter. Eritrea, adamant that the findings were to be final and binding, refused, and has become increasingly outraged that more international pressure has not been placed on Ethiopia to implement the agreement. Pressure on the two sides to reach compromise has produced no results. As the UN finally pulled out in 2007–8, the border was 'virtually' demarcated—a political nonsense which was nonetheless endorsed by Isaias. Relations with Ethiopia are not yet normalized, nor do they look like being normalized in the near future.[37] Cross-border incidents occur regularly, and at the time of writing the government-owned media in Eritrea regularly warns of further Ethiopian expansionist plans, even as thousands of Eritrean conscripts leak into both Ethiopia and Sudan in search of asylum. The spectre of war, whether real or imagined, continues to stalk Eritrea, and in truth the government has utilized the external threat in stalling demobilization, keeping society at a high level of military preparedness and justifying tight political discipline.

A great deal of attention has been paid, again, to the creation of hated enemies, the manipulation of ethnicity and nationalism, and the perception of the past in both Eritrea and Ethiopia, but particularly the latter, as the result of the war.[38] On the Ethiopian side, it is in fact a book that pre-dates the war, rather than anything that comes after it, which best demonstrates the sense of simmering antipathy toward the EPLF in particular, and perhaps the *kebessa* Tigrinya in general. Tekeste Negash's study of the federal period of the 1950s is in fact an ill-disguised condemnation of the EPLF, which, Tekeste suggests, embodies the fickleness and cynical Machiavellianism of the Christian highlanders.[39] Before the war, too, Alemseged Abbay tried a gentler tack by suggesting that Tigrayans on either side of the Mereb were the same people but the EPLF chose a 'divergent path', rejecting primordial links with their southern brothers and developing an 'instrumentalist' identity.[40] Certainly, regardless of any inter- or indeed intra-ethnic nuance, the pain of the loss of coastline once again coursed through the Ethiopian body politic, the amputation all the more traumatic as now the inherently aggressive, confrontational *sha'abiya* were once again on the march, the ungrateful recipients of Ethiopian political and economic *largesse*. Isaias' military hubris, apparently well known during the liberation struggle years, was rediscovered through hindsight and was now exposed for all to see. Eritrea was indeed, as one contemporary polemic had it, Ethiopia's 'problem child'.[41] Ethiopia was the victim of a northern militancy which—not content with the attainment of its sovereignty—had now gone so far as to encroach on Ethiopia's own sovereignty, much to the 'shock' and 'disappointment' of ordinary Ethiopians.[42] When the Eritrean government accepted the original OAU peace plan following its defeat on the Badme front in February 1999, it was rejected by Addis Ababa as a cynical and disingenuous ploy to buy time in the face of unexpected military setback. Eritrea and Eritreans could not be trusted—witness the ongoing expulsion of tens of thousands of 'Eritreans' from Ethiopia. This would be softened somewhat later on among many ordinary Ethiopians, who—like increasing numbers of exiled Eritreans—came to focus on the megalomania of Isaias himself, pitying their Eritrean 'brothers and sisters' who were now languishing under his dictatorial rule.[43]

For now, however, 'Eritrea' was a condition to be addressed as aggressively as it had erupted. Ethiopia's war was righteous, and just;[44] and in that sense the events of 1998-2000 fed easily into a pattern of celebratory militarism which had been a core element in the Ethiopian nation-building project since the mid-nineteenth century, and which had been a part of *habesha* political culture for several centuries. Days after Badme fell in late February 1999, there came the annual celebration of Adwa across Ethiopia.

In Addis Ababa, predictably, the event took on new meaning, and the public celebrations were frenetic. Once again, a northern invader had been put to flight; once again, Ethiopian troops had stood firm on the northern frontier.[45] Ultimately, victory over Eritrea was a 'second Adwa', and indeed placed clear psychological as well as physical distance between the Eritrean aggressor and the Ethiopian victor—a kind of 'firming up' of the northern boundary, although the creation of this would hardly bring stability, as we see below, but rather would merely institutionalize and formalize instability.[46] For some, there was resonance too with the Italian war of the mid-1930s, especially among the few surviving 'Patriots'.[47] There were, of course, overlapping pools of identity involved in this: Tigrayans could frame the war in very local terms, not least because of their proximity to the historic frontier zone and cultural affinity to the Tigrinya of the Eritrea plateau, for example; others (not least the EPRDF government itself) needed to appeal to a pan-Ethiopian nationalism, remarkable in its durability, and overriding ethnic or regional tensions. Tigray, for example, had fought many of its past wars with the Amhara, *not* exclusively with enemies lurking in the so-called *Mereb Melash*, the land beyond the Mereb. For the Amhara, the *sha'abiya* represented the loss of Eritrea and the culmination of the great northern war which had smashed their hold on power, for the time being; the TPLF, indeed, had inherited their losses. In any case it scarcely mattered: a generic tradition of heroic violence could be mobilized according to current needs, and tailored to current circumstances. It meant that, come the Eritrean war and the new ethno-political dispensation of the 1990s, there were various vintages of violence which could be carried up from the great cellars of public memory, and which all could sup, at least in principle.

On the Tigrayan side of the Mereb war zone, the response to the war was an ambiguous *melange* of shock, sadness, and prepared resignation.[48] Eritreans were interlinked with Tigray through a complex mesh of personal relationships, cultural and linguistic ties, and economic activities; but they were also aggressive, untrustworthy, haughty: characteristics writ large in the EPLF—and indeed ultimately in the person of Isaias himself, whom Tigrayans would have had to invent had he not already existed, as the perfect Eritrean caricature. Yet these ambiguities—characteristics, surely, of most frontier zones throughout human history—were mirrored on the *kebessa* side of the border, as I have demonstrated elsewhere.[49] At the larger level, Ethiopia—conceived as a monolith when the need arose—remained an expansionist empire-state, as it had been since the late nineteenth century, and remained unreconciled to the loss of Eritrea. In this context it did not matter *who* was at the helm in Addis Ababa. Yet on another level it clearly mattered a great deal. Tigrayans had been part of Eritrean communities along the border; there had been intermarriage and shared culture, and a rich common heritage; peoples on both sides of the Mereb, notably, had struggled against Amhara domination, and here they had much in common with western lowlanders, too. And yet Tigrayans were never to be fully trusted; they were venal, mean-spirited, and scheming, characteristics incarnate in the person of Meles Zenawi, just as Isaias was the personification of *kebessa* hubris. Tigrayans were, in short, despised. Indeed the closeness of Tigray appeared to make this war even more bitter than any past conflict with the Amhara far to the south—partly, indeed, because Tigrayans were commonly held in such contempt, while the Amhara were viewed as more 'natural', and more respected, opponents. The proximity, in the end, only made the differences starker and, it seemed, more deadly; the ambiguities of the Tigray–Tigrinya relationship were clearly more dangerous than any sharp edges.

From the middle of 1998, apparently deeply held feelings of contempt as well as the bitterest of memories were aroused in Eritrea, and were expressed both privately and publicly. Some writers reflected on Tigrayan expansionism from a historical point of view, and were drawn inexorably to comparisons of the TPLF with Yohannes IV.[50] Predictably, patterns of 'Eritrean' resistance were discerned in the distant past, patriotic spotlights cast into the dark corners of history much as they had been in the enemy's camp. Others recalled how the TPLF had been driven by deep-seated resentment, or were gripped by an unnerving inferiority complex, or had laid claim to Badme during the liberation struggle, long before (it was suggested) it became a serious issue.[51] Along the border, many expressed the view that the *Woyane* had been planning this for a long time, and that they were simply following a much deeper tradition of Tigrayan military leaders making violent incursions into the *kebessa*.[52] And of course, what clearer evidence was there of the TPLF's hatred for Eritreans than the deportations?[53]

The pact of forgetting was broken, and almost every view expressed on one side had its echo on the other: untrustworthiness; dangerous ambition; prior planning for this war; military aggression born of insecurity. So much of this was the inevitable product of highly charged emotion at a time of national crisis, clearly; and scholars need to exercise caution in the utilization of such testimony. But the alacrity with which communities and states alike presented their animus is telling. Real historical experience shaped views on both sides; the trans-Mereb relationship was one built on the region's major fault line, the epicentre of so much violent—and creative—instability, and therefore was both ambiguous and highly volatile. This was no disingenuous passion, but the reflection of a troubled association between communities, peoples, political organizations, and, ultimately, state structures. To a very real degree, the events of the late twentieth century were rooted in the violent century between 1850 and 1950. In their different but overlapping ways, each of the Eritrean, Tigrayan, and Oromo struggles developed out of past experience over the long term, and were the products of layered identities which were organic, even as they were increasingly exploited by modern state apparatuses. Too often the functional element has been exaggerated, leading scholars to think too much on the present at the expense of historical experience. Certainly, a great deal of the imagery was the product of modern states' manipulations; but wholly instrumentalist interpretations are misleading. The past mattered; lived experience was critical. This was now clearly manifest in the reality of Eritrea as the frontier society, the institutionalization of violence which was the outcome of both residual Ethiopian territorial and political ambition and, in particular, the EPLF's conquest of the contested Eritrean frontier zone. It is this to which we now turn.

Borderline nation: Eritrea as frontier society

The hope invested in the new state of Eritrea in the early 1990s—in truth, as much the product of relief at the ending of the long war as of any real understanding of the political culture of the EPLF—evaporated in the space of a decade, although in fact the real shift came quickly, in the space of a few months in 2001. The extraordinary clampdown on dissent in that year was in fact only a reprise of the 1973 'crisis' within the movement, when questions had been asked about the authoritarian tendencies of the leadership; but now, in the context of independent statehood, and in full view of a wary citizenry still recovering from the war, it took on rather more critical proportions. The immediate roots of the 2001 crisis are to be found in the war itself, for there had been growing dismay at Isaias' direct handling of operations which culminated, many senior figures believed, in the Ethiopian breakthrough in May 2000. Whether or not the stories of an imminent *coup* against Isaias at that point were accurate, his standing in the army protected him as the war reached its climax in the hills south of Asmara; but the dissidents were not to be silenced. The private newspapers, which had briefly flourished just prior to and during the war, became outlets for criticism of the leadership. In October 2000, a number of prominent Eritreans in the diaspora produced the so-called 'Berlin Manifesto' which criticized the President's increasingly personalized and dictatorial system of rule. Early in 2001, an 'open letter' to Isaias, written by several high-ranking political and military figures in the government and 'leaked' to the broader membership of the PFDJ, accused the President of autocratic and high-handed leadership, and of failing to consult either the Party or the National Assembly in terms of the direction the country was taking.[54] For a time, there was no public response from the President's Office; but it is now clear that plans were indeed being hatched, and doubtless many of the dissidents—all too familiar as they were with the autocratic and indeed at times paranoid political culture of the EPLF, for they had been part of it—anticipated detention. And so it came, in September 2001—a week after the attacks in the United States, notably—when 11 of the 15 key critics, who included some of the chief architects of the EPLF's victory in 1991, were arrested and imprisoned. (Three others were abroad at the time, and one recanted.) These dissidents remain in jail at the time of writing.[55] The private press was closed down, and journalists and editors arrested. Public debate was swiftly stifled. It signalled a new strategy of oppression and intolerance of opposition which shows no sign of abating.

In truth, of course, many in the EPLF may have seen something like this coming, for such behaviour was hardly unknown within the Front since its inception in the early 1970s. There was a recognition that certain senior figures, in their readiness to follow his leadership in the pursuit of the 'revolution', had ultimately facilitated the emergence of Isaias' own dominance. He might have been checked in the early 1990s, arguably, as the EPLF was dissolved and the PFDJ founded, or in the mid-1980s with shifts in the central leadership; but he was not, and the Isaias faction gradually strengthened its hand within the movement in the course of the 1990s. The entrenchment of the President's position would continue in the decade after the 2001 clampdown.[56] While through the 1990s, and during the struggle, there had been no real evidence of the personality cult, it was increasingly clear that such a creeping cult did indeed exist, and that Isaias had in fact carefully cultivated the image of the simple, selfless, and incorruptible leader, the only individual capable of guiding Eritrea into the future, the guardian of the achievements of the 'revolution'. He became an increasingly isolated figure, surrounding himself with those who were in complete concurrence with his views, and creating a series of rivalries and tensions among those below him. The President's Office, characterized by a heady conjunction of para-noia and self-righteousness, swiftly became the sole source of power in Eritrea. This sense of government under siege was reflected in society at large as the 'no-war, no-peace' situation looked ever more permanent. Prisons swelled with dissidents, critics, Pentecostal Christians, and Jehovah's Witnesses, with draft dodgers and deserters, with 'spies' and journalists, and suspiciously successful businessmen. The judiciary was rendered impotent, the media remained under the tightest of controls, the Orthodox Church was watched.[57] Movement in and out of the country—both for individuals and commodities, even of the most basic kind—was soon severely restricted. Within a few years, Eritrea was widely regarded as one of the most oppres-sive countries in the world, as well as one of the most militarized.[58] While there was little space for serious opposition to the government inside the country—with the partial exception of the shadowy armed movement of Islamic *jihad*ists operating in the Sudanese border areas—opposition move-ments proliferated abroad, and critics in exile increased in number and became more vocal. Disparate elements in Europe and North America con-tinually combined, split, and recombined to form a confusing constellation of opposition to the Isaias regime, but they were—and by and large remain—disorganized and disoriented.[59] They had little credibility inside Eritrea itself, as many long-suffering Eritreans regarded them sceptically as cut from much the same cloth as Isaias himself, while the decision of some to accept Ethiopian hospitality from time to time further undermined their integrity and authority in most Eritreans' eyes.

Much of this was against a background of, and was in many respects directly linked to, rapid economic deterioration. The war had devastated the fledgling Eritrean economy—fragile to begin with, following the neglect and destruction suffered between the 1950s and the 1980s, and hardly assisted by the government's centralist and regulatory interference during the 1990s. After 2000, trade was reduced to a trickle, inward investment was virtually non-existent, and the effects of massive unemployment were only partially and in any case temporarily masked by mass military and national service. Dependency on foreign aid—despite the increasingly shrill rhetoric related to self-reliance which had now become dangerous dogma—worsened in the wake of a series of bad harvests which compounded the material devastation wrought by the war itself. This was true despite the Eritrean government's deteriorating relationships with the European Union and the US, neither of which possessed the patience or the wherewithal to understand the journey which had led the country to its grim condition. As 2010 dawned, indeed, reports emerged that the Eritrean government was actually confiscating incoming food aid, declaring that such outside assistance made people 'lazy'.[60] The utilization of economic desperation for political ends appeared to be taking new and ever more brutal forms; but in fact food has long been politicized—both as a military target and as a weapon, by being withheld—and evidence of the intersection of food and violence abounds throughout the nineteenth and twentieth centuries. The destruction or the confiscation of food has long been used to destabilize or punish enemies across an environmentally fragile region; the EPLF, it seems, has learnt the lesson well, the enemy in this case being its own citizenry.

Ever greater distance opened up between government and populace, as the former maintained a high level of militarization—arguing, only partly disingenuously, for the need for vigilance against future Ethiopian aggression—and the latter increasingly faced a future bereft of hope or opportunity.[61] The system of fixed-term military service, begun in the early 1990s with the establishment of Sawa training camp in the western lowlands, was initially conceived as a nation-building project; in the early twenty-first century such service was actively undermining the nation. It had become indefinite, and most young people (and not a few older ones) thought only of how to escape. The government mistrusted its own population, especially youth, to a marked degree.[62] The University of Asmara, for example, had long been seen as a source of potential trouble, owing to the agitation of some students during the war, and the increasing activity of the bravely (but briefly) independent Students' Union immediately after it; its eventual closure stood in stark contrast to the massive expansion of Sawa, which in many ways was the real heart of the educational system. The University was replaced by a series of ill-developed 'colleges' around the country—a reflection of Isaias' own apparent distaste for Asmara, which was seen as corrupted and troublesome—where students lived in military conditions and received very little actual 'education'. Indeed the EPLF's anti-intellectualism was marked, and was reflected in the contempt expressed not simply for the University but for the 'so-called' scholars in exile who were increasingly critical of the movement. While Isaias declared that an ex-fighter could do the same job as someone with a university degree, others sought weakly to defend an education policy that claimed a developmental agenda but which appeared rather more motivated by control freakery and growing nervousness that young people were losing the 'values' of the struggle—forgetting, of course, that tens of thousands had been killed or maimed in the trenches between 1998 and 2000. That nervousness was reflected in the opening of a cadre school in Nakfa, where selected youths would be 'reminded' of those values; the government's fear of popular dis-engagement from politics, indeed, also led to the holding of public meet-ings in the course of 2005 to invite some degree of 'dialogue'. It was short-lived, and a resounding failure, but it provided a brief glimpse of concern in government circles.[63]

An oppressive, militarized social system led to a haemorrhaging of youngsters in the army across the border into Ethiopia and Sudan. It was a steady leakage of sovereignty, and a matter of political legitimacy much more serious than any squabble over the demarcation of a border. While asylum centres across the region, as well as in Europe and North America, swelled with young Eritreans, their supposed abandonment of the 'cause' confirmed in the minds of those still in Isaias' circle that only he possessed the character and direction to finish the job: 'the dogs bark', he was alleg-edly fond of saying, 'but the camel continues to march'. Few Eritreans were at all clear where exactly the camel was headed, or even if he knew himself; but the dwindling core of loyalists only had their mistrust of 'the people' confirmed, reinforcing the extraordinarily solipsistic belief within the movement that those who had not been in 'the struggle' could not truly understand it, or the sacrifices made. What I have elsewhere termed the 'Nakfa syndrome'[64]—the essentialist conviction that 'Eritrea' had been truly forged in the EPLF's struggle in the 1970s and 1980s, and that some-thing of an authoritarian utopia had been created in the rear base around Nakfa—had defined Eritrean society from the moment the EPLF entered Asmara in 1991. The celebration of the 'martyrs'—those who had given their lives in 'the field'—was an annual pageantry which was both pro-foundly emotional but also deeply political, for it represented the last word in all political discourse. Whatever might happen, whatever problems might be encountered, however occasionally disgruntled people might become, the EPLF was untouchable: the memory of the martyrs, and the sacrifices the movement had made on behalf of the people, guaranteed it. This was the culture that hardened into something altogether more malignant in the years after 2001. Independence Day and Martyrs' Day were once about the creation of national cohesion; in later years, they only served to accentuate the distance between the governing and the governed. It seemed that, after all, the Nakfa utopia had only been for the few who had actually *been there*; everyone else could, at best, only be associated with, but never truly part of, that great achievement. And so there were fighters, and there was everyone else; and yet after 2001 it seemed that neither could really be trusted by an ever mightier executive whose authority was rooted in military command, and a talent for intrigue.

A similar belligerence, the product of the bitter isolation of the EPLF's struggle, was evident in Eritrea's foreign relations.[65] Even apart from Ethiopia, independent Eritrea's relations with its neighbours were turbulent, leading to the frequently made charge that Eritrea is an aggressive and destabilizing force intent on building a hegemonic or at least spoiling role in the region. While this may be true to some extent, it has to be understood in the context of the Eritrean region's long-term historical experience, culminating in the political culture of the EPLF.[66] In fact, some of the problems with neighbours have not been of Eritrea's deliberate making, and in any case are comprehensible in the context of young nationhood. Nonetheless, at the very least, Eritrea's foreign policy has been characterized by a clumsy naivety, a reflection, in part, of the inexperienced diplomatic corps which was drawn from the same pool of ex-fighters making up the ranks of government. Eritrea's responses to foreign policy problems have invariably involved some degree of force, at least in the first instance. Regarded by outsiders as prickly and uncompromising, the government's position has always been that Eritrea's hard-won sovereignty will come first and foremost in policy considerations, and any perceived threat will be met with whatever force necessary; certainly, independent Eritrea's political establishment had become the domain of a liberation movement whose military skills were proven but whose willingness to negotiate and compromise was hardly a notable characteristic. A belief in the absolute primacy of armed force lay at the heart of that political establishment. The military hubris of the Eritreans was marked after 1991; their unconditional military triumph, and the attendant semi-mythology which grew quickly around it—they had defeated the superpower that was the Soviet Union, as well as Ethiopia with the largest army in Africa—had generated an extraordinary degree of self-belief. At the same time, however, it is important to remember that the Eritrean government was keenly aware of its potential vulnerability in a region dominated by two much larger, economically stronger, and better established powers, namely Ethiopia and Sudan. The attempt to destabilize its neighbours was in that sense a rational policy decision for Eritrea. It might also be pointed out that it has proved remarkably easy for outsiders to blame the Eritreans for a great many of the region's problems; a relative newcomer, Eritrea has lacked the pools of empathy or even knowledge among western observers and therefore has suffered somewhat in terms of representation.

Nonetheless, Eritrea did itself very few favours. Thus, early on there was distaste for the OAU and its failure to serve Eritrea's interests in particular and those of the continent more widely; Isaias declared that 'to mince our words now and applaud the OAU would neither serve the desired purpose of learning lessons from our past, nor reflect positively on our honesty and integrity'.[67] This initiated a difficult relationship which would haunt Eritrea during the war with Ethiopia, the latter having much greater influence within the organization, as well as being its permanent host. Relations with Sudan quickly collapsed and were problematic for the first decade or more of Eritrean independence;[68] the rise to power of the National Islamic Front in 1989, and the unfolding of its Islamist agenda, created severe strains in the relationship with independent Eritrea in the early 1990s. The EPLF, after all, had its roots in no small part in opposition to Sudanese Arabism and Islamism, and the two countries were soon providing succour to one another's rebels and political opponents in order to gain leverage over their internal and therefore their external affairs. Eritrea sponsored or supported the ongoing rebellions in southern and eastern Sudan through the 1990s, and would later do the same in Darfur; Sudan provided bases and ideological sustenance to *jihad*ist groups operating in the northern mountains, seeking the overthrow of the EPLF state.

Meanwhile, Eritrea clashed with Yemen over the Hanish Islands in 1996, although this was resolved by outside arbitration;[69] there were sporadic tensions with Djibouti, with whom diplomatic ties were cut during the 1998–2000 war, and there is a military standoff along a contested stretch of border at the time of writing.[70] There was adventurism in Somalia—after 2000, this was a means of instigating trouble on Ethiopia's southern flank—although the scale of the Eritreans' involvement was somewhat smaller than that of Ethiopia. In the years after 2002, when the boundary commission published its findings, Eritrean condemnations of the US, the EU, and ultimately the UN—all of whom Asmara saw as complicit in failing to place pressure on

Ethiopia to abide by the ruling—became ever more shrill. Relations with the US in particular reached a nadir by 2007,[71] when Washington—convinced, as it remains, that the Eritreans were essentially arming Somali terrorists—declared that it was considering placing Eritrea on the list of state sponsors of terrorism. At any rate, after vigorous lobbying by both IGAD and the AU, the UN Security Council in December 2009 imposed sanctions on Eritrea for its involvement in Somalia, an unprecedented experience for an African nation; Eritrea's isolation, notwithstanding its growing interest in friendships with such states as Iran, seemed complete. The sanctions, predictably, were greeted with angry outrage in Asmara, and it seemed that Isaias was at loggerheads with just about the whole of the 'international community'—and, moreover, that he was happiest in that position. Of course, it might be pointed out that over the last twenty years Ethiopia has hardly been more successful in terms of regional relations: a major war with Eritrea, military involvement in Somalia, border problems with Kenya. In that sense—so the Eritrean leadership would have it, at any rate—Ethiopia is the centrepiece of the region's instability. However, it is the Eritrean 'zone' which is in fact the epicentre of much of the area's conflict, while Eritrea itself is the most visible manifestation of the politics of the frontier. The EPLF inherited not a nation but a historical fault line, a thin arc of contested territory with a history of recurrent conflict and intrinsic instability. This environment, of which the movement itself was a product, profoundly influenced Eritrean foreign policy, and thus has had a major impact beyond Eritrea itself; but it also influenced Eritrea's domestic politics in ways which were not, perhaps, foreseeable at the point of liberation—many had their judgement clouded by euphoria—but which had become clear by the end of the decade. The EPLF's mistrust of the very space they had inherited, and its knowledge of the region's violent, unstable past, meant that they in turn governed through a violent militarism which suggested that Eritrea's own people were apparently not to be trusted any more than the country's rapacious neighbours.

In other words, contemporary Eritrea—in both foreign and domestic affairs—must be understood as much in terms of the politics of the fault line as of the failures of the post-colony. It is the case that recent analyses of Eritrea's increasing difficulties have tended to focus on the authoritarian proclivities of the EPLF;[72] the country's predicament, in sum, is the product of modern misgovernment, and is rooted in the political failures of the EPLF itself, and even more specifically, in the personality of Isaias Afeworki.

The nation may be battered from above, but it remains intact, and the central assumption is that a nation does indeed exist, or at least that there is a nation to be had in the future, given the requisite political guidance. These analyses are of course valid in their own right; but here I propose an alternative approach, related to historical experience and resultant political culture. Eritrea's politics, again, are those of the borderland, and the outcome of long-term instability; the pressures of the frontier zone, dating to the nineteenth century and perhaps earlier, have produced a politically unstable environment and a restless militarism. Eritrea cannot simply be understood to have 'failed' in the conventional post-colonial sense. The roots of its failure, rather, lie in its troubled and unstable history as a violent frontier zone, and the political tectonics which have shaped responses to particular problems. It was an extraordinarily fertile frontier, too; and that fertility—the vitality of violence, if we prefer—is critical to understanding the region's modern history.

Ethiopia remains the *sine qua non* of the Eritrean state. Ethiopia has been differently imagined by different sets of people at different points in time, but in the end no satisfactory solution has been reached in Eritrea about how to deal with either Tigray, or the Amhara, or the putative 'empire-state' as a whole. The EPLF has not yet developed a coherent or persuasive strategy—either at home or abroad—which is not at heart anti-Ethiopian. At the same time, of course, it must be remembered that Ethiopia does indeed constitute a 'threat', however distorted or exaggerated by the government in Asmara; multiple strands of what we might call the Ethiopian 'political establishment' do not accept Eritrean independence in its current form, and there is residual hostility from the TPLF and Amhara elites alike. In other words, although much blame for the troubled relationship might be laid at the feet of the EPLF, there is a very real and complex set of problems to be addressed which requires a degree of political creativity, flexibility, and imagination of which the current government in Asmara seems increasingly incapable. Yet in many respects Ethiopia is only the gatekeeper of *sha'abiya* anger: beyond it lies the global hinterland. Ethiopia reminds Eritrea of how the latter has been habitually betrayed and misunderstood; the repeated failure of the international community to do its duty, or even to pay attention—in the 1950s, in the early 1960s, during the struggle itself, and latterly during the 1998–2000 war and its immediate aftermath—has persuaded the leadership that Eritrea is always the victim of international intrigue and ignorance. National neurosis, perhaps, but unfortunately it is grounded in

some measure of historical reality—and needs to be taken rather more seriously by foreign representatives charged with dealing with the Eritrean government. Thus the logic of the militarized isolation of Sahel, and beyond:
the fortified and undemarcated border represents Eritrea's besieged and
beleaguered position in a hostile world. Much of this also explains the
export of the frontier war; the 'frontier on the move' is manifest in Eritrean
involvement in Somalia, and Darfur, and southern Ethiopia, policies aimed
at undermining both Sudan and Ethiopia. In this sense the EPLF is a form
of super-*shifta*, its foreign policy representing *shifta* rampant. The movement's regional adventurism is a reflection of the restless violence of the
historic Eritrean frontier, and at least in part symptomatic of its frustration
with and indeed contempt for the 'nation' it supposedly inherited.

The rise of the Eritrean armed nationalist movement represented, ultimately, an attempt to achieve mastery of the frontier through violence. It was
not, in the end, 'revolution', but evolution, in which the Tigrinya, not unnat-
urally, emerged pre-eminent, even if that was not how the liberation war
itself began; the militant identity thus created is the outcome of an attempt
to resolve a historically uncertain and ambiguous state of affairs, born of
mistrust and insecurity. The EPLF has attempted, further, to make the frontier a *moral state*, to weave a sense of morality around the experience of the
frontier, driven forward by the Front's own sense of militarized morality and
'revolutionary' zeal. In sum, it was a process which involved making a moral
virtue of *being Eritrean*, rooted in a sense of bitter experience on the contested frontier, with all its attendant sacrifice and suffering, the critical moral
elements of the frontier people. In effect, the EPLF represented a form of
militarized moral mastery of the frontier;[73] such mastery was not, as the
EPLF had it, in itself revolutionary—although clearly it comprised novel and
innovative elements—but rather profoundly evolutionary. Arguably the most
novel element, in fact, was the brutal imposition of a monopoly on the use
of violence across the Eritrean frontier zone, which was essential if the EPLF
was to succeed in 'modernizing'—i.e. creating a functioning nation from—
the contested space which it had captured. The Eritrea that the EPLF created, then, involved the modernization and institutionalization of a frontier.
However, it seems clear that even while striving for mastery, the Front did
not truly accept the viability of its estate, and certainly it could not take for
granted its stability; the roots of modern authoritarianism, thus, lie in the
long-term violent struggle to achieve control over an inherently unstable
environment—both internal and external.

Oromia

The OLF withdrew from the coalition in 1992, and shortly afterwards resumed its struggle for 'Oromia', the imagined homeland of the Oromo people. The profound divisions within the Oromo liberation movement notwithstanding, the exponents of the cause became ever more articulate, and were increasingly supported by an academic establishment in exile, determined to pursue its revision of the Ethiopian past—essentially an exercise in the demythologizing of the Menelik empire and its successors. Some of this work was more polemical than scholarly, but it was all aggressively revisionist.[74] The situation was horrendously complex, however: the very shape of the new federal state of Oromia indicated the scale of the problem, for it was flung like a splash of paint across the south and centre of the republic, wholly lacking in the geographical logic of Ethiopia, or Tigray, or even—for all its political and clan-related complexity—the Ogaden. Millions of Oromo, moreover, lived at relative peace with the Ethiopian state, unwilling to embrace the renewed armed struggle advocated by the OLF and the myriad other Oromo movements which soon emerged. But the fact remained that the withdrawal of Oromo fighters back to the proverbial bush was perhaps the most visible manifestation of the failure of the EPRDF's ethnic federalist experiment. At the time of writing, those fighters—of whatever faction—are some way from overthrowing the state, or anything approaching it; their main areas of activity are Wellega in the west, to some extent in Gambella region, and in southern Sidamo close to the Kenyan border. But they do have the *potential* to represent the single most dangerous internal challenge to the federal state, not least in that the Oromo nationalist movements purport to represent close to half the country's total population. Those who are contemptuously dismissive of the Oromo military challenge are missing the point, for as long as it exists, the Federal Democratic Republic of Ethiopia is inherently unstable. As the 1990s developed, Oromo nationalists situated their struggle in an ever more sophisticated historical context; the basic thesis, however, was relatively straightforward, viz. that Ethiopia was an imperial state created by Menelik, and the Oromo were the largest of a number of 'colonized peoples' under the *habesha* yoke since the late nineteenth century.[75] While the 'new' EPRDF regime made some effort to control Oromo hearts and minds, largely through the illusion of ethno-federalism and political partnership—from the mid-1990s, there was a significant

Oromo presence in the Ethiopian government—the proliferating nationalist movements advocated its violent overthrow and talked of redress for decades of persecution and oppression of the Oromo at the hands of the Amhara-Tigrayan political establishment.

The issue for Oromo activists has been one of unity. Already from the late 1980s the OLF was in competition with the Oromo People's Democratic Organisation (OPDO), formed in 1989 by a group of Oromo who had been cooperating with the TPLF. The OPDO accepted the pan-Ethiopianism of the EPRDF, while the OLF—which had long had uneasy relations with other Ethiopian guerrilla organizations—situated its struggle solely in terms of Oromo rights; certainly, at the very least, the OLF demanded that it be recognized as the sole representative of the Oromo people. When this was not forthcoming, and the TPLF favoured the OPDO, the OLF withdrew from the coalition, declaring that the OPDO was a government puppet organization which did not represent the interests of the Oromo population. In the years that followed, the OPDO was vigorously promoted as the Oromo 'official partner' in the new political dispensation, and any Oromo suspected of supporting rival movements, including the OLF, faced systematic persecution.[76] In 1997, talks between the government and the OLF broke down, the former inviting the latter back into its fold, but the latter stipulating that power in Oromia should be transferred from the OPDO to the OLF, something which the government could not countenance. There was a faith-based element, too, for the OLF leadership—predominantly Muslim—believed that Addis Ababa's US-assisted military operations against Islamic extremism (mostly Somali) in the mid-1990s ultimately rendered any serious dialogue between the secessionist OLF and the EPRDF pointless. The OLF was branded a terrorist organization bent on overthrowing the legitimate political system by force—as the EPRDF itself had done, but it seemed it was a matter of interpretation and context—and the state security apparatus was brought to bear on an Oromo population toward which the state itself remained suspicious and hostile.[77] The OPDO itself was subject to continual monitoring—there were major purges of its membership and leadership, for example, in 1997 and again in 2001, when former Ethiopian president Negasso Gidada was expelled—which was clearly important for the government, as it was through the OPDO that 'Oromia' would be administered, from the new federal capital at Adama (formerly Nazret). Sporadic public protests by Oromo activists were dealt with brutally; by the late 1990s and early 2000s, human rights organizations were reporting horrific stories of abuse of Oromo suspects in detention, with often entire communities being targeted owing to supposed OLF links and women in particular being subjected to sexual assault.[78] At the other end of the political scale, senior Oromo political leaders—accused, invariably, of 'narrow nationalism'—continue to be arrested and detained regularly at the time of writing.

Yet the response to 'state terrorism' has been splintered, and again the Oromo cause, if it can be thus singularly rendered, has been undermined by a chronic disunity which makes even the Eritrean opposition groups appear relatively cohesive. The proliferation of movements through the 1990s caused such consternation within the broad church of Oromo activism that various groups came together in 2000 to form the United Liberation Forces of Oromia (ULFO).[79] Strains quickly emerged, and by 2006 the movement had collapsed, the trigger being the formation of the rival Alliance for Freedom and Democracy (AFD), in which the OLF—apparently long suspicious of the rise of the ULFO—was involved. Confusingly, however, there were now three distinct movements using the nomenclature 'OLF'; there was also FIDO (the Front for Independent Democratic Oromia), UOPLF (United Oromo People's Liberation Front), FIO (Front for Independence of Oromia), and COPLF (Council for Oromia People's Liberation Front). By the time the Oromo Forum for Dialogue and Reconciliation emerged in exile in 2007–8 in an attempt to at least provide a context for open discussion, it was clearly badly needed, and there was more than a hint of desperation in the preamble: there needed to be an end to 'infighting, mistrust and innuendos', and a new unified struggle to halt 'the escalation of the suffering of the Oromo people and other colonized peoples at the hands of the TPLF minority government'.[80] To anyone acquainted with Ethiopian and Eritrean liberation politics in the 1970s and 1980s, it was a familiar tale. Meanwhile the actual numbers involved in the field of combat on the Oromo side had dropped from perhaps 15,000 in the early 1990s to something around 5000–6000.

The Eritreans would increasingly if surreptitiously lend their support— certainly moral, and allegedly material—to the cause, especially after 1998. The irony, but also the motivation, was that tens of thousands of the bodies scattered across the Eritrean battlefields of 1998, 1999, and 2000 belonged to Oromo soldiers in the Ethiopian army. With the eruption of the war in mid-1998, there had been a massive recruitment campaign across the south, especially in impoverished, rural Oromo communities; they were to become cannon-fodder, in the true Napoleonic sense, although many joined up because of the opportunities promised to them by recruitment officers.[81] Stories abounded of Oromo soldiers being marched over minefields in order to clear the way for more elite, glory-hunting *habesha* units; of Oromo units being deployed in hopeless or static situations, while Amhara and Tigrayan units were given rather more attractive postings; of Oromo being ill-trained and ill-equipped, and being deployed only to draw fire; or of Oromo dead being abandoned in mass graves by retreating Ethiopian forces without any but the most basic of markings, while Tigrayan and Amhara soldiers and officers were treated rather more carefully, often given individual graves or being carried back.[82] Whatever the precise truth of these stories, their very existence was suggestive of brutal ethnic differentiation within a military establishment now under new management, and of troubled attitudes more broadly. Disenfranchised, rural Oromo youth—as much a socio-economic group as an ethnic one—clearly provided EPRDF officers with a source of cheap and replaceable manpower, although perhaps their recruitment might also be seen as a form of the political co-option necessary to the great national (re)building of the 1990s. Nonetheless, where the project itself was evidently failing, the EPRDF reverted to the brutal control and repression of Oromo communities well learnt from earlier regimes.

In that sense, the great EPRDF-led nation-building project—supposedly greatly spurred by the 1998–2000 war—was a resounding failure, riddled as it was with deep-seated tensions.[83] While the Eritrean war was meant to galvanize Ethiopian patriots and enable the government to appeal to an ancient Ethiopian nationalism, it was clear that millions of Ethiopians—Oromo prominent among them—could scarcely endorse such a project. Many Oromo leaders themselves rejected completely the nationalist rhetoric deployed during the war, perceiving the conflict, rather, as an exclusively northern affair between Tigrinya rivals, which Meles was now manipulating to consolidate the TPLF's position in Ethiopia more broadly. From this perspective, arguably, the Eritrean war actually *heightened*, rather than reduced, simmering ethno-regional tensions within Ethiopia—because it led inevitably to the questions, *whose war is this and who stands to benefit?* Regardless of the inefficacy of the Oromo armed struggle and its political weaknesses, the fact remained that 'Oromia'—both as a concept and as a place—was also a fertile frontier within which creative new identities were being cultivated, and along which the true nature of the EPRDF state revealed itself.

It remains a frontier which may yet come to redefine the very polity of Ethiopia itself.

Continuities and transitions: Somalia and Ethiopia

The disintegration of Somalia between 1988 and 1991 stood in stark contrast, so it initially seemed, to the progressive state-building projects in Eritrea and Ethiopia in the early 1990s. It is not my purpose here to explore the Somali situation in the kind of depth which is in any case much better left to specialists;[84] rather, my aim is to briefly outline the manner in which Somalia came once again to constitute a major frontier of violence for both Ethiopia and Eritrea, though especially the former, and involved the continuation of the 1998–2000 war by proxy. While the Ethiopian involvement in Somalia is very much on the public record, as it were—even if they reject some of the accusations made regarding motive and behaviour—it should be pointed out that the Eritreans continue to reject allegations that they are involved, beyond offering 'moral support' for the 'Somali struggle'. Throughout the 1990s, the EPRDF government had naturally taken a close interest in the violence playing out along Ethiopia's historic southern frontier, with security operations being periodically conducted along the Somali border while the 'warlordism' of the Hawiye clans in southern central Somalia descended into violent competition over (as much as anything else) commercial opportunities. Between the fourteenth and the sixteenth centuries, Christian highlanders had forged statehood in struggles with Somali Islam; it was an ongoing contest in the nineteenth and early twentieth centuries. Now, Addis Ababa had the full support of the US in its mounting battle against Islamic extremism, and in particular against the fundamentalist *al-Ittihad* movement. As a 'failed state'—in the conventional sense of that increasingly utilized catchphrase—Somalia was seen as a fertile breeding ground, and a hiding place, for Muslim extremism, especially after September 2001, when US intelligence detected the presence of *al-Qaeda* cells there.[85] The US and Ethiopia had shared objectives in this respect throughout both the Clinton and the Bush administrations, even if they differed over strategy.

Ethiopian policy through much of the 1990s was to support certain key 'secular' warlords, notably Abdulahi Yusuf, in opposition to the Islamic groups; in the meantime, repeated reconciliation conferences were held in the attempt to bring together various Somali factions, usually in vain. The last of these gave rise to the Transitional National Government (TNG) in 2000.[86] This 'administration' lacked support from certain key Mogadishu warlords, while its Islamist leanings soon provoked Ethiopian hostility, and shortly another peace progress—led by the regional Intergovernmental Authority on Development (IGAD)—was in motion, ostensibly to reconcile the TNG with its Ethiopian-backed opponents. By the end of the process in 2004, however, the TNG had largely evaporated. Meles Zenawi was instrumental in the international negotiations leading to its replacement, the Transitional Federal Government (TFG), whose parliament (meeting in Kenya, not on Somali soil) elected Abdulahi Yusuf as president. The Ethiopians have long been forced to defend themselves against allegations that they bribed the parliament to do so. Increasingly, the TFG was something of a fiction, desperately casting around for wider Somali support; meanwhile, the Union of Islamic Courts (UIC), an umbrella organization for various loosely affiliated interests, including both moderate and more radical wings of political Islam, was becoming ever more influential and popular across southern Somalia. By early 2006, supporters of the UIC were increasingly hostile to the warlords, and especially some warlord factions' dominance of the profitable Mogadishu port business.

Clearly, external intervention further complicated the mire of Somali politics and allegiances. The Ogaden, of course, had long been a natural field of intrigue, dating to the era of the liberation struggle. The Ogaden National Liberation Front (ONLF), dating to 1984 when it took up the struggle of the earlier Western Somali Liberation Front, had long been a key ally of the EPLF in the region; Siad Barre had long hosted movements against the *Derg*, at least until the agreement of 1988, and both TPLF and EPLF leaders had travelled on Somali passports. The ONLF's main support was drawn from the southern Ogadeni clans, while the major northern clans, as well as the non-Ogadeni clans living in the Ogaden, including the Hawiye and Isaq, opposed the movement. Supported by the EPLF, it fought the *Derg* for several years before (briefly) enjoying legitimate status as a political party in the early 1990s; it followed the OLF out of the coalition, however, and returned to the bush, in the process absorbing a number of Muslim Oromo recruits. After independence, Eritrea sought further opportunities in Somalia: in 1998, it struck up a short-lived relationship with the key warlord Hussein Aideed before the latter transferred his loyalty to Addis Ababa. Eritrea also continued to support the ONLF, with rumours emerging by 2005 that ONLF fighters were being trained in Eritrea itself. Occasional bomb outrages in Addis Ababa and attacks on oil installations notwithstanding, the 'success' of the ONLF was limited—not least because of its apparent inability to develop broad support within the newly named 'Region 5' of the federal Ethiopian state. A complex interplay between Ethiopian and Somali authorities in the Ogaden had led to something approaching a stable political settlement there, or at least one in which 'resistance' to Ethiopian 'occupation' had been largely neutered.[87] Nonetheless, the Ogaden remained a key area of radical political activity, enabling Ethiopian forces to justify brutal security operations there,[88] and the region was a natural point of leverage against Ethiopia for Eritrea; when the UIC took control of Mogadishu in mid-2006, it greatly opened up Eritrea's access to the Ogaden and the ONLF.

Eritrea's problem—and, of course, Ethiopia's—was the growing Islamism within the region. Asmara had long discouraged the growth of Islamism in the ONLF, but it nonetheless developed links with radical Islamic leaders within the UIC, notably Sheikh Yosef Indohadde and Sheikh Hassan Dahir Aweys, and was reportedly training and arming UIC fighters. In sum, the profoundly fragmented 'arrangement' of a besieged and ineffectual TFG surrounded by an array of warlords was at least partially improved through the rise of the UIC, which briefly, in 2006, governed the southern region of Somalia rather more effectively than any administration since the end of the 1980s. An apparently popular revolt (precipitated by a long-running business rivalry) saw the warlords expelled from Mogadishu in mid-2006. The UIC itself was divided between moderates and hardliners, but it was the militant Islamist wing which held sway, for now. Their 'mistake', however, was to make threatening noises in the direction of Ethiopia, which feared both *shari'a* and *jihad* on its southern flank, a much more serious threat, in its way, than that posed by the Eritreans in the north. At the end of 2006 and the beginning of 2007, Ethiopia invaded. The US had reportedly advised against such a risky adventure, warning Meles that Somalia would become 'Ethiopia's Iraq', but once it had begun they supported it, materially and morally. And at first, Ethiopia seemed vindicated: the UIC forces scattered into the bush, and Ethiopian troops occupied Mogadishu with relative ease. But it was a remarkably wrongheaded war, apparently ignorant of history; few Somalis of whatever clan, or political or religious persuasion, would welcome Ethiopian troops as 'liberators' and guarantors of order, and a violent backlash was entirely predictable. Ethiopia was the ancient enemy, and radicalized Islam fuelled the violence of the response.

The insurgency grew in strength—again, the Eritreans were allegedly supporting it with small arms and basic training, although they refuted the charge—and the Ethiopian forces were increasingly beleaguered in their bases. Civilian casualties spiralled across southern Somalia, and a humanitarian crisis of shocking proportions loomed; meanwhile, Ethiopian troops were reportedly involved in appalling abuses of civilians and suspected fighters alike,[89] and did little to win over proverbial 'hearts and minds'—however unlikely that would have been in any case. There were reports that Ethiopian forces regularly and deliberately shelled civilian areas of Mogadishu in response to insurgent attacks, wiping out entire districts in what human rights organizations described as 'war crimes'. While for much of 2007 occupying Ethiopian forces reportedly behaved in a restrained and disciplined manner, in 2008 eye-witness accounts abounded of troops looting and pillaging, raping women, and carrying out on the spot executions, as well as firing live rounds into crowds of civilians and attacking mosques. There were also 'credible reports' that the Ethiopian military was diverting urgently needed food aid from drought-affected areas in order to flush out rebels.[90] There was nothing novel about such tactics, for they had been seen before, most recently in the tactics adopted by the armies of the *Derg*. If anything, however, atrocities in Somalia (as also in the Ogaden) took on the appearance of culture- and race-war, aimed at the decimation of the very economic and cultural bases of Somali existence.

Addis Ababa engineered the creation of a new administration, as 'transitional' and as ineffectual as that overthrown by the UIC, against the backdrop of mounting catastrophe. The invasion stoked up nationalist as well as Islamist hatred of the government in Addis Ababa. Somali Islamist insurgents—known popularly as *al-Shabaab*, literally 'the youth'—escalated their attacks through 2007 and 2008. There was a certain irony in Eritrea's support, as the government had long had problems of its own with Islamic extremism, and a wave of Islamism across the region was hardly in Asmara's long-term interests—but from Eritrea's point of view the policy was both logical and consistent.[91] The EPLF saw not allies but short-term interests and opportunities, a chance to undermine Ethiopia along a new front; it was decidedly *not* in Eritrea's interests to see Ethiopia succeed in Somalia. But the outcome was increasing international isolation—ironic, again, given that Eritrea's Somali policy was driven by the same self-interest and concern for self-defence that had motivated Ethiopia's aggression. The US, again, identified Eritrea as behaving in the manner of a state sponsor of terrorism, and indeed Asmara had become the meeting place for various strands of Somali opposition—UIC leaders, some warlords, elements of the former transitional administration. Most importantly, from the Americans' viewpoint, was Eritrea's hosting of the Alliance for the Re-Liberation of Somalia (ARS), which included Sheikh Hassan Dahir Aweys, a leader of the *al-Ittihad* Islamist group, and named in the UN list of persons linked to terrorism; its secretary-general was Sheikh Sharif Sheikh Ahmed, a key religious leader but regarded as something of a moderate. Eritrea supported the ARS in its refusal to work either with the temporary Somali government or the Ethiopians, and many of its members stayed away from the Djibouti conference in 2008 which brought some Somali groups together for preliminary negotiations. Indeed, the fact that Djibouti was treading on Eritrean 'political territory', as it were, was almost certainly one of the factors behind the confrontation which took place on the Eritrean–Djiboutian border that same year. Eritrea's isolation seemed complete at the time of writing in mid-2009 when the AU took the dramatic and unprecedented step of calling for international sanctions against Eritrea in view of the latter's support for Somali insurgents. These were imposed by the UN Security Council in December 2009.

Meanwhile Ethiopia became increasingly frustrated by the inability of the Somali administration to settle even their internal differences, never mind cope with the growing insurgency; Meles made threatening noises about pulling out if Ethiopia did not receive the anticipated international support, or indeed the gratitude which he believed he was due for 'dealing with' the Somali crisis. But direct UN intervention was ruled out, and only a token AU force was made available. It was enough for the Ethiopian government, which declared its mission achieved, and withdrew its troops at the beginning of 2009. Ethiopian forces remained close by, however, and reports soon emerged of military operations just inside the Somali border, activity which will surely continue for the foreseeable future. With the Ethiopian withdrawal, and a new Somali administration under former UIC and ARS leader Sheikh Sharif Sheikh Ahmed in place, Aweys (dubbed the 'kingmaker' by foreign journalists) returned to Mogadishu and there is, at the time of writing, a belief that Somalis are on the threshold of their best chance at a lasting political settlement for nearly two decades. But it is only a threshold: while it is hoped that increasing numbers of *al-Shabaab* might be lured into a ceasefire by a power-sharing arrangement with key Islamist leaders, in the meantime violence between government and Islamist forces continues.[92] There is clearly a long way to travel, while the conflict on land spills over onto sea lanes in the Gulf of Aden and Indian Ocean in the form of Somali piracy.[93] For perhaps obvious reasons, the upsurge in piracy has captured international attention, but it is ultimately only a reflection of the turmoil—and of economic collapse—on land.[94] Ethiopia and Eritrea, moreover, will continue to harness whatever forces within Somalia they see fit to further their own national interests—lessons well learnt from the era of liberation struggle.

Mention should be made, finally, of the self-proclaimed Republic of Somaliland, the territory of former British Somaliland, which has both distanced itself from the mayhem further south and made significant progress toward independent statehood.[95] Its campaign for international recognition has been as yet unsuccessful, for a range of reasons, some more difficult to understand than others; but to all intents and purposes Somaliland is already a functioning state, and the government in Hargeysa has a powerful claim to sovereign status which it must be hoped will be accepted sooner rather than later. Somaliland is by no means wholly free of the disturbances which have defined the south,[96] and it is not quite the haven depicted by some of its more ardent supporters; but it has established a relative stability much appreciated by Ethiopia which has developed a close relationship with its neighbour. At the time of writing, Ethiopia is reportedly preparing to champion Somaliland's cause, which will prove an extremely interesting and important development for the region. There can be little doubt that it is very much in Ethiopia's interests to have a 'friendly' Somali regime so close to hand, while it also further undercuts Eritrea's influence in the region; on this frontier, if on no other, Meles' strategy is proving markedly superior to that of Isaias, who would have done rather better to cultivate his own relationship with a government in Hargeysa that may yet play a major role in the stabilization of the region.

Epilogue

Armed Frontiers and Militarized Margins

From the early 1990s, there emerged across the region an extraordinary patchwork of conflict. Axes of violence and strategic machinations intermeshed and pulled peoples and places together in new ways. In truth some of these conflicts began as localized struggles and crises, and were not initially connected to others in the region: the collapse of Somalia at the beginning of the 1990s was one such example, having its causes and its own dynamics. But given that one of the key themes of the region's history in the second half of the twentieth century was the enlargement of scale in terms of violence, it was inevitable that such local battles should become others' battles, too. Each war represented someone else's foreign policy opportunity and formed part of a war being fought for other reasons somewhere else in the region. The Eritrean–Ethiopian war, various insurgencies in Ethiopia, in particular that in the Ogaden and Oromo territories, the civil war in Sudan and the conflict in Darfur, the escalating violence in Somalia: these were the interconnected frontiers of violence, the political tectonics which had come to define the region.

This was not how it was supposed to be, of course: the end of the Cold War was supposed to usher in a new era of democratic development, an era which saw greater efforts toward the resolution of conflict and the application of pragmatic solutions to long-standing problems—and all against the backdrop provided by the triumph of liberal, democratic, capitalist values. At the very least, there would be no superpower rivalry to spur on wars in Africa. It was a remarkably naive, not to say curiously patronising, approach to African warfare in the late twentieth century: it seemed that, in killing one another as much as in any other sphere, Africans required some kind of external inspiration. To many outsider observers, the death of the Siad Barre regime in Somalia and subsequent violent chaos was an unfortunate anomaly, and indeed reminded many of just how savage Africa might be, and had been; still, the US-led intervention would hopefully go some way to restoring order. And, more importantly, further north there were apparently reasons to be optimistic. In Isaias Afeworki's EPLF and Meles Zenawi's EPRDF, the region appeared to have organizations capable of engendering stability and political and economic development. The term 'pragmatic' was the one most often used to describe Isaias and Meles themselves—and certainly, the EPLF and EPRDF respectively appeared to offer solutions to problems which had plagued the Ethiopian region since the eighteenth century. One was the issue of the frontier zone of Eritrea and access to the coast, and the other was the question of 'nationalities' within Ethiopia itself. Events in Somalia no doubt fed the West's inertia when it came to the mass killing in Rwanda, and together the two crises darkened the international mood in the first few years after the supposed 'end of history'. Nonetheless, the optimism was still there in 1998 when US President Clinton declared his belief in an 'African renaissance', within which were included Isaias Afeworki and Meles Zenawi.

To suggest that such optimism that the end of the Cold War produced was misplaced would not merely be an understatement, it would in itself be a chronic misrepresentation of reality. This was an optimism which was underpinned by a criminal ignorance of the dynamics of the region's history and political processes; whether such ignorance was wilful is something which will only become clear to the historians of the future, but for certain it was born of a remarkable arrogance. The West saw what it wanted to see in the mid-1990s, and what it saw served its interests. Neo-imperialism now came in the guise of free-marketism and aggressive humanitarianism. The notion that Africans could now stop fighting because 'liberal capitalism' had supposedly won the last great battle of history was redolent of the same conceit which had driven the partition of Africa a century earlier. By its very nature it was a marginalization of Africans from the engines of change: they would be the dumb recipients of wisdoms developed in another place. Isaias Afeworki and Meles Zenawi were indeed pragmatic, but not quite in the way that Western governments had hoped: for these men, war was now a matter of unfinished business, an extension of national policy, and something over which their new-found sovereignty allowed them complete control. Liberation war would have multiple legacies in the region, but one of them was clearly the institutionalization of violence in the new states of Ethiopia and Eritrea. In both countries, governments which were led by and to a large extent comprised of former guerrillas could draw on long histories of violence and use these to craft notions of national destiny.

In the case of the 'new' nations, which both Ethiopia and Eritrea eventually became, these were not merely militarisms which were mutually antagonistic, but rather they were in many respects actually defined one against the other. The peculiar political and cultural systems of the Eritrean state can be explained by the fact that it was built on a historical fault line—and one which had come to fundamentally destabilize the entire region. The Ethiopian state was also profoundly militarized, and defined by its frontiers, *viz*. the pointed celebration of Adwa in March 1999, just days after the Ethiopian army's success in capturing Badme. This was an exercise in telescopic remembrance, in which Isaias Afeworki took the place of Oreste Baratieri. Regardless of the enemy, the 1999 commemoration of Adwa provided a meaningful glimpse into the role of militarism at the heart of the Ethiopian polity and public life. The epicentre of the region's instability lay along the Eritrean–Ethiopian border, and thus the roots of much modern conflict lay in the history of troubled relations between the EPLF and the TPLF; but they were also to be found in the difficult relationship between newly independent Eritrea and Sudan. Certainly it might be argued—and some in the region have been only too happy to make the argument—that much of the region's instability stems from the emergence of one of the most successful armed liberation movements in Africa, and perhaps anywhere in the world, namely the EPLF. The EPLF has had a profound impact on the political shape of the region, and thus it may be possible to see Eritrea as the pivot around which, and through which, so much contemporary violence occurs. The very presence of Eritrea has affected the political dynamics of the region; the EPLF itself is a complex, ambitious, and—until very recently—highly effective organization. It has had considerable regional reach. Yet the emergence of Eritrea is only part of the story, because of course the contemporary history of the region has been shaped by the 'success' not only of the EPLF, but also of the TPLF in Ethiopia and the SPLM in Sudan. Nationalism and ethnicity remain, at the time of writing, powerful shapers of regional destiny—but religion has also long been significant and, likewise, remains so today, perhaps more than ever. In particular, the clash between Christianity and Islam is potentially more violent than previously.

Above all, perhaps, the period between the 1970s and the early twenty-first century has witnessed a dramatic expansion in the scale of 'frontierism', especially since the early 1990s. It is the interconnectedness of various frontiers of violence across the region which is the single most important manifestation of 'modernity' in recent years. In particular, frontiers by proxy have opened up, or perhaps more aptly, frontiers have been co-opted within the region by parties wishing to extend their own confrontations in new ways. Ethiopia's hosting of a range of Eritrean opposition movements, and multi-faceted Eritrean involvement in Somalia, eastern Sudan, Darfur, and inside Ethiopia itself, has created a set of what we might term 'virtual borderlands', and the proliferation of these has been much more the product of the organic, restless militarism of the region—dating at least to the nineteenth century—than the result of any kind of transformative modernity or external intervention, either during the Cold War or after.

North-east Africa, then, in common with virtually all zones of human habitation, is characterized by peripheral areas with long histories of economic distress, political marginalization and oppression, social dislocation, and ultimately violent conflict.[1] These regions are but rarely glimpsed in contemporary reportage, unless they happen to advance on the centre; and when they do receive attention, these militarized margins often attract humanitarian interest—usually relating to refugee flows and attendant nutritional and medical issues—rather than attracting interest in the conflict itself, or even in the dynamics behind the marginalization of those zones in the first place. The upshot is often that the wars being fought there represent the grime on the underbelly of human progress, and seem curiously pointless and endless; descriptions of them are sometimes redolent of nineteenth-century depictions of endless cycles of borderland violence. Thus, while the Eritrean–Ethiopian war attracted a flurry of attention at the end of the 1990s, a host of 'smaller' conflicts were proliferating across the region—many of them, indeed, related at various removes to the Eritrean–Ethiopian war itself. Some were located in the turbulent Ethiopian–Sudanese borderlands, involving a range of local liberation fronts and rebel groups hoping to exert leverage on either Addis Ababa or Khartoum or indeed both. Other groups again operated in the southern extremities of Ethiopia, linked in different ways to the civil war in Sudan, or to the Oromo and Somali in northern Kenya and eastern Ethiopia. There was nothing new, for example, in the violent instability of the western-Ethiopia–eastern-Sudan frontier zone; cross-border violence had been endemic for much of the twentieth century. In this sense the area broadly had much in common with the Eritrean frontier zone. Nonetheless, owing to such specific factors as population density, and

political and ethnic 'visibility', these militarized margins were as yet unable
to produce the kind of cohesive and effective militarism witnessed in
Eritrea. But their importance was not less for that.

Indeed, many of the conflicts which have been at the centre of this study
started out as 'marginal', fizzling into life on the peripheries of major states;
this is true, for example, of the modern Eritrean and Tigrayan insurgencies,
dismissed by successive Ethiopian governments as mere *shifta*. Struggling on
the edges, they strove to make themselves heard. Both Eritrean and Tigrayan
insurgencies, of course, were ultimately successful, marching on the centre
and capturing the state. Yet our concern here is those struggles which do not
'succeed' in quite this manner—or at least, have not done so at the time of
writing—and which have not captured the state, or even much attention,
save from NGOs, anthropologists, and of course internal security forces.
Here, violence became a way of life, and life was violence, however 'low-
level'. Such violence was the product of the neglected place, often beginning in the proverbial backwaters of nineteenth-century polities and early
twentieth-century colonial states; these were backwaters, the 'wild places'
and frontier country of the fevered metropolitan imagination, often becoming caught between colonial territories as buffer zones, scarcely governed
and ill-developed. The inhabitants invariably acquired bad reputations, as
warlike and troublesome. Such rough places could be treated accordingly by
state militaries, which could behave there in ways unthinkable elsewhere. As
we have seen, a good example is the Northern Frontier District in Kenya,
prone to raids from the Ethiopian side of the border, a frontier zone where
the far, diluted reaches of British authority in Nairobi met the southernmost reaches of imperial Ethiopia. With shifting links across the border in
Italian Somaliland, to their episodic 'brothers' in the Ogaden and southern
Ethiopia, the inhabitants were regarded by the independent Kenyan government very much as the British had before them—wild, dangerous, unreliable in their loyalties, irreconcilable to modernity. Volatile and scarcely
visible, it was the proverbial militarized margin.

Conceptually, no doubt, these places are inevitable in human history, as
necessary to the functioning of society as any of the other brutal pillars on
which communities are raised; and they provide essential reference points
for states and metropoles in the processes of objectification which feed self-
image there. Such frontiers are often kept at arms' length, whether they are
armed against an external enemy, or whether they serve as an ugly reminder
of what society once was at some indeterminate point in time—yet, as

I have argued throughout this book, such frontiers are both fertile and primordial, the well-springs of both deep-seated insecurity and dynamic creativity. These are areas characterized by a delicate balance of local resources, notably access to water, healthy pasture, and arable farming land, and they are areas which are extremely vulnerable to environmental shifts which can have—and have had—catastrophic consequences. These are zones where conflict is easily sparked, sucking adjacent states into them, where economic war quickly becomes political, and vice versa.[2] Our region has long been crisscrossed by a series of these frontier zones, places where there exist groups at odds with 'law' and 'authority', places which are no-man's-lands, but also places which are zones of transition, where cultures and peoples meet, and new communities are formed. These have been places of refuge as well as resistance, and new or hybrid social structures appear; crucially, the states that persecute or neglect or lay claim to them have limited, if any, authority here, and as one travels further from the centres, the oxygen of state power becomes ever thinner.

These have also been places to which states may export wars started elsewhere—another key feature of our region's history, but especially visible in recent years. Eritrea has certainly diversified its responses to the 'Ethiopian problem', by simultaneously courting the southern Sudanese in terms of commercial and other links, and siding with Khartoum over such issues as a UN force for Darfur and the ICC arrest warrant for Bashir himself. A ruthless pragmatism lies behind Eritrea's 'foreign policy' initiatives in Darfur itself, and in Somalia and among the Oromo; Eritrean *realpolitik* has involved violent leverage in those spaces between states. While it is outside the scope of the present work, the Darfur region exemplifies the point.[3] Sudan under Nimeiri had been a relatively consistent supporter of the EPLF; under Bashir and the National Islamic Front from 1989, however, Sudan was an enemy. Eritrea sought to exert pressure on Khartoum, which, it was believed as early as 1994, was backing *jihad*ist rebels against Asmara. Following the severance of diplomatic relations between Eritrea and Sudan at the end of 1994, Isaias dispatched a mission to Chad in the attempt to persuade President Deby to open a 'Western Front' against Khartoum; when Deby demurred, Asmara had to content itself with supporting the SPLA in southern Sudan, and the Beja guerrillas in the north-east, known as the Beja Congress, composed mostly of Beni Amer. The latter were in alliance with a smaller group, the Rashaida Free Lions, under the banner of the 'Eastern Front'. These were brought together, under Eritrean supervision, within the anti-Khartoum National Democratic Alliance, and Eritrean support for Sudanese opposition movements intensified with Khartoum's increased assistance to Eritrean Islamist fighters—some of whom were trained and armed by Osama bin Laden, then active in north-east Sudan. The irony of Eritrea's later support for Somali Islamists, thus incurring the wrath of the US, clearly lies in the fact that the government in Asmara was doing battle with bin Laden long before most of the world had heard of him. When the Darfur rebellion erupted in 2003, the Eritreans were quick to take advantage, offering support to both the various factions of the Sudan Liberation Army (SLA) and the Justice and Equality Movement (JEM), while Asmara became an important conduit for supplies to the rebels. Isaias, it seemed, hoped to 'manage' the revolt and become the key intermediary between the rebels and Khartoum, and indeed the wider international community, rendering himself indispensible—hence his opposition to any kind of international peacekeeping force, which would clearly have undermined his own position. In a sense this was diplomacy not between 'states' *per se*, but between powerful organizations—the EPLF, TPLF, NIF, SPLM—with access to the resources and manpower and ultimately the leverage associated with states. They were the products of political tectonics, and their diplomacy was that of the fault line. For Eritrea, in particular, this was about the export of the frontier war—whether to Somalia, or Darfur, or any other volatile place where it might be successfully repackaged.

The Ethiopian–Sudanese borderlands also constituted a vast zone in which violence had become an increasingly marketable commodity against a backdrop of economic neglect; long a place of refuge for individuals and their followers fleeing from either Khartoum or Addis Ababa, in the 1990s and 2000s it continued to be characterized by low-level violent insurgency[4]—and a place where the true characters of the states involved were sharply revealed. Note should be made in particular of the Gambella and Benishangul regions, where the Gambella People's Liberation Movement (GPLM) and the Benishangul People's Liberation Movement (BPLM) operated in defiance of metropolitan authority. While Eritrean–Sudanese relations swiftly deteriorated in the early 1990s, the relationship between Khartoum and Addis Ababa was rather more ambiguous: initially, the EPRDF sought more positive dealings with Bashir's regime—although, like the Eritreans, the Ethiopians were also concerned with the export of Islamic radicalism from Sudan. The assassination attempt on Egypt's President Mubarak in Addis Ababa in 1995 seemed to bear these fears out. Meles kept dialogue open with Khartoum, but simultaneously offered support to the SPLM who were able to operate from bases inside the Ethiopian border. On the Sudanese side, Islamist foreign policy directives emerged within the NIF under the leadership of Hassan al-Turabi with the aim of cultivating clients in the border areas who were hostile to the EPRDF. Thus the BPLM, with its major support from the Muslim Berti group, fell under Khartoum's influence, and by the mid-1990s was engaged in 'irredentist' (i.e. pro-Sudan) violence across the Benishangul region. Further south, in Gambella, violent competition between the two dominant groups, the Nuer and the Anuak, was the key dynamic: because a Nuer elite had leaned toward the *Derg*, the Anuak-dominated GPLM had become a key ally of the EPRDF forces in the region, a relationship which continued into the 1990s. But it collapsed when, amid allegations of corruption, Addis Ababa instituted direct rule and effectively sidelined the GPLM; moreover, a 1994 EPRDF-run census concluded that the Nuer were the majority group in the region, a finding angrily rejected by the Anuak who thus became ever more alienated from the new Ethiopian regime.[5]

The outbreak of the Eritrean–Ethiopian war in 1998 signalled a new phase in cross-border dynamics. Ethiopia was ever more anxious to repair relations with Sudan, which was happy to oblige considering its own insecurities—and economic and strategic agreements involved the ending of, or at least the reduction in support for one another's dissidents and rebels. This, for a time at least, weakened the position of both the BPLM and the OLF. Nonetheless, the GPLM received Eritrean support from 2000 onwards. Meanwhile the EPRDF created the joint Anuak–Nuer front, the Gambella People's Democratic Front, largely controlled by Addis Ababa; the Anuak responded by forming the Gambella People's Democratic Congress, whose espoused aim was the expulsion of both Nuer and *habesha* settlers from the region. Indeed tension in the area is multi-dimensional, with that between Nuer and Anuak playing out against the larger issue of local groups' hostility toward highland (Amhara, Tigrayans, and Oromo) settlement in the region. Most of these movements, however, were crippled by internal factionalism and their impact, in the end, has been negligible. Nonetheless, Ethiopian security forces carried out operations against the Anuak in late 2003, when several hundred civilians were massacred, demonstrating the willingness of the state to make its presence felt at the edge in the most violent manner and to bring to heal recalcitrant groups.[6]

Coffee-rich Sidamo region, too, has found itself the focus of unwelcome attention from central authority. Here, a tradition of violent resistance to interference from Addis Ababa—the peasant uprising in Gedeo in 1960 was in response to the seizure of coffee-producing land by highland settlers, and was brutally crushed[7]—evolved into the Sidama People's Democratic Organisation (SPDO) which took up arms against the *Derg*. The SPDO became part of the Southern Ethiopian People's Democratic Front (SEPDF), which was itself part of the EPRDF coalition. From the early 1990s, however, the attempt by central government to dominate politics in outlying areas such as Sidamo, and the consequent persecution of Sidama groups which oppose it, intensified considerably. In the early 2000s, much disturbance was centred on the move by the government to alter the federal status of Sidamo, bringing it under the regional government and thus under closer central control. In May 2002, a demonstration against these proposals took place in Awassa, the federal capital of Sidamo, and was apparently peaceful until security forces opened fire, killing at least twenty-five people and wounding many others. In the days that followed, scores of the demonstrators and others who supported the demonstration were arrested and allegedly tortured while in detention. While the southern region government set up an enquiry into the demonstration, the enquiry was not independent—in other words it was dominated by central government—and no report was published.[8] Further repercussions followed in August 2002, when several leading figures in the SPDO were dismissed from the party and arrested, accused by central government of fomenting the May violence; however, the president of the SPDO, Girma Chuluko, openly condemned the security forces for opening fire unprovoked, and strongly opposed the change in Sidamo's status.[9] The SPDO has found itself harassed and pressurized by central government since that time. The alacrity and force with which the Ethiopian state imposes itself on frontier zones—often in the pursuit of economic goals—has also recently been demonstrated by the Gibe dam project on the Omo river. Here, local needs and environmental concerns are swept aside in the name of state-led modernization—in this case, increased electricity production.

Other small wars proliferate in contested frontier zones across the region—often brutal at the local level, but fought beneath the horizon of visibility, among groups long neglected and marginalized. Thus, Afar guerrillas—the Afar Liberation Front, or the Red Sea Front—continue to operate in the politically and physically hostile geography of the Danakil region, for example, and might be utilized by the Ethiopian military should the need arise at any point in the future; yet the Eritreans provide backing to other shadowy Afar groups set against the Ethiopian government, including *Ugugumo* ('revolution'), and the Afar Revolutionary Democratic Front. Finally, we need to note the degree to which—in time honoured fashion, it must be said—both Eritrea and Ethiopia host a range of armed groups opposed to the other. These are movements which are in the truest sense 'stateless', lacking even a physical space of their own except that which is provided by host governments; it is on the whole a precarious and sorry existence, although not necessarily entirely hopeless—for they all hope that one day their moment will come, and that they too will march as an armed frontier on the sinister centre. Ethiopia provides 'hospitality'—in the loosest sense of that term—to a range of Eritrean opposition movements of variable efficacy, strength, and secrecy, including the ELF-Revolutionary Council, the Democratic Movement for the Liberation of Eritrea, the National Alliance of Eritrean Forces, the Eritrean Democratic Alliance, and the Eritrean Revolutionary Democratic Front. The list goes on, somewhat tragically. For their part, the Eritreans support the Ethiopian People's Patriotic Front—reportedly a few hundred Amhara, and perhaps some Oromo, soldiers operating around Gondar—and the Tigrayan National Alliance for Democracy, which appears to exploit provincial differences within Tigray itself. At the time of writing, again, the opposition movement known as *Ginbot 7* appeared to be attempting to draw together various armed groups in a common front against the EPRDF, and reports were emerging that talks were taking place with the Eritrean government, if only at the lower level. In August 2009, an Ethiopian court found several key opposition leaders guilty of treason, and in December they were sentenced to death, mostly in absentia.

While, in truth, we lack the space here to provide the doubtless deserved level of detail on the various movements along the Ethiopia–Sudan border and their dizzying recent histories of shifting allegiance, it is sufficient to note here some key aspects of the story. At the 'international' level, many of the ongoing conflicts remain extremely vulnerable to the interests of distant actors—the Ethiopian, Eritrean, and Sudanese governments—willing to intervene in the pursuit of larger agendas. At the local level, recurrent violence frequently takes place around the issue of access to resources—increasingly, land and water—while cattle-raiding is common. Local groups also compete for access to the power represented by local administrations; but these are also, and have long been, ill-governed regions as far as metropolitan centres are concerned, far from the centres of power which purport to control them. This is true, of course, until the state decides that certain regions are worth large-scale economic—and thus political and military—investment, at which point the state presence becomes rather more visible, and invariably brutal, as in the case of the Gibe dam project. At that point, hostility toward the state may increase still further, when compared to local attitudes toward the arm's-length patronage—a rough-hewn version of colonial-era indirect rule—which preceded the new interventionism. Firearms, moreover, proliferate across the borderlands, acquired from a myriad of sources, including the region's governments themselves, who often supply arms to groups in the interests of local 'security'—the SPLM, and individuals in the adjacent Ethiopian and Sudanese armies. It is hardly controversial to suggest that guns do much to heighten the capacity for, and thus the desirability of, violent conflict. Thus, heavily armed pastoralists fight for cattle and pasture; and in turn, it seems safe to say, cultures of violence have been created, or at least enhanced, as resources become scarcer, or as political exigencies shift. Of course, many of these conflicts date back decades, and have their roots in the nineteenth century with the creation of 'Sudan' on the one side, and the expansion of the *habesha* polity on the other; it is impossible to say with any degree of certainty whether the frontier violence we see today is any more intense than it was in the past, but what we can say is that it represents a deeply destabilizing vortex, both for the indigenous peoples of the areas themselves as well as the adjacent states.

Even close watchers of the region know little about many of these indistinct organizations, which seem to function in a curious political gloaming. Yet they provide clues to the origins of the current political situation in north-east Africa, and we may look on them in the way that astronomers examine dust and dark matter for clues to the origins of the universe. They echo the war cries, the rhetoric, and indeed the nomenclature of the movements of the 1960s and 1970s, and as political organisms they remind us of how it all began—in the ideological tribalism of people's democratic revolution, and in the violence necessary in the pursuit of regional, or ethnic, or national liberation. They, too, are the products of fertile frontiers; but this political harvest is less impressive, to date, in terms of the advance of the cause, and it is for the historians of the future to assess the conversion of potential to kinetic energy, and the march of these armed and vibrant frontiers on decadent and dying centres.

Endnotes

PROLOGUE

1. See for example K. Menkhaus, 'Somalia: a country in peril, a policy nightmare', *ENOUGH Strategy Paper* (September, 2008) p.8.
2. S. Healy, *Lost Opportunities in the Horn of Africa: How Conflicts Connect and Peace Agreements Unravel* (London, 2008).

CHAPTER I

1. The term *habesha* refers loosely to Amharic- and Tigrinya-speaking (i.e. Semitic) peoples, and is commonly how these peoples describe themselves. In certain contexts, notably those prior to the late nineteenth century, I consider it preferable to terms such as 'Ethiopia' and certainly 'Abyssinia'.
2. See for example C. Clapham, 'Boundary and Territory in the Horn of Africa', in A. I. Asiwaju and P. Nugent (eds.), *African Boundaries: Barriers, Conduits and Opportunities* (London, 1996) p.245.
3. J. Young, *Armed Groups Along Sudan's Eastern Frontier: An Overview and Analysis* (Geneva, 2007) pp.22, 26, 38.
4. Although see C. Ehret, *Ethiopians and East Africans: The Probem of Contacts* (Nairobi, 1974).
5. Gadaa Melbaa, *Oromia: An Introduction* (Khartoum, 1988).
6. See also D. Crummey, 'Society, state and nationality in the recent historiography of Ethiopia', *Journal of African History*, 31:1 (1990).
7. D. L. Donham and W. James (eds.), *The Southern Marches of Imperial Ethiopia* (Oxford, 2002; 1986).
8. J. Markakis, *National and Class Conflict in the Horn of Africa* (Cambridge, 1987).
9. B. K. Holcomb and Sisai Ibssa, *The Invention of Ethiopia: The Making of a Dependent Colonial State in Northeast Africa* (Trenton, NJ, 1990).
10. J. Sorenson, *Imagining Ethiopia: Struggles for History and Identity in the Horn of Africa* (New Brunswick, NJ, 1993).
11. W. James, D. Donham, E. Kurimoto, and A. Triulzi (eds.), *Remapping Ethiopia: Socialism and After* (Oxford, 2002).
12. See for example D. Connell, *Conversations with Eritrean Political Prisoners* (Trenton, NJ, 2005); Kidane Mengisteab and Okbazghi Yohannes, *Anatomy of an African*

Tragedy: Political, Economic and Foreign Policy Crisis in Post-independence Eritrea (Trenton, NJ, 2005); and my own 'The politics of silence: interpreting apparent stasis in contemporary Eritrea', *Review of African Political Economy*, 36:120 (2009).

13. Ezekiel Gebissa (ed.), *Contested Terrain: Essays on Oromo Studies, Ethiopianist Discourse, and Politically Engaged Scholarship* (Trenton, NJ, 2009), offers some interesting insights into the rancour that has dogged the scholarly dimension of the Oromo struggle.

14. D. Levine, *Greater Ethiopia* (Chicago, 2000; 1974) pp.36–9.

15. E. Gellner, *Nations and Nationalism* (Cambridge, 2005; 1983) p.85.

16. Bairu Tafla (ed.), *Eritrean Studies Review*, 5:1 (2007).

17. See for example P. R. Schmidt, M. C. Curtis and Zelalem Teka (eds.), *The Archaeology of Ancient Eritrea* (Trenton, NJ, 2008).

18. I. M. Lewis, *A Modern History of the Somali* (Oxford, 2002).

19. D. Crummey, *Land and Society in the Christian Kingdom of Ethiopia: From the Thirteenth to the Twentieth Century* (Oxford, 2000).

20. Donham and James, *Southern Marches*.

21. For example, Mohammed Hassen, *The Oromo of Ethiopia: A History, 1570–1860* (Cambridge, 1990; Trenton, NJ, 1994); Asafa Jalata, *Oromia and Ethiopia: State Formation and Ethnonational Conflict, 1868–1992* (London and Boulder, CO, 1993); P. T. W. Baxter, J. Hultin, and A. Triulzi (eds.), *Being and Becoming Oromo: Historical and Anthropological Enquiries* (Uppsala, 1996).

22. A partial (and largely unconvincing) exception is Semere Haile, 'Historical background to the Ethiopia–Eritrea conflict', in B. Davidson and L. Cliffe (eds.), *The Long Struggle of Eritrea for Independence and Constructive Peace* (Trenton, NJ, 1988). Various other studies of the liberation struggle in the 1980s devoted introductory chapters to antiquity.

23. K. Fukui and J. Markakis (eds.), *Ethnicity and Conflict in the Horn of Africa* (London, 1994); E. Kurimoto and S. Simonse (eds.), *Conflict, Age and Power in North East Africa: Age Systems in Transition* (Oxford, 1998).

24. P. Marsden, *The Barefoot Emperor: An Ethiopian Tragedy* (London, 2007).

25. For example J. C. McCann, *People of the Plow: An Agricultural History of Ethiopia, 1800–1990* (London, 1995).

26. I. Orlowska, 'Re-imagining empire: Ethiopian political culture under Yohannis IV (1872–89)', PhD thesis, School of Oriental and African Studies (London, 2006).

27. R. J. Reid, *War in Pre-Colonial Eastern Africa* (Oxford, 2007) pp.8ff.

28. For example, S. Rubenson, 'Adwa 1896: the resounding protest', in R. Rotberg and A. Mazrui (eds.), *Protest and Power in Black Africa* (New York, 1970); for a contemporary view, see G. F.-H. Berkeley, *The Campaign of Adowa and the Rise of Menelik* (New York, 1969; first pub., 1902).

29. D. Gerhard, 'The frontier in comparative view', *Comparative Studies in Society and History*, 1:3 (1959).

30. I. Kopytoff, 'The internal African frontier: the making of African political culture', in I. Kopytoff (ed.), *The African Frontier: The Reproduction of Traditional African Societies* (Bloomington and Indianapolis, 1987).

31. Donham and James, *Southern Marches*; James *et al.*, *Remapping Ethiopia*; M. Leopold, *Inside West Nile: Violence, History and Representation on an African Frontier* (Oxford, 2005); Nene Mburu, *Bandits on the Border: The Last Frontier in the Search for Somali Unity* (Trenton, NJ, 2005); Young, *Armed Groups*; Clapham, 'Boundary and territory', *passim*.

32. See for example F. Barth (ed.), *Ethnic Groups and Boundaries: The Social Organisation of Culture Difference* (London, 1969); and for a summation, P. Lawrence, *Nationalism: History and Theory* (Harlow, 2005) p.187.

CHAPTER 2

1. Schmidt *et al.*, *Ancient Eritrea*.

2. Yosief Libsekal, 'Eritrea', in *International Council on Monuments and Sites (ICOMOS): World Report 2001–02 on Monuments and Sites in Danger* (Paris, 2002).

3. D. Phillipson, *Ancient Ethiopia. Aksum: Its Antecedents and Successors* (London, 1998) pp.111*ff*.

4. Taddesse Tamrat, *Church and State in Ethiopia, 1270–1527* (Oxford, 1972) pp.54*ff*.

5. An affordable and accessible edition is M. Brooks (ed. and tr.), *A Modern Translation of the* Kebra Negast (*The Glory of the Kings*) (Lawrenceville, NJ, 1995).

6. G. W. B. Huntingford (ed. and tr.), *The Glorious Victories of Amda Seyon, King of Ethiopia* (London, 1965); Taddesse Tamrat, *Church and State*, chapters 3–5.

7. Levine, *Greater Ethiopia*.

8. See for example Huntingford, *Glorious Victories*; R. Pankhurst (ed.), *The Ethiopian Royal Chronicles* (Addis Ababa, 1967).

9. Brooks, *Modern Translation*, p.127. See also Reid, *War*, and R. J. Reid, 'War and remembrance: orality, literacy and conflict in the Horn', *Journal of African Cultural Studies*, 18:1 (2006).

10. Lewis, *Modern History*, pp.20*ff*.

11. D. Robinson, *Muslim Societies in African History* (Cambridge, 2004) pp.114*ff*; M. Abir, *Ethiopia and the Red Sea: The Rise and Decline of the Solomonic Dynasty and Muslim–European Rivalry in the Region* (London, 1980) pp.10–13; and for a useful contemporary account, see Arab Faqih (tr. P. L. Stenhouse), *The Conquest of Abyssinia* (Hollywood, 2003).

12. See Crummey, *Land and Society*, pp.50–1 and *passim*.

13. Bahrey's account is contained in C. F. Beckingham and G. W. B. Huntingford (trs. and eds.), *Some Records of Ethiopia 1593–1646: Being Extracts from 'The History of High Ethiopia or Abassia', by Manoel de Almeida* (London, 1954).

14. H. Salt, *A Voyage to Abyssinia and Travels into the Interior of that Country* (London, 1814) pp.299, 306.

15. S. Gobat, *Journal of Three Years' Residence in Abyssinia* (New York, 1969; first pub., 1851) p.52.

16. H. Blanc, *A Narrative of Captivity in Abyssinia* (London, 1970; first pub., 1868) p.290.

17. C. R. Markham, *A History of the Abyssinian Expedition* (London, 1869) pp.39–40.

18. Although see for example Holcomb and Ibssa, *The Invention of Ethiopia*, and Sorenson, *Imagining Ethiopia*. For more recent insights into current debates in Oromo studies, see the collection of essays in Ezekiel Gebissa, *Contested Terrain*.

19. Mohammed Hassan, *The Oromo of Ethiopia*, pp.18*ff*; M. Abir, 'Ethiopia and the Horn of Africa', in R. Gray (ed.), *Cambridge History of Africa: Vol. 4, from c.1600 to c.1790* (Cambridge, 1975) pp.537*ff*.

20. In particular, see the work of Asmarom Legesse: *Gada: Three Approaches to the Study of African Society* (New York, 1973); and *Oromo Democracy: An Indigenous African Political System* (Trenton, NJ, 2006).

21. Crummey, *Land and Society, passim*.

22. Levine, *Greater Ethiopia*, p.82.

23. H. S. Lewis, *Jimma Abba Jifar, an Oromo monarchy: Ethiopia 1830–1932* (Lawrenceville, NJ, 2001); Mohammed Hassen, *The Oromo of Ethiopia*.

24. Crummey, *Land and Society*, pp.67*ff*.

25. E. A. Wallis Budge, *A History of Ethiopia, Nubia and Abyssinia* (London, 1928) II, pp.445*ff*.

26. Pankhurst, *Chronicles*, pp.121*ff*.

CHAPTER 3

1. The best detailed accounts are still S. Rubenson, 'Ethiopia and the Horn', in J. E. Flint (ed.), *Cambridge History of Africa: Vol. 5, c.1790–c.1870* (Cambridge, 1976); S. Rubenson, *The Survival of Ethiopian Independence* (London, 1976); M. Abir, *Ethiopia: The Era of the Princes* (London, 1968). See also H. Weld Blundell, *The Royal Chronicle of Abyssinia, 1769–1840* (Cambridge, 1922).

2. Pankhurst, *Chronicles*, pp.140–2.

3. See for example UK National Archives Foreign Office Series (hereafter NA FO) 1/1 Valentia and Salt: letters and documents. H. Salt, inclosure re. maps, London, 22 August 1811.

4. J. Bruce, *Travels to Discover the Source of the Nile, in the Years 1768, 1769, 1770, 1771, 1772, and 1773* (Edinburgh, 1790) Vol. 2, p.696.

5. Ibid., p.680.

6. M. Abir, 'Ethiopia and the Horn of Africa', in R. Gray (ed.), *Cambridge History of Africa: Vol. 4, from c.1600 to c.1790* (Cambridge, 1975) pp.571–7; Abir, *Ethiopia: The Era of the Princes*, especially chapter 2.

7. Rubenson, 'Ethiopia and the Horn', pp.57*ff*.

8. See also Reid, *War*, pp.13–20 *passim*.

9. R. J. Reid, 'Warfare and urbanisation: the relationship between town and conflict in pre-colonial eastern Africa', in A. Burton (ed.), *The Urban Experience in Eastern Africa, c.1750–2000* (Nairobi, 2002).

10. Ibid., pp.288*ff.*

11. W. C. Plowden, *Travels in Abyssinia and the Galla Country* (London, 1868) p.74.

12. Blanc, *Captivity*, pp.294–5.

13. See for example Salt, *Voyage*, pp.486–95; Plowden, *Travels*, pp.75–7. For the early use of firearms, see Merid Wolde Aregay, 'A reappraisal of the impact of firearms in the history of warfare in Ethiopia, c.1500–1800', *Journal of Ethiopian Studies*, 14 (1980).

14. Gobat, *Residence*, p.441.

15. Plowden, *Travels*, esp. chapters III and IV.

16. Ibid., p.133.

17. M. Parkyns, *Life in Abyssinia: Being Notes Collected During Three Years' Residence and Travels in that Country* (London, 1966; first pub. 1853, 1868) p.xxi.

18. R. A. Brown, quoted in M. Howard, *War in European History* (Oxford, 2009) p.1.

19. Plowden, *Travels*, p.38.

20. Quoted in Howard, *War*, p.23.

21. Plowden, *Travels*, p.45.

22. NA FO 1/1 Valentia and Salt: letters and documents. H. Salt, 'Extracts from original observations', Chelicut, April 1810.

23. Among the best accounts are Mohammed Hassen, *The Oromo of Ethiopia* and Lewis, *Jimma Abba Jifar*; see also M. Abir, 'The emergence and consolidation of the monarchies of Enarea and Jimma in the first half of the nineteenth century', *Journal of African History*, 6:2 (1965). For the unabashedly Oromo nationalist interpretation—both of the nineteenth century and everything later, including 'Abyssinian colonialism' and the anti-colonial struggle—see for example Gadaa Melbaa, *Oromia*.

24. Lewis, *Jimma Abba Jifar*, especially chapter 2.

25. Abir, 'Emergence and consolidation'.

26. See Abir, *Ethiopia: The Era of the Princes*.

27. D. Crummey, 'Society and ethnicity in the politics of Christian Ethiopia during the Zamana Masfent', *International Journal of African Historical Studies*, 8:2 (1975) p.278.

28. A. Hoben, *Land Tenure Among the Amhara: The Dynamics of Cognatic Descent* (Chicago, 1973); Levine, *Greater Ethiopia*; D. Crummey, 'Abyssinian feudalism', *Past and Present*, 89 (1980); J. Goody, *Technology, Tradition and the State in Africa* (London, 1971) pp.30–2.

29. A. Moore-Harell, 'Economic and political aspects of the slave trade in Ethiopia and the Sudan in second half of the nineteenth century', *International Journal of African Historical Studies*, 23:2–3 (1999).

30. J. H. Arrowsmith-Brown (ed. and tr.), *Prutky's Travels in Ethiopia and Other Countries* (London, 1991) pp.25, 152, 179; see also Gobat, *Residence*, p.39.

31. Plowden, *Travels*, p.20.

32. Arrowsmith-Brown, *Prutky's Travels*, pp.152, 179.

33. Parkyns, *Life in Abyssinia*, pp.155–6.

34. Ibid., p.441; H. Dufton, *Narrative of a Journey Through Abyssinia in 1862–63* (Westport, 1970, 1ˢᵗ ed. 1867) pp.42–3.

35. Gobat, *Residence*, pp.401–2.

36. J. Bruce, *Travels*, III, p.88.

37. Salt, *Voyage to Abyssinia*, p.426.

38. H. Stern, *Wanderings Among the Falashas in Abyssinia* (London, 1968, 1ˢᵗ ed. 1862) p.146.

39. A. B. Wylde, *Modern Abyssinia* (London, 1901) pp.71, 73.

40. Ibid., pp.125, 127.

41. For the basics, see S. Rubenson, *King of Kings: Tewodros of Ethiopia* (Addis Ababa and Nairobi, 1966); D. Crummey, 'Tewodros as reformer and moderniser', *Journal of African History*, 10:3 (1969); D. Crummey, 'The violence of Tewodros', in B. A. Ogot (ed.), *War and Society in Africa* (London, 1972).

42. D. Crummey, 'Banditry and resistance: noble and peasant in nineteenth-century Ethiopia', in D. Crummey, *Banditry, Rebellion and Social Protest in Africa* (London, 1986) p.133; in the same volume, see also T. Fernyhough, 'Social mobility and dissident elites in northern Ethiopia: the role of banditry, 1900–1969'. Much of the analysis in the Crummey volume itself owes something to E. Hobsbawm, *Bandits* (London, 2000).

43. Crummey, 'Banditry and resistance', p.135.

44. See the excellent account by R. Caulk, 'Bad Men of the Borders: shum and shifta in northern Ethiopia in the nineteenth century', *International Journal of African Historical Studies*, 17:2 (1984).

45. Stern, *Wanderings*, pp.64–6.

46. Rubenson, 'Ethiopia and the Horn', pp.65*ff*; Crummey, 'The violence of Tewodros', pp.67*ff*.

47. Stern, *Wanderings*, pp.68–75; Dufton, *Narrative*, pp.122–31.

48. Dufton, *Narrative*, pp.113–14.

49. Reid, 'War and remembrance'; Reid, *War*, especially chapter 2.

50. Stern, *Wanderings*, p.122.

51. Ibid., p.128.

52. Ibid., p.129.

53. Dufton, *Narrative*, p.105.

54. Markham, *History*, pp.84–5.

55. Blanc, *Captivity*, p.5.

56. NA FO 881/1609 Account of Mission to Abyssinia, by H. Rassam to Lord Stanley, 1 September 1868, p.4.

57. Blanc, *Captivity*, pp.7, 8–9.

58. Ibid., pp.333–5.

59. Tewodros to Hormuzd Rassam, [28 January 1866], in S. Rubenson (ed.), *Acta Aethiopica II: Tewodros and his Contemporaries 1855–1868* (Addis Ababa, 1994).

60. NA FO 881/1609 Account of Mission to Abyssinia, by H. Rassam to Lord Stanley, 1 September 1868, pp.2, 7.

61. Parkyns, *Life in Abyssinia*, p.xxiii.

62. For example, Reid, *War*, pp.147–8; Blanc, *Captivity*, p.315; Assegahhen to d'Abbadie, 14 January 1866 and 28 November 1868, in Rubenson, *Acta Aethiopica II*; NA FO 881/1493 Merewether to Stanley, 15 February 1867.

63. Pankhurst, *Chronicles*, p.151.

64. Crummey, 'The violence of Tewodros', p.71.

65. NA FO 881/1493 Merewether to Stanley, 15 February 1867.

66. Crummey, 'The violence of Tewodros', p.72.

67. The best accounts of the expedition itself remain D. Bates, *The Abyssinian Difficulty* (Oxford, 1979), and more recently Marsden, *The Barefoot Emperor*. There was a rush of publications through the 1860s, and especially around the Abyssinian expedition, replete with breathless wonder at the crazed genius that was Tewodros. A selection would include: Blanc, *Captivity*; Dufton, *Narrative*; Markham, *History*; Plowden, *Travels*; H. Rassam, *Narrative of the British Mission to Theodore, King of Abyssinia* (London, 1869); H. M. Stanley, *Coomassie and Magdala: the story of two British campaigns in Africa* (London, 1874); Stern, *Wanderings*.

68. I. M. Lapidus, *A History of Islamic Societies* (Cambridge, 2002) pp.771–2.

69. Gellner, *Nations*, p.84.

70. K. S. Vikor, 'Sufi brotherhoods in Africa', in N. Levtzion and R. L. Pouwels (eds.), *The History of Islam in Africa* (Oxford, 2000) p.468.

71. Iqbal Jhazbhay, 'Islam and stability in Somaliland and the geo-politics of the war on terror', *Journal of Muslim Minority Affairs*, 28:2 (2008) p.179, drawing on the work of Said Samatar among others. See also the collection of essays in A. de Waal (ed.), *Islamism and its Enemies in the Horn of Africa* (London, 2004), especially chapters 1 and 4 in this context.

72. A good overview can be found in L. Kaptjeins, 'Ethiopia and the Horn of Africa', in Levtzion and Pouwels, *History of Islam*.

73. Abir, 'Emergence and consolidation', p.211.

74. See for example Hussein Ahmed, *Islam in Nineteenth-Century Wallo, Ethiopia: Revival, Reform and Reaction* (Leiden, 2001).

75. Parkyns, *Life in Abyssinia*, p.276.

76. Blanc, *Captivity*, p.2.

77. Dufton, *Narrative*, pp.114–18.

78. Ibid., p.116.

79. NA FO 1/30 'Abyssinia…' Memo on Abyssinia by Sir E.Baring, to Granville, February 1884.

80. For example, see NA FO 1/27B Yohannes to Victoria, 10 August 1872; Yohannes to Alexander II, 19 June 1879, in S. Rubenson (ed.), *Acta Aethiopica Vol. III:*

Internal Rivalries and Foreign Threats, 1869–1879 (Addis Ababa, 2000); also
A. Bulatovich (ed. and tr. R. Seltzer), *Ethiopia Through Russian Eyes: Country in
Transition, 1896–98* (Lawrenceville, NJ, 2000) p.53.
81. Bulatovich, *Ethiopia Through Russian Eyes*, p.94.
82. See also the account in E. Paice, *Tip and Run: The Untold Tragedy of the Great War
in Africa* (London, 2007) pp.212ff.

CHAPTER 4

1. See for example Gebru Tareke, *Ethiopia: Power and Protest. Peasant Revolts in the
Twentieth Century* (Lawrenceville, NJ, 1996) pp.109, 116, 118; J. Young, *Peasant
Revolution in Ethiopia: The Tigray People's Liberation Front, 1975–1991* (Cambridge,
1997) p.99; Alemseged Abbay, *Identity Jilted or Re-Imagining Identity? The Divergent
Paths of the Eritrean and Tigrayan Nationalist Struggles* (Lawrenceville, NJ, 1998)
passim; and, rather more disparagingly, the Eritrean nationalist viewpoint in
Jordan Gebre-Medhin, 'Eritrea (Mereb-Melash) and Yohannes IV of Abyssinia',
Eritrean Studies Review, 3:2 (1999).
2. NA FO 1/1 Valentia and Salt: letters and documents. 'Observations on the trade
of the Red Sea', by Valentia, p.9.
3. A good contemporary account of the early years of the nineteenth century is
provided in Salt, *Voyage to Abyssinia*, pp.269ff.
4. Gobat, *Residence*, pp.396–407.
5. The most exhaustive account remains Zewde Gabre-Selassie, *Yohannes IV of
Ethiopia: A Political Biography* (Oxford, 1975). See also Bairu Tafla (ed. and tr.),
A Chronicle of Emperor Yohannes IV (1872–89) (Wiesbaden, 1977).
6. By Donald Crummey, see 'Orthodoxy and imperial reconstruction in Ethiopia,
1854–1878', *Journal of Theological Studies*, 29:2 (1978); and 'Imperial legitimacy
and the creation of neo-Solomonic ideology in 19th-century Ethiopia', *Cahiers
d'Etudes Africaines*, 28 (1988).
7. Wylde, *Modern Abyssinia*, p.29.
8. Ibid., pp.33, 44; also NA FO 1/27B Abyssinia: Mission of General Kirkham.
Yohannes to Victoria, 10 August 1872.
9. This can be seen in the various correspondence from and about him contained
in Rubenson, *Acta Aethiopica III*.
10. R. J. Reid, 'The challenge of the past: the quest for historical legitimacy in
independent Eritrea', *History in Africa*, 28 (2001).
11. The best study of Massawa to date is J. Miran, *Red Sea Citizens: Cosmopolitan
Society and Cultural Change in Massawa* (Bloomington and Indianapolis,
2009).
12. H. Erlich, *Ras Alula and the Scramble for Africa: A Political Biography. Ethiopia and
Eritrea, 1875–1897* (Lawrenceville, NJ, 1996) pp.ix, xiii.
13. Quoted in ibid., p.17.
14. G. H. Portal, *My Mission to Abyssinia* (London, 1892) p.81.

15. Salt, *Voyage to Abyssinia*, pp.307, 488; NA FO 1/1 Salt to Cullen Smith, September 1811.
16. NA FO 1/1 *Ras* Welde Selassie to HM The King, 25 February 1811.
17. Gobat, *Residence*, p.39.
18. Ibid., pp.37–8.
19. Ibid., pp.389–90.
20. Plowden, *Travels*, pp.24–5, 27, 39.
21. Ibid., p.39.
22. Ibid., p.131.
23. Parkyns, *Life in Abyssinia*, pp.55, 98.
24. Plowden, *Travels*, p.22.
25. Salt, *Voyage*, p.213.
26. Ibid., p.200; Plowden, *Travels*, pp.25–6.
27. Salt, *Voyage*, pp.361–2.
28. NA FO 1/1 Salt to Cullen Smith, 4 March 1811.
29. NA FO 1/1 Salt, 'Extracts', April 1810.
30. Wube to Louis Philippe, 24 May 1845, in S. Rubenson (ed.), *Acta Aethiopica I: Correspondence and Treaties, 1800–1854* (Evanston, IL, and Addis Ababa, 1987).
31. Wube to Louis-Napoleon Bonaparte, 2 October [1849], in ibid.
32. Salt, *Voyage*, pp.305*ff*.
33. Crummey, 'The violence of Tewodros', pp.71–2, 75.
34. Birru Petros to Antoine d'Abbadie, 26 November 1858, in Rubenson, *Acta Aethiopica II*.
35. See the Treaty between Simen-Tigray and France, 29 December 1859, in ibid.
36. Aregawi Subagadis to Theodore Gilbert, 30 December 1860, in ibid.
37. Blanc, *Captivity*, pp.8–9.
38. Ibid., p.50.
39. Ibid., pp.90–1.
40. Asseggahen to Antoine d'Abbadie, 14 January 1866 and 15 April 1867, in Rubenson, *Acta Aethiopica II*.
41. Afe Werq and Welde Mesqel to Alemayyehu Tewodros, 21 August 1869, in Rubenson, *Acta Aethiopica III*.
42. NA FO 1/27B Abyssinia: Mission of General Kirkham: Yohannes to Victoria, 4 June 1873.
43. NA FO 1/27B Yohannes to Granville, dated 1872.
44. NA FO 1/27B Kirkham's Mission, statement for Granville, 31 October 1872.
45. NA FO 1/27B Kirkham to Granville, 13 May 1873.
46. Yohannes IV to Isma'il Ibrahim, [31 July 1872], in Rubenson, *Acta Aethiopica III*.
47. Yohannes IV to Victoria, 13 August 1872, in ibid.
48. Yohannes IV to E. Choquin de Sarzec, 24 March 1873, in ibid.
49. Yohannes IV/J.C. Kirkham to Granville, 13 May 1873, in ibid.
50. Yohannes IV to Granville, 15 May 1873, in ibid.

51. For example, Yohannes IV to Victoria, 4 June 1873, in ibid.

52. NA FO 881/3058 Governor of Massawa to Khairy Pasha, 2 September 1875.

53. NA FO 881/3058 Ismail to Arendrup, 17 September 1875.

54. NA FO 881/3058 Stanton to Derby, 14 November 1875.

55. NA FO 881/3058 Stanton to Derby, 27 November 1875.

56. See for example Bahru Zewde, *A History of Modern Ethiopia 1855–1991* (London, 2001) pp. 51ff.

57. NA FO 881/1610 Cameron to Stanley, 28 September 1868.

58. Hailu Tewelde Medhin to Ismail Ibrahim, [14 November 1867], in Rubenson, *Acta Aethiopica III*.

59. NA FO 881/1522 Munzinger's 'Notes and Route Observations' (1867).

60. Welde Mikael Solomon to Napoleon III, 22 August 1869, in Rubenson, *Acta Aethiopica III*.

61. Kasa Mircha to Munzinger, 17 November [1869], in ibid.

62. NA FO 1/29 Report by Lt Carter [1868?], appendix by Holdich.

63. Samuel Giyorgis *et al.* to E. Choquin de Sarzec, 13 March 1873, in Rubenson, *Acta Aethiopica III*.

64. See also H. Marcus, *The Life and Times of Menelik II: Ethiopia 1844–1913* (Oxford, 1975) pp. 40, 42.

65. NA FO 881/3058 Stanton to Derby, 31 January 1876.

66. NA FO 881/3058 Extract from the *Moniteur Egyptien*, 3 December 1875.

67. NA FO 881/3058 Ismail to Governor of Massawa, 17 September 1875.

68. Yohannes IV to Hasan Ismail and Muhammad Ratib, 12 March 1876, in Rubenson, *Acta Aethiopica III*.

69. Yohannes IV to Muhammad Ratib, [22 March 1876], in ibid.

70. See for example Welde Mikael Solomon to Muhammad Ratib *et al.*, [March 1876], and Welde Mikael Solomon to Muhammad Ratib, [July 1876], in ibid. See also Johannes Kolmodin, *Traditions de Tsazzega et Hazzega* (Uppsala, 1915).

71. For example, Welde Mikael Solomon to Muhammad Ratib, [September? 1876], in Rubenson, *Acta Aethiopica III*.

72. The population of Se'azega to Charles Gordon, [March 1877], and Barya'u Gebre Sadiq to Charles Gordon, 11 May 1878, in ibid.

73. Kasa Mircha to Munzinger, 17 November [1869], in ibid.

74. Asseggahen to Antoine d'Abbadie, [July–August?] 1866, in Rubenson, *Acta Aethiopica II*.

75. NA FO 1/30 'Abyssinia...' Baker to Granville, 5 January 1884; also Marcus, *Life and Times*, p. 79.

76. For example, Salt, *Voyage*, pp. 227–9.

77. Zekkariyas Tesfa Mikael to Guillaume Lejean, 5 July 1864, in Rubenson, *Acta Aethiopica II*.

78. Portal, *Mission*, p. 28.

79. Ibid., pp. 7, 34.

80. NA FO 1/30 'Abyssinia...' Baker to Granville, 5 and 7 January 1884.

81. Ibid., 7 January 1884; see also Wylde, *Modern Abyssinia*, pp. 30–1.

82. Portal, *Mission*, pp.5–6.

83. P. M. Holt, 'Egypt and the Nile valley', in J. E. Flint (ed.), *Cambridge History of Africa, Vol. 5: c.1790–c.1870* (Cambridge, 1976) pp.22*ff*; see also R. Gray, *A History of the Southern Sudan 1839–1889* (London, 1961).

84. A useful overview is in P. M. Holt and M. W. Daly, *A History of the Sudan* (Harlow, 2000), chapter 4.

85. Wendy James' work remains crucial. A selection would include: '*KWANIM PA: The Making of the Uduk People. An Ethnographic Study of Survival in the Sudan–Ethiopian Borderlands* (Oxford, 1979); 'War and "ethnic visibility": the Uduk on the Sudan–Ethiopian border', in K. Fukui and J. Markakis (eds.), *Ethnicity and Conflict in the Horn of Africa* (London, 1994); 'Local centres on the Western Frontier, 1974–97: a case study of Kurmuk', in K. Fukui *et al.* (eds.), *Ethiopia in Broader Perspective: Papers of the XIIIth International Conference of Ethiopian Studies Vol. II* (Kyoto, 1997); 'No place to hide: flag-waving on the western frontier', in W. James *et al.* (eds.), *Remapping Ethiopia: Socialism and After* (Oxford, 2002).

86. A. Triulzi, *Salt, Gold and Legitimacy: Prelude to the History of a No-man's-land, Bela Shangul, Wallagga, Ethiopia (ca.1800–1898)* (Naples, 1981).

87. Sahle Dingil *et al.* to Louis Philippe, [June 1838], in Rubenson, *Acta Aethiopica I*.

88. Parkyns, *Life in Abyssinia*, p.177.

89. Plowden, *Travels*, p.20.

90. Parkyns, *Life in Abyssinia*, pp.182–5.

91. Ibid., p.187.

92. Plowden, *Travels*, p.19.

93. Ibid., pp.8–9.

94. NA FO 1/27B Stanton to Granville, 12 August 1872.

95. NA FO 1/27B Memo by Cherif Pasha, n.d., encl. in Stanton to Granville, 28 November 1872.

96. NA FO 1/31 Mason Bey to Nubar to Pasha, 7 May 1884.

97. NA FO 1/31 'Abyssinia...' Hewett to Secretary to the Admiralty, 22 June 1884, and 'Despatch from Hewett to Cairo', 16 June 1884.

98. NA FO 1/30 'Abyssinia...' Memo on Abyssinia by Sir E. Baring, to Granville, February 1884.

99. Portal, *Mission*, p.7.

100. Wylde, *Modern Abyssinia*, p.40.

101. See for example Berkeley, *Campaign*, p.379; Bahru Zewde, *Modern Ethiopia*, p.58; Holt and Daly, *History of the Sudan*, pp.94–5.

102. Marcus, *Life and Times*, chapters 2 and 3.

103. Ibid., chapter 4.

104. Ibid., chapter 5; Rubenson, *Survival*, pp.384*ff*; G. N. Sanderson, 'The Nile basin and the eastern Horn, 1870–1908', in R. O. Oliver and G. N. Sanderson (eds.), *Cambridge History of Africa, Vol. 6: from 1870 to 1905* (Cambridge, 1985) pp.656*ff*.

105. Portal, *Mission*, p.248.

106. Gobat, *Residence*, p.446.
107. Blanc, *Captivity*, pp.296–7.
108. Bulatovich, *Russian Eyes*, p.68.
109. Ibid., p.68.
110. Ibid., p.47.
111. Ibid., p.51.
112. Ibid., p.177.
113. Again, a great deal of rich contemporary detail on these campaigns is provided by Bulatovich.
114. For a useful overview, see Bahru Zewde, *Modern Ethiopia*, pp.85*ff*; and on the statuses of *neftennya* and *gabbar* in various local contexts, see Donham and James, *Southern Marches*, *passim*.
115. Wylde, *Modern Abyssinia*, pp.56, 214–15.
116. Ibid., p.365.
117. Ibid., pp.174, 220–1.
118. Berkeley, *Campaign*, p.27.
119. R. Caulk, 'Armies as predators: soldiers and peasants in Ethiopia, *c.*1850–1935', *International Journal of African Historical Studies*, 11:3 (1978); J. Dunn, ' "For God, Emperor, and Country!" The evolution of Ethiopia's nineteenth-century army', *War in History*, 1 (1994).
120. Reid, *War*, pp.79–106.
121. Berkeley, for example, suggests that an actual army might be rendered half as large again by women and slaves: Berkeley, *Campaign*, p.9.
122. See also R. Caulk, 'Firearms and princely power in Ethiopia in the nineteenth century', *Journal of African History*, 13:4 (1972) pp.609–10.
123. Wylde, *Modern Abyssinia*, p.5; see also NA FO 881/5530X 'The Abyssinian Army', Lt Gleichen, 28 December 1887, pp.2–3.
124. Portal, *Mission*, pp.165–6.
125. Wylde, *Modern Abyssinia*, pp.7–9, 165.
126. NA FO 881/5530X 'The Abyssinian Army', Lt. Gleichen, 28 December 1887, p.1.
127. Bulatovich, *Russian Eyes*, p.100.

CHAPTER 5

1. Rubenson, *Survival*, pp.384–99.
2. C. Giglio (tr. R. Caulk), 'Article 17 of the Treaty of Uccialli', *Journal of African History*, 6:2 (1965).
3. R. Pateman, *Eritrea: Even the Stones are Burning* (Lawrenceville, NJ, 1990, 1998) p.50.
4. See R. Pankhurst and D. Johnson, 'The great drought and famine of 1888–92 in northeast Africa', in D. Johnson and D. M. Anderson (eds.), *The Ecology of Survival: Case Studies from Northeast African History* (London, 1988) pp.47–57; McCann, *People of the Plow*, pp.89, 91–2.

5. NA FO 881/5530X 'The Abyssinian Army', by Lt. Gleichen.

6. Berkeley, *Campaign*, p.8.

7. Caulk, 'Firearms and princely power'.

8. One of the best accounts remains Rubenson, 'Adwa 1896'; and see also Rubenson, *Ethiopian Independence*, pp.399–406.

9. See also R. J. Reid, 'The Trans-Mereb Experience: perceptions of the historical relationship between Eritrea and Ethiopia', *Journal of Eastern African Studies*, 1:2 (2007) pp.240–6.

10. The idea recurs in virtually all of the key texts on modern Eritrean history. See for example: Jordan Gebre-Medhin, *Peasants and Nationalism in Eritrea* (Trenton, NJ, 1989) pp.56–69; Pateman, *Eritrea*, esp. pp.47–66; Ruth Iyob, *The Eritrean Struggle for Independence: Domination, Resistance, Nationalism 1941–1993* (Cambridge, 1995) p.4; Redie Bereketeab, *Eritrea: the making of a nation, 1890–1991* (Trenton, NJ, 2007) pp.75–132.

11. A good overview can be found in Redie Bereketeab, *Eritrea*, chapter 4.

12. Foreign Office (UK), *Handbook [on Eritrea] prepared under the direction of the historical section of the Foreign Office*, No.126 (London, 1920).

13. Jordan Gebre-Medhin, *Peasants and Nationalism*, pp.56ff.

14. Foreign Office, *Handbook*.

15. Ibid.

16. See for example F. Locatelli, 'Oziosi, vagaboni e pregiudicati: labour, law and crime in colonial Asmara, 1890—1941', *International Journal of African Historical Studies*, 40:2 (2007); and her 'Beyond the Campo Cintato: prostitutes, migrants and "criminals" in colonial Asmara (Eritrea), 1890–1941', in F. Locatelli and P. Nugent (eds.), *African Cities: Competing Claims on Urban Spaces* (Leiden, 2009).

17. Uoldelul Chelati Dirar, 'Colonialism and the construction of national identities: the case of Eritrea', *Journal of Eastern African Studies*, 1:2 (2007).

18. For example, R. Caulk, 'Ethiopia and the Horn', in A. D. Roberts (ed.), *Cambridge History of Africa: Vol. VII* (Cambridge, 1986) pp.724–5.

19. Ibid., p.725.

20. Ibid.

21. Foreign Office, *Handbook*.

22. Caulk, 'Ethiopia and the Horn', p.725.

23. Ibid., p.726; see also Pateman, *Eritrea*, pp.58ff.

24. See for example W. C. Young, 'The Rashayida Arabs vs the State: the impact of European colonialism on a small-scale society in Sudan and Eritrea', *Journal of Colonialism and Colonial History*, 9:2, Fall 2008.

25. Ibid.

26. Ibid.

27. In Tekeste Negash, *No Medicine for the Bite of a White Snake* (Uppsala, 1986), pp.41–2; Kolmodin, *Traditions*, pp.281–3.

28. Tekeste Negash, *No Medicine*, p.44; Pateman, *Eritrea*, pp.51–2; Kolmodin, *Traditions*, pp.284–5.

29. See R. Caulk, ' 'Black snake, white snake': Bahta Hagos and his revolt against Italian overrule in Eritrea, 1894', in D. Crummey (ed.), *Banditry, Rebellion and Social Protest in Africa* (London, 1986).

30. Pateman, *Eritrea*, p.52.

31. Tekeste Negash, *No Medicine*, p.45.

32. Redie Bereketeab, *Eritrea*, pp.120ff.

33. Foreign Office, *Handbook*.

34. Tekeste Negash, *No Medicine*, pp.45ff; also Tekeste Negash, *Italian Colonialism in Eritrea, 1882–1941: policies, praxis and impact* (Uppsala, 1987) pp.127ff.

35. Tekeste Negash, *Italian Colonialism*, p.127.

36. Alemseged Tesfai, *Aynefalale* (Asmara, 2001) pp.267–8.

37. The best military account is A. J. Barker, *Eritrea 1941* (London, 1966).

38. Ibid., p.109.

39. Quoted in S. Pankhurst, *British Policy in Eritrea and Northern Ethiopia* (Woodford Green, 1946). 'Benadir' or 'Benaadir' was the term applied to southern Italian Somaliland.

40. It is the opening gambit in M. Wrong, *I Didn't Do It For You: How the World Betrayed a Small African Nation* (London and New York, 2005).

41. Lewis, *Modern History*, chapter 1.

42. L.V. Cassanelli, *The Shaping of Somali Society: Reconstructing the History of a Pastoral People, 1600–1900* (Philadelphia, 1982) pp.201ff.

43. Ibid., pp.203–4.

44. R. Robinson and J. Gallagher, *Africa and the Victorians: The Official Mind of Imperialism* (London, 1981) p.331.

45. Mburu, *Bandits*, pp.23ff; see also Markakis, *National and Class Conflict*, pp.43–4.

46. It is beyond the scope of this book to explore the clans in detail; suffice to say here that the history of relations between the main groupings—Dir, Isaq, Ogaden, Darod, Rahanweyn, Hawiye, and Digil—has been characterized by both necessarily peaceful cooperation and sporadically violent competition over material and political resources.

47. See Lewis, *Modern History*, pp.63–91; also R. L. Hess, 'The poor man of God: Muhammad Abdullah Hassan', in N. R. Bennett (ed.), *Leadership in Eastern Africa* (Boston, 1968).

48. To the British, naturally, he was the 'Mad Mullah'. For a detailed account of the military campaigns, see H. Moyse-Bartlett, *The King's African Rifles: A Study in the Military History of East and Central Africa, 1890–1945* (Aldershot, 1956) II, pp.160–94; II, 419–33.

49. Paice, *Tip and Run*, pp.212ff.

50. Said S. Samatar, *Oral Poetry and Somali Nationalism: The Case of Sayyid Mahammad 'Abdille Hasan* (Cambridge, 1982).

51. L. Farago, *Abyssinia on the Eve* (London, 1935) pp.258ff.

52. Record of the British Military Administration in Eritrea and Somalia, *The First to be Freed* (London, 1944) pp.49–53.

53. Quoted in ibid., p.50.

54. C. Barnes, 'The Somali Youth League, Ethiopian Somalis and the greater Somalia idea, *c*.1946–48', *Journal of Eastern African Studies*, 1:2 (2007).

55. Lewis, *Modern History*, pp.161*ff.*

56. Two accessible collections of documents from the British perspective, both edited by Peter Woodward, are: *British Documents on Foreign Affairs: Reports and Papers from the Foreign Office Confidential Print. Part III, from 1940 through 1945. Series G, Africa* (Bethesda, MD, 1998); and *British Documents on Foreign Affairs: Reports and Papers from the Foreign Office Confidential Print. Part IV, from 1945 through 1950. Series G, Africa* (Bethesda, MD, 1999—).

57. Pateman, *Eritrea*, pp.67*ff*; Jordan Gebre-Medhin, *Peasants and Nationalism*, chapter 5; Redie Bereketeab, *Eritrea*, chapter 5, *passim.*

58. See also the range of opinion expressed in contemporary British analysis: S. Pankhurst, *Eritrea on the Eve: The Past and Future of Italy's 'First-born' Colony, Ethiopia's Ancient Sea Province* (Woodford Green, 1952) p.59; S. Longrigg, *A Short History of Eritrea* (Oxford, 1945) pp.169–70; S. F. Nadel, *Races and Tribes of Eritrea* (Asmara, 1944) pp.71, 78; S. Longrigg, 'The future of Eritrea', *African Affairs* 45(180) (1946) pp.122, 126; M. Perham, *The Government of Ethiopia* (London, 1948) pp.434–5; G. K. N. Trevaskis, *Eritrea: A Colony in Transition, 1941–52* (London, 1960) p.130.

59. L. Ellingson, 'The emergence of political parties in Eritrea, 1941–1950', *Journal of African History*, 18:2 (1977); Ruth Iyob, *Eritrean Struggle*, chapter 4.

60. See for example Alazar Tesfa Michael, *Eritrea To-Day: Fascist Oppression Under the Nose of British Military* [sic] (Woodford Green, *c*.1946) p.5.

61. See Pankhurst, *British Policy*; Pankhurst, *Eritrea on the Eve*; and with her son R. Pankhurst, *Ethiopia and Eritrea: The Last Phase of the Reunion Struggle, 1941–1952* (Woodford Green, 1953). For a breezily refreshing commentary on Sylvia Pankhurst's obsession with Ethiopia, see W. B. Carnochan, *Golden Legends: Images of Abyssinia, Samuel Johnson to Bob Marley* (Stanford, 2008).

62. See by Alemseged Abbay, 'The trans-Mereb past in the present', *Journal of Modern African Studies*, 35:2 (1997); and *Identity Jilted, passim.*

63. Markakis, *National and Class Conflict*, p.64; see also Longrigg, 'The future of Eritrea', p.126.

64. This was the short-lived Bevin-Sforza plan, which rested on the idea that the highlands of Eritrea might belong to Ethiopia, but the western lowlands should really be annexed to Sudan. The southern Afar lowlands were also to go to Ethiopia.

65. Longrigg, 'The future of Eritrea', p.126.

66. Okbazghi Yohannes, *Eritrea: A Pawn in World Politics* (Gainesville, FL, 1991) chapters 4 and 5.

67. Ellingson, 'Emergence'.

68. Jordan Gebre-Medhin, *Peasants and Nationalism*, p.80.

69. Ruth Iyob, *Eritrean Struggle*, pp.65–6.

70. Fernyhough, 'Social mobility', p.165 and *passim*.
71. Jordan Gebre-Medhin, *Peasants and Nationalism*, pp.108*ff*.
72. Ruth Iyob, *Eritrean Struggle*, chapter 4, *passim*.
73. D. Cumming, 'The UN disposal of Eritrea', *African Affairs*, 52:207 (1953) p.131.
74. Much information comes from Trevaskis, both in *Eritrea*, especially pp.103*ff*; and his report on the issue, 'A Study of the Development of the Present Shifta Problem and the Means Whereby it can be Remedied' (June 1950), Research and Documentation Centre (Asmara), Box/293 File SH/20 Vol. II Acc 13406.
75. Plowden, *Travels*, chapter 2.
76. Trevaskis provides considerable detail on this in 'Shifta Problem', appendix B, pp.12*ff*.
77. Ibid.
78. See also Jordan Gebre-Medhin, *Peasants and Nationalism*, chapter 6, *passim*.
79. See the 'sitreps' (situation reports) contained in the UK National Archives War Office (WO) 230 Series, containing details of anti-*shifta* activities. Also N. Mburu, 'Patriots or bandits? Britain's strategy for policing Eritrea, 1941–1952', *Nordic Journal of African Studies*, 9:2 (2000).
80. See for example RDC Box / 287 File 70 / B / 9 Acc.13339. The Amnesty—a progress report. Enclosed letter to Senior Divisional Officers, 30 July 1951.
81. Trevaskis, *Eritrea*, pp.70–1.
82. J.-B. Gewald, 'Making tribes: social engineering in the Western province of British-administered Eritrea, 1941–1952', *Journal of Colonialism and Colonial History*, 1:2 (2000).
83. RDC Box / 287 File 70 / B / 9 Acc.13339, Address by His Excellency the Chief Administrator, 16 June 1951.
84. Okbazghi Yohannes, *Eritrea*, provides an in-depth examination. See also Ruth Iyob, *Eritrean Struggle*, pp.73*ff*; and Bereket Habte Selassie, 'From British rule to federation and annexation', in B. Davidson, L. Cliffe, and Bereket Habte Selassie (eds.), *Behind the War in Eritrea* (Nottingham, 1980).
85. The full text is in Tekeste Negash, *Eritrea and Ethiopia: The Federal Experience* (Uppsala, 1997) pp.188–208.

CHAPTER 6

1. For an excellent overview, see Caulk, 'Ethiopia and the Horn', pp.707*ff*.
2. Bahru Zewde, *Modern Ethiopia*, p.121.
3. There are a number of detailed accounts of these events. See for example the excellent essay by R. Caulk, 'Ethiopia and the Horn', in A. D. Roberts (ed.), *Cambridge History of Africa, Vol. 7: from 1905 to 1940* (Cambridge, 1986); Marcus, *History*, pp.116*ff*; P. Henze, *Layers of Time: A History of Ethiopia* (London, 2000), pp.188*ff*; Bahru Zewde, *Modern Ethiopia*, pp.111*ff*. See also Haile Selassie's own account of his early life in E. Ullendorff (ed. and tr.), *The Autobiography of Emperor Haile Selassie I: 'My Life and Ethiopia's Progress', 1892–1937* (London, 1976).

4. Marcus, *History*, p.120.

5. Abdusammad H. Ahmad, 'Trading in slaves in Bela-Shangul and Gumuz, Ethiopia: border enclaves in history, 1897–1938', *Journal of African History*, 40:3 (1999).

6. See also R. Pankhurst, *Economic History of Ethiopia, 1800–1935* (Addis Ababa, 1968) pp.108ff.

7. See Bahru Zewde, *Pioneers of Change in Ethiopia: The Reformist Intellectuals of the Early Twentieth Century* (Oxford, 2002); and, for a useful summary, Bahru Zewde, *Modern Ethiopia*, pp.103–11.

8. Ullendorff, *Autobiography*, pp.156ff; Henze, *Layers of Time*, pp.202ff.

9. W. Thesiger, *The Danakil Diary: Journeys Through Abyssinia, 1930–34* (London, 1998) p.3.

10. Lewis, *Jimma Abba Jifar*, p.46.

11. Bahru Zewde, *Modern Ethiopia*, p.91.

12. Thesiger, *Danakil Diary*, pp.21, 99, and *passim*.

13. A. H. M. Jones and E. Monroe, *A History of Ethiopia* (Oxford, 1935) p.173.

14. Bahru Zewde, *Modern Ethiopia*, p.137.

15. Evelyn Waugh, *Waugh in Abyssinia* (Baton Rouge, 2007; first pub. 1936) p.24.

16. Ibid., pp.222–3, 239.

17. See for example Farago, *Abyssinia*.

18. Jones and Monroe, *Ethiopia*, pp.173–4; also Tibebe Ashete, 'Towards a history of the incorporation of the Ogaden: 1887–1935', *Journal of Ethiopian Studies*, 27:2 (1994).

19. U. Almagor, 'Institutionalising a fringe periphery: Dassanetch–Amhara relations', in Donham and James, *Southern Marches*.

20. Sir P. Mitchell, *African Afterthoughts* (London, 1954) p.271.

21. Moyse-Bartlett, *King's African Rifles*, II, p.209.

22. D. A. Low, 'Uganda: the establishment of the Protectorate, 1894–1919', in V. Harlow and E. M. Chilver (eds.), *History of East Africa* (Oxford, 1965) II, pp.106–7.

23. D. A. Low, 'British East Africa: the establishment of British rule, 1895–1912', in Harlow and Chilver, *History of East Africa*, II, pp.30–1.

24. Moyse-Bartlett, *King's African Rifles*, II, pp.447–9.

25. Ibid., p.467.

26. For a study of these shifts in the recent past, see for example G. Schlee, 'Brothers of the Boran once again: on the fading popularity of certain Somali identities in northern Kenya', *Journal of Eastern African Studies*, 1:3 (2007).

27. Sir H. Macmichael, *The Anglo-Egyptian Sudan* (London, 1934) p.97.

28. D. Johnson, 'On the Nilotic frontier: imperial Ethiopia in the southern Sudan, 1898–1936', in D. Donham and W. James (eds.), *The Southern Marches of Imperial Ethiopia* (Oxford, 2002, 1986) p.240.

29. Ibid.

30. Macmichael, *Anglo-Egyptian Sudan*, pp.177–9, 182–6.

31. Ibid., p.178; P.Garretson, 'Vicious cycles: ivory, slaves and arms on the new Maji frontier', in Donham and James, *Southern Marches*.

32. Macmichael, *Anglo-Egyptian Sudan*, pp.182–3.

33. For example T. M. Coffey, *Lion by the Tail: The Story of the Italian–Ethiopian War* (London, 1974); A. Mockler, *Haile Selassie's War: The Italian–Ethiopian Campaign, 1935–1941* (London, 1984).

34. Coffey, *Lion by the Tail*, pp.3ff.

35. See for example A. Hilton, *The Ethiopian Patriots: Forgotten Voices of the Italo-Abyssinian War 1935–41* (Stroud, 2007).

36. C. Zoli, 'The organisation of Italy's East African Empire', *Foreign Affairs*, 16:1 (1937) pp.81–2.

37. E. M. Robertson, *Mussolini as Empire-Builder: Europe and Africa 1932–36* (London, 1977) p.9.

38. H. Erlich, 'Tigrean politics, 1930–35, and the approaching Italo-Ethiopian war', in H. Erlich, *Ethiopia and the Challenge of Independence* (Boulder, CO, 1986) p.141.

39. For example Bahru Zewde, *Modern Ethiopia*, p.147.

40. See for example Howe to Eden, 5 July 1943, in P. Woodward (ed.), *British Documents on Foreign Affairs: Reports and Papers from the Foreign Office Confidential Print. Part III, from 1940 through 1945. Series G, Africa* (Bethesda, MD, 1998) (hereafter *BDFA*, III) Vol. III (Africa, April–December 1943).

41. Zoli, 'Italy's East African Empire', pp.83–4.

42. Erlich, *Challenge of Independence*, especially pp.129–34, 135–65.

43. A. Triulzi, 'Italian colonialism and Ethiopia', *Journal of African History*, 23:2 (1982).

44. A. Sbacchi, *Ethiopia under Mussolini: Fascism and the Colonial Experience* (London, 1985); Haile Larebo, *The Building of an Empire: Italian Land Policy and Practice in Ethiopia* (Trenton, NJ, 2006; first pub. 1994).

45. Zoli, 'Italy's East African Empire', pp.80–1.

46. Ibid., p.84.

47. Ibid., pp.81–2.

48. Ibid., p.86.

49. Ibid., p.87.

50. Waugh, *Waugh in Abyssinia*, pp.234–5.

51. Henze, *Layers of Time*, p.226.

52. Waugh, *Waugh in Abyssinia*, pp.237–8.

53. Bahru Zewde, *Pioneers*, pp.42, 46, 86–8.

54. 'Ethiopian personalities', enclosure in Howe to Eden, 11 December 1942, in *BDFA*, III, Vol. II, (Africa, January 1942–March 1943).

55. Mitchell, *Afterthoughts*, pp.202, 204.

56. H. Marcus, *The Politics of Empire: Ethiopia, Great Britain and the United States, 1941–1974* (Lawrenceville, NJ, 1995; first pub. 1983) pp.8ff.

57. Foreign Office, 'Policy for Ethiopia', 20 January 1942, in *BDFA*, III, Vol. II (Africa, January 1942–March 1943).

58. Young, *Peasant Revolution*, pp.51*ff*; Gebru Tareke, 'Peasant resistance in Ethiopia: the case of *Weyane*', *Journal of African History*, 25:1 (1984); Gebru Tareke, *Ethiopia: Power and Protest*, pp.89–124; H. Erlich, ' 'Tigrean nationalism', British involvement, and Haile Selassie's emerging absolutism: northern Ethiopia, 1941–1943', *Asian and African Studies*, 15:2 (1981).

59. Young, *Peasant Revolution*, pp.53–4; J. Hammond, *Fire From the Ashes: A Chronicle of Revolution in Tigray, Ethiopia, 1975–1991* (Lawrenceville, NJ, 1999) pp.165, 244–5.

60. Gebru Tareke, 'Peasant resistance', p.77.

61. Ibid., pp.79, 81–7.

62. 'Ethiopia: Political Review for 1943', enclosure in Howe to Eden, 13 June 1944, in *BDFA*, III, Vol. IV (Africa, 1944).

63. E. A. Chapman-Andrews, 'Political memorandum on Eritrea', 27 October 1940, in *BDFA*, III, Vol. I (Africa, 1940–1).

64. Marcus, *Politics of Empire*.

65. These can be followed in minute detail in the five volumes which make up P. Woodward (ed.), *British Documents on Foreign Affairs: Reports and Papers from the Foreign Office Confidential Print. Part IV, from 1945 through 1950. Series G, Africa* (Bethesda, MD, 1999) (hereafter *BDFA*, IV). See also Tibebe Eshete, 'The root causes of political problems in the Ogaden, 1942–1960', *Northeast African Studies*, 13:1 (1991).

66. R. Greenfield, *Ethiopia: A New Political History* (London, 1965) pp.306*ff*.

67. Bahru Zewde, *Pioneers*, offers the best account of this.

68. For example, 'Ethiopia: Annual Review for 1948', enclosure in Lascelles to Bevin, 9 February 1949, in *BDFA*, IV, Vol. IV (Africa, January 1948–December 1949).

69. 'Ethiopia: Annual review for 1949', enclosure in Lascelles to Bevin, 8 May 1950, in *BDFA*, IV, Vol. V (Africa, January–December 1950).

70. See J. Iliffe, *The African Poor: A History* (Cambridge, 1987) p.157.

71. See for example H. Erlich, 'The Ethiopian Army and the 1974 Revolution', in M. Janowitz (ed.), *Armed Forces and Society* (Chicago, 1983).

72. Messay Kebede, *Radicalism and Cultural Dislocation in Ethiopia, 1960–1974* (Rochester, NY, 2008).

73. Arguably the finest account of these events is still the late Richard Greenfield's *Ethiopia*.

74. For example, Addis Hiwet, *Ethiopia: From Autocracy to Revolution* (London, 1975).

75. H. Erlich, 'The Eritrean autonomy, 1952–1962: its failure and its contribution to further escalation', in Y. Dinstein (ed.), *Models of Autonomy* (New York, 1981).

76. Jordan Gebre-Medhin, *Peasants and Nationalism*, pp.144*ff*.

77. J. Markakis, 'The nationalist revolution in Eritrea', *Journal of Modern African Studies*, 26:1 (1988) p.54.

78. Okbazghi Yohannes, *Eritrea*, pp.189*ff*.

79. T. Killion, 'Eritrean workers' organisation and early nationalist mobilisation: 1948–1958', *Eritrean Studies Review*, 2:1 (1997).

80. Markakis, 'Nationalist revolution', p.54.

81. See also Ruth Iyob, *Eritrean Struggle*, pp.98*ff*.

82. Othman Saleh Sabbe (tr. Muhamad Fawaz al-Azem), *The History of Eritrea* (Beirut, n.d. [c.1974?]) p.249.

83. Erlich, 'Eritrean autonomy', pp.178–9.

84. D. Johnson, *The Root Causes of Sudan's Civil Wars* (Oxford, 2003) pp.29*ff*.

85. Markakis, 'Nationalist revolution', pp.55; D.Pool, *From Guerrillas to Government: the Eritrean People's Liberation Front* (Oxford, 2001) pp.36–7.

86. Pool, *Guerrillas*, pp.49*ff*.

87. Gaim Kibreab, 'Eritrean–Sudanese relations in historical perspective', in R. J. Reid (ed.), *Eritrea's External Relations: Understanding its Regional Role and Foreign Policy* (London, 2009) pp.72*ff*.

88. Wolde-Yesus Ammar, 'The role of Asmara students in the Eritrean nationalist movement, 1958–68', *Eritrean Studies Review*, 2:1 (1997).

89. Pool, *Guerrillas*, p.52.

90. See the engrossing account given by Haile Wold'ensae to Dan Connell in the latter's *Conversations*, pp.25*ff*.

91. Markakis, 'Nationalist revolution', pp.56–61; Pool, *Guerrillas*, pp.49–58; Ruth Iyob, *Eritrean Struggle*, pp.109–17.

92. Pool, *Guerrillas*, p.52

93. Lewis, *Modern History*, pp.178*ff*.

94. Markakis, *National and Class Conflict*, pp.175–80.

95. The best of a very small pool of work on this is Mburu, *Bandits*; see also Lewis, *Modern History*, pp.183*ff*.

96. I am grateful to Hannah Whittaker, a doctoral research student at the School of Oriental and African Studies in London, for this analysis.

97. Mburu, *Bandits*, pp.182, 202–3.

98. Ibid., p.78.

99. Gebru Tareke, *Power and Protest*, pp.125*ff*.

100. Ibid., pp.160*ff*.

101. See the wonderfully thoughtful account of the Ethiopian situation in Messay Kebede, *Radicalism and Cultural Dislocation*.

CHAPTER 7

1. Messay Kebede, *Radicalism and Cultural Dislocation*.

2. For a remarkably sympathetic contemporary assessment, see P. Schwab, *Ethiopia: Politics, Economics and Society* (London, 1985). For more critical, in-depth analyses from the 1980s—including a spate of studies published in 1988, virtually on the eve of the regime's collapse—see F. Halliday and M. Molyneux, *The Ethiopian Revolution* (London, 1981); C. Clapham, *Transformation and Continuity in*

Revolutionary Ethiopia (Cambridge, 1988); J. W. Harbeson, *The Ethiopian Transformation: The Quest for the Post Imperial State* (Boulder and London, 1988); and E. J. Keller, *Revolutionary Ethiopia: From Empire to People's Republic* (Bloomington and Indianapolis, 1988). Arguably the best single account—and certainly the best by an Ethiopian scholar—is Andargachew Tiruneh, *The Ethiopian Revolution, 1974–1987: A Transformation from an Aristocratic to a Totalitarian Autocracy* (Cambridge, 1993).

3. S. Decalo, *Coups and Army Rule in Africa: Motivations and Constraints* (New Haven and London, 1990) pp.33–4, 293–4.

4. See for example A. Gavshon, *Crisis in Africa: Battleground of East and West* (New York, 1981) pp.258*ff*.

5. C. Legum and B. Lee, *The Horn of Africa in Continuing Crisis* (New York and London, 1979).

6. Quoted in Bahru Zewde, *Modern Ethiopia*, p.255.

7. Gebru Tareke, *The Ethiopian Revolution: War in the Horn of Africa* (New Haven and London, 2009) chapter 4.

8. Andargachew Tiruneh, *Ethiopian Revolution*, pp.345–6.

9. Ibid., pp.211–12; also M. Dines, 'The Ethiopian 'Red Terror'', in Davidson *et al.*, *Behind the War*, pp.60–1.

10. Markakis, *National and Class Conflict*, pp.237ff; Andargachew Tiruneh, *Ethiopian Revolution*, chapter 3, *passim*.

11. Dines, 'The Ethiopian "Red Terror"', p.61; R. Pateman, 'Drought, famine and development', in L. Cliffe and B. Davidson (eds.), *The Long Struggle of Eritrea for Independence and Constructive Peace* (Trenton, NJ, 1988) pp.169*ff*.

12. G. Hancock, *Ethiopia: The Challenge of Hunger* (London, 1985); R. D. Kaplan, *Surrender or Starve: Travels in Ethiopia, Sudan, Somalia and Eritrea*, 2nd edn. (New York, 2003) pp.20*ff*.

13. For an excellent overview, see Gaim Kibreab, 'Eritrean–Sudanese relations'.

14. See Young, *Armed Groups*, pp.18*ff*.

15. Ibid., pp.21–2.

16. The EPDM later became part of the EPRDF coalition, and changed its name to the Amhara National Democratic Movement (ANDM).

17. Again see Gaim Kibreab's work on Eritrean refugees in Sudan, notably *People on the Edge in the Horn* (Oxford, 1996); and *Critical Reflections on the Eritrean War of Independence* (Trenton, NJ, 2008).

18. Again, Young, *Armed Groups*, provides the best overview; see also the illuminating piece by Eisei Kurimoto, 'Fear and Anger: female versus male narratives among the Anywaa', in James *et al.*, *Remapping Ethiopia*.

19. James, 'No place to hide'.

20. Ibid., pp.263–4.

21. Holt and Daly, *History of the Sudan*, pp.187*ff*.

22. Gebru Tareke, 'The Ethiopia–Somalia war of 1977 revisited', *International Journal of African Historical Studies*, 33:3 (2000); Lewis, *Modern History*, pp.231–48.

23. Gebru Tareke, *Ethiopian Revolution*, chapter 6 *passim*; Markakis, *National and Class Conflict*, pp.225*ff*.

24. Legum and Lee, *Horn of Africa*, pp.68 *ff*.

25. Lewis, *Modern History*, pp.239–48.

26. A. Triulzi, 'Competing views of national identity in Ethiopia', in I. M. Lewis (ed.), *Nationalism and Self-Determination in the Horn of Africa* (London, 1983).

27. M. Dines, 'Ethiopian violation of human rights in Eritrea', in Cliffe and Davidson, *Long Struggle*, p.148.

28. C. Clapham (ed.), *African Guerrillas* (Oxford, 1998).

29. Sorenson, *Imagining Ethiopia*, p.62.

30. Mohammed Hassan, 'Conquest, tyranny and ethnocide against the Oromo: a historical assessment of human rights conditions in Ethiopia, ca.1880s–2002', in Ezekiel Gebissa, *Contested Terrain*, pp.30–1.

31. See H. S. Lewis, 'The development of Oromo political consciousness from 1958 to 1994', in P. T. W. Baxter *et al.*, *Being and Becoming Oromo* for an insightful overview. In the same collection, see also Gemetchu Megerssa, '*Oromumma*: tradition, consciousness and identity'; and Mohammed Hassan, 'The development of Oromo nationalism'; as well as P. Baxter, 'The creation and constitution of Oromo nationality', in K. Fukui and J. Markakis (eds.), *Ethnicity and Conflict in the Horn of Africa* (London, 1994).

32. Hassan, 'Conquest', pp.31–2.

33. Asafa Jalata, *Oromia and Ethiopia*, pp.179–80.

34. Hassan, 'Conquest', pp.33–6.

35. Levine, *Greater Ethiopia*.

36. The point is well made in Clapham, 'Boundary and territory', p.245.

37. As Gunther Schlee has shown, however, even this can be complicated, as identities and senses of belonging shift from time to time between 'Somali' and 'Oromo': see for example Schlee, 'Brothers of the Boran'; also his *Identities on the Move: Clanship and Pastoralism in Northern Kenya* (Manchester, 1989), and 'Gada systems on the meta-ethnic level: Gabbra / Boran / Garre interactions in the Kenyan / Ethiopian borderland', in Kurimoto and Simonse, *Conflict, Age and Power*.

38. Asafa Jalata, *Oromia and Ethiopia*, p.193.

39. Ibid., pp.193–5.

40. Mohammed Hassan, 'The development of nationalism', p.69.

41. Bahru Zewde, *Pioneers of Change*, p.133.

42. Young, *Peasant Revolution*, pp.44–9, 99.

43. J. Young, 'The Tigray and Eritrean Peoples' Liberation Fronts: a history of tensions and pragmatism', *Journal of Modern African Studies*, 34:1 (1996) p.106.

44. The term 'Agame' as a pejorative for Tigrayan came to have widespread currency, even among Amhara: see Alemseged Abbay, *Identity Jilted*, pp.140, 142; Young, *Peasant Revolution*, p.69. The antiquity of the concept is unclear. In 1901, Wylde noted the 'saying' that 'nothing ever good came out of Agame': Wylde, *Modern Abyssinia*, p.200.

45. Young, *Peasant Revolution*, pp.87, 92ff; Markakis, *National and Class Conflict*, pp.253ff; Gebru Tareke, *Ethiopian Revolution*, chapter 3.

46. Young, *Peasant Revolution*, chapter 4 *passim*.

47. A vivid first-hand account of this later period is provided by Hammond, *Fire from the Ashes*.

48. Gebru Tareke, *Ethiopian Revolution*, chapter 9.

49. Pool, *Guerrillas*, pp.87ff; Ruth Iyob, *Eritrean Struggle*, pp.123ff.

50. The history of the ELF–EPLF civil war remains shrouded, and it will be some time before a fuller picture of it becomes clear; but see for example Gaim Kibreab, *Critical Reflections*.

51. Pool, *Guerrillas*, chapter 3 *passim*.

52. Ibid., pp.67ff; Gaim Kibreab, *Critical Reflections*, chapter 5 *passim*: Markakis, *National and Class Conflict*, pp.131ff.

53. Bereket Habte Selassie, *The Crown and the Pen: The Memoirs of a Lawyer Turned Rebel* (Trenton, NJ, 2007) pp.299ff.

54. Pool, *Guerrillas*, pp.76ff; Gaim Kibreab, *Critical Reflections*, chapter 7; Kidane Mengisteab and Okbazghi Yohannes, *Anatomy*, pp.46ff.

55. Andargachew Tiruneh, *Ethiopian Revolution*, pp.77–8.

56. For example, see Dines, 'Ethiopian violation'.

57. Ibid., pp.149–52.

58. Interesting contemporary analysis is offered by R. Sherman, *Eritrea: The Unfinished Revolution* (New York, 1980).

59. Awet Weldemichael, 'The Eritrean long march: the strategic withdrawal of the Eritrean People's Liberation Front (EPLF), 1978–79', *Journal of Military History*, 73:4 (2009).

60. For a rare published memoir dealing with these events, see Tekeste Fekadu, *Journey from Nakfa to Nakfa: Back to Square One, 1976–1979* (Asmara, 2002).

61. Gebru Tareke, *Ethiopian Revolution*, chapter 7; for a personal account of military action in this period, see Alemseged Tesfai, *Two Weeks in the Trenches: Reminiscences of Childhood and War in Eritrea* (Lawrenceville, NJ, 2002) pp.43ff.

62. Pool, *Guerrillas*, Pateman, *Eritrea*; and D. Connell, *Against All Odds: A Chronicle of the Eritrean Revolution* (Lawrenceville, NJ, 1997). See also D. Pool, 'Eritrean nationalism', in Lewis, *Nationalism and Self-Determination*; and J. Harding, *Small Wars, Small Mercies: Journeys in Africa's Disputed Nations* (London, 1993) chapter 6.

63. Press Department, Ethiopian Ministry of Information, *Historical Truth About Eritrea* (Addis Ababa, 1988).

64. Tekeste Fekadu, *The Tenacity and Resilience of Eritrea, 1979–1983* (Asmara, 2008); Connell, *Against All Odds, passim*; Pool, *Guerrillas*, part II *passim*.

65. Pateman, *Eritrea*, chapter 9.

66. T. Redeker Hepner, *Soldiers, Martyrs, Traitors, and Exiles: Political Conflict in Eritrea and the Diaspora* (Philadelphia, 2009).

67. For a useful summary, see D. Pool, 'The Eritrean People's Liberation Front', in Clapham, *African Guerrillas*.

68. The 'National Democratic Programme of the EPLF', (January 1977), in Davidson *et al.*, *Behind the War*, pp.143–50.

69. The key source is the excellent piece by Dan Connell, 'Inside the EPLF: the origins of the "People's Party" and its role in the liberation of Eritrea', *Review of African Political Economy*, 89 (September 2001). It is also appended in Connell's *Conversations*, and indeed it is based on information derived from those interviews.

70. R. Leonard, 'Popular participation in liberation and revolution', in Cliffe and Davidson, *Long Struggle*.

71. See R.J. Reid, 'Old Problems in New Conflicts: some observations on Eritrea and its relations with Tigray, from liberation struggle to inter-state war', *Africa*, 73:3 (2003); and R.J. Reid, ' "Ethiopians believe in God, *Sha'abiya* believe in mountains": the EPLF and the 1998–2000 war in historical perspective', in D. Jacquin-Berdal and M. Plaut (eds.), *Unfinished Business: Ethiopia and Eritrea at War* (Lawrenceville, NJ, 2005). See also Young, 'The Tigray and Eritrean Peoples' Liberation Fronts'.

72. Exceptions, again, are Young, 'The Tigray and Eritrean Peoples' Liberation Fronts'; Alemseged Abbay, *Identity Jilted*; and, from an earlier era, the prescient analysis in P. Gilkes, 'Centralism and the PMAC', in Lewis, *Nationalism and Self-Determination in the Horn of Africa*.

73. Most markedly, perhaps, Roy Pateman, who in the second edition of his major book on the Eritrean struggle in 1997–8 unwisely declared that there was no military threat to Eritrea from Ethiopia as long as the EPRDF remained in power: Pateman, *Eritrea*, p.264.

74. Tekeste Negash and K. Tronvoll, *Brothers at War: Making Sense of the Eritrean–Ethiopian War* (Oxford, 2000).

75. Reid, 'Old problems', pp.376*ff*; Alemseged Tesfai, ' "The March of Folly" re-enacted: a personal view', *Eritrean Studies Review*, 3:2 (1999) p.216; D. Connell, 'Against more odds: the second siege of Eritrea', *Eritrean Studies Review*, 3:2 (1999) p.197.

76. Young, 'The Tigray and Eritrean Peoples' Liberation Fronts', p.105.

77. Publications of the EPLF: 'The TPLF and the development of its relations with the EPLF' (c.1984). Research and Documentation Centre, Asmara (hereafter RDC), Acc. No. 05062/Rela/3 p.4.

78. Publications of the TPLF: 'The Eritrean struggle, from where to where? An assessment' (1985). RDC Acc. No. Rela/10359 pp.42–3.

79. RDC Acc. No. 05062/Rela/3 p.20.

80. Ibid., pp.19–20, 27.

81. RDC Acc. No. Rela/10359 pp.161–2.

82. RDC Acc. No. 05062/Rela/3 p.8; Young, 'The Tigray and Eritrean peoples' liberation fronts', p.106.

83. RDC Acc. No. Rela/10359 p.51.

84. RDC Acc. No. 05062/Rela/3 pp.4, 13.

85. Ibid., p.18.
86. RDC Acc. No. Rela/10359 pp.81–2.
87. Foreign Relations Bureau of the TPLF: 'On our Differences with the EPLF' (1986). RDC Acc. No. 2399 p.3.
88. Clapham, *Transformation and Continuity*, p.212.
89. 'National Democratic Programme, Eritrean People's Liberation Front' (March 1987), in Cliffe and Davidson, *Long Struggle*, pp.205–13.
90. Tekeste Fekadu, *Tenacity and Resilience*, pp.207ff.
91. Gebru Tareke, *Ethiopian Revolution*, chapter 7; Alemseged Tesfai, *Two Weeks*, pp.99ff.
92. Quoted in Connell, *Against All Odds*, p.228.
93. Gebru Tareke, *Ethiopian Revolution*, chapter 10.

CHAPTER 8

1. Ruth Iyob, *Eritrean Struggle*, pp.137ff.
2. Ibid., pp.138–40; Pool, *Guerrillas*, pp.161ff.
3. Ruth Iyob, *Eritrean Struggle*, pp.141–2.
4. Quoted in ibid., p.143.
5. The spirit of this period is captured in Connell, *Against All Odds*, pp.263ff and 279ff; Pateman, *Eritrea*, chapter 11; and Ruth Iyob, *Eritrean Struggle*, chapters 8 and 9.
6. Connell, *Against All Odds*, pp.287ff.
7. In ibid., p.251.
8. The Constitutional Commission of Eritrea, *Information on Strategy, Plans and Activities* (Asmara, October 1995).
9. Gaim Kibreab, *Eritrea: a dream deferred* (Woodbridge, 2009) chapter 2 *passim*.
10. Pateman, *Eritrea*, pp.248, 250, 260–1; Connell, *Against All Odds*, pp.294ff.
11. The single best analysis to date is D. Turton (ed.), *Ethnic Federalism: the Ethiopian experience in comparative perspective* (Oxford, 2006). See also, for example, J. Abbink, 'Breaking and making the state: the dynamics of ethnic democracy in Ethiopia', *Journal of Contemporary African Studies*, 13:2 (1995); J. Abbink, 'Ethnicity and constitutionalism in contemporary Ethiopia', *Journal of African Law*, 41 (1997); J. M. Cohen, '"Ethnic federalism" in Ethiopia', *Northeast African Studies*, 2:2 (1995); J. Young, 'Ethnicity and power in Ethiopia', *Review of African Political Economy*, 23:70 (1996); Kidane Mengisteab, 'New approaches to state building in Africa: the case of Ethiopia's ethnic-based federalism', *African Studies Review*, 40:3 (1997).
12. For example, Henze, *Layers of Time*.
13. Marcus, *History*, pp.231ff.
14. Ibid., p.240.
15. J. Prendergast and M. Duffield, 'Liberation politics in Ethiopia and Eritrea', in T. M. Ali and R. O. Matthews (eds.), *Civil Wars in Africa: Roots and Resolution* (Montreal and Kingston, 1999) p.49.

16. D. Donham, 'Introduction', in James *et al.*, *Remapping Ethiopia*, p.6.

17. For example, Merera Gudina, 'Contradictory interpretations of Ethiopian history: the need for a new consensus', in Turton, *Ethnic Federalism*; various contributions to James *et al.*, *Remapping Ethiopia*; K. Tronvoll, 'Human rights violations in federal Ethiopia: when ethnic identity is a political stigma', *International Journal on Minority and Group Rights*, 15 (2008).

18. K. Tronvoll, 'Ambiguous identities: the notion of war and "significant others" among the Tigreans of Ethiopia', in V. Broch-Due (ed.), *Violence and Belonging: The Quest for Identity in Post-colonial Africa* (London, 2005); and his *War and the Politics of Identity in Ethiopia: The Making of Enemies and Allies in the Horn of Africa* (Oxford, 2009).

19. S. Pausewang, K. Tronvoll, and L. Aalen (eds.), *Ethiopia since the Derg: A Decade of Democratic Pretensions and Performance* (London, 2002).

20. Marcus, *History*, p.244; Young, *Peasant Revolution*, pp.211ff.

21. The author was told by General Tsadkan Gebretensae that he felt he was denied the opportunity to complete the mission in Eritrea: interview (Addis Ababa, 14 September 2005). The split, indeed, divided Tigrayans more generally, and gave rise to new opposition groups in exile. An example is the 'Tigrayan International Solidarity for Justice and Democracy', which has accused the Ethiopian government of giving away Ethiopian territory to the 'tyrant' Isaias.

22. See for example Human Rights Watch, '"Why am I still here?" The 2007 Horn of Africa renditions and the fate of those still missing' (1 October 2008); and A. Mitchell, 'US agents interrogating terror suspects held in Ethiopian prisons', *International Herald Tribune* (4 April 2007); and A. Mitchell, 'US agents visit secret Ethiopian jails', *Mail and Guardian Online* (4 April 2007).

23. R. Paz, 'The youth are older: the Iraqization of the Somali Mujahidin Youth Movement', *The Project for the Research of Islamist Movements: Occasional Papers*, 6:2 (2008); R. Marchal, 'Islamic political dynamics in the Somali civil war', in de Waal, *Islamism*.

24. R. J. Reid, 'A fierce race', *History Today*, 50:6 (2000); R. J. Reid, 'Revisiting primitive war: perceptions of violence and race in history', *War and Society*, 26:2 (2007); Reid, *War*, esp. chapter 1.

25. Most obviously, Tekeste Negash and Tronvoll, *Brothers at War*.

26. P. Gilkes and M. Plaut, *War in the Horn: The Conflict between Eritrea and Ethiopia* (London, 1999); D. Jacquin-Berdal and M. Plaut (eds.), *Unfinished Business: Ethiopia and Eritrea at War* (Lawrenceville, NJ, 2005); Tronvoll, *War and the Politics of Identity*; Ruth Iyob, 'The Ethiopian–Eritrean conflict: diasporic vs. hegemonic states in the Horn of Africa, 1991–2000', *Journal of Modern African Studies*, 38:4 (2000).

27. See Pateman, *Eritrea*, pp.235ff; Ruth Iyob, *Eritrean Struggle*, pp.136–7.

28. See appendices 1 and 2 in Tekeste Negash and Tronvoll, *Brothers at War*; Amare Tekle, 'The basis of Eritrean–Ethiopian cooperation', in Amare Tekle (ed.), *Eritrea and Ethiopia: From Conflict to Cooperation* (Lawrenceville, NJ, 1994).

29. D. Styan, 'Twisting Ethio-Eritrean economic ties: misperceptions of war and the misplaced priorities of peace, 1997–2002', in Jacquin-Berdal and Plaut, *Unfinished Business*.

30. Tekeste Negash and Tronvoll, *Brothers at War*, pp.23–9.

31. Appendix 3 in ibid.

32. More detailed accounts can be found in Tekeste Negash and Tronvoll, *Brothers at War*; and Gilkes and Plaut, *War in the Horn*.

33. Interview with General Tsadkan Gebretensae (Addis Ababa, 14 September 2005).

34. In 1999, the author conducted extensive research among Ethiopians living in Asmara as part of a report for the International Labour Organisation in Geneva.

35. Much of this analysis is based on personal observation, as the author was resident in Eritrea throughout this period.

36. This extensive document can be viewed at http://www.un.org/NewLinks/eebcarbitration/EEBC-Decision.pdf .

37. A number of useful interim reports have been produced, including International Crisis Group, *Ethiopia and Eritrea: Preventing War*, Africa Report No.101 (22 December 2005); and S. Hally and M. Plaut, *Ethiopia and Eritrea: Allergic to Persuasion* (London, 2007).

38. P. Gilkes, 'Violence and identity along the Eritrean–Ethiopian border', in Jacquin-Berdal and Plaut, *Unfinished Business*; Tronvoll, 'Ambiguous identities'; Tronvoll, *War and the Politics of Identity*.

39. Tekeste Negash, *Eritrea and Ethiopia*.

40. Alemseged Abbay, *Identity Jilted*.

41. Addis Birhan, *Eritrea: A Problem Child of Ethiopia* (Addis Ababa, 1998).

42. This is the basic purpose behind the ostensibly 'independent' Walta Information Centre's publication of *Chronology of the Ethio-Eritrean Conflict and Basic Documents* (Addis Ababa, 2001).

43. This was repeated to me on many occasions by Tigrayan and Amhara informants in Addis Ababa during trips in 2005 and 2006.

44. Medhane Tadesse, *The Eritrean–Ethiopian War: Retrospect and Prospects* (Addis Ababa, 1999).

45. Tronvoll, *War and the Politics of Identity*, pp.139ff.

46. A. Triulzi, 'The past as contested terrain: commemorating new sites of memory in war-torn Ethiopia', in P. Kaarsholm (ed.), *Violence, Political Culture and Development in Africa* (Oxford, 2006). But for a somewhat quirkier, more polemical interpretation, see Mesfin Araya, 'Contemporary Ethiopia in the context of the battle of Adwa, 1896', in Paulos Milkias and Getachew Metaferia (eds.), *The Battle of Adwa* (New York, 2005).

47. Hilton, *Ethiopian Patriots*, pp.68–70, 185; also Tronvoll, *War and the Politics of Identity*, chapters 5 and 6, *passim*.

48. Tronvoll, *War and the Politics of Identity*, pp.61–84.

49. Reid, 'Old problems'.

50. Tekie Fessehatzion, 'Eritrea and Ethiopia: from conflict to cooperation to con-flict' and Jordan Gebre-Medhin, 'Eritrea (Mereb-Melash)', both in *Eritrean Studies Review*, 3:2 (1999).

51. Alemseged Tesfai, '"The March of Folly"' and D.Connell, 'Against more odds'.

52. These views, gathered during extensive periods of fieldwork in Eritrea, are presented in Reid, 'Old problems'.

53. For example, Gaim Kibreab, 'Mass expulsion of Eritreans and Ethiopians of Eritrean origin from Ethiopia and human rights violations', *Eritrean Studies Review*, 3:2 (1999).

54. The full text is in Connell, *Conversations*.

55. Gaim Kibreab, *Eritrea*, pp.36*ff*.

56. This is well documented, for example, in Kidane Mengisteab and Okbazghi Yohannes, *Anatomy*; and, again, the rich material in Connell, *Conversations*.

57. Another high profile victim, indeed, was the Orthodox *Abuna*, the head of the Church, arrested and detained in 2006. See for example United States Commission on International Religious Freedom, *Annual Report* (Washington, DC, May 2009) pp.28*ff*.

58. See Human Rights Watch, *Service for Life: State Repression and Indefinite Conscription in Eritrea* (New York, April 2009); and a number of contributions in D. O'Kane and T. Redeker Hepner (eds.), *Biopolitics, Militarism and Development: Eritrea in the Twenty-First Century* (New York and Oxford, 2009).

59. Gaim Kibreab, *Eritrea*, pp.310*ff*.

60. 'Eritrea's controversial push to feed itself', BBC News, 24 December 2009.

61. I explore this in more detail in my 'Caught in the headlights of history: Eritrea, the EPLF and the post-war nation-state', *Journal of Modern African Studies*, 43:3 (2005), and in a follow-up to that piece, 'The politics of silence'.

62. See for example T. Muller, 'Human resource development and the state: higher education in post- revolutionary Eritrea', and M. Treiber, 'Trapped in adoles-cence: the post-war urban generation', both in O'Kane and Redeker Hepner, *Biopolitics*.

63. Reid, 'The politics of silence', *passim*.

64. Reid, 'Caught in the headlights', p.478.

65. See the various contributions in Reid, *Eritrea's External Relations* for an in-depth exploration of these issues.

66. See also R.J. Reid, 'Eritrea's regional role and foreign relations: past and present perspectives', in ibid.

67. Quoted in Connell, *Against All Odds*, pp.282–3.

68. Gaim Kibreab, 'Eritrean-Sudanese relations', *passim*.

69. For a summary, see Kidane Mengisteab and Okbazghi Yohannes, *Anatomy*, pp.216*ff*.

70. Institute for Security Studies Situation Report, *The Eritrea–Djibouti Border Dispute* (15 September 2008).

71. D. Connell, 'Eritrea and the United States: towards a new US policy', in Reid, *Eritrea's External Relations*, pp.135ff.

72. Foremost among these critiques are: Gaim Kibreab, *Critical Reflections* and his sequel to that volume, *Eritrea*; Kidane Mengisteab and Okbazghi Yohannes, *Anatomy*; and Yohannes Gebremedhin, *The Challenges of a Society in Transition: Legal Development in Eritrea* (Trenton, NJ, 2004).

73. Readers familiar with it will perhaps observe that I owe much in the way of inspiration here to John Lonsdale's work on Mau Mau: see, in particular, B. Berman and J. Lonsdale, *Unhappy Valley: Conflict in Kenya and Africa. Book Two: Violence and Ethnicity* (London, 1992).

74. Again, see in particular Sorenson, *Imagining Ethiopia*; Holcomb and Ibssa, *Invention of Ethiopia*; Gebissa, *Contested Terrain*; Baxter *et al.*, *Being and Becoming Oromo*.

75. The case is made, for example, in Holcomb and Ibssa, *Invention of Ethiopia*. The rather more complex interaction between Amhara, Tigrinya, and Oromo over the preceding 300 years was of less interest to nationalists.

76. See for example 'Oromo talks', *Africa Confidential*, 38(21) (October 1997).

77. A useful overview can be found in International Crisis Group, *Ethiopia: ethnic federalism and its discontents*, Africa Report No.153 (4 September 2009).

78. For example, Amnesty International, 'Ethiopia', in Annual Report 2003 (London, 2003). See also Mohammed Hassan, 'Conquest'; Asafa Jalata, *Oromia and Ethiopia*, pp.229ff.

79. Oromo Forum for Dialogue and Reconciliation, *A Proposal for the Consolidation of Oromo Forces for Liberation, Peace and Prosperity in the Horn of Africa* (Melbourne, 2008).

80. Ibid., p.3.

81. The author interviewed Oromo prisoners of war near Nakfa, northern Eritrea, in September 2000.

82. This was evident on several trips made by the author to the former front line areas in July and August 2000.

83. Tronvoll, *War and the Politics of Identity*, pp.189ff.

84. A useful overview of the 1990s and early 2000s is in Lewis, *Modern History*, chapter 11; see also M. Bradbury, *Becoming Somaliland* (Oxford, 2008), and of course the excellent work continually produced by Ken Menkhaus, including *Country in Peril*, and shorter pieces in the *Horn of Africa Bulletin*, notably January 2008 and August 2008.

85. K. Menkhaus, 'Somalia and Somaliland: terrorism, political Islam and state collapse', in R. I. Rotberg (ed.), *Battling Terrorism in the Horn of Africa* (Washington, DC, 2005); Paz, 'The youth are older'.

86. An excellent overview of a complicated situation is provided in Healy, *Lost Opportunities*, pp.20ff.

87. See for example T. Hagmann, 'Beyond clannishness and colonialism: understanding political disorder in Ethiopia's Somali region, 1991–2004', *Journal of Modern African Studies*, 43:4 (2005).

88. Human Rights Watch, *Collective Punishment: War Crimes and Crimes against Humanity in the Ogaden Area of Ethiopia's Somali Region* (New York, June 2008).

89. For example, Human Rights Watch, 'Ethiopia's Dirty War' (5 August 2007), and 'Somalia: war crimes devastate population' (8 December 2008); Amnesty International, *Routinely Targeted: Attacks on Civilians in Somalia* (London, May 2008). See also Menkhaus, *Country in Peril*.

90. Human Rights Watch, 'Ethiopia', January 2009, available at: <http://www.hrw.org/sites/default/files/related_material/Ethiopia.pdf>.

91. D. Connell, 'Eritrea: on a slow fuse', in Rotberg, *Battling Terrorism*; D. Connell, 'The EPLF/PFDJ Experience: how it shapes Eritrea's regional strategy', in Reid, *Eritrea's External Relations*.

92. A. McGregor, *Who's Who in the Somali Insurgency: A Reference Guide* (Washington, DC: The Jamestown Foundation, September 2009).

93. Among the best accounts to date are R. Middleton, *Piracy in Somalia: Threatening Global Trade, Feeding Local Wars.* Chatham House Briefing Paper (London: Chatham House, October 2008); and K. Menkhaus, 'Dangerous waters', *Survival*, 51:1 (2009).

94. K. Menkhaus, J. Prendergast and C. Thomas-Jensen, 'Beyond Piracy: Next Steps to Stabilise Somalia', *Enough!* (Washington, DC, May 2009).

95. The best account remains Bradbury, *Becoming Somaliland*.

96. Iqbal Jhazbhay, 'Islam and stability'.

EPILOGUE

1. Many such communities are examined in much greater detail than can be offered here in: Donham and James, *Southern Marches* and its successor volume, James *et al.*, *Remapping Ethiopia*; and Fukui and Markakis, *Ethnicity and Conflict*.

2. See for example R. Love, *Economic Drivers of Conflict and Cooperation in the Horn of Africa: A Regional Perspective and Overview*, Chatham House Briefing Paper (London, December 2009).

3. See a number of the contributions to A. de Waal (ed.), *War in Darfur and the Search for Peace* (London, 2007); and G. Prunier, *Armed Movements in Sudan, Chad, CAR, Somalia, Eritrea and Ethiopia*, Center for International Peace Operations (Berlin, 2008).

4. The best recent survey is provided by Young, *Armed Groups*.

5. See also J. Young, 'Along Ethiopia's western frontier: Gambella and Benishangul in transition', *Journal of Modern African Studies*, 37:2 (1999).

6. Human Rights Watch, *Targeting the Anuak: Human Rights Violations and Crimes Against Humanity in Ethiopia's Gambella Region* (New York, March 2005).

7. J. Markakis, 'Ethnic conflict and the state in the Horn of Africa', in Fukui and Markakis, *Ethnicity and Conflict*, p.221.

8. Amnesty International, *Annual Report 2003*; '"Deaths" in Ethiopian demonstration', BBC News (Africa, 24 May 2002).

9. 'Ethiopian Officials Held Over Violence', by Nita Bhalla, BBC News (Africa, 21 August 2002).

Bibliography

A NOTE ON ORAL INFORMANTS AND PERSONAL INFORMATION

Much of the analysis in this book, particularly that in Part IV, is based on numerous conversations and interviews—informal and otherwise—with a range of groups and individuals in both Eritrea and Ethiopia since 1997. It is neither possible nor politic to list them here; the majority, indeed—especially in Eritrea—must remain anonymous. Where appropriate I have noted oral sources in endnotes.

I ARCHIVAL COLLECTIONS

National Archives of the United Kingdom, London, UK:

Foreign Office (FO) 1 and 881 series.
War Office (WO) 230 series.

Research and Documentation Centre, Asmara, Eritrea:
Box/293 File SH/20
Box/287 File 70
Rela/10359
05062/Rela/3
Box/2399

II PUBLISHED PRIMARY SOURCES

Alazar Tesfa Michael. *Eritrea To-Day: Fascist Oppression Under the Nose of British Military* (Woodford Green: New Times Book Dept, *c*.1946).

Alemseged Tesfai. *Two Weeks in the Trenches: Reminiscences of Childhood and War in Eritrea* (Lawrenceville, NJ: Red Sea Press, 2002).

Amnesty International. 'Ethiopia', *Annual Report 2003* (London: Amnesty International, 2003).

Amnesty International. *Routinely Targeted: Attacks on Civilians in Somalia* (London: Amnesty International, May 2008).

Arab Faqih. *The Conquest of Abyssinia* (tr. P. L. Stenhouse) (Hollywood, CA: Tsehai, 2003).

Arrowsmith-Brown, J. H. (ed. and tr.). *Prutky's Travels in Ethiopia and Other Countries* (London: The Hakluyt Society, 1991).

Bairu Tafla (ed. and tr.). *A Chronicle of Emperor Yohannes IV (1872–89)* (Wisbaden: Franz Steiner Verlag GMBH, 1977).

Beckingham, C. F. and G. W. B. Huntingford (eds. and trs.). *Some Records of Ethiopia 1593–1646: Being Extracts From 'The History of High Ethiopia or Abassia', by Manoel de Almeida* (London: Hakluyt Society, 1954).

Bereket Habte Selassie. *The Crown and the Pen: The Memoirs of a Lawyer Turned Rebel* (Trenton: Red Sea Press, 2007).

Berkeley, G. F.-H. *The Campaign of Adowa and the Rise of Menelik*, 2nd edn. (New York: Negro Universities Press, 1969).

Blanc, H. *A Narrative of Captivity in Abyssinia*, 2nd edn. (London: Frank Cass, 1970).

Brooks, M. (ed. and tr.). *A Modern Translation of the* Kebra Negast *(The Glory of the Kings)* (Lawrenceville: Red Sea Press, 1995).

Bruce, J. *Travels to Discover the Source of the Nile, in the Years 1768, 1769, 1770, 1771, 1772, and 1773*, 5 vols. (London: G. G. J. and J. Robinson, 1790).

Budge, E. A. Wallis. *A History of Ethiopia, Nubia and Abyssinia*, 2 vols. (London: Methuen, 1928).

Burton, R. *First Footsteps in East Africa, Or, An Exploration of Harar* (New York: Dover, 1987).

Bulatovich, A. *Ethiopia Through Russian Eyes: Country in Transition 1896–1898* (ed. and tr. R. Seltzer) (Lawrenceville: Red Sea Press, 2000).

Connell, D. *Against All Odds: A Chronicle of the Eritrean Revolution*, 2nd edn. (Lawrenceville: Red Sea Press, 1997).

Connell, D. *Conversations with Eritrean Political Prisoners* (Trenton: Red Sea Press, 2005).

Constitutional Commission of Eritrea. *Information on Strategy, Plans and Activities* (Asmara, October 1995).

Cumming, D. 'The UN disposal of Eritrea', *African Affairs*, 52:207 (1953).

Dufton, H. *Narrative of a Journey Through Abyssinia in 1862–63*, 2nd edn. (Westport: Negro Universities Press, 1970).

Eritrean People's Liberation Front. 'National democratic programme of the EPLF', January 1977, in B. Davidson *et al.* (eds.), *Behind the War in Eritrea* (Nottingham: Spokesman, 1980).

Eritrean People's Liberation Front. 'National democratic programme', March 1987, in L. Cliffe and B. Davidson (eds.), *The Long Struggle of Eritrea for Independence and Constructive Peace* (Trenton: Red Sea Press, 1988).

Farago, L. *Abyssinia on the Eve* (London: Putnam, 1935).

Foreign Office (UK). *Handbook [on Eritrea] Prepared Under the Direction of the Historical Section of the Foreign Office*, No.126 (London: H.M. Stationery Office, 1920).

Gobat, S. *Journal of Three Years' Residence in Abyssinia*, 2nd edn. (New York: Negro Universities Press, 1969).

Hammond, J. *Fire From the Ashes: A Chronicle of Revolution in Tigray, Ethiopia, 1975–1991* (Lawrenceville: Red Sea Press, 1999).

Hancock, G. *Ethiopia: The Challenge of Hunger* (London: Gollancz, 1985).

Harding, J. *Small Wars, Small Mercies: Journeys in Africa's Disputed Nations* (London: Viking, 1993).

Harmsworth, G. *Abyssinian Adventure* (London: Hutchinson, 1935).

Hilton, A. (ed.). *The Ethiopian Patriots: Forgotten Voices of the Italo-Abyssinian War, 1935–41* (Stroud: Spellmount, 2007).

Human Rights Watch. *Targeting the Anuak: Human Rights Violations and Crimes Against Humanity in Ethiopia's Gambella Region* (New York, March 2005).

Human Rights Watch. 'Ethiopia's dirty war' (5 August 2007).

Human Rights Watch. *Collective Punishment: War Crimes and Crimes Against Humanity in the Ogaden Area of Ethiopia's Somali Region* (New York, June 2008).

Human Rights Watch. 'Somalia: war crimes devastate population' (8 December 2008).

Human Rights Watch. *Service for Life: State Repression and Indefinite Conscription in Eritrea* (New York, April 2009).

Huntingford, G. W. B. (ed. and tr.). *The Glorious Victories of Amda Seyon, King of Ethiopia* (London: Oxford University Press, 1965).

Kaplan, R. D. *Surrender or Starve: Travels in Ethiopia, Sudan, Somalia and Eritrea*, 2nd edn. (New York: Vintage, 2003).

Kolmodin, J. (tr.). *Traditions de Tsazzega et Hazzega* (Uppsala: Archives d'Etudes Orientales, 1915).

Longrigg, S. H. *A Short History of Eritrea* (Oxford: Clarendon Press, 1945).

Longrigg, S. H. 'The future of Eritrea', *African Affairs*, 45(180) (1946).

Macmichael, Sir H. *The Anglo-Egyptian Sudan* (London: Faber and Faber, 1934).

Markham, C. R. *A History of the Abyssinian Expedition* (London: Macmillan, 1869).

Ministry of Information, UK. *The First to be Freed: The Record of British Military Administration in Eritrea and Somalia, 1941–1943* (London: H.M. Stationery Office, 1944).

Ministry of Information, Ethiopia. *Historical Truth About Eritrea* (Addis Ababa: Ethiopian Ministry of Information, 1988).

Mitchell, Sir P. *African Afterthoughts* (London: Hutchinson, 1954).

Nadel, S. F. *Races and Tribes of Eritrea* (Asmara: British Military Administration, 1944).

Oromo Forum for Dialogue and Reconciliation. *A Proposal for the Consolidation of Oromo Forces for Liberation, Peace and Prosperity in the Horn of Africa* (Melbourne, August 2008).

Othman Saleh Sabbe. *The History of Eritrea* (tr. Muhamad Fawaz al-Azem) (Beirut: n.p., c.1974?)

Pankhurst, R. (ed.). *The Ethiopian Royal Chronicles* (Addis Ababa: Oxford University Press, 1967).

Pankhurst, S. *British Policy in Eritrea and Northern Ethiopia* (Woodford Green: n.p., 1946).

Pankhurst, S. *Eritrea on the Eve: The Past and Future of Italy's 'First-born' Colony, Ethiopia's Ancient Sea Province* (Woodford Green: New Times and Ethiopia News Books, 1952).

Pankhurst, S. and R. Pankhurst. *Ethiopia and Eritrea: The Last Phase of the Reunion Struggle, 1941–1952* (Woodford Green: Lalibela House, 1953).

Parkyns, M. *Life in Abyssinia: Being Notes Collected During Three Years' Residence and Travels in that Country*, 3rd edn. (London: Frank Cass, 1966).

Perham, M. *The Government of Ethiopia* (London: Faber and Faber, 1948).

Plowden, W. C. *Travels in Abyssinia and the Galla Country* (ed. T. C. Plowden) (London: Longmans, Green, 1868).

Portal, G. H. *My Mission to Abyssinia*, 2nd edn. (New York: Negro Universities Press, 1969).

Rassam, H. *Narrative of the British Mission to Theodore, King of Abyssinia*, 2 vols. (London: John Murray, 1869).

Rubenson, S. *et al.* (eds. and trs.). *Acta Aethiopica I: Correspondence and Treaties, 1800–1854* (Evanston: Northwestern University Press, 1987).

Rubenson, S. *et al.* (eds. and trs.). *Acta Aethiopica II: Tewodros and his Contemporaries, 1855–1868* (Addis Ababa: Addis Ababa University Press, 1994).

Rubenson, S. *et al.* (eds. and trs). *Act Aethiopica III: Internal Rivalries and Foreign Threats, 1869–1879* (Addis Ababa: Addis Ababa University Press, 2000).

Salt, H. *A Voyage to Abyssinia and Travels into the Interior of that Country* (London: F. C. and J. Rivington, 1814).

Stanley, H. M. *Coomassie and Magdala: The Story of Two British Campaigns in Africa* (New York: Harper and Brothers, 1874).

Stern, H. *Wanderings Among the Falashas in Abyssinia*, 2nd edn. (London: Frank Cass, 1968).

Tekeste Fekadu. *Journey from Nakfa to Nakfa: Back to Square One, 1976–1979* (Asmara: n.p., 2002).

Tekeste Fekadu. *The Tenacity and Resilience of Eritrea, 1979–1983* (Asmara: Hidri, 2008).

Thesiger, W. *The Danakil Diary: Journeys Through Abyssinia* (London: Flamingo, 1998).

Thomson, B. *Ethiopia: The Country that Cut Off Its Head. A Diary of the Revolution* (London: Robson Books, 1975).

Trevaskis, G. K. N. *Eritrea: A Colony in Transition* (London: Oxford University Press, 1960).

Ullendorff, E. (ed. and tr.). *The Autobiography of Emperor Haile Selassie I: 'My Life and Ethiopia's Progress', 1892–1937* (London: Oxford University Press, 1976).

United States Commission on International Religious Freedom. *Annual Report* (Washington, May 2009).

Walta Information Centre. *Chronology of the Ethio-Eritrean Conflict and Basic Documents* (Addis Ababa: Walta Information Centre, 2001).

Waugh, E. *Waugh in Abyssinia* (Baton Rouge: Louisiana State University Press, 2007).

Weld Blundell, H. *The Royal Chronicle of Abyssinia, 1769–1840* (Cambridge: Cambridge University Press, 1922).

Woodward, P. (ed.). *British Documents on Foreign Affairs: Reports and Papers from the Foreign Office Confidential Print. Part III, from 1940 through 1945. Series G, Africa.* 5 vols. (Bethesda: University Publications of America, 1998).

Woodward, P. (ed.). *British Documents on Foreign Affairs: Reports and Papers from the Foreign Office Confidential Print. Part IV, from 1945 through 1950. Series G, Africa.* 5 vols. (Bethesda: University Publications of America, 1999–).

Wylde, A. B. *Modern Abyssinia*, 2nd edn. (Westport: Negro Universities Press, 1970).

Zoli, C. 'The organisation of Italy's East African empire', *Foreign Affairs*, 16:1 (1937).

III OTHER SOURCES

Abbink, J. 'Breaking and making the state: the dynamics of ethnic democracy in Ethiopia', *Journal of Contemporary African Studies*, 13:2 (1995).

Abbink, J. 'Ethnicity and constitutionalism in contemporary Ethiopia', *Journal of African Law*, 41 (1997).

Abir, M. 'The emergence and consolidation of the monarchies of Enarea and Jimma in the first half of the nineteenth century', *Journal of African History*, 6:2 (1965).

Abir, M. *Ethiopia: the era of the princes* (London: Longmans, 1968).

Abir, M. 'Ethiopia and the Horn of Africa', in R. Gray (ed.), *Cambridge History of Africa: Vol. 4, from c.1600 to c.1790* (Cambridge: Cambridge University Press, 1975).

Abir, M. *Ethiopia and the Red Sea: The Rise and Decline of the Solomonic Dynasty and Muslim–European Rivalry in the Region* (London: Frank Cass, 1980).

Addis Birhan. *Eritrea: A Problem Child of Ethiopia* (Addis Ababa: Marran Books, 1998).

Addis Hiwet. *Ethiopia: From Autocracy to Revolution* (London: Review of African Political Economy, 1975).

Ahmad, Abdussamad H. 'Trading in slaves in Bela-Shangul and Gumuz, Ethiopia: border enclaves in history, 1897–1938', *Journal of African History*, 40:3 (1999).

Ahmed, H. *Islam in Nineteenth-Century Wallo, Ethiopia: Revival, Reform and Reaction* (Leiden: Brill, 2001).

Alemseged Abbay. 'The trans-Mereb past in the present', *Journal of Modern African Studies*, 35:2 (1997).

Alemseged Abbay. *Identity Jilted or Re-Imagining Identity? The Divergent Paths of the Eritrean and Tigrayan Nationalist Struggles* (Lawrenceville: Red Sea Press, 1998).

Alemseged Tesfai. '"The March of Folly" re-enacted: a personal view', *Eritrean Studies Review*, 3:2 (1999).

Alemseged Tesfai. *Aynefalale* (Asmara: Hidri Publishers, 2001).

Almagor, U. 'Institutionalising a fringe periphery: Dassanetch-Amhara relations', in D. Donham and W. James (eds.), *The Southern Marches of Imperial Ethiopia*, 2nd edn. (Oxford: James Currey, 2002).

Amare Tekle. 'The basis of Eritrean–Ethiopian cooperation', in Amare Tekle (ed.), *Eritrea and Ethiopia: From Conflict to Cooperation* (Lawrenceville: Red Sea Press, 1994).

Andargachew Tiruneh. *The Ethiopian Revolution, 1974–1987: A Transformation from an Aristocratic to a Totalitarian Autocracy* (Cambridge: Cambridge University Press: 1993).

Anonymous. 'Oromo talks', *Africa Confidential*, 38(21) (October 1997).

Asafa Jalata. *Oromia and Ethiopia: State Formation and Ethnonational Conflict, 1868–2004*, 2nd edn. (Trenton: Red Sea Press, 2005).

Asmarom Legesse. *Gada: Three Approaches to the Study of African Society* (New York: Free Press, 1973).

Asmarom Legesse. *Oromo Democracy: An Indigenous African Political System* (Trenton: Red Sea Press, 2006).

Awet Weldemichael. 'The Eritrean Long March: the strategic withdrawal of the Eritrean People's Liberation Front (EPLF), 1978–79', *Journal of Military History*, 73:4 (2009).

Bahru Zewde. *A History of Modern Ethiopia, 1855–1991* (Oxford: James Currey, 2001).

Bahru Zewde. *Pioneers of Change in Ethiopia: The Reformist Intellectuals of the Early Twentieth Century* (Oxford: James Currey, 2002).

Bairu Tafla (ed.). 'Eritrea on the Eve of Colonial Rule', special issue of *Eritrean Studies Review*, 5:1 (2007).

Barker, A. J. *Eritrea 1941* (London: Faber and Faber, 1966).

Barnes, C. 'The Somali Youth League, Ethiopian Somalis and the Greater Somalia idea, c.1946–48', *Journal of Eastern African Studies*, 1:2 (2007).

Bates, D. *The Abyssinian Difficulty: the Emperor Theodorus and the Magdala Campaign, 1867–68* (Oxford: Oxford University Press, 1979).

Baxter, P. 'The creation and constitution of Oromo nationality', in K. Fukui and J. Markakis (eds.), *Ethnicity and Conflict in the Horn of Africa* (London: James Currey, 1994).

Baxter, P., J. Hultin and A. Triulzi (eds.). *Being and Becoming Oromo: Historical and Anthropological Enquiries* (Uppsala: Nordiska Afrikainstitutet, 1996).

Bereket Habte Selassie. 'From British rule to federation and annexation', in B. Davidson, L. Cliffe and Bereket Habte Selassie (eds.), *Behind the War in Eritrea* (Nottingham: Spokesman, 1980).

Berman, B. and J. Lonsdale. *Unhappy Valley: Conflict in Kenya and Africa. Book Two: Violence and Ethnicity* (London: James Currey, 1992).

Bradbury, M. *Becoming Somaliland* (Oxford: James Currey, 2008).

Carnochan, W. B. *Golden Legends: Images of Abyssinia, Samuel Johnson to Bob Marley* (Stanford: Stanford University Press, 2008).

Cassanelli, L. V. *The Shaping of Somali Society: Reconstructing the History of a Pastoral People, 1600–1900* (Philadelphia: University of Pennsylvania Press, 1982).

Caulk, R. 'Firearms and princely power in Ethiopia in the nineteenth century', *Journal of African History*, 13:4 (1972).

Caulk, R. 'Armies as predators: soldiers and peasants in Ethiopia, c.1850–1935', *International Journal of African Historical Studies*, 11:3 (1978).

Caulk, R. 'Bad men of the borders: shum and shifta in northern Ethiopia in the nineteenth century', *International Journal of African Historical Studies*, 17:2 (1984).

Caulk, R. 'Ethiopia and the Horn', in A. D. Roberts (ed.), *Cambridge History of Africa, Vol. 7: 1905–1940* (Cambridge: Cambridge University Press, 1986).

Caulk, R. '"Black snake, white snake": Bahta Hagos and his revolt against Italian overrule in Eritrea, 1894', in D. Crummey (ed.), *Banditry, Rebellion and Social Protest in Africa* (London: James Currey, 1986).

Clapham, C. *Transformation and Continuity in Revolutionary Ethiopia* (Cambridge: Cambridge University Press, 1988).

Clapham, C. 'Boundary and territory in the Horn of Africa', in A. I. Asiwaju and P. Nugent (eds.), *African Boundaries: Barriers, Conduits and Opportunities* (London: Pinter, 1996).

Clapham, C. *Africa and the International System: The Politics of State Survival* (Cambridge: Cambridge University Press, 1996).

Clapham, C. (ed.). *African Guerrillas* (Oxford: James Currey, 1998).

Cliffe, L. and B. Davidson (eds.). *The Long Struggle of Eritrea for Independence and Constructive Peace* (Trenton: Red Sea Press, 1988).

Coffey, T. M. *Lion by the Tail: The Story of the Italian–Ethiopian War* (London: Hamish Hamilton, 1974).

Cohen, J. M. '"Ethnic federalism" in Ethiopia', *Northeast African Studies*, 2:2 (1995).

Connell, D. 'Against more odds: the second siege of Eritrea', *Eritrean Studies Review*, 3:2 (1999).

Connell, D. 'Inside the EPLF: the origins of the "People's Party" and its role in the liberation of Eritrea', *Review of African Political Economy*, 89 (2001).

Connell, D. 'Eritrea: on a slow fuse', in R.I.Rotberg (ed.), *Battling Terrorism in the Horn of Africa* (Cambridge and Washington: World Peace Foundation / Brookings Institution Press, 2005).

Connell, D. 'The EPLF / PFDJ Experience: how it shapes Eritrea's regional strategy', in R. J. Reid (ed.), *Eritrea's External Relations: Understanding its Regional Role and Foreign Policy* (London and Washington: Chatham House, 2009).

Crummey, D. 'Tewodros as reformer and moderniser', *Journal of African History*, 10:3 (1969).

Crummey, D. 'The violence of Tewodros', in B. A. Ogot (ed.), *War and Society in Africa* (London: Frank Cass, 1972).

Crummey, D. 'Society and ethnicity in the politics of Christian Ethiopia during the Zamana Masfent', *International Journal of African Historical Studies*, 8:2 (1975).

Crummey, D. 'Orthodoxy and imperial reconstruction in Ethiopia, 1854–1878', *Journal of Theological Studies*, 29:2 (1978).

Crummey, D. 'Abyssinian feudalism', *Past and Present*, 89 (1980).

Crummey, D. 'Banditry and resistance: noble and peasant in nineteenth-century Ethiopia', in D. Crummey (ed.), *Banditry, Rebellion and Social Protest in Africa* (London: James Currey, 1986).

Crummey, D. (ed.). *Banditry, Rebellion and Social Protest in Africa* (London: James Currey, 1986).

Crummey, D. 'Imperial legitimacy and the creation of Neo-Solomonic ideology in 19th-century Ethiopia', *Cahiers d'Etudes Africaines*, 28 (1988).

Crummey, D. 'Society, state and nationality in the recent historiography of Ethiopia', *Journal of African History*, 31:1 (1990).

Crummey, D. *Land and Society in the Christian Kingdom of Ethiopia: From the Thirteenth to the Twentieth Century* (Oxford: James Currey, 2000).

Davidson, B., L. Cliffe and Bereket Habte Selassie (eds.). *Behind the War in Eritrea* (Nottingham: Spokesman, 1980).

de Waal, A. (ed.). *Islamism and its Enemies in the Horn of Africa* (London: Hurst, 2004).

de Waal, A. 'Darfur's elusive peace', in A. de Waal (ed.), *War in Darfur and the Search for Peace* (London: Justice Africa/Global Equity Initiative, Harvard University, 2007).

Decalo, S. *Coups and Army Rule in Africa: Motivations and Constraints* (New Haven and London: Yale University Press, 1990).

Dines, M. 'The Ethiopian "Red Terror"', in B. Davidson, L. Cliffe and Bereket Habte Selassie (eds.), *Behind the War in Eritrea* (Nottingham: Spokesman, 1980).

Dines, M. 'Ethiopian violation of human rights in Eritrea', in L. Cliffe and B. Davidson (eds.), *The Long Struggle of Eritrea for Independence and Constructive Peace* (Trenton NJ: Red Sea Press, 1988).

Donham, D. and W. James (eds.). *The Southern Marches of Imperial Ethiopia*, 2nd edn. (Oxford: James Currey, 2002).

Dunn, J. '"For God, Emperor, and Country!" The evolution of Ethiopia's nineteenth-century army', *War in History*, 1 (1994).

Ehret, C. *Ethiopians and East Africans: The Problem of Contacts* (Nairobi: East African Publishing House, 1974).

Ellingson, L. 'The emergence of political parties in Eritrea, 1941–1950', *Journal of African History*, 18:2 (1977).

Erlich, H. ' "Tigrean nationalism", British involvement, and Haile Selassie's emerging absolutism: northern Ethiopia, 1941–1943', *Asian and African Studies*, 15:2 (1981).

Erlich, H. 'The Eritrean autonomy, 1952–1962: its failure and its contribution to further escalation', in Y. Dinstein (ed.), *Models of Autonomy* (New York: Transaction Books, 1981).

Erlich, H. 'The Ethiopian Army and the 1974 Revolution', in M. Janowitz (ed.), *Armed Forces and Society* (Chicago: University of Chicago Press, 1983).

Erlich, H. 'Tigrean politics, 1930–35, and the approaching Italo-Ethiopian war', in H. Erlich, *Ethiopia and the Challenge of Independence* (Boulder: Lynne Reinner, 1986).

Erlich, H. *Ras Alula and the Scramble for Africa: A Political Biography. Ethiopia and Eritrea, 1875–1897* (Lawrenceville: Red Sea Press, 1996).

Ezekiel Gebissa (ed.). *Contested Terrain: Essays on Oromo Studies, Ethiopianist Discourse, and Politically Engaged Scholarship* (Trenton: Red Sea Press, 2009).

Fernyhough, T. 'Social mobility and dissident elites in northern Ethiopia: the role of banditry, 1900–1969', in D. Crummey (ed.), *Banditry, Rebellion and Social Protest in Africa* (London: James Currey, 1986).

Firebrace, J. [*et al.*]. *Never Kneel Down: Drought, Development and Liberation in Eritrea* (Trenton: Red Sea Press, 1985).

Fukui, K. and J. Markakis (eds.). *Ethnicity and Conflict in the Horn of Africa* (London: James Currey, 1994).

Gadaa Melbaa. *Oromia: An Introduction* (Khartoum: n.p., 1988).

Gaim Kibreab. *People on the Edge in the Horn: Displacement, Land Use and the Environment in the Gedaref Region, Sudan* (Oxford: James Currey, 1996).

Gaim Kibreab. 'Mass expulsion of Eritreans and Ethiopians of Eritrean origin from Ethiopia and human rights violations', *Eritrean Studies Review*, 3:2 (1999).

Gaim Kibreab. *Critical Reflections on the Eritrean War of Independence* (Trenton: Red Sea Press, 2008).

Gaim Kibreab. *Eritrea: A Dream Deferred* (Woodbridge: James Currey, 2009).

Gaim Kibreab. 'Eritrean–Sudanese relations in historical perspective', in R. J. Reid (ed.), *Eritrea's External Relations: Understanding its Regional Role and Foreign Policy* (London and Washington: Chatham House/Brookings Institution Press, 2009).

Garretson, P. 'Vicious cycles: ivory, slaves and arms on the new Maji frontier', in D. Donham and W. James (eds.), *The Southern Marches of Imperial Ethiopia*, 2nd edn. (Oxford: James Currey, 2002).

Gavshon, A. *Crisis in Africa: Battleground of East and West* (New York: Pelican, 1981).

Gebru Tareke. 'Peasant resistance in Ethiopia: the case of *Weyane*', *Journal of African History*, 25:1 (1984).

Gebru Tareke. *Ethiopia: Power and Protest. Peasant Revolts in the Twentieth Century* (Cambridge: Cambridge University Press, 1991).

Gebru Tareke. 'The Ethiopia–Somalia war of 1977 revisited', *International Journal of African Historical Studies*, 33:3 (2000).

Gebru Tareke. *The Ethiopian Revolution: War in the Horn of Africa* (New Haven and London: Yale University Press, 2009).

Gellner, E. *Nations and Nationalism* (Oxford: Blackwell, 1983).

Gemetchu Megerssa. '*Oromumma*: tradition, consciousness and identity', in P. Baxter *et al.* (eds.), *Being and Becoming Oromo: Historical and Anthropological Enquiries* (Uppsala: Nordiska Afrikainstitutet, 1996).

Gerhard, D. 'The frontier in comparative view', *Comparative Studies in Society and History*, 1:3 (1959).

Gewald, J.-B. 'Making tribes: social engineering in the Western province of British-administered Eritrea, 1941–1952', *Journal of Colonialism and Colonial History*, 1:2 (2000).

Giglio, C. 'Article 17 of the Treaty of Uccialli' (tr. R. Caulk), *Journal of African History*, 6:2 (1965).

Gilkes, P. 'Centralism and the PMAC', in I. M. Lewis (ed.), *Nationalism and Self-determination in the Horn of Africa* (London: Ithaca Press, 1983).

Gilkes, P. 'Eritrea: historiography and mythology', *African Affairs*, 90:361 (1991).

Gilkes, P. 'Violence and identity along the Eritrean–Ethiopian border', in D. Jacquin-Berdal and M. Plaut (eds.), *Unfinished Business: Ethiopia and Eritrea at War* (Lawrenceville: Red Sea Press, 2005).

Gilkes, P. and M. Plaut. *War in the Horn: The Conflict Between Eritrea and Ethiopia* (London: Royal Institute of International Affairs, 1999).

Goody, J. *Technology, Tradition and the State in Africa* (London: Cambridge University Press, 1971).

Gray, R. *A History of the Southern Sudan 1839–1889* (London: Oxford University Press, 1961).

Greenfield, R. *Ethiopia: A New Political History* (London: Pall Mall Press, 1965).

Hagmann, T. 'Beyond clannishness and colonialism: understanding political disorder in Ethiopia's Somali region, 1991–2004', *Journal of Modern African Studies*, 43:4 (2005).

Haile Larebo. *The Building of an Empire: Italian Land Policy and Practice in Ethiopia*, 2nd edn. (Trenton: Red Sea Press, 2006).

Halliday, F. and M. Molyneux. *The Ethiopian Revolution* (London: Verso, 1981).

Harbeson, J. W. *The Ethiopian Transformation: The Quest for the Post Imperial State* (Boulder and London: Westview Press, 1988).

Healy, S. and M. Plaut. *Ethiopia and Eritrea: Allergic to Persuasion* (London: Chatham House, 2007).

Healy, S. *Lost Opportunities in the Horn of Africa: How Conflicts Connect and Peace Agreements Unravel* (London: Chatham House, 2008).

Henze, P. *Layers of Time: A History of Ethiopia* (London: Hurst, 2000).

Hess, R. L. 'The Poor Man of God: Muhammad Abdullah Hassan', in N. R. Bennett (ed.), *Leadership in Eastern Africa* (Boston: Boston University, 1968).

Hoben, A. *Land Tenure Among the Amhara: The Dynamics of Cognatic Descent* (Chicago: University of Chicago Press, 1973).

Hobsbawm, E. *Bandits* (London: Abacus, 2000).

Holcomb, B. K. and Sisai Ibbsa. *The Invention of Ethiopia: The Making of Dependent Colonial State in Northeast Africa* (Trenton: Red Sea Press, 1990).

Holt, P. M. 'Egypt and the Nile valley', in J. E. Flint (ed.), *Cambridge History of Africa, Vol. 5: c.1790–c.1870* (Cambridge: Cambridge University Press, 1976).

Holt, P. M. and M. W. Daly. *A History of the Sudan* (Harlow: Longmans, 2000).

Howard, M. *War in European History*, 2nd edn. (Oxford: Oxford University Press, 2009).

Iliffe, J. *The African Poor: A History* (Cambridge: Cambridge University Press, 1987).

Institute for Security Studies Situation Report. *The Eritrea–Djibouti Border Dispute* (15 September 2008).

International Crisis Group. *Ethiopia and Eritrea: Preventing War*, Africa Report No. 101 (22 December 2005).

International Crisis Group. *Ethiopia: Ethnic Federalism and Its Discontents*, Africa Report No. 153 (4 September 2009).

Jacquin-Berdal, D. and M. Plaut (eds.). *Unfinished Business: Ethiopia and Eritrea at War* (Lawrenceville: Red Sea Press, 2005).

James, W. *'KWANIM PA: The Making of the Uduk People. An Ethnographic Study of Survival in the Sudan–Ethiopian Borderlands* (Oxford: Clarendon Press, 1979).

James, W. 'War and "ethnic visibility": the Uduk on the Sudan–Ethiopia border', in K. Fukui and J. Markakis (eds.), *Ethnicity and Conflict in the Horn of Africa* (London: James Currey, 1994).

James, W. 'Local centres on the Western Frontier, 1974–97: a case study of Kurmuk', in K. Fukui *et al.* (eds.), *Ethiopia in Broader Perspective: Papers of the XIIIth International Conference of Ethiopian Studies*, Vol. II (Kyoto: Shokado Book Sellers, 1997).

James, W., D. Donham, E. Kurimoto, and A. Triulzi (eds.). *Remapping Ethiopia: Socialism and After* (Oxford: James Currey, 2002).

James, W. 'No place to hide: flag-waving on the western frontier', in W. James *et al.* (eds.), *Remapping Ethiopia: Socialism and After* (Oxford: James Currey, 2002).

Jhazbhay, I. 'Islam and stability in Somaliland and the geo-politics of the war on terror', *Journal of Muslim Minority Affairs*, 28:2 (2008).

Johnson, D. 'On the Nilotic frontier: imperial Ethiopia in the southern Sudan, 1898–1936', in D. Donham and W. James (eds.), *The Southern Marches of Imperial Ethiopia*, 2nd edn. (Oxford: James Currey, 2002).

Johnson, D. *The Root Causes of Sudan's Civil Wars* (Oxford: James Currey, 2003).

Johnson, D. and D. M. Anderson (eds.). *The Ecology of Survival: Case Studies from Northeast African History* (London: Lester Crook, 1988).

Jones, A. H. M. and E. Monroe. *A History of Ethiopia* (Oxford: Clarendon Press, 1935).

Jordan Gebre-Medhin. *Peasants and Nationalism in Eritrea: A Critique of Ethiopian Studies* (Trenton: Red Sea Press, 1989).

Jordan Gebre-Medhin. 'Eritrea (Mereb-Melash) and Yohannes IV of Abyssinia', *Eritrean Studies Review*, 3:2 (1999).

Kaptjeins, L. 'Ethiopia and the Horn of Africa', in N. Levtzion and R. L. Pouwels (eds.), *The History of Islam in Africa* (Oxford: James Currey, 2000).

Keller, E. J. *Revolutionary Ethiopia: From Empire to People's Republic* (Bloomington and Indianapolis: Indiana University Press, 1988).

Kidane Mengisteab. 'New approaches to state building in Africa: the case of Ethiopia's ethnic-based federalism', *African Studies Review*, 40:3 (1997).

Kidane Mengisteab and Okbazghi Yohannes. *Anatomy of an African Tragedy: Political, Economic and Foreign Policy Crisis in Post-independence Eritrea* (Trenton: Red Sea Press, 2005).

Killion, T. 'Eritrean workers' organisation and early nationalist mobilisation: 1948–1958', *Eritrean Studies Review*, 2:1 (1997).

Kopytoff, I. 'The internal African frontier: the making of African political culture', in I. Kopytoff (ed.), *The African Frontier: The Reproduction of Traditional African Societies* (Bloomington and Indianapolis: Indiana University Press, 1987).

Kurimoto, E. 'Fear and Anger: female versus male narratives among the Anywaa', in W.James *et al.* (eds.), *Remapping Ethiopia: Socialism and After* (Oxford: James Currey, 2002).

Kurimoto, E. and S. Simonse (eds.). *Conflict, Age and Power in North East Africa: Age Systems in Transition* (Oxford: James Currey, 1998).

Lapidus, I. *A History of Islamic Societies* (Cambridge: Cambridge University Press, 2002).

Legum, C. and B. Lee. *The Horn of Africa in Continuing Crisis* (New York and London: Africana Publishing Co., 1979).

Leonard, R. 'Popular participation in liberation and revolution', in L. Cliffe and B. Davidson (eds.), *The Long Struggle of Eritrea for Independence and Constructive Peace* (Trenton: Red Sea Press, 1988).

Leopold, M. *Inside West Nile: Violence, History and Representation on an African Frontier* (Oxford: James Currey, 2005).

Levine, D. *Greater Ethiopia: The Evolution of a Multi-ethnic Society*, 2nd edn. (Chicago: University of Chicago Press, 2000).

Lewis, H. S. 'The development of Oromo political consciousness from 1958 to 1994', in P. Baxter *et al.* (eds.), *Being and Becoming Oromo: Historical and Anthropological Enquiries* (Uppsala: Nordiska Afrikainstitutet, 1996).

Lewis, H. S. *Jimma Abba Jifar, an Oromo monarchy: Ethiopia 1830–1932*, 2nd edn. (Lawrenceville: Red Sea Press, 2001).

Lewis, I. M. (ed.). *Nationalism and Self-Determination in the Horn of Africa* (London: Ithaca Press, 1983).

Lewis, I. M. *A Modern History of the Somali*, 4th edn. (Oxford: James Currey, 2002).

Locatelli, F. 'Oziosi, vagabondi e pregiudicati: labour, law and crime in colonial Asmara, 1890–1941', *International Journal of African Historical Studies*, 40:2 (2007).

Locatelli, F. 'Beyond the Campo Cintato: prostitutes, migrants and "criminals" in colonial Asmara (Eritrea), 1890–1941', in F. Locatelli and P. Nugent (eds.), *African Cities: Competing Claims on Urban Spaces* (Leiden: Brill, 2009).

Love, R. *Economic Drivers of Conflict and Cooperation in the Horn of Africa: A Regional Perspective and Overview*, Chatham House Briefing Paper (London, December 2009).

Low, D. A. 'Uganda: the establishment of the Protectorate, 1894–1919', in V. Harlow and E. M. Chilver (eds.), *History of East Africa, Vol. II* (Oxford: Clarendon Press, 1965).

Low, D.A. 'British East Africa: the establishment of British rule, 1895–1912', in V. Harlow and E. M. Chilver (eds.), *History of East Africa, Vol. II* (Oxford: Clarendon Press, 1965).

Marchal, R. 'Islamic political dynamics in the Somali civil war', in A. de Waal (ed.), *Islamism and its Enemies in the Horn of Africa* (London: Hurst, 2004).

Marcus, H. *The Life and Times of Menelik II: Ethiopia, 1844–1913* (Oxford: Clarendon Press, 1975).

Marcus, H. *The Politics of Empire: Ethiopia, Great Britain and the United States, 1941–1974* (Berkeley: University of California Press, 1983).

Marcus, H. *A History of Ethiopia*, 2nd edn. (Berkeley: University of California Press, 2002).

Markakis, J. *National and Class Conflict in the Horn of Africa* (Cambridge: Cambridge University Press, 1987).

Markakis, J. 'The nationalist revolution in Eritrea', *Journal of Modern African Studies*, 26:1 (1988).

Markakis, J. 'Ethnic conflict and the state in the Horn of Africa', in K. Fukui and J. Markakis (eds.), *Ethnicity and Conflict in the Horn of Africa* (London: James Currey, 1994).

Marsden, P. *The Barefoot Emperor: An Ethiopian Tragedy* (London: Harper, 2007).

Mburu, N. 'Patriots or Bandits? Britain's strategy for policing Eritrea, 1941–1952', *Nordic Journal of African Studies*, 9:2 (2000).

Mburu, N. *Bandits on the Border: The Last Frontier in the Search for Somali Unity* (Trenton: Red Sea Press, 2005).

McCann, J. C. *People of the Plow: An Agricultural History of Ethiopia, 1800–1990* (London: University of Wisconsin Press, 2005).

McGregor, A. *Who's Who in the Somali Insurgency: A Reference Guide* (Washington, DC: The Jamestown Foundation, September 2009).

Medhane Tadesse. *The Eritrean-Ethiopian War: Retrospect and Prospects* (Addis Ababa: n.p., 1999).

Menkhaus, K. 'Somalia and Somaliland: terrorism, political Islam, and state collapse', in R. I. Rotberg (ed.), *Battling Terrorism in the Horn of Africa* (Cambridge/Washington, DC: World Peace Foundation / Brookings Institution Press, 2005).

Menkhaus, K. 'The crisis in Somalia: tragedy in five acts', *African Affairs*, 106:424 (2007).

Menkhaus, K. 'Somalia: a country in peril, a policy nightmare', *Enough! Strategy Paper* (September 2008).

Menkhaus, K. 'Dangerous waters', *Survival*, 51:1 (2009).

Menkhaus, K., J. Prendergast, and C. Thomas-Jensen. 'Beyond piracy: next steps to stabilise Somalia', *Enough!* (May 2009).

Merera Gudina. 'Contradictory interpretations of Ethiopian history: the need for a new consensus', in D. Turton (ed.), *Ethnic Federalism: The Ethiopian Experience in Comparative Perspective* (Oxford: James Currey, 2006).

Merid Wolde Aregay. 'A reappraisal of the impact of firearms in the history of warfare in Ethiopia, c.1500–1800', *Journal of Ethiopian Studies*, 14 (1980).

Mesfin Araya. 'Contemporary Ethiopia in the context of the battle of Adwa, 1896', in Paulos Milkias and Getachew Metaferia (eds.), *The Battle of Adwa: Reflections on Ethiopia's Historic Victory Against European Colonialism* (New York: Algora Publishing, 2005).

Messay Kebede. *Radicalism and Cultural Dislocation in Ethiopia, 1960–1974* (Rochester: University of Rochester Press, 2008).

Middleton, R. *Piracy in Somalia: Threatening Global Trade, Feeding Local Wars*. Chatham House Briefing Paper (London: Chatham House, October 2008).

Miran, J. *Red Sea Citizens: cosmopolitan society and cultural change in Massawa* (Bloomington and Indianapolis: Indiana University Press, 2009).

Mockler, A. *Haile Selassie's War: The Italian–Ethiopian Campaign, 1935–1941* (London: Random House, 1984).

Mohammed Hassan. *The Oromo of Ethiopia: A History, 1570–1860* (Cambridge: Cambridge University Press, 1990).

Mohammed Hassan. 'The development of Oromo nationalism', in P. Baxter *et al.* (eds.), *Being and Becoming Oromo: Historical and Anthropological Enquiries* (Uppsala: Nordiska Afrikainstitutet, 1996).

Mohammed Hassan. 'Conquest, tyranny and ethnocide against the Oromo: a historical assessment of human rights conditions in Ethiopia, ca.1880s–2002', in Ezekiel Gebissa (ed.), *Contested Terrain: Essays on Oromo Studies, Ethiopianist Discourse, and Politically Engaged Scholarship* (Trenton: Red Sea Press, 2009).

Moore-Harell, A. 'Economic and political aspects of the slave trade in Ethiopia and the Sudan in second half of the nineteenth century', *International Journal of African Historical Studies*, 23:2–3 (1999).

Moyse-Bartlett, H. *The King's African Rifles: A Study in the Military History of East and Central Africa, 1880–1945*, 2 vols. (Aldershot: Gale and Polden, 1956).

Muller, T. 'Human resource development and the state: higher education in post-revolutionary Eritrea', in D. O'Kane and T. Redeker Hepner (eds.), *Biopolitics, Militarism and Development: Eritrea in the Twenty-First Century* (New York and Oxford: Berghahn, 2009).

O'Kane, D. and T. Redeker Hepner (eds.). *Biopolitics, Militarism and Development: Eritrea in the Twenty-First Century* (New York and Oxford: Berghahn, 2009).

Okbazghi Yohannes. *Eritrea: A Pawn in World Politics* (Gainesville: University of Florida Press, 1991).

Orlowska, I. 'Re-Imagining Empire: Ethiopian political culture under Yohannis IV (1872–89)', PhD thesis (London, 2006).

Paice, E. *Tip and Run: The Untold Tragedy of the Great War in Africa* (London: Phoenix, 2007).

Pankhurst, R. *Economic History of Ethiopia, 1800–1935* (Addis Ababa: Haile Sellassie I University, 1968).

Pankhurst, R. and D. Johnson. 'The great drought and famine of 1888–92 in northeast Africa', in D. Johnson and D. M. Anderson (eds.), *The Ecology of Survival: Case Studies from Northeast African History* (London: Lester Crook, 1988).

Patemam, R. 'Drought, famine and development', in L. Cliffe and B. Davidson (eds.), *The Long Struggle of Eritrea for Independence and Constructive Peace* (Trenton, NJ: Red Sea Press, 1988).

Pateman, R. *Eritrea: Even the Stones are Burning*, 2nd edn. (Lawrenceville: Red Sea Press, 1998).

Paulos Milkias and Getachew Metaferia (eds.). *The Battle of Adwa: Reflections on Ethiopia's Historic Victory Against European Colonialism* (New York: Algora Publishing, 2005).

Pausewang, S., K. Tronvoll, and L. Aalen (eds.). *Ethiopia Since the Derg: A Decade of Democratic Pretensions and Performance* (London: Zed Books, 2002).

Paz, R. 'The Youth are Older: the Iraqization of the Somali Mujahidin Youth Movement', *The Project for the Research of Islamist Movements: Occasional Papers*, 6:2 (2008).

Phillipson, D. *Ancient Ethiopia. Aksum: Its Antecedents and Successors* (London: The British Museum Press, 1998).

Pool, D. 'Eritrean nationalism', in I. M. Lewis (ed.), *Nationalism and Self-determination in the Horn of Africa* (London: Ithaca Press, 1983).

Pool, D. 'The Eritrean People's Liberation Front', in C. Clapham (ed.), *African Guerrillas* (Oxford: James Currey, 1998).

Pool, D. *From Guerrillas to Government: The Eritrean People's Liberation Front* (Oxford: James Currey, 2001).

Prendergast, J. and M. Duffield. 'Liberation politics in Ethiopia and Eritrea', in T. M. Ali and R. O. Matthews (eds.), *Civil Wars in Africa: Roots and Resolution* (Montreal and Kingston: McGill-Queen's University Press, 1999).

Prunier, G. *Armed Movements in Sudan, Chad, CAR, Somalia, Eritrea and Ethiopia* (Berlin: Center for International Peace Operations, 2008).

Redeker Hepner, T. *Soldiers, Martyrs, Traitors, and Exiles: Political Conflict in Eritrea and the Diaspora* (Philadelphia: University of Pennsylvania Press, 2009).

Redie Bereketeab. *Eritrea: The Making of a Nation, 1890–1991* (Trenton: Red Sea Press, 2007).

Reid, R. J. 'A Fierce Race', *History Today*, 50:6 (2000).

Reid, R. J. 'The challenge of the past: the quest for historical legitimacy in independent Eritrea', *History in Africa*, 28 (2001).

Reid, R. J. 'Warfare and urbanisation: the relationship between town and conflict in pre-colonial eastern Africa', in A. Burton (ed.), *The Urban Experience in Eastern Africa, c. 1750–2000* (British Institute in Eastern Africa: Nairobi, 2002).

Reid, R. J. 'Old problems in new conflicts: some observations on Eritrea and its relations with Tigray, from liberation struggle to inter-state war', *Africa*, 73:3 (2003).

Reid, R. J. 'Caught in the headlights of history: Eritrea, the EPLF and the post-war nation-state', *Journal of Modern African Studies*, 43:3 (2005).

Reid, R. J. ' "Ethiopians believe in God, Sha'abiya believe in mountains": the EPLF and the 1998–2000 war in historical perspective', in D. Jacquin-Berdal and M. Plaut (eds.), *Unfinished Business: Ethiopia and Eritrea at War* (Lawrenceville: Red Sea Press, 2005).

Reid, R. J. 'War and remembrance: orality, literacy and conflict in the Horn of Africa', *Journal of African Cultural Studies*, 18:1 (2006).

Reid, R. J. *War in Pre-colonial Eastern Africa: The Patterns and Meanings of State-level Conflict in the Nineteenth Century* (Oxford: James Currey, 2007).

Reid, R. J. 'The Trans-Mereb experience: perceptions of the historical relationship between Eritrea and Ethiopia', *Journal of Eastern African Studies*, 1:2 (2007).

Reid, R. J. 'Revisiting primitive war: perceptions of violence and race in history', *War and Society*, 26:2 (2007).

Reid, R. J. 'The politics of silence: interpreting apparent stasis in contemporary Eritrea', *Review of African Political Economy*, 36:120 (2009).

Reid, R.J. (ed.). *Eritrea's External Relations: Understanding its Regional Role and Foreign Policy* (London: Chatham House, 2009).

Robertson, E. M. *Mussolini as Empire-builder: Europe and Africa 1932–36* (London: Macmillan, 1977).

Robinson, D. *Muslim Societies in African History* (Cambridge: Cambridge University Press, 2004).

Robinson, R. and J. Gallagher. *Africa and the Victorians* (London: Macmillan, 1961).

Rotberg, R. I. (ed.). *Battling Terrorism in the Horn of Africa* (Cambridge / Washington, DC: World Peace Foundation / Brookings Institution Press, 2005).

Rubenson, S. *King of Kings: Tewodros of Ethiopia* (Addis Ababa and Nairobi: Oxford University Press, 1966).

Rubenson, S. 'Adwa 1896: the resounding protest', in R. Rotberg and A. Mazrui (eds.), *Protest and Power in Black Africa* (New York: Oxford University Press, 1970).

Rubenson, S. 'Ethiopia and the Horn', in J. E. Flint (ed.), *Cambridge History of Africa: Vol. 5, c.1790–c.1870* (Cambridge: Cambridge University Press, 1976).

Rubenson, S. *The Survival of Ethiopian Independence* (London: Heinemann, 1976).

Ruth Iyob. *The Eritrean Struggle for Independence: Domination, Resistance, Nationalism 1941–1993* (Cambridge: Cambridge University Press, 1995).

Ruth Iyob. 'The Ethiopian–Eritrean conflict: diasporic vs. hegemonic states in the Horn of Africa, 1991–2000', *Journal of Modern African Studies*, 38:4 (2000).

Samatar, Said S. *Oral Poetry and Somali Nationalism: The Case of Sayyid Mahammad 'Abdille Hasan* (Cambridge: Cambridge University Press, 1982).

Sanderson, G. N. 'The Nile basin and the eastern Horn, 1870–1908', in R. O. Oliver and G. N. Sanderson (eds.), *Cambridge History of Africa, Vol. 6: from 1870 to 1905* (Cambridge: Cambridge University Press, 1985).

Sbacchi, A. *Ethiopia under Mussolini: Fascism and the Colonial Experience* (London: Zeb Books, 1985).

Schlee, G. *Identities on the Move: Clanship and Pastoralism in Northern Kenya* (Manchester: Manchester University Press, 1989).

Schlee, G. 'Gada systems on the meta-ethnic level: Gabbra / Boran / Garre interactions in the Kenyan / Ethiopian borderland', in E. Kurimoto and S. Simonse (eds.), *Conflict, Age and Power in North East Africa: Age Systems in Transition* (Oxford: James Currey, 1998).

Schlee, G. 'Brothers of the Boran once again: on the fading popularity of certain Somali identities in northern Kenya', *Journal of Eastern African Studies*, 1:3 (2007).

Schmidt, P., M. Curtis, and Zelalem Teka (eds.). *The Archaeology of Ancient Eritrea* (Trenton: Red Sea Press, 2008).

Schwab, P. *Ethiopia: Politics, Economics and Society* (London: Frances Pinter, 1985).

Semere Haile. 'Historical background to the Ethiopia–Eritrea conflict', in B. Davidson and L. Cliffe (eds.), *The Long Struggle of Eritrea for Independence and Constructive Peace* (Trenton: Red Sea Press, 1988).

Sherman, R. *Eritrea: The Unfinished Revolution* (New York: Praeger, 1980).

Sorenson, J. *Imagining Ethiopia: Struggles for History and Identity in the Horn of Africa* (New Brunswick: Rutgers University Press, 1993).

Styan, D. 'Twisting Ethio-Eritrean economic ties: misperceptions of war and the misplaced priorities of peace, 1997–2002', in D. Jacquin-Berdal and M. Plaut (eds.), *Unfinished Business: Ethiopia and Eritrea at War* (Lawrenceville: Red Sea Press, 2005).

Taddesse Tamrat. *Church and State in Ethiopia, 1270–1527* (Oxford: Clarendon Press, 1972).

Tekeste Negash. *No Medicine for the Bite of a White Snake: Notes on Nationalism and Resistance in Eritrea, 1890–1940* (Uppsala: University of Uppsala, 1986).

Tekeste Negash. *Italian Colonialism in Eritrea, 1882–1941: Policies, Praxis and Impact* (Uppsala: University of Uppsala, 1987).

Tekeste Negash. *Eritrea and Ethiopia: The Federal Experience* (Uppsala: Nordiska Afrikainstitutet, 1997).

Tekeste Negash and K. Tronvoll. *Brothers at War: making sense of the Eritrean-Ethiopian war* (Oxford: James Currey, 2000).

Tekie Fessehatzion. 'Eritrea and Ethiopia: from conflict to cooperation to conflict', *Eritrean Studies Review*, 3:2 (1999).

Tibebe Eshete. 'The root causes of political problems in the Ogaden, 1942–1960', *Northeast African Studies*, 13:1 (1991).

Tibebe Eshete. 'Towards a history of the incorporation of the Ogaden: 1887–1935', *Journal of Ethiopian Studies*, 27:2 (1994).

Treiber, M. 'Trapped in adolescence: the post-war urban generation', in D. O'Kane and T. Redeker Hepner (eds.), *Biopolitics, Militarism and Development: Eritrea in the Twenty-First Century* (New York and Oxford: Berghahn, 2009).

Triulzi, A. *Salt, Gold and Legitimacy: Prelude to the History of a No-man's-Land, Bela Shangul, Wallagga, Ethiopia (ca. 1800–1898)* (Naples: Istituto Universitario Orientale, 1981).

Triulzi, A. 'Italian colonialism and Ethiopia', *Journal of African History*, 23:2 (1982).

Triulzi, A. 'Competing views of national identity in Ethiopia', in I. M. Lewis (ed.), *Nationalism and Self-determination in the Horn of Africa* (London: Ithaca Press, 1983).

Triulzi, A. 'The past as contested terrain: commemorating new sites of memory in war-torn Ethiopia', in P. Kaarsholm (ed.), *Violence, Political Culture and Development in Africa* (Oxford: James Currey, 2006).

Tronvoll, K. 'Ambiguous identities: the notion of war and "significant others" among the Tigreans of Ethiopia', in V. Broch-Due (ed.), *Violence and Belonging: The Quest for Identity in Post-colonial Africa* (London: Routledge, 2005).

Tronvoll, K. 'Human rights violations in federal Ethiopia: when ethnic identity is a political stigma', *International Journal on Minority and Group Rights*, 15 (2008).

Tronvoll, K. *War and the Politics of Identity in Ethiopia: The Making of Enemies and Allies in the Horn of Africa* (Oxford: James Currey, 2009).

Turton, D. (ed.). *Ethnic Federalism: The Ethiopian Experience in Comparative Perspective* (Oxford: James Currey, 2006).

Uoldelul Chelati Dirar. 'Colonialism and the construction of national identities: the case of Eritrea', *Journal of Eastern African Studies*, 1:2 (2007).

Vikor, K. S. 'Sufi brotherhoods in Africa', in N. Levtzion and R. L. Pouwels (eds.), *The History of Islam in Africa* (Oxford: James Currey, 2000).

Wolde-Yesus Ammar. 'The role of Asmara students in the Eritrean nationalist movement, 1958–68', *Eritrean Studies Review*, 2:1 (1997).

Wrong, M. *I Didn't Do It For You: How the World Betrayed a Small African Nation* (London and New York: Fourth Estate, 2005).

Yohannes Gebremedhin. *The Challenges of a Society in Transition: Legal Development in Eritrea* (Trenton: Red Sea Press, 2004).

Yosief Libsekal. 'Eritrea', in *International Council on Monuments and Sites (ICOMOS): World Report 2001–02 on Monuments and Sites in Danger* (Paris: ICOMOS, 2002).

Young, J. 'The Tigray and Eritrean Peoples' Liberation Fronts: a history of tensions and pragmatism', *Journal of Modern African Studies*, 34:1 (1996).

Young, J. 'Ethnicity and power in Ethiopia', *Review of African Political Economy*, 23:70 (1996).

Young, J. *Peasant Revolution in Ethiopia: The Tigray People's Liberation Front, 1975–1991* (Cambridge: Cambridge University Press, 1997).

Young, J. 'Along Ethiopia's western frontier: Gambella and Benishangul in transition', *Journal of Modern African Studies*, 37:2 (1999).

Young, J. *Armed Groups Along Sudan's Eastern Frontier: An Overview and Analysis*. HSBA Working Paper 9 (Geneva: Small Arms Survey, 2007).

Young, W. C. 'The Rashayida Arabs vs. the State: the impact of European colonialism on a small-scale society in Sudan and Eritrea', *Journal of Colonialism and Colonial History*, 9:2 (2008).

Zewde Gabre-Selassie. *Yohannes IV of Ethiopia: a political biography* (Oxford: Clarendon Press, 1975).

Index

Abba Bagibo 46
Abba Jifar I 46
Abeba Aregai 145
Aberra, *Dejazmach* 105
Acholi 137
Adal 28–9, 33
Adwa 49, 192
  battle of (1896) 89, 90, 92, 98, 105,
    223–4, 248
Afar 5, 12, 29, 61, 71, 86, 89, 110, 135,
    143, 160, 254–5
Agame 73, 189
Agaw 11, 25
Ahmed ibn Ibrahim ('Gran') 29–30,
    63–4
Akele Guzay 49, 71, 72, 73, 75, 76, 77,
    105, 195
Al-Beshir, Omar 181, 251
Algiers Agreement 1
Ali, *Ras* 45
All Amhara People's Organisation
    (AAPO) 213
Alula, *Ras* 70, 75, 78, 83, 85, 96, 202
Aman Andom 175, 197
Amda Tsion 27–8
Amhara 3, 5, 11, 134, 136, 137, 138, 143,
    216, 234
  activism in 1990s 213, 214
  defining features of 13–14
  during *zemene mesafint* 42, 43
  expansion under Menelik II 84–6, 87
  political role in twentieth-century
    Ethiopia 106, 115, 117, 131, 133,
    135, 146, 147, 154, 160, 210, 215,
    224–5

tensions with other groups 98, 186,
    188, 239, 253
Anuak 11, 138, 180, 253
Arsi 88
ascari 97, 102, 108, 119, 122, 144, 158
Asfeha Woldemichael, *Dejazmach* 155,
    156
Aussa sultanate 135, 160–1
Axum 24–5
Azebo 89, 143, 149

Bahta Hagos 100, 105, 107
Bale 154, 165–6, 177
banda 146, 149, 152
baria 11, 48, 81–2, 174
Begemeder 44, 134, 142, 145
Beja 11–12, 179
Beni Amer 11, 83, 104, 125, 156, 160,
    161, 196
Benishangul 11, 179, 180, 181,
    252–3
Benishangul People's Liberation
    Movement (BPLM) 14, 252–3
Berta 11, 139, 180, 253
Britain 56, 67, 107–8, 112–13,
    146–8, 149, 150–1
  see also Eritrea, British Military
    Administration (BMA); Northern
    Frontier District, Kenya (NFD);
    Somaliland, British

Christianity, Orthodox 13, 25–30, 52,
    59–60, 62–5, 68–9, 119, 131, 154,
    161–2
Cushitic culture and people 11–12, 14